The COMPSTAT Paradigm

Management Accountability in Policing, Business and the Public Sector

By Vincent E. Henry
Foreword by William J. Bratton

43-08 162nd Street
Flushing, NY 11358
www.LooseleafLaw.com   800-647-5547

Library of Congress Cataloging-in-Publication Data

    The COMPSTAT paradigm : management accountability in policing, business and the public sector / By Vincent E. Henry ; Foreword by William J. Bratton.
    p. cm.
Includes index.
 ISBN 1-889031-15-1 (Paperback)
 1. Police administration--New York (State)--New York. 2. New York (N.Y.). Police Dept. 3. Police administration--United States. 4. Mathematical statistics--Data processing. I. Title.
 HV8148.N5 H46 2001
 363.2'068--dc21

2002001835

Printed in the United States of America

1 2 3 4 5 6 7 8 9 10

Cover design by: Joanne Scannello
                         josamba@aol.com

Dedication

For my wife, Lydia Staiano
My best secret weapon.

And for my mother, Joan Henry
She lived to know that it would happen.

Acknowledgments

I would like to express my gratitude to the many people whose guidance, knowledge and assistance made this book possible. First, I am indebted to those members of the NYPD I was fortunate enough to work with over the years and who generously shared their knowledge, expertise and experience to help shape my understanding of police work and police management.

Foremost among them is William J. Bratton, whose passion for innovation, commitment to excellence and antipathy for organizational inertia inspired a generation of men and women in the NYPD. His principled leadership and vision of what policing can and should be gave us our brief shining moment. He has always given generously of his time to listen, to discuss, and to offer insight into the events and activities that are the substance of this book.

Others who had a profound influence, at least in terms of writing this book and understanding how innovation works, include Michael Farrell, Peter LaPorte, Mike Julian, Charles Campisi, Aaron Rosenthal, Leo Callaghan, Bill Andrews and Joe Lovelock. All of them became friends as well as mentors. Bill Gorta and especially John Yohe – wonderful friends and co-conspirators in addition to being original members of the Compstat Unit – were always generous in sharing their time, their expertise, their insights and their excitement about the tremendous changes they helped make possible in the NYPD.

Many difficulties and obstacles were encountered in bringing this book to publication, and in such difficult times one learns a great deal about the nature of true friendship, commitment, and integrity. My publishers, Mary and Mike Loughrey, were exceptionally patient and understanding of those difficulties. I am also indebted to Rosemary Carroll and Alan Friess, who advocated strongly on my behalf and gave me a great deal of candid advise and counsel. The tremendous love, support and wisdom given by my mother-in-law and father-in-law, Ruth and Lou Staiano, has always sustained me during even the most difficult times. Joanne Scannello Dziuk, another cherished friend, conceived of and designed the book's cover. Thanks also to Pedro Bernal, Dennis O'Loughlin and Paul Kennedy – the Three Wise Men – whose wisdom, knowledge and integrity I greatly admire.

A special debt of gratitude is also owed to Jack Maple, whose extraordinarily brilliant career as a crime-fighter, innovator and iconoclast ended prematurely when he succumbed to cancer in August 2001. The Jackster had, and continues to have, a profound impact on crime in America, and he will be remembered as one of the most important figures in American policing in this century.

Table of Contents

Foreword

By *William J. Bratton, former NYPD Police Commissioner*

New York City Mayor Rudolph Giuliani was elected to office in November 1993 largely as a result of his campaign promises to reduce crime, disorder and fear so as to allow for a restoration of confidence and quality of life in America's largest city. Upon my appointment as his first Police Commissioner in January 1994, it was my challenge, and that of the extraordinary team of police and civilian professionals and managers that I quickly recruited, to re-engineer the New York City Police Department (NYPD) to achieve these goals – and to achieve them quickly, effectively and creatively. How we achieved that turnaround transforming a reactive, risk-averse organization, that for most of its history had been organized around avoiding risk and failure, to one that is organized and managed for results while rewarding risk-taking and initiative, is chronicled fully in this thoughtful and intimately researched book by Vincent Henry. As somebody who was "there" from the beginning, he has been able to create the most accurate accounting yet published of the "revolution" that occurred within the NYPD beginning in 1994 and the impact of the "Compstat Paradigm" on not only that department, but on policing and criminal justice systems in the United States and abroad.

The true impact of Compstat is only beginning to be felt and this book will go a long way toward institutionalizing the community policing/problem solving revolution that it is helping to energize and drive. At the same time, readers of this book, whether criminal justice practitioners, observers or collaborators, need to understand that this is not a "how-to" or cookbook about the technology or the dynamics that shape and drive Compstat, its meetings and related processes. Rather, it presents a fairly broad descriptive view of the overall management dynamic and the quality of interactions that should take place to maximize its multi-faceted potential and effectiveness. Since leaving the NYPD in 1996, I have written, spoken and consulted frequently around the world about the New York "miracle" and the role of Compstat in achieving New York's historic crime declines. In all those venues I constantly stress that while Compstat is transferable, compatible and replicable in any organization or environment, it cannot be successfully implemented by merely using a cookie cutter approach. In fact, such an approach will almost certainly doom the effort to failure. Henry quite accurately argues that if the Compstat-supported management style created, internalized and practiced by the NYPD for the last seven years is to succeed and its proven benefits are to accrue, then the specific policing programs and initiatives must emanate from within the organization, taking into account local influences, restrictions and circumstances. Indeed, one of Compstat's great strengths is its adaptability to constantly changing conditions.

A central theme of "The Compstat Paradigm" is that Compstat remains largely misunderstood in policing and in the criminal justice community and academia. Henry's book is appropriately named the "Compstat Paradigm" in that it reflects the fact that New York's policing revolution is really about a different mindset about police work, police management, Compstat meetings, philosophy and technology. Henry emphasizes that they are simply management tools that reflect and facilitate the larger overall paradigm. The paradigm emphasizes accountability and discretion at all levels of the organization, strategic and time-sensitive identification and response to management problems (not only crime, disorder and quality of life, but also internal management issues); capitalization of the expertise and input of all personnel, both inside and outside the organization; and continuous organizational restructuring or re-engineering to remove impediments to high performance.

A parallel theme is that because it is a paradigm rather than simply a crime fighting tool, it is applicable to a host of management issues in municipal, state and federal government as well as the private sector.

Various chapters deal with the historical forces (e.g. the Professional Model, Problem-Oriented Policing and Community Policing Model) that have shaped the contours and direction of contemporary policing, the processes of organizational reengineering and the directions it is likely to take in the future. Throughout the book, Henry sketches out and discusses the broad issues that affect (and have affected) policing in general, and then he leads his reader to focus more narrowly upon how these issues were manifested in the NYPD.

Henry details how, since January 1994, the NYPD has been engaged in a department-wide, full-scale, strategic attack on crime and disorder in New York City. Instead of merely reacting to individual crimes as they occur, the department established proactive strategies for confronting the problems of guns, youth crime, drugs, domestic violence, disorder in public spaces, auto-related theft and police corruption. Backed by sweeping changes in many department procedures and by a policy of decentralizing management to the precinct level, these strategies have achieved by far the largest drops in New York City felony crime in a quarter century.

As described by Henry, Compstat and its documented results reflect a sea change in the way the New York Police Department does business. Like many large bureaucracies, the NYPD had been organized around avoiding risk and failure. For years, precinct commanders had been constrained on every side by regulations and procedures. Many police operations, such as prostitution sweeps and executing search warrants, could only be conducted by centralized units, reflecting an abiding distrust of precinct personnel and resources. Yet, despite all the micro-management, the department was providing very little in the way of genuine strategic direction. It was clear what precinct commanders and personnel weren't allowed to do, but much less clear what they *ought* to be doing to combat crime, disorder and fear.

Beginning in 1994, my command staff and I made major changes in the management style of the NYPD. Precinct commanders were granted far more latitude in initiating their own operations and running their own shops. Uni-formed patrol cops were authorized to make drug arrests and to assertively enforce quality-of-life laws, things they hadn't been doing for more than 20 years. At the same time, the central strategic direction of the department became far stronger and the lines of accountability far clearer. Avoiding failure was no longer a formula for success. Instead, the positive efforts of commanders and cops at reducing crime, disorder and fear were recognized and encouraged.

For the first time in its history, the NYPD used crime statistics and regular meetings of key enforcement personnel to direct its enforcement efforts. In the past, crime statistics often lagged events by months and so did the sense of whether crime control initiatives had succeeded or failed. Now, there is a daily turnaround in the Compstat numbers, as the crime statistics are called, and NYPD commanders watch weekly crime trends with the same hawk-like attention private corporations pay to profit and loss. Crime statistics have become the department's bottom line, the best indicator of how the police are doing, precinct-by-precinct and citywide.

The results speak for themselves, and it is these results and the paradigm that helped to create them that Henry so ably chronicles and explores. His is not the first book, nor will it be the last, about the Compstat "revolution," but it will certainly be one of the most important.

About the Author

Vincent Henry, a twenty-year veteran of the NYPD, has held a wide variety of patrol, plain clothes, investigative, administrative and management positions. He holds the rank of Sergeant, Special Assignment in the NYPD, has been an Adjunct Professor in the Criminal Justice Department of Long Island University since 1991 and Adjunct Professor at St. John's University since 2001.

Sgt. Henry received his BA and MS degrees in Criminal Justice from Long Island University, and his M.Phil. and Ph.D. degrees in Criminal Justice from John Jay College/City University of New York. He also holds the Certified Protection Professional (CPP) credential conferred by the American Society for Industrial Security.

In 1989, Vincent Henry became the first American police officer to be named a Fulbright Scholar, and he spent one year as Visiting Fellow at Griffith University's Centre for Australian Public Sector Management in Brisbane, Australia studying comparative patterns of police corruption and reform, and as Visiting Fellow at the Queensland (Australia) Police Academy.

Among his other academic honors are the City University's 1995-1996 Kenneth B. and Mamie Phipps Clark Fellowship for the dissertation proposal showing the greatest potential for social policy impact, the 1995 Arthur Niederhoffer Memorial Fellowship for outstanding doctoral candidate at John Jay, and the John A. Reisenbach Foundation Dissertation Award.

Sgt. Henry has been a consultant to police agencies in the United States, Australia and Japan as well as to private security entities in the United States and abroad.

Chapter 1
Introduction and Overview

Oone of the most remarkable stories in law enforcement and in criminal justice today is the tremendous decline in crime achieved in New York City since 1993. According to New York Police Department figures, the total number of reported crimes for the seven major crime categories[1] declined an unprecedented 57.26 percent in calendar year 2000 from the levels reported in calendar year 1993. Only 184,000 of these major crimes occurred in 2000, as compared to 429,460 in 1993, and the calendar year 2000 figures represent the lowest annual number of total complaints for the seven major crimes in well over three decades. One of the most remarkable declines occurred in the Murder category, which fell 65.18 percent between 1993 and 2000. The 671 murders recorded in New York City in 2000 represented a 70 percent decline from 1990 - the year homicides peaked in New York City with 2,245 murders. Robberies fell 62.49 percent between 1993 and 2000, Felony Assaults declined 37.15 percent, Grand Larcenies fell 42.42 percent, Burglaries decreased by 62.16 percent, and Grand Larceny Autos and forcible Rapes respectively declined 68.08 percent and 35.91 percent (NYPD website – http//:www.nyc.gov.html/nypd/pdf/chdept/cshist.pdf).

According to the FBI's Uniformed Crime Report data for calendar year 1999[2], New York City's rate of Index Crimes per 100,000 population ranked 165th of the 217 American cities with a population over 100,000 that reported their crime statistics to the FBI. This showed a great improvement over the first six months of 1996, when New York City ranked 144th, and a vast improvement over the comparable 1993 period when it ranked 87th of 181 large cities reporting their crime statistics to the FBI. By way of comparison, St. Louis' crime rate in 1999 was 240 percent higher than New York's; Orlando's was 238 percent higher; Atlanta's was 229 percent higher;

---

1 Murder, Robbery, First Degree (forcible) Rape, Felony Assault, Burglary, Larceny, and Grand Larceny Auto, as defined in New York State Penal Law.

2 Uniformed Crime Report (UCR) data is based on slightly different offense definitions. These offense categories and definitions provide a basis for comparing data across jurisdictions. The UCR definitions and the New York State Penal Law definitions vary slightly, but the two measures are roughly comparable.

Flint, Michigan's was 164 percent higher; Salt Lake City's was 151 percent higher; Washington, D.C.'s was almost 94 percent higher; and Denver's crime rate was almost thirty percent higher than New York City's 1999 crime rate. New York City is the safest American city with a population over one million (City of New York, Mayor's Management Report - Fiscal 2000).

The UCR statistics show that crime has been falling in large cities across the nation over the past few years, but New York City's decline in reported crime has been significantly greater – in all crime categories – than the national averages. New York City's crime decline has not only surpassed the national average reduction, but it has actually pulled the national averages down. Between 1993 and 1999, for example, the UCR data show that the number of Murders and Non-Negligent Manslaughters occurring in US cities with a population over 100,000 (excluding New York City) fell 37 percent, while these crimes fell 66 percent in New York City. The 36 percent drop in New York City's Aggravated Assaults was nearly twice the national average decline (19 percent). Robberies in these cities fell 35 percent between 1993 and 2000, but fell 58 percent in New York City. New York City's decline in the Forcible Rape category (40 percent) was more than double the decline in other cities (17 percent), and New York City's 59 percent decline in Burglary was also more than twice the national average decline (26 percent). New York City's 65 percent reduction in Motor Vehicle Thefts over this period was more than double the 24 percent national decline, and its 40 percent drop in Larceny Theft was almost quadruple the national big-city decline of 11 percent. While the overall Total Index Crime in cities with a population over 100,000 (excluding New York City) fell 17 percent between 1993 and 1999, New York City's Total Index Crime reduction was an astounding 50.1 percent (Mayor's Management Report, Fiscal 2000).

The quality of life enjoyed by those who visit and live in New York City has also improved tremendously, and there is a palpable positive change in the sense of safety and civility throughout the city. The city's public image has also improved dramatically. A nation-wide Harris Poll released in July 1997 and a USA Today-Gallup Poll released in September of the same year each listed New York City as the most desirable place to live in the United States (Mayor's Message of September 29, 1997). A nation-wide *New York Times* poll of 782 adults – ninety-eight percent of them were *not* New Yorkers – conducted in March 1998 showed that more than sixty percent of those surveyed had a good image of the city, compared to forty percent only two years earlier. The percentage of poll respondents mentioning "crime" as New York City's most salient attribute was less than half of what it had been in 1996 (Johnson and Connelley, 1988).

Although quality of life indicators are eminently more difficult to quantify than reported crimes, it seems clear that New Yorkers see less graffiti, they encounter fewer hooligans with loud "boom-box" radios, and they are far less frequently accosted by aggressive panhandlers and "squeegee pests" than they were just a few years ago. A WCBS-TV/New York Times poll conducted in New York City in June 1994 (five months into Mayor Rudolph Giuliani's administration) revealed that thirty-two percent of New Yorkers thought crime increased city-wide in the previous year, seventeen percent thought it decreased, and forty-eight percent thought it stayed about the same. It actually *decreased* almost eleven percent in the year preceding the poll. In addition, the number of shooting incidents taking place in the city declined almost fourteen percent and the number of shooting victims fell almost twelve percent from the levels one year earlier (City of New York, 1997). The same WCBS/New York Times poll showed that crime was the issue of overwhelming concern to most New Yorkers at that time, and the issue they felt the Giuliani administration needed to address most vigorously. Fully 41 percent of the survey respondents chose "crime" from a list of twenty urban problems as the highest priority issue facing the city, slightly more than four times the next-highest priority issue of education. These results were practically identical to a poll sponsored by the same organizations several weeks before the November 1993 mayoral election.

By way of illuminating the tremendous changes that have taken place since that time as well as the tremendous difference in perceptions of safety in New York City, a poll conducted by the Mayor's Office in late December 1996 and early January 1997 revealed that 70 percent of respondents felt safer than they did in 1993 (Mayor's Home Page, http://www.ci.nyc.ny.us/mayor). The two polls were conducted by different pollsters using different methodologies and sampling methods, so the results should be viewed with a bit of caution, but despite this caveat the magnitude of change is impressive. Not only do New Yorkers have a statistically much lower likelihood of becoming a crime victim, but they feel safer as well. Although a host of factors influence electoral preferences, public satisfaction with the administration's anti-crime achievements are also reflected in Giuliani's November 1997 re-election by a wide margin over his challenger.

These and other data illustrate the remarkable changes that have taken place in New York City over the past several years, and the changes are in large measure the result of a revolution in the way the New York Police Department conducts its business, as well as a revolution in the way municipal government as a whole operates there. The NYPD has been transformed in this relatively brief period from a rather passive and reactive agency that lacked energy and focus to an agency that responds quickly and strategically to crime and quality of life trends with an unprecedented vigor. Emerging patterns of crime and quality of life problems are identified almost as they occur, and once identified the NYPD reacts immediately and aggressively to address them and does not diminish its efforts until the problem is solved. The NYPD uses timely and accurate intelligence to identify emerging problems, swiftly deploys personnel and other resources to bring a comprehensive array of effective tactics to bear on the problem, and relentlessly follows up and assesses results to ensure that the problem is truly solved. This revolution in the way the NYPD conducts its business reflects the overall patterns of public-sector management in New York City during the Giuliani administration, and is largely the result of a radically new and thoroughly dynamic police management process known as Compstat.

Because the Compstat process is an intrinsic part of the NYPD's revolution, it has attracted a great deal of attention in the local, national and international media as well as the attention of police practitioners and academics in the criminal justice field. Compstat is one of the most talked-about issues in the field of policing today, despite many misconceptions about it.

Many prominent criminal justice academicians and police leaders have become convinced that the innovative and strategic problem solving processes developed and refined in the NYPD over the past several years are primarily responsible for New York City's falling crime rates (see, generally, Kelling and Coles, 1996; Kelling, 1995; Silverman, 1999). This attention and optimism has not been limited to police and academic criminology circles, though. The NYPD's revolutionary management control and problem solving processes were described in feature articles in *Business Week*, *Forbes*, *The Economist*, *The Wall Street Journal*, *Newsweek*, and a host of other electronic and print media outlets which do not typically cover issues related to police management. The attention Compstat and the new style of results-oriented police management continues to receive in these outlets attests not only to their effectiveness but to their applicability in organizations and industries beyond policing. Compstat's influence is also evidenced by the tremendous number of police executives and academicians who have visited the NYPD to study its innovative management methods and problem-solving activities.

Because it is such an effective and successful management tool, Compstat was named one of five recipients of the prestigious Innovations in American Government Awards in 1996. This prestigious award, conferred jointly by the Ford Foundation and Harvard University's John F. Kennedy

School of Government, selected Compstat from among 1,500 applicant programs nationwide as one of the five most innovative and successful initiatives at any level of American government. The Civil Enforcement Initiative, another program in the NYPD's integrated repertoire of tactical solutions to problem solving, crime reduction and quality of life improvement, was one of five winning finalists in 1995. One reason the Civil Enforcement Initiative has been so successful in achieving its results is the way the Compstat process has been used to manage and direct it.

Despite all the accolades and attention it has received, Compstat has also been greatly misunderstood. Compstat has been variously portrayed as a high-pressure meeting between executives and middle-managers, as a technology system, as a computer program, and as a system for sharing important management information. Compstat management involves all of these things and a great deal more, and this book is an attempt to clear up many of the misconceptions that surround it.

It should be clearly understood at the outset that Compstat, *per se*, is a management process through which the NYPD identifies problems and measures the results of its problem-solving activities. Compstat involves meetings between executives and managers and it uses computer-based technology and other technology systems, but these elements are simply components in a much larger system or paradigm of management that seems to have taken hold throughout New York City's municipal government. Compstat meetings have been a key element in crime reduction, but they are only the tip of the iceberg – a great deal more goes on and has gone on behind the scenes to bring these unprecedented crime reductions and improvements in New York's quality of life to fruition. Without these other efforts and without a fundamental transformation in the agency's organizational structure, culture and mindset, the crime reductions and quality of life improvements could never have been achieved.

Compstat – Winner of the 1996
Innovations in American Government Award

Compstat was one of five winning finalists in the 1996 Innovations in American Government Award Program sponsored by the Ford Foundation and the John F. Kennedy School of Government at Harvard University. Over 1,500 innovative programs developed at the federal, state and municipal government levels apply for the prestigious award each year, but only five programs win a $100,000 finalist award.

This is how Compstat is described on the Kennedy School's web site:

New York City's two-year-old computer-coordinated attack on crime has been "like a shot of adrenaline to the heart of law enforcement," says Howard Safir, the city's Police Commissioner. In the last two years, the city has seen reductions in all categories of crime - petty to serious - with a drop in major felonies of 30 percent. Murders alone have plummeted more than 50 percent.

The key, Safir says, is "Compstat," short for "computer comparison statistics," a system that allows police to track crime incidents almost as soon as they occur. Included are information on the crime, the victim, the time of day the crime took place, and other details that enable officials to spot emerging crime patterns. The result is a computer-generated map illustrating where and when crime is occurring citywide. With this high-tech "pin-mapping" approach, the police can quickly identify trouble spots and then target resources to fight crime strategically.

Although other police departments nationwide are using computers to map crime and improve crime-fighting methods, the New York City Police Department took one other essential step in its anti-crime drive. While it was developing Compstat, the department was also undergoing a major management overhaul aimed at bringing the city's 76 precinct commanders and top departmental management closer together. In the process, it knocked down traditional walls between patrol officers, detectives, and narcotics investigators. Where isolation and even turf protection previously reigned, the department now holds weekly meetings that bring together a broad spectrum of police officials to review the computer data and discuss ways to cut crime in specific places. At these meetings, local commanders are held accountable by requiring them to report on steps they have taken and their plans to correct specific conditions. Also essential to the Compstat process are continual follow-up and assessment of results. Finally, building on its community-policing program, the department often invites to the meetings a variety of interested parties from school officials to neighborhood groups to local business leaders to help fashion a comprehensive response in crime-ridden areas.

Source: Kennedy School of Government website - http://ksgwww.harvard.edu/innovat/winners/cony96.htm

It is also absolutely essential to point out that despite Compstat's effectiveness as a management tool, the dramatic declines in crime would doubtless never have occurred without the political support and the coordination provided by the administration of Mayor Rudolph Giuliani as well as the legislative support of the City Council. It would be wrong and misleading to intimate that these changes were solely the work of the Police Department, just as it would be wrong to intimate they resulted solely from Compstat. In order to be effective and to achieve such dramatic results, Compstat must be seen as one facet of a comprehensive and carefully orchestrated array of management strategies and practices.

One should never conceive of an agency of government - perhaps especially a criminal justice agency - as operating independently of other agencies. Within the criminal justice enterprise, for example, police agencies regularly and flexibly interact with prosecutors, courts, corrections, probation and parole agencies, and to some extent each of these agencies and all of their personnel are interdependent upon the others. If a serious breakdown of communications occurs, or if necessary resources and activities in any sphere of the criminal justice enterprise are not forthcoming, the entire system of justice administration could grind to a halt. These interactions are far more complicated than one might first imagine, since they deal not merely with passing along resources and information but with tailoring each agency's protocols and policies in such a way that they do not conflict or interfere with the policies and protocols guiding the activities of other agencies. In this way, Criminal Justice should be viewed as an enterprise of government involving the coordinated interaction of numerous spheres of interest, function and responsibility, rather than as a complex of separate and discrete agencies each independently pursuing its own goals and agendas.

A schematic depiction of all the lines of communication and interaction among these agencies would resemble a web, with multiple interconnecting lines extending from each agency to every other agency. While these lines have always existed – that is, there has always been communication and some degree of coordination between the spheres of the criminal justice system – many more of them were forged in New York City since 1994 than at any time in the past. A great deal of the increased efficiency and effectiveness of the Criminal Justice enterprise in New York City over the past several years can be credited to the coordination and direction provided by the mayoral administration, which used its influence over these agencies to facilitate enhanced interaction. What was once simply a web of interconnecting lines has come to resemble a network of complimentary policies, practices and strategies that combine to make the Criminal Justice enterprise in New York City reach a new level of effectiveness. This effectiveness is predicated on the need to ensure that all of the agencies are, so to say, reading from the same page of music.

A simplistic example of the need for cooperation and coordination among agencies might be when a police department plans to conduct a major Driving While Intoxicated crackdown over a holiday weekend. If the police agency arrests a large number of violators but the agencies responsible for detaining them (often a municipal corrections agency or sheriff's department), prosecuting them, arraigning them and making arrangements for pre-trial release do not have sufficient staff on hand, the police department will encounter serious problems that may backlog the entire system for an extended period. Prior coordination, cooperation and communication ensure that the system operates more smoothly and with greater efficiency and effectiveness.

Going beyond this generic example, we can easily see how other governmental agencies and entities become involved in the criminal justice process without actually being a part of the system. Municipal budget offices are involved in allocating the necessary fiscal resources to criminal justice agencies, and their operations and actions must be coordinated as well if the system is to work smoothly and systemic bottlenecks and breakdowns are to be avoided. It often becomes necessary to enact specific kinds of legislation that enables criminal justice agencies to perform certain functions or enforce certain offenses more effectively, and it becomes extremely difficult for police agencies to successfully lobby state or local legislative bodies for these changes without the assistance and committed political support of the executive branch. Such enabling legislation may be particularly important for police agencies operating in a problem-solving mode and attacking crime as well as quality of life offenses (see, for example, Kelling, 1995). In many jurisdictions including New York City, police until recently lacked the legal power to prevent sales of spray paint to minors who used it for graffiti, or to take enforcement action against teens carrying box-cutter razor knives that were often used in assaults, robberies and other crimes. The NYPD, the City Council and the Mayor's Office of Legislative Affairs worked together to draft and pass legislation which empowered police officers to take action in these and other cases.

A host of other examples could be given, but the basic point here is that any police agency's success in fulfilling its basic mission and in conducting its business depends greatly upon the kind of commitment, support, interest and coordination provided by its political leadership.

One of the most important reasons why Compstat has functioned so well to reduce crime and improve the quality of life in New York City – that is, to make the Criminal Justice enterprise operate as it should – is because Compstat has political support. From the beginning, the Giuliani administration accepted as its mandate the public's demand for a reduction in crime and a restoration of order in a city that seemed to be out of control. Many believed (erroneously as it turned out) that the City of New York was intrinsically unmanageable. Crime and disorder were major campaign issues in New York City's 1993 mayoral campaign, as was the seeming incapacity of incumbent David Dinkins administration to effect substantive positive change in this area.

Shortly after his inauguration in January 1990, Dinkins and Police Commissioner Lee Brown introduced a vision of Community Policing to the NYPD and set about making it the agency's dominant philosophy. Following the record-breaking levels of murder and other violent crime in New York in 1990, Dinkins expended considerable political capital to achieve passage of the Safe Streets, Safe City Act in the State Legislature. The Safe Streets Act, passed by the Legislature in February 1991, raised taxes throughout the State of New York to provide a $1.8 billion revenue stream over a five year period to increase the size of the NYPD and the Transit and Housing Police Departments (which were separate entities until their 1995 mergers with the NYPD). The Safe Streets legislation mandated that a minimum 19,747 officers would be assigned to patrol duties and also funded a host of social programs, most of them community-based, to facilitate Community Policing.

Based upon the NYPD's Staffing Needs Report of October 1990 (NYPD, 1990), Commissioner Lee Brown determined that in order to implement Community Policing the NYPD's total uniformed headcount should be 31,351 sworn personnel. Including the Transit and Housing Police, the Safe Streets Act provided a revenue stream to raise the total headcount to 38,310 officers among the three agencies (McKinley, 1994; Strong and Queen, 1994). Given the fairly high rate of attrition and retirement at the time and a number of admitted "fiscal gimmicks" used by the Dinkins administration to delay hiring in order to defer the City's share of the hiring costs, the agency's actual growth was fairly slow. The 38,310 Safe Streets benchmark was not reached until 1996. Because it increased the number of new hires and reduced the minimum hiring age to 20, the agency found that the average age and level of experience among its uniformed patrol force declined significantly.

Three significant events – the Crown Heights riots of August and September 1991 (resulting from a vehicle accident in which a young African-American child was struck and killed by an auto driven in the motorcade of a prominent Hasidic rabbi), the Washington Heights riots of July 1992 (resulting from the shooting death of an armed drug dealer in a gun battle with a plainclothes officer), and the Mollen Commission report on police corruption – did little to enhance public confidence in the police or in the capacity of the Dinkins administration to manage the city. Crime, disorder and the declining quality of life in New York City became the bellwether issues of the 1993 mayoral election. Rudolph Giuliani defeated David Dinkins by a slim two percent margin, but he took these issues as his mandate and made good on his election pledge to vigorously attack them.

Giuliani appointed William Bratton, the highly-regarded former chief of the New York City Transit Police[3] and several police agencies in his native Boston, as Police Commissioner. Bratton immediately set about rousing the department's executive corps from their bureaucratic malaise, and after requesting resignations from the entire upper level of the executive corps (all but one of the agency's top five chiefs were replaced in the first few weeks of the new administration), he assembled a top-notch staff of fairly young but well-seasoned executives who were aggressive risk takers (McQuillan, 1994; Krauss, 1994a; Bratton and Knobler, 1998). At his swearing-in speech,

---

3 At that time, the Transit Police was a separate agency under the jurisdiction of the Metropolitan Transportation Authority rather than the City of New York. Similarly, the Housing Police Department operated under the aegis of the New York City Housing Authority. The Transit and Housing Police Departments were merged with the NYPD in 1995.

Bratton took the opportunity to begin setting the tone for the agency's new direction and mandate. Bratton invoked John Paul Jones' request to the Continental Congress: "give me a fast ship, for I intend to sail in harm's way." The words and the sentiment behind them rang true with police officers, who saw themselves as "sailing in harm's way" at work each day. They welcomed a leadership that sought to join them in this struggle.

From the beginning of the Giuliani/Bratton administration, the message to managers was clear: just two weeks after Bratton took office, a senior police planning officer commented in the *New York Times* that the new administration would give precinct commanders "direct control over resources to carry out enforcement operations, to address chronic crime locations and suppress the low-level irritants to their communities (Krauss, 1994a, p. B3)." Once the Compstat meetings began to take shape, Bratton used them in conjunction with other key performance indicators to identify which mid-level managers should be replaced or transferred and which managers should be promoted to positions with additional responsibilities. Within the new administration's first year, more than two thirds of the department's seventy-six precinct commanders were been replaced – either by moving them to positions more suited to their less-assertive management style or promoting them to more challenging positions (Silverman, 1996; Bratton and Knobler, 1998). The key strategy here was to match up particular positions with the commanders who had the requisite skills, experience, expertise and personality to manage them proficiently. As we will see, Compstat meetings proved to be an essential tool in identifying individual managers' strengths and weaknesses.

The shake-up was calculated to shake off the lethargy, passivity and drift that had characterized the NYPD's executive corps. Just as importantly, Giuliani and Bratton began immediately to articulate and to demonstrate their belief in the idea that the New York Police Department and the City of New York as a whole could be managed, and that unprecedented levels of performance could be achieved.

One of the first orders of business was the development of Compstat. As described more fully in subsequent chapters, until the advent of Compstat in the early days of the Bratton administration the NYPD had no functional system in place to rapidly and accurately capture crime statistics or use them for strategic planning. Although the department collected crime statistics, they were often three to six months old by the time they were compiled and the methods used to analyze them were rudimentary at best. Six-month-old crime data is of little use to any police executive, since they say nothing about when and where crimes are occurring today. The fact that NYPD executives in previous administrations never bothered or never saw a compelling need to get accurate and timely crime intelligence is emblematic of the overall lassitude and lack of concern that characterized many of the agency's managers.

This is not to say that every member of the NYPD's management cadre was timid, indecisive, or unconcerned with effectively addressing the kind of crime and quality of life issues that plagued the city. Indeed, the agency had many fine and highly skilled managers, but it was only when a sufficient number of less-effective managers were weeded out or marginalized that an important shift took place in the agency's management culture. By removing or neutralizing indecisive, unimaginative and ineffective managers, the number and percentage of the strong managers who were most capable of leading the department reached a critical mass, and the inept managers no longer impeded the agency's progress.

Achieving this critical mass of dedicated, decisive and innovative managers was an important element in changing the agency's management culture, and its impact was akin to what Malcolm Gladwell (1995, 2000) calls a "tipping point." This concept of "tipping points," a term Gladwell borrowed from epidemiology, involves the idea that some social phenomena – including, Gladwell (1995) argues, some forms of crime and social disorder – behave like infectious agents. That is, the frequency of certain social phenomena and certain behaviors increases gradually and in a linear fashion until they reach a certain threshold or critical mass, at which point they begin to explode – to increase rapidly and exponentially throughout the population. Medical epidemiologists use the term "tipping point" to describe the particular threshold at which the frequency of an infectious disease within a population suddenly tips the balance and takes off to become a full-blown epidemic.

In one interview (Lester, 2000), Gladwell summed up the connection between the tipping points principle and the "Broken Windows theory" approach William Bratton and others in the Transit Police Department applied in the late 1980s and early 1990s to dramatically reduce crime in New York City's rapid transit system:

> Crime in New York is a very important example. I don't think the people who set to work cleaning up the subway ever in their wildest dreams imagined that they'd have the kind of influence that they did. They based their work on

James Q. Wilson and George Kelling's "Broken Windows"
theory – which is just a version, really, of a tipping-point
argument – and they decided that what they had to focus on
was graffiti and turnstile jumping, and a reduction in crime
would follow. That was not an intuitive move at all. They
were setting out to engineer an end to a major behavioral
epidemic – crime on the subway – by what we consider to
be little things... Crime went down. A change in the context
led to a change in behavior (Lester, 2000).

Gladwell (1995, 2000) points out that, just like infectious diseases, the
key to restoring order and reducing crime is to bring crime and disorder to
within manageable limits – below the tipping point that caused it to explode
in the first place. In the case of the subways, such low-level quality-of-life
offenses as graffiti and turnstile jumping were the tipping points or "broken
windows" that invited more serious crime: using enforcement strategies
instituted by William Bratton and based on the "broken windows" approach,
serious felony crime on the subway system plummeted more than fifty
percent between 1990 and 1995. He also cites the tremendous decline in
homicides in Brooklyn's 75th Precinct (from 126 homicides in 1993 to 44
homicides in 1995) as evidence that sustained, aggressive and highly coordinated enforcement aimed at reducing low-level quality-of-life offenses can
tip the balance on serious violent crime.

The same tipping point argument, though, applies to police management:
by creating a critical mass of creativity, innovation and dedication at the
executive level as well as in middle management and among the rank-and-
file, the police chief executive can tip the balance to create an "epidemic" of
organizational creativity, innovation, and dedication that yields remarkable
results. A great deal of this book discusses how and why this "epidemic" of
creativity and innovation occurred in the NYPD in the years after 1994, but
we must also bear in mind that inept or indifferent chief executives can just
as easily tip the balance in the other direction to plunge the organization into
a state of despair.

The dedicated, decisive and innovative executives Bratton assembled
understood the tremendous importance of accurately measuring performance.
Perhaps few executives in earlier NYPD administrations saw the necessity
for accurate and timely crime statistics because few actually believed that
they could use them to fight crime and public disorder more effectively. They
lacked the vision and the focus, and were more concerned with avoiding the
kind of scandals that could cost them their jobs than with fighting crime. The

new administration's mandate to assertively address crime and disorder was the impetus for the revolutionary Compstat process, and within a few weeks the first affirmative steps were taken to develop appropriate technology systems, policies and practices that would ultimately and permanently transform the way the NYPD looked at and responded to crime and disorder problems.

Eli Silverman (1996) summarizes and describes the process, noting that

the most significant aspect of the department's organizational changes within the past few years has been the process known as Compstat... Compstat was originally a document, referred to as the Compstat book, which included current year-to-date statistics for criminal complaints, arrests for major felony categories and gun violations, compiled on a citywide, patrol borough and precinct basis. The initial versions of the Compstat book, which improved steadily over time with regard to overall sophistication and degree of detail, developed from a computer file called "Compare Stats," hence Compstat...

Compstat, through the weekly headquarters meetings, provides the dynamics for precinct and borough accountability, and an arena for testing the mettle of field commanders. As a management tool, Compstat melds upgraded quantitative information on crime locations and times with police deployment arrangements and qualitative quality-of-life information. Precinct problem-solving can be weighed against available resources, and the responsibilities, information-sharing and interaction of different department units can be gauged (Silverman, 1996).

For the first time in the agency's long history, key members of the organization began gathering each week to examine various sources of crime information at a meeting devoted solely to the issue of reducing crime and improving the quality of life enjoyed by New York City's residents (Silverman, 1996).

Compstat: A new management paradigm

It should be emphatically stated at the beginning that Compstat meetings and Compstat technology are management tools – nothing more, nothing less – that are employed to great effect within a radically new and potentially revolutionary management paradigm. Because the NYPD's overall management paradigm and the dynamics of the twice-weekly Compstat meetings reflect essentially similar themes and approaches, and because the meetings and the management system are intrinsically linked, throughout this book the emerging management style is referred to as the "Compstat paradigm."

"Revolutionary" is a term that is frequently bandied about in management circles and frequently misused in common discourse. In reality, true revolutions in management (perhaps especially police management) or in any other area of human endeavor are few and far between, and so this term is used advisedly. Nevertheless, Compstat *is* a revolutionary method of police management because it involves a fundamental shift in the NYPD's management paradigm, and although it has been adopted and practiced in the NYPD and a few other municipal police agencies it has yet to become standard practice across the landscape of American police management. The Compstat paradigm will become a true revolution when it is widely accepted and practiced in police management circles, and when it brings about the same kind of results in other jurisdictions.

The terms revolution and paradigm are used here in the same sense that scientific historian Thomas Kuhn (1970) applied them when he addressed the idea of revolutions in science and scientific thought. Paradigms are a sort of mindset or a collection of organizing principles and fundamental viewpoints around which we organize our basic understanding of the world. Paradigms can be compared to ideologies, belief systems, philosophical principles, or cognitive models that shape our understanding of something, and because they determine the kind of problems and issues we consider important as well as the way we approach the problems, they influence our behavior as well. In terms of management, paradigms are a sort of general point of view about human nature and human behavior, and about how human organizations operate. They also prescribe the management issues we deem most important and the way we approach their resolution. Our paradigm or outlook on management determines the kind of results we seek to achieve as well as the methods and tools we use to achieve them.

Kuhn (1970) pointed out that under ordinary conditions (what he called 'normal science') paradigms guide the development and direction of new knowledge, and knowledge increases incrementally within the paradigm's boundaries. Scientists are guided by the paradigms they follow, and they seldom venture far from them to intellectually consider or experiment with dramatically new ideas. Scientific revolutions occur, Kuhn explained, when paradigms shift radically or when a new paradigm emerges and proves to explain some scientific phenomena better. As other scientists begin to operate within the new paradigm, they stretch the boundaries of knowledge and develop new theories and new technology based on the paradigm. The paradigm of Newtonian physics, for example, prevailed in science until Einstein's theory of relativity successfully challenged its basic assumptions about the physical world. The theory of relativity eventually supplanted Newton's ideas about physics because it more accurately reflected our knowledge of the world, better explained the physical universe, and opened up new and more productive avenues for scientific research.

Paradigms also guide police managers and executives and shape the way they develop new and innovative approaches to the problems they face. For the most part, the approach many police executives and managers continue to take today is not very different from what they and others have done in the past. Because they continue to operate within a narrow management paradigm that generally does not encourage innovation and generally does not strive to stretch the potential boundaries of performance, most police executives are satisfied with incremental improvements. The paradigm with which many police executives operate, for example, does not truly embrace one of the Compstat paradigm's most important underlying principles and beliefs – that police officers and police agencies can really have a substantial positive impact on the crime and quality of life problems facing the communities they serve.

Scientific (and management) revolutions occur when a radical paradigm shift takes place – when there emerge a new set of ideas, ideologies or controlling principles around which we organize our understanding of a phenomena. The new understanding of the phenomena, in turn, points up new insights and better practices. The new paradigm takes hold and gains acceptance when it proves effective – when it does a better job at explaining a phenomena and when its methods achieve more positive results than the paradigm preceding it.

In similar fashion, the Compstat paradigm presents police managers and executives with a new way of looking at police organizations and police activities. It is radically different from the ideologies and practices that have guided police management through most of this century, and it points to new methods and strategies police can use to pursue their goals. As illustrated in the examples and statistics cited at the beginning of this chapter, the Compstat paradigm's effectiveness in achieving results can scarcely be denied.

To many casual observers, Compstat appears to be simply a meeting at which executives and managers discuss the latest information about emerging crime trends, develop specific tactical plans to address them, and monitor the results of the actions previously undertaken. In one sense, Compstat *is* a meeting. Each week, the commanders of all operational units in a given geographic area of New York City gather in the NYPD's Command and Control Center at Police Headquarters to give an accounting of themselves and their officers' activities for the past month (Kelling, 1995; Silverman, 1996; Bratton and Knobler, 1998; Maple, 1999)[4]. The Command and Control Center, informally dubbed the "war room" for its resemblance to the Pentagon's nerve center, is a high-tech conference facility equipped with numerous computer systems, video monitors, video projection screens, and communications equipment. The equipment in the room makes it possible to run virtually the entire City of New York from one central location during major operations, natural disasters and other events requiring central coordination and rapid response.

As will be discussed in subsequent chapters, this level of technology is not absolutely essential for Compstat's effectiveness – the meetings were initially run in a small room equipped only with easels and flip charts, and they nevertheless produced startling results. Police agencies need not assume that Compstat requires a tremendous investment in hardware or software to achieve its results, since even a complete Compstat technology package that will suit the needs of ninety-nine percent of American police agencies can be assembled for just a few thousand dollars.

Each precinct commander takes his or her turn at the Command and Control Center's podium to present their activities and accomplishments and to be closely questioned – some might say interrogated – by the Police Commissioner, several Deputy Commissioners, the Chief of Department, Chief of Detectives, Chief of Patrol, and other top executives. Precinct commanders are accompanied by detective squad supervisors, narcotics and vice squad commanders, and ranking personnel from just about every

---

4 For administrative purposes, the NYPD divides the five Boroughs of the City into eight Patrol Boroughs. The seventy-six precincts, twelve Transit Division Districts and nine Housing Bureau Police Service Areas are about equally apportioned among the eight geographic Patrol Boroughs.

operational and investigative unit within their geographic area of responsibility. Because of their intensity and the technology involved (including computerized pin mapping, comprehensive crime trend analyses and other graphic presentations of data) Compstat meetings permit the agency's executives to have an unprecedented level of in-depth knowledge about the specific crime and quality of life problems occurring at specific locations in each of the NYPD's seventy-six precincts. With this wealth of highly specific knowledge, executives can ask commanders and managers probing questions about the particular activities and tactics they are using to address these problems at specific locations. Crime and quality of life trends and patterns can be more easily discerned through the discussions, and connections between seemingly disparate events and issues are more easily identified. Commanders are expected to have answers and to demonstrate results, and to show how they cooperate and coordinate their activities with other operational entities. The focus is on performance and results at Compstat meetings (Kelling, 1995; Kelling & Coles, 1996; Jener, 1997; Wilson, 1997; Newcombe, 1997; Witkin, 1998; Bratton and Knobler, 1998; Silverman, 1999).

But Compstat is much more than a meeting, and Compstat meetings provide executives with an in-depth knowledge of other management performance data beyond just enforcement and productivity information related to crime and quality of life conditions. Executives focus on each commander's efforts to ensure that officers in his or her command interact with citizens and with other members of the department in a courteous, professional and respectful manner. Executives can effectively gauge the morale in each command by examining sick rates, the number and type of disciplinary actions taken, the number of civilian complaints made against officers, and a host of other data. Each commander's performance in managing such important functions as overtime expense, traffic safety, and even the number of automobile accidents involving department vehicles can be evaluated at Compstat meetings. Executives can and do focus on virtually any area of management responsibility, comparing each commander's performance to that of his or her peers. Performance comparisons can easily be made to other similar commands or to Patrol Borough and City-wide averages as well. Changes over time can be calculated and charted for graphical presentation on practically any crime or quality of life performance criteria within the commander's scope of responsibility (Kelling, 1995; Wilson, 1997; Bratton and Knobler, 1998; Silverman, 1999). In short, the Compstat meetings amount to intensive monthly performance evaluations for every commander of practically every operational unit in the agency.

Compstat – A Tactical Analogy

In describing Compstat technology's capacity for tactical crime fighting and for achieving dramatic results against seemingly-over-whelming odds, Police Commissioner William Bratton often used the analogy of the Royal Air Force's victory in the Battle of Britain during World War II. During the early stages of the war, the British were under air siege from the Luftwaffe. Thousands of German long-range bombers were able to cross the English Channel from bases in Germany and France with impunity, and their nightly bombing raids not only laid waste to England's infrastructure and the factories it needed to produce war materiel, but they were having a devastating impact on the morale of the British people. In particular, the Blitzkrieg in London seemed to imply that no one was safe.

Due to inadequate planning before the war and to ineffective tactics during its earlier stages, the RAF was down to only 450 fighter planes with which to intercept the thousands of bombers that crossed the channel each night. The problem was not that the RAF fliers lacked the skills and determination to wage an effective battle, but that they were simply overwhelmed by Germany's numerical advantage and their inability to predict when, where, and how many waves of bombers would cross the Channel.

When things seemed the worst, the British unveiled their new secret weapon: RADAR. With RADAR, the RAF was able to pinpoint when and where the German bomber waves were taking off, and it was able to intercept them over the Channel. Armed with only 450 fighter planes flown by courageous, determined and highly skilled pilots, the British were able to predict where the German bombers would be, to lie in wait for them, and pick them off before they could do much damage. The small fighter planes seemed no match for the heavily-armed German bombers, but highly focused tactics and operations gave the RAF an advantage far beyond its numbers. When the newly-developed RADAR systems alerted the RAF to the fact that bombers were taking off, fighter squadrons across England scrambled to meet them, and they attacked relentlessly. RADAR gave the RAF the ability to predict the enemy's location and its strength, to quickly develop the kinds of tactics it needed to win the air battle, and to have its determined and highly skilled pilots in the right place at the right time.

In short order, the RAF used RADAR, along with effective tactics, pinpoint accuracy and unrelenting effort, to turn the tide of the Battle of Britain. German bombers were no longer able to cross the Channel, war production resumed, and the morale of the British people was given a much-needed boost – the British people again had faith that the war was winnable. Once the advantage was gained, the continued use of RADAR (along with effective tactics and determined leadership) played a significant role in the course of the war. As Churchill remarked after the Battle of Britain, never have so many owed so much to so few.

The same principles apply to the NYPD's use of Compstat technology to turn the tide of crime in New York City. Because Compstat technology gives executives and middle managers the ability to predict with great accuracy where the criminals will be and the kind of activities they are engaging in, they are able to meet them with appropriate personnel and resources. When Compstat raised the alert that a new crime pattern has emerged or that a new trend is developing, Precinct Commanders and their officers scramble to meet and defeat the threat to the City's safety. Just as in the Battle of Britain, a relatively small number of officers armed with accurate and timely crime intelligence, effective tactics, rapid deployment and unrelenting effort can turn what seems to be an overwhelming tide of crime and disorder.

Commanders who fail to achieve results or who otherwise do not make the grade may find that they are no longer commanders, but those who excel and achieve results find promotion and advancement. Compstat meetings have introduced a unique element of competition among the department's management cadre, and they are a stimulus to achieve results that has never before existed in the NYPD.

Because the Compstat meetings are also attended by commanders of support units, local prosecutors, and representatives of other criminal justice agencies with whom commanders interact, they allow information to be widely disseminated to appropriate parties. Although the support unit commanders and other attendees may not be asked to make presentations, their presence at the meeting allows for the immediate development of integrated plans and strategies. A precinct commander who intends to commence a major enforcement effort, for example, can get on-the-spot commitments for the resources and assistance he or she needs from ancillary and operational units (Kelling, 1995; Wilson, 1997; Newcombe, 1997;

Witkin, 1998). Details of the plan can be worked out without crossing bureaucratic lines or scheduling a prolonged series of meetings.

Compstat meetings, then, are also about supporting and empowering commanders, sharing information and crime intelligence, communicating management's values and objectives, and ensuring accountability. But again, Compstat meetings are just a part of the story behind the NYPD's transformation and its performance, and the meetings are simply a tool used within the larger Compstat paradigm.

A host of other organizational, structural and philosophical changes have been implemented in the NYPD to support its mission, and in conjunction with the support and cooperation received from the mayoral administration and other city criminal justice agencies they made the crime reductions and quality of life improvements possible by enhancing discretion and by changing the dimensions of power, responsibility, authority and accountability throughout the agency. Without these fundamental systemic and philosophical changes within the department and without the support and direction provided by the administration to the police and other criminal justice agencies, the transformation would not have been possible and the dramatic results would not have been achieved. One can scarcely overstate the importance of these structural and philosophical transformations to the agency's overall success. By themselves and without adoption of other elements of the overall Compstat paradigm, Compstat meetings are not only unlikely to achieve more than temporary results, but they could potentially incur long-term damage and possibly undermine the organization's viability as an effective law enforcement agency. The organizational, structural and philosophical changes are as much a part of the Compstat paradigm and the NYPD's transformation as the Compstat meetings themselves.

Compstat meetings permit executives and managers to monitor practically every aspect of the agency's activities – from fulfilling the primary mission of reducing crime and making the city's streets safer to closely observing and controlling virtually every systemic change instituted in the agency's systems, practices, structures and culture. Compstat meetings are, in a sense, a window through which the department's executives and managers can glimpse every aspect of its operations as well as the progress and directions of every change taking place. They are also a mechanism by which the agency's operations and practices can be continually assessed and fine-tuned to ensure their continued success, and through which important messages can be subtly or overtly transmitted and reinforced.

As will become more apparent in subsequent chapters, the Compstat meetings also present opportunities for the agency to temporarily (and, in a sense, artificially) break free of the constraints typically imposed by bureaucracy and by rigid hierarchical organizational structures. Instead of operating within a framework where lines of communication, authority and responsibility are precisely defined by straight horizontal and vertical lines on an organizational chart, for the duration of the Compstat meeting the organizational structure changes to one resembling what Bratton called a "seamless web" (see Henry, 2000). In this seamless web – a structure that facilitates brainstorming, innovative problem solving, and the development of effective strategies and plans – every individual, every unit and every function can communicate immediately and directly with every other individual, unit or function. Once the meeting concludes and decisions have been formulated, the structure reverts to one resembling a hierarchical bureaucratic structure – the kind of structure that is particularly well tailored to carrying plans through to fruition.

This book will provide a description of the Compstat meetings and the kind of interactions that take place in them, it will generally describe the kind of technology used at the meetings and throughout the agency, and it will provide a broader framework of the new management paradigm as a means for conceptually appreciating how and why the Compstat process works. Although the overall contours of the Compstat paradigm apply to the way the City of New York as a whole is managed, we will focus most closely upon the way the NYPD uses Compstat and the principles of the Compstat paradigm to manage crime.

Intrinsic to grasping how and why the Compstat paradigm and process work so well is understanding that the paradigm and process work at every level of the agency and beyond it as well. To remain prepared for the Compstat meetings at Headquarters, most or all Patrol Borough and Precinct Commanders convene their own in-house Compstat-style meetings with key personnel. Accountability and responsibility for achieving results is not just placed on managers by executives, but by managers upon supervisors and to some extent by supervisors upon rank-and-file members of the department. These formal or informal meetings within the agency were never officially mandated, but the Compstat meetings set such a good example that other managers began to emulate them, and they have had a profound influence over the way other meetings are conducted. Because these formal and informal meetings emulate Compstat, a high degree of communication and a sharp focus on achieving results pervade the organization.

The Compstat paradigm closely resembles the overall practices that guide municipal management in the Giuliani administration as a whole, and Mayor Giuliani holds his agency commissioners as accountable for their agencies' activities as the Police Commissioner holds his Patrol Borough and Precinct Commanders. On a weekly basis, the Police Commissioner and several top police executives meet with the mayor to report on their own performance. As a management paradigm – a way of organizing our ideas about the nature of human organizations and their management – Compstat has applicability throughout the public and private sectors. The paradigm has been successfully adapted, for example, to manage New York City's jail system (O'Connell and Straub, 1999), and the city of Baltimore has implemented a "Citistat" program based on the Compstat paradigm for managing the entire city and all its agencies (Clines, 2001; Swope, 2001; www.baltimorecity.gov).

Most of what is contained in this book, though, is fairly closely and narrowly related to policing. There are several reasons for this, including the fact that law enforcement is the function of government administration with which the author is most familiar. Compstat continues to evolve and find broader application in other spheres of public sector administration, but its roots are firmly planted in policing. Compstat continues to bring about remarkable changes in other public sector spheres, but its most tangible, quantifiable and dramatic impact has been in the area of crime reduction. This exploration of the Compstat paradigm is also confined to police management because it involves some rather complex concepts that are difficult enough to convey without venturing too far from one's field of expertise.

The Compstat meetings and the developing paradigm are inextricably linked, but in the interests of clarity it is necessary to distinguish between them. Throughout this book, the term *Compstat meeting* refers to the actual assemblage of personnel and the interactions that take place twice each week at headquarters, the term *Compstat process* refers to the preparations, interactions and activities that are related to Compstat meetings but do not necessarily take place at the meetings, and what we call the *Compstat paradigm* refers to the overall management philosophy that shapes the direction and scope of operations and practices throughout the agency.

A Hybrid Management Style

The Compstat paradigm is a hybrid management style that combines the best and most effective elements of several organizational models as well as the best elements of the philosophies that support them. Compstat retains the best practices of traditional policing, for example, but also incorporates insights and practices from the Community Policing and Problem Solving policing styles. It also utilizes the kind of strategic management approaches used by successful corporate entities that thrive in highly competitive industries. Because the Compstat paradigm is so flexible and because it emphasizes the rapid identification and creative solution of problems, it can be applied in virtually any goal-driven human organization.

Although Compstat police management draws on the strengths of the traditional Professional model of policing as well as the Community Policing and Problem Solving Policing models, it also differs from each in important ways. The NYPD has based its approach to crime reduction and quality of live improvement on the "Broken Windows" theory articulated by George Kelling and James Q. Wilson (1982) – an approach that many Community Policing theorists have also championed. This important theory will be explored in greater depth in subsequent chapters, but in essence it takes the position that quality of life problems such as graffiti, public intoxication, loud radios, urban decay, and a host of other petty annoyances of modern urban life are in themselves criminogenic – when left untended they subtly and overtly convey a message that disorder and incivility prevail, that social controls have broken down, and that no one really cares about the neighborhood in which they occur. This message often translates to the idea that such conditions are somehow acceptable, and because minor offenses are acceptable, more serious ones must be as well. Ultimately, if minor offenses are left unchecked they lead to more serious crime (Wilson & Kelling, 1982, 1989; Wilson 1983, 1997; Kelling & Coles, 1996, 1997; Kelling, 1987, 1991, 1992, 1995).

The postulates of the Broken Windows theory are central to many Community Policing ideologies and practices, although many leading Community Policing theorists and practitioners place the burden for identifying and remedying a neighborhood's crime and quality of life problems on the beat officer. In order to empower the beat officer and support effective Community Policing, they say, the agency must be thoroughly decentralized so that power can be almost completely devolved to those at the bottom of the organizational pyramid.

In the NYPD, though, the burden of identifying and solving problems has been placed squarely in the shoulders of middle managers – the agency's seventy-six Precinct Commanders. Based on its experience during the late

1980s and early 1990s in implementing a version of Community Policing which emphasized the primacy of the beat officer, the NYPD recognized that it is unfair and unreasonable to expect beat cops to disentangle and successfully address entrenched social problems whose solutions have confounded social scientists and criminal theorists for years. Despite their best efforts and, in many cases, their skills and expertise, beat-level police officers simply cannot muster the organizational resources needed to attack these problems.

Decentralizing and Establishing Accountability

Former Police Commissioner William Bratton explained his rationale for devolving power from the top to the middle of the organizational and rank structures in an address to the Heritage Foundation in October 1996:

> I gave away many of my powers not – as my predecessors wanted – to the cop on the beat, but rather to the precinct commander. I did not want to give more power to the cops on the beat. They were, on the average, only 22 years of age. Most of them never held a job before becoming New York City police officers, and had only high school or GED qualification. These kids, after six months of training, were not prepared to solve the problems of New York City; sorry, but it just was not going to work that way. However, my precinct commanders typically had an average of 15 years of service, and they were some of the best and the brightest on the police force. All of them were college educated; all were very sophisticated; and they were at the appropriate level in the organization to which power should be decentralized.

> My form of community policing, therefore… put less emphasis on the cop on the beat and much more emphasis on the precinct commanders, the same precinct commanders who met with community councils and with neighborhood groups. They were empowered to decide how many plain clothes officers to assign, how many to put in community policing, on bicycle patrols, and in robbery squads. They were empowered to assign officers as they saw fit – in uniform or in plain clothes – to focus on the priorities of that neighborhood… Whatever was generating the fear in their precinct, they were empowered to address it by prioritizing their responses. We decentralized the organization, and I eliminated a few levels in the organization of the force and in the hierarchy as well (Bratton, 1996).

Closely related to the NYPD's decentralization was the redistribution of power in the agency. The five bases of power operating within a police organization - coercive, legitimate, expert, reward and referent power – need to be realigned if the agency and its members are to achieve their full potential. In traditionally-managed agencies, the majority of power is concentrated among the executive cadre, and because others have almost no access to coercive, legitimate or reward power, they cannot easily obtain or apply the agency's resources to address problems. We will explore the dimensions of power and authority in greater depth in Chapter 2.

The Compstat paradigm's effectiveness also derives from the emphasis it places on mobilizing expertise and good practice – in many cases the expertise and good practices of experienced patrol officers – and making them the norm throughout the agency. This, too, is a tenet of Problem Solving policing, but as an organizational reality it has often proven to be an illusory goal in American policing. The NYPD's executives gathered together experts from throughout the agency as well as from outside it and drew upon their knowledge and experience to develop a series of crime control and quality of life strategies. The strategies, specifically crafted to be flexible and adaptable to the local community's particular needs and conditions, addressed specific types of crime and disorder problems and were promulgated throughout the department. Every Precinct Commander was mandated to adapt and implement them, and Compstat meetings are one way to ensure that they have been implemented effectively. We will examine some of these crime control and quality of life strategies in subsequent chapters.

As a practical matter, the strategies all proceeded from the Broken Windows theory's basic position that many serious crimes will be prevented and serious problems avoided if we attend to minor offenses as they occur or soon afterward. The strategies also primarily use enforcement tactics to suppress these lower-level offenses and quality of life problems. Some Community Policing adherents eschew enforcement as a means to reduce crime and disorder, or at best they express ambivalence about how effectively enforcement tactics work to reduce crime. Their position, in a nutshell, is that the police should become agents of change who empower and build communities to police themselves. Other Community Policing advocates rarely deal with the idea of *actually* reducing crime, preferring instead to emphasize that the perceived *fear* of crime in a community can be reduced through more positive police-community interactions. These Community Policing theorists have been criticized by more traditional thinkers for placing more emphasis on the *appearance* of public safety than upon substantive crime reduction. Highly focused enforcement activities were always a goal of the Professional Model that dominated American policing for most of this century, but they were nevertheless a rarely-achieved goal. Through the Compstat paradigm and the Compstat meetings, the NYPD has had great success with the use of enforcement in the Broken Windows context.

It is important to recognize, though, that although the results the NYPD achieved depended greatly on enforcement activities, the Compstat management paradigm can be used equally well to manage an agency in which enforcement has a lower priority. That agency may or may not achieve the magnitude of crime reduction accomplished in New York City – indeed, some agencies may not face the compelling crime problems the NYPD did – but the agency will improve its performance on any criteria it deems important if it implements the paradigm cogently. If the agency's prevailing philosophy is that the number and quality of police-citizen encounters are of primary importance and that enforcement has little value, Compstat paradigm management can be adapted and used to tremendously improve the quality and number of those positive encounters. As will become more apparent in subsequent chapters, the converse is also true: there is a great danger that the Compstat model could be adapted and applied in other nations and other police systems to repress the citizenry and deprive the public of basic human rights. Regardless of the agency's specific goals and objectives, implementing the basic principles of the Compstat paradigm will dramatically increase the likelihood they will be attained.

As practiced in New York City, the Compstat paradigm also articulates a bold new philosophy – an unwavering belief in the capacity of police officers to make a difference and to reduce crime. Police officials in the NYPD and elsewhere have, of course, spoken to this philosophy for years, but in fact their words often amounted to mere platitudes and in many cases were betrayed by their actions. As we will discuss in subsequent chapters, this perceived or real insincerity combines with other factors to foment cynicism, to drive a divisive wedge between street cops and management cops, and to undermine the legitimacy of managers as well as their capacity to effectively manage and direct their department's affairs.

Patrick Murphy on Transforming a Police Organization

In the early 1970s, Police Commissioner Patrick V. Murphy faced the daunting task of transforming the NYPD in the aftermath of a devastating corruption scandal. Murphy set about this transformation by focusing on changing the management cadre – the 300 or so members of the department in the rank of Captain or above. His approach was for the most part quite successful – managers and executive were made strictly accountable for any corruption taking place within their commands, he imposed effective systems to monitor and prevent corruption, and the types of corruption that existed at that time practically disappeared from the agency. Managers who controlled corruption were rewarded with promotion and advancement, and those who failed to act aggressively enough were pushed aside or out of the organization. New waves of corrupt activity swept the agency in the late 1980s and early 1990s, but that corruption was of a very different type than existed twenty years earlier. This less pervasive but far more insidious corruption resurfaced for the same reason: management again became complacent. Executives and managers failed to recognize new and emerging corruption problems and failed to respond to them aggressively.

Patrick Murphy frequently said that about ten percent of the department's members at the beginning of his tenure were thoroughly corrupt, and that they would rise to any corrupt situation they encountered. They had to be identified and separated from the department through termination or some other means, if only so that their influence on other officers was neutralized. Another ten percent or so, he said, were scrupulously honest - they could always be trusted to do the right thing and would never succumb to the temptations of corruption. The remaining eighty percent were men and women of good impulse who sincerely wanted to be honest, but they would go whichever way management and their peer groups led them.

The same basic approach – akin to the "tipping point" argument – applies to the NYPD's transformation in the mid-1990s. Some small percentage of cops were thoroughly lazy and demoralized and would actively seek to do as little work as possible. Deputy Commissioner Jack Maple dubbed these officers "Conscientious Objectors:" they showed up for work, but didn't get involved in the fighting. Another group could always be counted on to do the job to the best of their abilities and to maintain the highest levels of performance despite the lack of supportive leadership and the cynicism of other cops. The majority of the department wanted to be good and assertive cops, but instead of leading them to greatness, management placed obstacles in their way, and they became satisfied with a level of performance that was merely adequate. By empowering and transforming management through the imposition of accountability systems like Compstat and by forging alliances with the best and most effective operational cops, the NYPD's executive corps of the mid-1990s transformed the agency into one in which the highest standards of performance became the norm.

At the heart of the Compstat paradigm is a realistic appreciation for the wealth of expertise and experience held by effective police officers. Expert officers of every rank worked together to create and implement the crime and quality of life strategies that helped reinvigorate the NYPD, and they worked together in the reengineering committees that restructured twelve important functional areas. In far too many agencies, including the NYPD, managers and executives have subtly or overtly devalued operational officers and their contribution to the agency. Good and effective cops exist in every agency, and the Compstat management paradigm insists that managers and executives capitalize on that expertise and use this essential resource effectively.

Quite frankly, this often demands that executives and middle managers put aside their own deficiencies to acknowledge that in many instances street cops may have greater expertise and greater knowledge than they. In far too many agencies, including the NYPD, some managers and executives have been too timid to take the kind of risks that might compromise their own careers, and they have concentrated a disproportionate share of their energies on restraining and controlling operational officers.

This is by no means to say that executives, managers and supervisors should exert no restraints on officers' behavior and conduct, but that as often as not the restraints have taken the form of broad policies and blanket practices that put unnecessary and burdensome restrictions on all cops, without regard to their capabilities. Managers and executives often impose unnecessary impediments to good police work, but Compstat management not only demands that these obstacles to performance be removed in order to let good cops flourish and influence others around them to do the same, but it helps identify and reward the officers who perform best.

Another central tenet of the new management philosophy is a belief in
the idea that police *can* make a difference and that police *can* reduce crime.
A great deal more will be said about this idea throughout this book, but at
this point it should be pointed out that a great many criminologists,
politicians and police executives seem to equivocate about whether the police
really make a difference in terms of crime. When a police officer performs
a creditable act or when the agency performs well, executives laud it as an
example of the kind of difference police can make. When crime rises, though,
many are unwilling to acknowledge their own managerial inadequacies or
failures, and they begin looking about for other explanations. They may
never directly articulate a *disbelief* in the capacity of police officers to make
a difference by reducing crime and improving the quality of life enjoyed in
their communities, but their failure to maintain a consistent approach often
casts them as self-serving and undermines their legitimacy in the eyes of
officers. In the world of policing, the disjuncture between words and actions
often breeds suspicion and distrust, and such subtleties rarely go unnoticed
by cops. The Compstat paradigm rejects this pessimistic and cynical management view and optimistically asserts without question that conscientious
police officers in a well managed police organization can make a remarkable
difference.

The Structure of this Book: Possibilities and Constraints

This book is written with several rather diverse audiences in mind, and
that fact raises the sometimes-difficult task of trying to provide enough
information to satisfy the needs of each audience without boring or
overwhelming the others. This book is primarily directed toward college-
level students of policing and police management, and the author is keenly
aware that this audience can itself be quite diverse in terms its members'
familiarity with police organizations and practices. This audience ranges
from those with no direct first-hand experience with policing to highly
experienced police practitioners, who may themselves range from operational
officers to police executives. Beyond this academic audience, others
including students of organizational management, business or private security
management may be interested in applying the Compstat paradigm in various
other public-sector and private-sector organizations. This book is also written
for police practitioners – ranging from operational officers and patrol cops
to ranking executives – who wish to improve their own performance and the
performance of their agency or who wish to enhance their understanding of
cutting-edge police management practices.

The changes in the NYPD over the past few years were shaped by internal and external forces and historical trends which emanate from the internal and external political environments, from the history and culture of the agency, and from trends taking place across the landscape of American policing as a whole. The changes were also affected by the personalities and career insights of key players involved in developing Compstat and each of the strategy elements it supports. If the author is to fulfill his responsibility to this diverse audience and provide an understanding of how the NYPD was so fundamentally transformed in so brief a period of time, we must address these forces and themes. Without understanding the larger context and some of the possibilities and constraints the agency encountered along the way, it would be as difficult to grasp the true dimension of change as it would be for other organizations to successfully adapt these principles to their own environments. Because many of the themes discussed in this book seem to resonate through other police agencies, they may also help the reader to conceptualize applications closer to home.

Certainly, an important practical constraint is the need to provide a comprehensive explanation of Compstat and the Compstat paradigm without delving into minutia. Multiple chapters could be written just on the attempted implementation of one vision of the Community Policing model in New York during the late 1980s and early 1990s, for example, and it would be possible to describe in detail how each of the forces in each of the environments noted above shaped the vision's implementation as well as subsequent efforts to break free of it. That implementation effort provided important lessons about policing and about the NYPD in particular, and the lessons ultimately informed and impelled the agency's shift toward the management style and set of management practices that comprise the Compstat paradigm. Similarly, it is possible to go on in great detail about the subtleties and nuances of how the Compstat paradigm was developed and how it took hold in the agency, or about the lessons learned from specific types of interactions at the Compstat meetings. The author could describe in great detail the specific elements and practices that comprise each of the NYPD's crime and quality of life strategies. To do so, however, would be misleading and ultimately it would do a disservice to readers.

Having examined police practices in the NYPD and in other police agencies across the nation and around the world, the author is convinced that a great many problems in contemporary policing are the result of what might be called "cookie cutter management." That is, there is a distinct tendency throughout policing to find some policy or practice that another agency has put to good use and to appropriate it. Agencies borrow these policies from another agency comprised of different people with a different organizational culture and structure and a different set of environmental and political forces working upon them, pressing the borrowed policy down on their own agency as if it were a cookie cutter or template. In one fairly large police agency, for example, the newly-appointed chief executive "borrowed" the NYPD's entire 800-plus page Patrol Guide of rules and regulations several years ago, had it retyped on a new letterhead with absolutely minimal changes, and adopted it lock, stock and barrel. These unimaginative managers wind up trying to make the agency fit the policy or practice, rather than the other way around.

Experience and close observation of police agencies and systems in the United States and overseas shows that in the vast majority of cases, a home-grown policy or practice will work much better than an imported policy or practice precisely because it was developed in conformance with the reality of the department. These policies and practices also work better because they are developed by people who are intimately familiar with the agency, its history and culture, and the capabilities of its personnel. The same is true of the Compstat paradigm's adoption: the general principles outlined in this book must be carefully tailored to the specific conditions, situations and realities faced by other agencies in other contexts.

A related management practice that seems to affect American police management is what we might call "cargo cult management." The notion of "cargo cult management" derives from the millennial cults that developed in Melanesia and the South Pacific islands during and after the Second World War and continue to exist today. In essence, members of these primitive cultures had no exposure to the outside world, and as a function of their insularity the cultures were permeated with a deep strain of magical thinking and a propensity to attribute results to rituals rather than to their actual causes. These cultures had their first real exposure to outsiders during the war, when foreigners (Allied military personnel) arrived and began to carve out long flat strips of jungle. The foreigners engaged in such rituals as marching around in formation with unusual devices made of wood and metal over their shoulders. The foreigners built towers and spoke odd words into strange boxes, and shortly thereafter large bird-like flying machines came out of the sky laden with all sorts of good stuff the foreigners called "cargo." The foreigners eventually departed but left behind some of the cargo – Coca Cola, various ingenious machines, and building materials that were far superior to anything the tribes had known before. To this day cargo cultists continue to carve out strips of jungle, march around with tree limbs over their shoulders, build bamboo towers or climb trees and repeat "roger, over and out" into coconuts as they await the return of the cargo-bearing magical flying machines.

The analogies of "cookie cutter management" and "cargo cult management" to the expanding use of Compstat-like programs is clear. Gootman (2000), for example, noted that 235 police agency representatives visited NYPD Compstat meetings in the first ten months of 2000, while 221 visited in 1999 and 219 visited in 1998. There is no doubt that many of these representatives are highly experienced practitioners and fine managers, but based upon their too-brief exposure to the Compstat meetings, we can expect that many will return to their agencies with only a rudimentary and very superficial understanding of the Compstat process and even less knowledge of the Compstat paradigm as a whole. There is a distinct possibility that some proportion of these representatives will not fully grasp how and why the process works in terms of motivation, strategy development, the dissemination of knowledge and expertise, or organizational and cultural transformation. Nor will they comprehend the important activities (such as reengineering and training) that were undertaken to support it. They may convene Compstat-type meetings where executives apply a heavy hand where a gentle touch is required, and in many cases they will not go beyond the statistical data to identify important qualitative management issues that should be of concern to competent police executives.

Some police executives who see the wonderful things Compstat can bring to the organization (and to them personally) may engage in ritualistic repetition of the overt behaviors they've witnessed while the larger picture eludes them. This certainly may not be the case in all situations, but the overall pervasiveness of "cookie cutter management" and "cargo cult management" in American police management certainly illuminates the potential harm that Compstat can do when unenlightened executives wield such a powerful management tool. Perhaps the greatest danger lies in the fact that the organizational and cultural damage they do remains submerged, creating a host of concealed difficulties with which future generations of police officers and executives will have to grapple. Moreover, once locked-in to this pseudo-Compstat mindset, future generations of managers in these agencies may lack the capacity or the experience to easily recognize or respond effectively to the subtleties and nuances of the problems they confront. Wittingly or unwittingly, far too many police chief executives seem willing to enter into the Faustian bargain of selling their souls to achieve immediate results without regard for the long-term organizational and social consequences or the management burdens that others will have to assume when they've moved on.

There are certainly useful templates or blueprints one might borrow to structure or design a policy, a practice or an entire police organization, but the key to the success and applicability of the Compstat paradigm is the fact that its principles are eminently adaptable to any police agency. It is not necessary or desirable to create an NYPD Compstat-clone to achieve remarkable results. Compstat is too good and too effective a management tool to be cheapened and misused in this way. Instead, in writing this book, the goal has been to try to set out the broad perimeters of the Compstat paradigm and to describe, in fairly general terms, how it works. The goal is not to describe how the NYPD does it, *per se*, so much as to describe the transformations in a fairly systematic and comprehensible way that students of policing and management can readily understand, and so that other agencies can effectively apply the principles in their own municipalities.

Each chapter in this book begins with a brief introduction of the chapter's content and ends with a brief summary highlighting the important points contained in it. Each chapter also provides a series of questions for discussion or debate and a listing of additional readings for those who desire to learn more about a particular issue. From time to time, sidebars or brief items apart from the text present a particular view or explore a particular issue in greater depth.

The first several chapters in this book deal with general issues that have historically influenced policing and police management and which set the stage for the Compstat paradigm's revolution. They set the stage for the next few chapters, which focus upon Compstat technology, Compstat meetings, and the Compstat process. The final chapters deal with the future of Compstat, how and where it may be applied in policing in the 21st Century, and how it may be applied in other public sector organizations.

Readers interested in learning more about Compstat should visit the Compstat website: www.compstat.com. The site, maintained by John Yohe (one of the original members of the NYPD's Compstat Unit, architect of the technology system that supports the Compstat process, and currently a consultant to numerous police and public sector agencies that utilize Compstat), has a great deal of information about Compstat as well as links to many of the primary source documents referenced in this book.

Recommended Readings

Former Police Commissioner William Bratton provides an excellent and highly readable insider's account of the creation of Compstat and the overall process of transforming NYPD's management practices between 1994 and 1996 in his book (with Peter Knobler) **Turnaround: How America's Top Cop Reversed the Crime Epidemic**. One of Bratton's top advisors, former Deputy Commissioner for Operations Jack Maple, has also written an insightful and very colorful analysis of the NYPD and its transformation in his 1999 autobiography **The Crime Fighter**. Both books take an autobiographical approach to demonstrate how the authors developed their management styles through real-world police experience in very different environments.

Bratton, William J. with Peter Knobler **Turnaround: How America's Top Cop Reversed the Crime Epidemic**, New York: Random House, 1998.

Maple, Jack with Chris Mitchell **The Crime Fighter: Putting the Bad Guys out of Business**, New York: Doubleday, 1999.

These articles by Wilson and Kelling are the basic starting points for an exploration of the Broken Windows theory:

Wilson, James Q. and George Kelling "Broken Windows," *Atlantic Monthly* (March 1982), pp. 29-38.

Wilson, James Q. and George Kelling "Making Neighborhoods Safe," *Atlantic Monthly* (February 1989), pp. 46-52.

The following books and articles authored or co-authored by George Kelling show the application of Broken Windows theory, especially the way it has been applied in New York City:

Kelling, George L. and Catherine M. Coles **Fixing Broken Windows: Restoring Order and Reducing Crime in Our Communities**, New York: Touchstone (Simon & Schuster), 1996.

Kelling, George "Measuring What Matters: A New Way of Thinking About Crime and Public Order," *City Journal*, 2, 3 (Spring 1992), pp. 21-33.

Kelling, George L. "Acquiring a Taste for Order: The Community and the Police," *Crime and Delinquency*, 33, 1 (January 1987), pp. 90-102.

Kelling, George L. "How to Run a Police Department," *City Journal*, 5, 4 (Autumn, 1995), pp. 34-45.

Kelling, George L. "Reclaiming the Subway," *City Journal*, I, 2 (Winter 1991), pp. 17-28.

Eli Silverman, a Professor in the Department of Law, Police Science and Criminal Justice at John Jay College of Criminal Justice in New York, has been studying Compstat and its impact on crime and quality of life for several years. He is the author of the following:

Silverman, Eli B. **NYPD Fights Crime: Innovative Strategies in Policing**, Boston, MA: Northeastern University Press, 1999.

Silverman, Eli B. "Mapping Change: How the New York City Police Department Reengineered Itself to Drive Down Crime," *Law Enforcement News*, December 15, 1996. [Available Online: http://www.lib.jjay.cuny.edu/len/96/15dec/ html/12.html].

A wealth of information about crime and quality-of-life issues in New York City can be found at the City of New York's official website (www.ci.nyc.ny.us). In addition to providing links to and information about the NYPD and other city agencies, the site has an extensive archive of mayoral statements, press releases and statistical data.

Questions for Debate or Discussion

1. In the discussion above, an example was given of how something as simple as a DWI enforcement initiative could cause a logjam in the Criminal Justice system unless the various agencies involved communicate and act in a coordinated fashion. Other than a sudden shift in workload and resources as described here, what other types of problems can the system face when agencies fail to communicate and coordinate? What government agency or entity should take the lead in coordinating and directing the activities of other Criminal Justice agencies, and under what authority can it determine the policies and practices of other autonomous agencies? Does such an agency or entity currently exist in your jurisdiction?

2. Police executives are sometimes held accountable to the public (i.e., they lose their jobs) when crime, fear of crime and public disorder problems reach critical proportions. Under what conditions are elected officials – specifically the officials who appointed or hired the police executives – held publicly accountable for the police executive's failures?

3. In this chapter, the author stated that the introduction of highly-focused, high-pressure Compstat-style meetings to hold managers accountable for the performance of the officers they command could incur significant long-term damage to the agency if they are not supported with other systemic changes. In what specific ways could this cause long-term harm to the agency and its capacity to function effectively?

4. Some basic features of the Compstat meetings and the Compstat paradigm were described in this chapter, and they will be fleshed out in subsequent chapters. Given what you know at this point, how could the paradigm and the process be applied by the supervisor of, say, a detective squad? By the supervisor of a Highway Patrol unit? By a patrol supervisor?

5. How much of a difference do the police really make in the crime equation? Aren't crime rates really determined by demographic, economic and social trends?

6. What specific kinds of formal and informal restraints do police managers (or managers in any organization, for that matter) exercise to limit the effectiveness and efficiency of police officers (or employees in other

organizations)? Why would they want to impose limits on police officers' activities?

7. Obviously, some restrictions have to be placed on police behavior in order to prevent the purposeful or inadvertent trampling of civil liberties. Can police managers ensure that police officers do not violate civil liberties without relying on strict rules and harsh disciplinary sanctions?

8. This chapter briefly discussed the notion of "cookie cutter management," in which managers attempt to impose on their own organization a policy, practice or strategy that has proven successful in other jurisdictions. Other than the examples given in this chapter, what kinds of long-term organizational and operational problems does "cookie cutter management" create?

Chapter 2
Management Theory

T his book is about a revolution in the way the New York Police Department has come to fulfill its core mission of reducing crime and improving the quality of life experienced by New Yorkers, and about how other police agencies can apply the principles that gave shape and form to that revolution to bring about similar changes within their own jurisdictions. In this sense, the book is not about the NYPD, *per se*. While it focuses on the NYPD and the particular problems, issues and organizational impediments that faced that agency and that inhibited organizational change, the goal is not merely to present a case study detailing the recent history and problems of one police department or the lessons that might be drawn from its experience. Rather, the goal is to integrate these experiences and lessons in such a way as to permit a broader and more comprehensive understanding of the problems shared by many police agencies, both in the United States and abroad. The goal is also to provide effective illustrations as to how the Compstat management paradigm addressed these issues and how it can be applied in virtually any policing environment, in private security, and in other organizations in the public and private sectors.

At first glance, these goals presents a somewhat daunting array of challenges, since there are in excess of 17,000 local, state and federal law enforcement agencies n the United States (Bureau of Justice Statistics, 1995; Reeves, 1995). At the local level, for example, these agencies range in size from one-officer departments (indeed, in some one-officer agencies the officer is a part-time employee) to large municipal agencies with several thousand officers. The largest American police department, the NYPD had a headcount of nearly 42,300 sworn officers and almost 9,000 civilian employees in 1999, but nearly 6,400 agencies (or 54 percent of the total) employ fewer than ten officers. There are nearly twice as many one-officer police agencies in the United States as there are agencies with one hundred or more officers (Reeves, 1995).

Along with the problem of tailoring this text to address agencies of varying sizes, there exists the related problem of complexity: larger agencies, which account for a relatively small number of the total 17,000 (only 38 local police agencies employ one thousand or more officers), tend to be more complex in terms of the missions and functions they perform and the methods they practice in pursuit of their goals. In addition, it is quite clear that many variants of policing styles are practiced in America and abroad, and that there are intrinsic differences between urban, suburban and rural policing (McDonald, Wood and Pflug, 1996; Thurman and McGarrell, 1997).

It would be foolish and somewhat arrogant to presume that because the NYPD is the largest and arguably the most complex American police department, the problems and management issues it faced (and continues to face) are representative of all police agencies, or that these problems are the only management issues worth considering. However, based upon extensive contacts with officers in other departments in the United States and abroad – particularly Japan, Great Britain, Ireland and Australia – and based upon an understanding of policing and of organizational management in other jurisdictions, the author believes that certain unifying themes, principles and universal problems are to some extent evident in virtually all police agencies.

In most cases, these themes, principles and problems derive from the fact that the enterprise of police work, in its essence and regardless of the social and political environments in which it takes place, concerns the regulation of social behavior through the enforcement of law. Police agencies tend to have similar organizational structures, and they generally conform to a bureaucratized, quasi-military management system. The basic goals and objectives of all police agencies – at least those in Western liberal democracies – can be distilled and summarized as fulfilling the mission of reducing crime and improving the quality of life enjoyed by the citizens they serve. While many police agencies perform functions in addition to these core roles, these two roles lay at the heart of policing and all other functions flow from them.

Although these themes, principles and problems outlined here may vary from agency to agency in terms of their extent or dimensions, to greater or lesser extent every police officer and every police executive encounters them on a regular basis. They are universal elements of policing.

In order to assist the reader who may be unfamiliar with the NYPD and the problems it has historically faced to understand the tremendous changes that have taken place over the past several years, it is important to set forth in broad terms some basic concepts about how the NYPD and other police agencies operate. We will use the NYPD as a sort of template to illustrate the process and the possibilities of change, and the template may be particularly useful because the NYPD's problems were so complex and so entrenched.

To paraphrase the popular song about New York, if we can change it there, we can change it anywhere.

It is important to again point out that while the NYPD is used as an exemplar or template for understanding organizational problems in policing, the author does not advocate, suggest or advise that the winning tactics, strategies and processes developed by the NYPD to achieve such startling results should be adopted *in their entirety* in other agencies. Police management should not be a cookie cutter operation, and the principles and processes outlined in this book will work most effectively only if they are carefully adapted and flexibly implemented according to the needs, structures, and conditions operating in other venues.

The principles and concepts set forth in this chapter will be referenced throughout the book, so discussing them at the beginning seems both pragmatic and necessary. By putting the process of changing police organizations into a broad theoretical framework of general principles, they hopefully become more comprehensible to readers and more generalizable to other police agencies and settings. The first several chapters of this book address some of the more salient problems confronting the NYPD prior to the advent of Compstat and Strategic Policing. They deal with concrete and specific problems and issues. Other chapters deal with the solutions to those problems. Both the problems and the solutions, though, can be best understood if they are embedded in a solid framework of management theory.

The Biggest Secret in Policing: the Police Can and Do Make a Difference.

To many academic criminologists, the idea that police activity can have a substantial positive impact on crime and the problems of social disorder is anathema. Many (but fortunately, not all) criminologists believe that crime, social disorder, and the other social problems that typically fall within the purview of the police are exclusively caused by social problems such as unemployment, economic trends, a poorly educated or insufficiently socialized populace, or other factors that are simply beyond the immediate capacity of the police to address. Some of these criminologists are possessed of a seemingly unshakable ideology that the vast majority of society's problems – including the very problems that police are most often called upon to solve – result from fundamental flaws in the social fabric or in the structure of society itself, and that the solution to these problems must therefore result from restructuring society. Because these "root cause" problems are so deeply entrenched, they say, the police are simply incapable of achieving lasting and permanent change. Moreover, some of these theorists see the police as a repressive mechanism of social control whose mandate and function is the preservation of the *status quo*.

Another group of academic criminologists agree that crime and social disorder problems are related to social and economic issues, but they contend that police *can* have an impact by organizing and working with communities to effect change. They propose that the police adopt the role of social reformer in order to restore a sense of order and safety to communities, and their ideas formed the basis for much of the early literature of community-based policing. This group of criminologists tends to operate from a political science perspective – their paradigm leads them to see society in political terms and therefore to see social problems as having political solutions. Their work and their theories are generally more concerned with grass-roots political action and community mobilization than with political change at the electoral level. While the support and the resources necessary to bring about change in policing are absolutely essential and must come from elected officials, Community Policing theorists emphasize change at the neighbor-hood or community level. Many Community Policing theorists believe that the entire institution of policing must be radically transformed if society is to reap the benefits of Community Policing. Police officers, in their view, must become agents of change.

In their view, the goals of policing should include working with neigh-borhoods and communities to achieve consensus, to mobilize and apply com-munity-based resources, and ultimately to reduce crime and disorder by empowering communities to police themselves. There is much to be said for this perspective, which underlies that philosophy of policing that has been variously dubbed Community Policing, Community-Oriented Policing, Neighborhood-Oriented Policing, etc. Indeed, one of the problems with the Community Policing concept is its lack of substantive definition – even avid Community Policing theorists like Herman Goldstein (1993) admit that the term is widely used without regard for its substance. Some police and political leaders latch onto the label for the positive images it evokes but do not invest in the concept itself, while others resist it because they see it as an attempt to appease segments of the community that are intent on imposing additional controls over police activities. The term Community Policing is being used to describe practically all innovations in policing, according to Goldstein (1993), and there is a danger that it will be perceived as a panacea for a host of intractable social problems.

Although the community-based policing model has great appeal and potentially great merit, the experience of many jurisdictions show that Community Policing may be difficult to implement and that it may have limited immediate impact on crime and quality of life. Without an immediate and tangible impact, it becomes difficult to sustain the community's interest and participation in Community Policing, and raises the possibility that the venture will fail. We shall revisit these issues and problems in our discussion of New York City's early attempts to implement Community Policing, but it should be sufficient at this point to note that communities are particularly difficult to organize and empower when their members believe, justifiably or not, that they are under siege from the criminal element.

Regardless of their perspective or ideology, though, relatively few criminologists believe that police, especially police adhering to the traditional model of municipal law enforcement, can make a difference in terms of actually reducing crime. One can scarcely argue with the conclusions reached in the research studies they have conducted. They point out that no empirical studies or experiments have ever demonstrated that the number of police officers deployed within a given area actually reduces reported crime. A host of studies have shown that saturation patrol tactics can reduce the number of crimes taking place on the street within a target area, where the crimes are visible to police, but increasing the number of police deployed within an area has little or no impact upon crimes taking place indoors or in locations that are not visible to patrolling officers (Kelling, Pate, Diekman and Brown, 1974).

Further, none of the police patrol experiments, including some controlled quasi-experimental research designs, have eliminated the possibility that the target zone reduction may be due to the displacement of street crime to other geographic areas rather than to true deterrence. Indeed, some of the studies showed that apparent short-term reductions were actually displacements – crime declined in the target area but increased in nearby areas outside the saturation zone. James Q. Wilson (1985, pp. 62-64) describes two such saturation deployment studies in New York City in 1954 and 1966, and he points out that while these studies demonstrated significant short term reductions in "outside" or "street" crime, neither study could adequately determine how much of the reduction was due to the deterrent effect of an increased police presence and how much was due to displacement. The studies also demonstrated little or no impact on crimes occurring indoors or where they were otherwise invisible to patrolling officers.

In his book **Sense and Nonsense About Crime**, Samuel Walker (1985) echoes the same theme. He admits that a uniformed police presence has some limited deterrent value, and that specific deterrence is achieved when an individual criminal is arrested and incarcerated, but he is emphatic in asserting that "even the most superficial evidence suggests no relationship between the number of cops and the crime rate (p. 104)."

Samuel Walker is absolutely correct in stating that there is no credible evidence to suggest that increasing the number of cops will decrease the crime rate. Yet time and again we have seen politicians and police executives, when backed into a corner by public outrage at increasing crime, offer the same trite and impractical solution: hire more cops. These politicians and police executives know well that the simple expedient of hiring additional officers, *per se*, will have little impact on reducing crime, but the ploy permits them some diversionary "tough on crime" posturing and rhetoric, and it buys them time. By the time the officers are hired, trained and deployed, public attention will most likely shift to other issues. Simply hiring more officers and then training and deploying them in the traditional manner – that is, essentially pointing them toward the door and saying, "OK, now go out there and randomly patrol" – is not a viable strategy.

At least in this regard, the criminologists are correct: as the empirical evidence suggests, we should not expect that merely increasing the number of officers within an area will reduce crime. The essential point these criminologists miss, however, is that the important thing is not *how many* officers are deployed, but *what they are doing* that matters. Indeed, after summarizing and critiquing the frequent misinterpretation of the empirical research on police patrol effectiveness, James Q. Wilson (1985) notes quite cogently that "*what* the police do may be more important than how many there are, that patrol focused on particular persons or locations may be better than random patrol, and that speed may be less important than information (p. 71, emphasis in original)." As we shall see, these precepts underscore and illuminate the principles put into place by the NYPD to reduce crime by more than half in about seven years.

Police Commissioner William Bratton made a very similar point at the American Society of Criminology's Annual Meeting in November 1995 as well as at a National Institute of Justice conference later that month, offering a simple intuitive example to refute the criminologists' tenaciously-held assumption that police can have no impact on crime:

Consider the following story: A series of robberies is taking place in a neighborhood and giving the local area a steeply rising crime rate. It just so happens that this neighborhood has enough political clout to have an elite police unit, expert at apprehending robbers, assigned to the problem. With all its special skill, the unit identifies the robbery patterns, deploys its resources, and systematically apprehends the members of two loosely knit robbery gangs. The robbery rate and the crime rate in the neighborhood plummet. Did the police cause the drop in the local neighborhood crime rate? Of course they did.

But I can hear the arguments now. A police department could never apply that level of skill and that level of resources to an entire city. Neighborhoods without clout – poor and minority neighborhoods especially – would be slighted. Crime would be displaced from the places where elite units were active to the neighborhoods where they were not. And so on… (Bratton, November 1995, p. 2).

The assertion that New York City's decline in crime is attributable to massive agency-wide replication of the methods used by elite units – timely intelligence, rapid deployment, effective tactics, and relentless follow-up – would inevitably be met with skepticism, but this is precisely what happened in New York City. No displacement effect occurred – as reflected in the city-wide crime statistics, overall crime declined dramatically in every one of the agency's seventy-six precincts, and the greatest percentage decreases were found in precincts where the levels of crime and public disorder were the highest. It should also be noted that the criminals did not simply move *en masse* to the suburbs – a statistical survey of Uniformed Crime Reports data in contiguous Nassau County, for example, showed that the overall crime rate there declined about two percent from 1994 to 1995 (Kushner, 1995; 1996).

In essence, Bratton's example explains in microcosm precisely what the NYPD achieved on an immensely broader scale: crime trends and "hot spots" where minor offenses and quality of life violations occur are identified almost contemporaneous with their occurrence; effective multifaceted tactical plans based on previous experience and innovative new ideas are developed; sufficient personnel and other necessary resources are rapidly deployed to the target locations to implement the tactical plans; and relentless follow-up and assessment is conducted to ensure that all violators have been apprehended and that the strategic plans have effectively and completely addressed the problem (Bratton, 1995).

Why is it a problem that some criminologists have derided the capacity of the police to reduce or control crime? Most importantly, because it gives inadequate or incompetent police executives an excuse or a justification for their poor performance. Many police executives and politicians (and, to be fair, some rank-and-file officers) engage in a kind of double-talk when they speak about crime – they are willing to take credit when crime goes down, but when it goes up they point to the criminologists' dictums that crime is primarily driven by social and economic engines that lie beyond the scope of the police to address. This same rhetoric leads to cynicism among rank-and-file officers and, as described more fully below, contributes to organizational divisiveness and the creation of two cultures of policing. The rank-and-file interpret such rhetoric as an executive cop-out, just as they see a police executive who tries to take all the credit for a crime decline as ignoring the hard work and personal sacrifices made by police officers, supervisors and middle managers. The rank-and-file officers tend to believe that they *do* make a difference, and they interpret this equivocal rhetoric as a lack of support from their leaders.

Good, effective police officers have always known that on a case-by-case basis, they make a difference. Despite the stifling bureaucracy and the often-illogical regulations that may inhibit them from properly exercising their discretion, good cops have always known that they make a difference in peoples' lives. It is true that the public may not always recognize or acknowledge the impact police officers have on their lives, just as it is true that police executives may not fully appreciate the contributions individual officers make. Notwithstanding this, in the interests of honesty we should also point out that there are a great many instances where police officers make little or no difference. This may be because they are inadequately trained or equipped to do the difficult job asked of them, it may be because they feel little support from their leaders, or it may be because they simply do not care to go beyond what is minimally required of them.

But what would happen, one might ask, if the vast majority of police officers – that is, those who really want to make a difference – were freed from some of the encumbering administrative rules and duties that serve little purpose? What if they had the committed support of their leaders, and if they were given the opportunity and the direction to work cooperatively with other like-minded cops to focus their efforts on important problems that affect peoples lives in a meaningful way? If we were able to reach this critical tipping point, we might have an entire agency that was capable of making an enormous difference.

Can the police make a difference in reducing crime? The author, along with tens of thousands of police officers across the United States believe they can, and they believe that the difference the police can make is primarily limited by the expectations the police have of themselves. As William Bratton noted in his National Institute of Justice paper, in order to answer the question of whether we should expect police activities to impact on crime, disorder and fear, we should begin by turning the question around:

> If we *don't* expect police activities and police departments to have an impact on crime disorder and fear, they almost certainly *won't*. By accepting the prevailing image of police departments as slow moving and relatively ineffectual bureaucracies and by assuming that nothing can be done to change them, we are, in effect, making a self-fulfilling prophesy. No organization, whether it's a police department or a private business, is going to achieve high performance results in an atmosphere of such low expectations (Bratton, 1995, p. 1; italics in original).

Evidence to support the optimistic view that the police have the capacity to positively impact crime, to reduce fear and disorder and to improve the quality of life enjoyed by members of the public can be found in the experience of the NYPD and in other jurisdictions where Compstat-like management principles have been applied. It must be clearly stated that this optimism and respect for the capabilities of officers must never be assumed or taken for granted. One of the unique features of policing that sets it apart from virtually every other line of work is the spirit of idealism and sense of purpose that initially motivated many or most of its members to become part of the policing enterprise. Police work is different from other lines of work because people *aspire* to be police officers. How many children aspire to be accountants or bankers or shopkeepers, viewing those occupations as noble endeavors that provide the opportunity to do great things for the betterment of society?

For some individuals, the desire to be a police officer takes shape early in life, and their view of what policing is and what policing should be are seen through a filter of romance and youthful idealism. They aspire to become police officers because they truly believe that the police can make a difference and do make a difference, and they altruistically want to be a part of the policing enterprise. Others drift into policing because it is steady work or because it pays well, but most of them soon discover that there is something magical and seductive about the possibilities of police work. As Arthur Niederhoffer described in his classic study of police cynicism,

Behind the Shield (1967), though, shortly after joining the agency many enthusiastic young officers confront an organization that stifles their best impulses and a public that regards them with ambivalence, and they begin to lose faith in their own capacity to make a difference. Their eroded idealism is replaced by the protective mantle of cynicism, and they see the world with a jaundiced eye.

Idealism and the belief in one's own ability to make a difference can be a powerful motivator to police officers, and one of the most important elements of the NYPD's success was the ability to allow officers to recapture their positive outlook and their enthusiasm for good police work. Once some of the organizational impediments to good police work were removed, and once officers saw their activities start to restore order and turn crime around, many recaptured a measure of their faith and they delved into police work with all the enthusiasm of their rookie years. Coupled with the wisdom of experience, that enthusiasm became an impetus for more commitment, more action, and more pride in oneself and in the agency. As crime began to decline and as order and civility was restored to New York City streets, cops began to stand a bit taller and walk with a bit more spring in their steps. Even some of the dead wood – the so-called "conscientious objectors" who came to work every day but did not really engage in the struggle – began to get back into the game.

Power, Authority and Discretion in Police Organizations

Police agencies cannot hope to fulfill their core missions of fighting crime, solving problems, maintaining order, reducing fear and improving the quality of life within their jurisdiction unless power, authority, and discretion are vested in the individuals, positions and ranks where they can achieve the greatest result. The individuals who are designated to take the lead in the agency's problem-solving effort need not (and probably should not) be at the pinnacle of the organization's hierarchy, but the designated leaders must have the power and the influence to motivate others within the organization – to motivate those above them as well as below them in the organizational structure. Motivating those who hold a higher place in the organizational pyramid can be tricky business, but as we shall see, the Compstat process and Compstat meetings provide a venue in which this can be accomplished. At minimum, the individuals charged with the responsibility to lead the prob- lem-solving activities must have the requisite knowledge, skills, authority and discretion to intelligently identify problems and construct viable tactical responses to them, as well as the organizational power to marshal and apply resources to solve the problems.

The fundamental organizational changes that took place in the NYPD, as well as the tremendous results the NYPD achieved, are intrinsically linked to the strategic realignment of the agency's power and authority structure.

In discussing the various dimensions and bases of power in police organizations, it is perhaps most useful to define power in its simplest and most generic terms: power is the ability of one individual to influence the behavior of another individual in order to get something done. Authority, a related concept, refers to the right to command and to utilize power. While several typologies or descriptions of power bases in organizations have been described, the classic typology used by Raven and French (1959) to describe the exercise of power in organizations seems particularly appropriate to police agencies. Raven and French (1959) describe five bases of power: legitimate; coercive; reward; expert; and referent power.

Legitimate power is related to the individual's position within the organization's formal authority structure, and therefore equates with rank. Rank and position implicitly convey the expectation that one's orders, directives and commands will be obeyed. The higher one's rank in the police department, the greater the legitimate expectation that commands and orders will be obeyed by subordinates. As in any quasi-military organization, one's rank and position in the organizational structure dictates the amount and quality of authority and legitimate power he or she has to direct the activities of others. Generally speaking, sergeants have the legitimate authority to direct police officers, lieutenants have the legitimate authority to direct sergeants and police officers, and captains have the legitimate authority to direct the activities of lieutenants, sergeants and police officers, so long as these individuals are in the same chain of command. Depending upon a number of factors including the agency's written policies and/or rules and procedures, a lieutenant or captain in the patrol division may or may not have the legitimate authority to direct the activities of a detective sergeant or detective. In policing, the amount of legitimate power one has as well as the spheres in which he or she may apply that power are determined by the rules and regulations. Those officers situated at the upper end of the rank hierarchy – the agency's executive cadre – have the greatest access to the agency's quotient of legitimate power. People accede to legitimate power simply because the organization's rank structure and rules and procedures stipulate that the other person has a greater right to be obeyed.

Legitimate power extends beyond directing the activities of individuals within the chain of command. Legitimate power and authority also provide access to other important resources, such as patrol cars and equipment, personnel, overtime for special operations and arrests, and other necessities that are essential to fulfilling the agency's mission. These organizational assets do not "belong to" the official (although many act as if they did) but the agency's formal rules and regulations give the legitimate power holder control over a certain quantity of resources and give them the authority to make discretionary decisions about their distribution and use. This discretionary capacity to distribute or withhold the resources under his or her control thus provides some of the ranking officer's basis for coercive and reward power.

In their discussion of the consequences of using power in police organizations, Roberg and Kuykendall (1990) point out that managers may initially depend upon their legitimate power in order to influence the behavior of subordinates, but protracted or sole exercise of legitimate power ultimately leads to dissatisfaction, frustration, and resistance among the rank-and-file. While a reliance upon legitimate authority may allow managers to obtain effective performance in the short term, they must access and utilize expert and referent power if the highest levels of performance are to be achieved and sustained (Roberg and Kuykendall, 1990, p. 195).

Coercive power involves the subordinate's recognition that if orders are not obeyed or if the individual does not fully comply with the superior's wishes, he or she will be punished (officially or unofficially) by the ranking officer, who again has the legitimate right to invoke the formal disciplinary process and to mete out punishment for violating orders. The coercive nature of punishment power can also be exercised when an individual has discretionary control over some tangible or intangible thing of value (an agency resource) as well as the discretion to control its distribution or use. By withholding some thing of value, the individual effectively coerces another person into acceding to his or her demands. A superior may exercise coercive power, for example, by withholding or limiting overtime, by assigning an individual to perform an unpleasant or less desirable task or duty, or by refusing to approve a transfer to a desired unit or assignment.

Again, one's access to the punishment power of the disciplinary system is determined by rank and position within the organizational structure. Rank implicitly confers the right to commence formal disciplinary action against a subordinate, and position in the organizational structure defines the chain of command in which the punishment power may be used. Punishment power is not exercised only through the actual use of disciplinary action - the mere threat of punishment or the knowledge that a superior has the capacity to invoke disciplinary action is usually enough to ensure compliance with orders and directives.

Like every other power base, legitimate power and coercive power have their limitations, and management based primarily on the exercise of legitimate, rank-based power has its shortcomings. Legitimate power and coercive power afford a superior officer

the ability to exercise control over subordinates' continued employment, salary increases, work hours, assignments, promotions, and infinite other rewards and punishments. The superior does not, however, own the subordinate, nor can he/she hope for much more than a rather limited control. It is the subordinate, in the end, who decides whether or not it is worth it - in fact, whether or not he should report for work at all. Thus the legitimate/coercive power in a police organization, while absolutely essential, has its limitations (Whisenand and Ferguson, 1973, pp. 144-145).

As many police supervisors or executives who rely too heavily or too exclusively on their legitimate power have come to learn, the subordinate can often undermine legitimate authority and power by exercising his or her lawful discretion or by interfering in some other way with the attainment of the superior officer's goals. Individuals as well as groups of officers who become alienated by the strict and unwavering imposition of legitimate power and punishment power may band together in a subtle conspiracy to weaken the superior's authority, to embarrass the superior and therefore depreciate his or her referent power, or to collectively diminish the quality or quantity of the work they perform. Subordinates who possess some sort of expert power the superior officer needs may also inhibit the superior officer's attainment of his or her goals by withholding their expertise. Perhaps the most typical response to an overbearing superior is the practice of reducing summons enforcement for parking infractions and moving violations, although subordinates usually have a host of other potential responses within their repertoire.

Because coercive power and the disciplinary system are important means of motivating and directing the actions of police personnel, the NYPD reengineered its entire disciplinary system to ensure that the middle-level commanders it was attempting to empower could effectively impose discipline within their commands. Like so many other functions and processes in the NYPD, the power to administer discipline came to be centralized and bureaucratized over the years, and commanders needed greater latitude in terms of the types of infractions for which they could impose sanctions as well as the severity of the sanctions. Some infractions carried mandatory penalties, so the best and most productive officer in a precinct would be mandated to receive exactly the same penalty for losing his or her memo book as the least productive officer. The disciplinary system's reengineering greatly expanded the number and type of violations a commander could adjudicate without referring the matter to a higher authority, and it broadened the range and scope of the discretionary penalties the commander could impose. More will be said of this disciplinary reengineering in subsequent chapters.

Reward power is derived from one individual's discretionary capacity to formally or informally compensate or provide another individual with some desired benefit, and is sort of the flip side of coercive power. In police organizations, the reward can take many forms including official letters of commendation, the recognition bestowed by medals or awards for excellence, a positive evaluation or choice assignment, or access to paid overtime. Like punishment power, reward power equates with rank but is more closely tied to the number, type, and value of organizational resources one controls and the amount of discretion one has in distributing these scarce resources.

If, for example, a sergeant was given absolute control over parking spaces in the headquarters garage and the absolute discretion to allot those spaces as he or she saw fit, the sergeant would be in a position of great reward power. The discretion to allot or give access to any scarce resources over which he or she has control – whether the resources are parking spaces, new computers, special training sessions, particularly desirable duty assignments or a quick glance at the list of upcoming promotions – conveys power. Because the discretionary ability to distribute scarce resources leads to power, and because reward power is an especially potent source of motivation, in most police organizations it is highly unlikely that a mere sergeant would remain in charge of allotting valuable parking spaces – a more likely scenario is that a ranking manager or executive would assert his or her legitimate authority and assume that responsibility.

In most or all police agencies, as in most or all organizations based upon the military model, reward and punishment power (along with legitimate power) tend to be consolidated in upper management. Although line supervisors and middle managers have some power to reward and punish - mostly through awarding or withholding discretionary assignments and formally invoking disciplinary action - their power tends to be ephemeral and impermanent. Line supervisors and middle managers rarely if ever have the power to permanently promote or demote subordinates, and any disciplinary action they commence for serious infractions or rule violations is usually administered by members of the executive cadre. Line supervisors and middle managers typically lack the authority and power to permanently affect a subordinate's working conditions, because that power is retained by executives.

Although reward power allows the manager to exert a potent influence over subordinates' activities and behaviors, it is important to point out that the number, type, and relative potency of tangible rewards may be limited by a variety of factors. These factors include budgetary constraints, which are often imposed from outside the police organization and which may limit the availability of overtime, merit increases or other monetary inducements to performance. Also complicating this issue is the fact that the available rewards may not appeal to some individuals: while some officers may work hard and long for a letter of commendation, others may be motivated almost entirely by the prospect of promotion to detective, with a concomitant increase in salary and status. The key to resolving this problem is to have a variety of rewards and reward systems available to the manager.

Increasing the range, value and scope of the available incentives for performance became an objective of the NYPD's reengineering process, and a reengineering committee made several recommendations in this area. The recommendations included the creation of several new discretionary ranks, with appropriate remuneration, to recognize outstanding performers. In a time of fiscal austerity in all City agencies, though, and in light of fairly restrictive collective bargaining arrangements with the various police unions, many of the recommendations dealing with tangible or financial rewards were never brought to fruition. Nevertheless, precinct commanders were encouraged to develop and utilize a host of other reward systems, including "Cop of the Month" ceremonies, etc.

The failure to create a viable reward system based upon tangible benefits or salary increases for top performers below the rank of captain was, of course, somewhat paradoxical because such a system had long existed for executives. Indeed, one of the reasons the NYPD was able to achieve such a turnaround in such a relatively short period of time is the fact that top-performing executives were rewarded with promotions and raises. One can only wonder what kind of gains might have been achieved if a similar motivation package existed for supervisors and street cops.

Referent power is based upon the individual's personal qualities, such as innate charisma, the respect and admiration others hold for him or her, or the ability to persuade through personal charm and interpersonal social skills. Unlike legitimate, reward and punishment power, its source is not linked to rank or the written rules and procedures of the organization or the ability to make life pleasant or difficult for subordinates. Rather, referent power derives from the personal qualities of the person who wields it. We are motivated to do something for such an individual simply because we respect and like him or her as a person. In police organizations, referent power is closely tied to the organizational culture – respect and admiration typically equate with police experience and with the extent to which an individual shows respect for other officers as well as for the police culture's value system. People accede to referent power simply because they like the individual and want to be liked by him or her, or because they consider the individual a friend or role model.

In this regard, referent power is not necessarily the province of upper management. In every police organization, there seem to be officers of relatively low rank who possess a disproportionately high amount of referent power in relation to others. At times, these valued officers may seem to have more real power - more ability to see their goals and objectives come to fruition - than most ranking officers. Through their network of contacts, friends and connections, their personal charm and prestige, and their ability to cajole and inspire others to agree with them and go along with their wishes, these officers have profound influence within the organization. While their influence seems particularly great within their own peer group, those with a high degree of referent power can usually influence the actions and behaviors of those above and below them in the organizational structure. Referent power is *not* intrinsically linked to rank or to the control of resources, and indeed some ranking officers may have little or no referent power simply because few members of the organization like or respect them as cops or as individuals. When a ranking officer (i.e., one who has significant legitimate, reward and punishment power) is able to add referent power to his repertoire, though, he or she becomes particularly powerful in the organization. The increased power comes not only from the added "juice" provided them by their personal influence, but because they often do not have to resort to expending their other power sources to gain compliance. They achieve compliance without alienating others and without "pulling rank" simply because people who like them will gladly do what they ask.

Individuals with low rank but high referent power may have a fairly high profile in the organization (in larger agencies, for example, they may hold positions in unions or fraternal organizations), but they may just as often operate in the background. Wise police executives identify and cultivate these key organizational players, enlisting them as allies in the management process. Wise police executives know that the influence these key players wield can either undermine or facilitate the success of an initiative or program. The example comes to mind of a respected older sergeant whose indifferent or dismissive tone of voice communicates that the policy directive he reads to the officers at roll call is unimportant. The chief executive may have devoted considerable time and effort and may have expended considerable resources in developing the policy, but the respected sergeant who holds greater referent power over cops can easily undermine all the chief's efforts.

At the same time, due to their extensive contacts inside and outside the agency, individuals with high referent power can be an absolutely essential source of feedback about the pace, direction and acceptance of change within the organization. They can provide the executive with formal or informal advice about organizational problems and their remedies, and because their opinions often reflect the opinions of a significant number of officers, the wise executive uses them as a sounding-board to assess new ideas and potential projects. Forging alliances with these individuals does not, by the way, diminish the executive's reserves of power in any other sphere – the basis for the alliance can simply be that the executive, like others in the organization, has respect for the individual's point of view. Often, this simple affirmation of respect can add a new and particularly powerful member to the executive's coalition for change.

If the manager or executive wins the individual over, his or her effectiveness and power to achieve organizational objectives is magnified substantially. If the manager or executive ignores the potential for alliances with these power bases, he or she misses out on a tremendous opportunity to consolidate power and achieve change, and allows the power bases to operate independently of his or her vision for the agency. Finally, if the executive or manager attempts to quash these referent and expert power bases, he or she will merely expend what precious little power he or she has in other spheres. The risk of alienating large numbers of the rank-and-file is too certain and the chances of successfully quashing these power bases is too low for this to be a viable tactic for any but the most reckless executive.

One of the problems with referent power, though, is that it is easily manipulated for personal gain. Individuals can use referent power to benefit themselves even when doing so is not in the best interests of the agency.

Individuals can use their referent power, for example, to prevail upon ranking officers and obtain promotions or assignments for which they are neither qualified or entitled, reinforcing the age-old refrain that "it's who you know, not what you know or how well you do it that matters." There can be few things more demoralizing or more debilitating to a police agency than the cynical perception that personal politics pave the road to success and promotions.

Expert power accrues when others recognize that an individual possesses some unique or high level of competence, skill, knowledge or experience that informs his or her professional judgments. Within the "street cop" culture, one's expert power tends to equate with the extent and quality of practical police experience he or she has amassed, and it is therefore the primary power base to which the patrol officer or detective may lay claim. Expert power is often related to referent power because police organizational cultures usually place great value and emphasis on experience and expertise, and because cops tend to admire those who have developed a reputation for expertise and the "street wisdom" that goes along with it.

That police officers tend to have great respect for experience is evidenced by the fact that younger and less experienced officers will often seek the counsel and guidance of an older officer who has "seen it all" when they are confronted with a problem or dilemma. "Street experience" or enforcement experience is afforded a particularly high value, but administrative assignments do not count for much among the rank-and-file patrol officers. The value placed on expertise can also be glimpsed in some typical interactions between officers when they meet for the first time. Irrespective of rank, cops tend to "size up" other officers by making subtle or overt inquiry into their previous assignments and street experience, and they make judgments based upon the amount and type of street experience he or she has amassed. To a large extent, these judgments determine the amount of expert power the officer will wield within the unit or the organization as a whole.

Expert power is not intrinsically linked to rank, and as described below, "street cops" may regard "management cops" as so far removed from the realities of the street that they do not deserve the expert power to which they may lay claim. Among street cops, enforcement experience and proficiency in the tasks and duties of policing are the route to expert power, but specialized knowledge and access to information is a source of expert power within the "management cop" culture. The old saw that "knowledge is power" certainly rings true in police management circles.

An officer of comparatively low rank who possesses a scarce or particularly valuable skill often has a disproportionate amount of power relative to others of the same rank. For example, a police officer or sergeant with an expertise in computer programming, a facility for writing speeches, a law degree or some other specialized skill becomes a valuable asset to executives, who are often willing to expend their own legitimate, coercive or reward power in order to exploit the officer's expertise.

One of the great misconceptions about police management is that executives actually possess all the expertise to which they lay claim. To outsiders, and even to those who are within the organization but are unfamiliar with the inner workings of headquarters bureaucracies, the chiefs and executives may seem to possess a great quantity of in-depth knowledge about the complexities and intricacies of the organization. They may also seem to be deeply involved in managing the agency's street-level operations. Especially in larger organizations, such executives are the exception. In reality, chiefs usually rely on a small group of mid-level advisors of relatively low rank to manage the day-to-day affairs of the organization, and they concern themselves mostly with policy issues. Often, they simply do not have the time or the communication structures that would permit them to remain apprized of and involved in the street-level operations, even if they possessed the expertise.

Executives do not typically broadcast or proclaim the fact that others may have greater expertise than they, for to do so would destroy the illusion of expert power they want and need to maintain. In turn, the sergeants and lieutenants on the chief's staff have a synergistic relationship with the executive and are often given the unofficial authority to use his or her legitimate power to manage the organization: when Sergeant Jones of the Chief's Office calls a precinct commander to discretely suggest a particular course of action, the precinct commander knows (or should know) that the sergeant's suggestion is as good as the chief's command. If the precinct commander does not comply, the chief will soon learn of it and will possibly invoke one or more of his sources of power to ensure compliance. In this respect, some relatively low-ranking members of the organization with special expertise or knowledge may possess disproportionately great power to effect change so long as ranking managers do not quash or undermine them. Successful and effective police executives, like successful executives in business and industry, surround themselves with trusted experts who have greater specific knowledge about a complex issue than they do, and give them broad discretion to act independently.

Street cops have virtually no access to sources of power other than referent and expert power, though. They lack the formal rank, the capacity to impose discipline, and the control of valuable organizational resources that make legitimate, coercive and reward power the exclusive province of superior officers. On the other hand, ranking management cops automatically have access to three power bases, and those with well-developed interpersonal management skills and a great deal of enforcement experience may have access to referent and expert power as well. Not surprisingly, managers who have access to all five bases of power have tremendous influence and tremendous capacity to get things done according to their agenda. They are the individuals who are most capable of bringing about change in the organization.

The dimensions and the allocation of power within the police organization are determined both by written policy and by the tone and tenor of the overall management philosophy espoused by the agency's chief executive. When the chief executive or police commissioner demonstrates that he or she places importance and value on experience and expertise, and when he or she demonstrates a commitment to change, the experts in the organization will ascend in importance and overall power almost regardless of their rank. They will have access to upper management, upper management will rely upon their expertise, and the potential for a symbiotic relationship will occur.

A rigid and bureaucratic management style that relies primarily on rank, discipline and the threat of negative reinforcement in order to achieve organizational goals is, of course, inimical to such symbiotic relationships. It is also inimical to innovation, improvement, change, and the attainment of organizational goals. An executive cadre that is intimidated by or dismissive of the potential expert power residing within members of lower ranks will usually fail to generate positive change, but then again an executive cadre with these characteristics is not usually interested in meeting the challenge of innovation.

Expert power is optimized when it coexists with coercive and reward power, but it is diminished by bureaucratic administrative procedures or other factors that decrease personal autonomy and discretion. A tightly controlled, rigidly bureaucratic police organization will necessarily place greatest emphasis on legitimate, reward and punishment power, while a more collegial management style will have greater tolerance and appreciation for the use of expert and referent power. The rigid and tightly controlled executive is, generally speaking, typically more concerned with maintaining the *status quo* while the collegial and flexible manager is usually geared toward transformation and change.

Taking these observations one step further, we can see that rigid bureaucratic management styles tend to be predicated upon the same kind of assumptions that underlie McGregor's (1960) so-called "Theory X," while more open and collegial management styles tend to embrace "Theory Y" assumptions. The rigid and bureaucratic Theory X management style tends to assume that workers generally dislike work and will try to avoid it as much as possible, and that organizational goals can only be attained in a highly directed and controlled atmosphere in which coercion and the threat or reality of punishment are the primary sources of human motivation.

On the other hand, open and collegial Theory Y managers have a more optimistic view of human motivation, and they assume that workers who have a personal commitment to the organizational goals will be highly motivated to achieve them. Personal commitment to organizational goals take hold, they believe, when tangible and intangible rewards and inducements that reinforce the goals are available to workers. They also believe that the ability to use imagination, ingenuity and creativity in the course of one's work is itself motivating, and that under the proper conditions human beings learn not only to accept but to actively seek additional responsibility. Theory X assumes that people work primarily to satisfy their physiological and safety needs, while Theory Y assumes that employees seek personal fulfillment in their work.

Of course, McGregor (1960) used the Theory X and Theory Y constructs to represent poles at either end of a philosophical and behavioral continuum, and did not conceive of them as separate, discrete or mutually exclusive theories. For example, few police officers – few workers in any field, for that matter – show up for work every day *just* to satisfy their physiological needs by getting a paycheck, and few show up *solely* to find personal fulfillment. Theory X and Theory Y are parts of an intellectual model or paradigm for understanding and analyzing managerial and organizational behavior, rather than as a true and accurate representation of human behavior. In reality, management philosophies, behaviors and attitudes towards workers usually fall somewhere along the continuum. As we shall see throughout this book, the NYPD's shift to a more open and collegial management style involved a fundamental shift toward the Theory Y perspective. That shift required a fundamental realignment of power bases, particularly in the areas of reward and expert power.

Roberg and Kuykendall (1990) point out that managers who

combine legitimate with referent or expert power are often the most
influential persons in a police organizations. However, managers and
subordinates may disagree on who has the real "expertise." One of
the most frequent complaints voiced by patrol officers about
managers is that managers lose their understanding of "street reality"
and become more concerned with their own political and
organizational survival... Supposedly, the higher in the organization
a manager goes, the less expertise and understanding he or she has
about the "street" (p. 194).

As we will see, this central disagreement over the use of power and the
value of expertise often lies at the heart of a fractionalized and alienated
police agency. The police manager who honestly admits his or her areas of
weakness and openly relies upon the advice and expertise of others will
garner more respect (i.e., more referent power) from the rank-and-file than
the manager who pretends to be an expert. Moreover, public recognition of
a subordinate's expertise tends to generate allegiance to the manager and can
be a powerful source of motivation as well. Cops are a rather perceptive
group, and the rank-and-file will quickly discover and marginalize the
pretender regardless of his or her rank and position. By withholding the
attribution of referent and expert power, they will effectively disempower the
pretender and force him or her to rely solely upon legitimate, coercive and
reward power.

Two Cultures of Policing:
"Street Cops" and "Management Cops"

Treatises on policing and police management often refer to the notion of
a police culture whose values, rituals, and behaviors communicate information and shape the behavior of its members. Comprehending the dimensions
and characteristics of the organizational or occupational culture should be a
matter of great concern and attention for the cogent manager, since cultures
are a sort of mechanism or filter through which people give meaning to their
experiences. Cultures entail a set of taken-for-granted attitudes, assumptions
and belief systems, and these dramatically affect the way we perceive the
world and our place in it. The shared belief systems and assumptions are a
sort of glue that holds the culture together.

Most often, police culture is referenced in a pejorative sense – a great
deal of the literature of police corruption, for example, tends to simplistically

attribute corrupt and protective activities (the notorious "blue wall of silence") to the culture itself. When some writers are hard-pressed to cogently explain subtle or arcane aspects of police behavior, they attribute them to the mysteries of the police culture. These police activities and values, they say in effect, are transmitted through and within the culture and become part of the police officer's operational repertoire.

Such broad characterizations of police officers, police behavior and police culture are unfortunate and inaccurate, as is the simplistic linking of police culture with corrupt activities. They ignore an entire range of important, productive and desirable attributes encompassed by the police culture, and by referring to a single generic and monolithic culture they mislead the uninformed and unsophisticated reader by painting all police officers in all police agencies with the same brush. They characterize police officers, as well as their behaviors and their values, as primarily responsive to a sort of sheep-like obedience to the dictates of a vague and mysterious culture. The ominous overtones of an insular and secretive police culture are unavoidable, and the imprecation that the powers of the police are more beholden to the customs of culture than to the rule of law can truly be frightening in a democratic society.

Finally, and perhaps most importantly in terms of understanding organizational change, they characterize the police culture as a singular and static entity that remains constant and inflexible, when in fact the culture exists in a constant state of evolution as it responds to innumerable forces and factors within the agency as well as outside it.

Organizational cultures evolve and change as new individuals and new ideas are introduced. When new individuals become part of the culture, they import new ideas, experiences, and values that may initially conflict with the *status quo*, but ultimately the conflicts result in the emergence of a new and slightly different value system. The process of change in police cultures is ongoing and dynamic, and is shaped by a raft of factors including historical events that impact on the agency, recruitment and hiring practices, and shifts in the value systems of the larger society or culture.

The culture of the NYPD (specifically the "street cop" culture) underwent a series of dramatic changes in the mid-1970s and early 1980s, and these changes later impacted upon the management culture and the management revolution of the mid-1990s. Between 1975 and 1980, the NYPD sustained severe budget cuts and massive personnel cutbacks as the result of New York City's fiscal crisis. For the first time in its history, the NYPD actually began laying-off rookie police officers in July 1975 and the layoffs continued until about 5,000 officers, or about fifteen percent of the agency, were ultimately furloughed. The agency's budgeted headcount of sworn officers shrunk from around 35,200 officers to around 27,200 actual officers in less than a month. Some officers were re-hired almost immediately, but no new personnel joined the department until the last of the furloughed officers were reinstated in 1980. The NYPD did not again reach its pre-July 1975 staffing levels until the mid-1990s. Former NYPD Chief Anthony Bouza (1990) describes the impact of the lay-offs on the agency's workforce, cogently noting that due to seniority concerns the officers most affected by the layoffs also tended to be the best and most aggressive in the agency.

> The upper ranks remained unscathed. The hard disciplinary cases, the winos, the psychologically unfit, the malingerers, the chronic sick, and the incompetent were left untouched. No business man could have faced the prospect of a 20 percent cut being aimed only at the active workers. Paring, trimming, economizing, disciplining, or self-sacrifice weren't even mentioned. The comforts, privileges and conveniences that attended the mandarins remained undisturbed. Random attrition and the rights of seniority carried the day for this exceedingly orthodox, conservative, cautious police administration (Bouza, 1990, p. 16).

Many of the laid-off officers were eventually re-hired, but many took positions in other police agencies or simply found other lines of work. Many of those who returned were bitter and cynical about police work in general and about the department's management in particular. The layoffs of the late 1970s also had a powerful impact on the amount and quality of experience among the agency's street cops. As the result of a massive hiring program in the early 1980s, within a few years more than half of the agency's patrol force would have less than five years experience and tenure in the agency.

The massive influx of young people into the agency changed its culture in many ways, and there were inevitable conflicts between younger and older cops. Generally speaking, the younger cops were more highly educated than older cops, and the age difference had also exposed them to a different set of social, generational, and cultural influences during their formative years. Many NYPD officers during the 1970s had been "children of the fifties," but the "cops of the eighties" were most often "children of the sixties." (for a more comprehensive exploration of this cultural strain, see Bahn, 1984). The clash of cultures might not have been so extreme if the change had taken place more gradually, but the hiring hiatus led to significant and rapid alteration of the agency's demographics. The younger, better educated, more ethnically and socially diverse officers hired after the lay-offs also tended to have less regard for the agency's conservative administrative style. By the mid-1990s, when members of this cadre rose to supervisory and managerial positions, they would indelibly alter the face of management in the NYPD.

The pace and direction of cultural change can also be tremendously affected by the type and quality of communication taking place between executives and the rank and file. A chief executive who fails to maximize the communications potential or fails to articulate and transmit his or her vision of policing to the rank-and-file is certainly forgoing a signal opportunity to shape the culture. In a typical bureaucratic police organization, though, communication channels usually flow vertically down the chain of command, and executives may lack the insight or the volition to break the chain of command to communicate directly with the troops. By maintaining a high level of communication with officers, including the use of personal one-on-one communication and the media (police officers read newspapers, too), the wise police executive limits the possibility that his or her message will be distorted as it flows down the organizational pyramid. He or she also stays in touch with the street cop's experience and culture, and gets direct feedback as to how well his or her policies are being accepted and implemented. Direct communication keeps the executive apprized of what operational officers are thinking, what problems and issues they face, and the areas where they feel change is most needed. No police manager can be an effective communicator or an effective leader unless he or she regularly gets out of the office and into the streets. Especially in larger police organizations, where the tendency is to view executives as aloof and distant "downtown" types (creating a built-in impediment to change and to amassing expert and referent power), direct personal communication with the rank-and-file humanizes management and increases the executive's referent and possibly expert power.

One of the reasons William Bratton was so effective an agent of organizational change, for example, was the fact that he always maintained close communication with operational cops. Bratton frequently rode the subways (both as Chief of the Transit Police and later as NYPD Police Commissioner) and walked the streets, engaging the cops he encountered in one-on-one dialogue about the agency, its problems, and the officer's perception of what could be done to remedy the problems. This practice enhanced his referent power and his standing within the street cop culture – he genuinely seemed to understand street cops and was interested in their views and concerns – and his in-depth knowledge of street conditions enhanced his expert power (see, generally, Bratton and Knobler, 1998). We will consider the notion of maintaining a high degree of communication and its role in organizational change in greater depth in subsequent chapters.

An important inference or conclusion can be drawn from the fact that police occupational cultures are in a constant state of evolution and flux. The police manager who has at his or her disposal the knowledge, the power and the organizational support to shape and direct the agency's culture can have profound influence upon the type and direction of change. Because virtually every change in the work environment and every alteration to policies and procedures will have some subtle or conspicuous impact upon the culture, the effective police executive will carefully consider the impact each and every one of his or her policy decisions will have on the culture. The effective police manager will also give careful consideration to the ways in which the values and prescribed behaviors of police culture will affect the actual implementation of the policies he or she develops.

It should also be recognized that the occupational culture within a particular police agency may communicate a set of perceptions and beliefs that have little or no basis in fact or objective reality, but members of the culture nevertheless believe in them emphatically. For all intents and purposes, these belief systems have the credibility and weight of objective reality, and members of the culture have an unquestioning allegiance to them. Once these erroneous beliefs take hold and are subscribed to, they become resilient and difficult to extinguish.

Organizational cultures are a sort of second set of informal rules and procedures that operate in the background of police agencies, and although they are not officially prescribed or written down in a particular place, they nevertheless play a potent role in determining behavior. We may pay little conscious attention to the demands and dictates of our culture, but cultures help us to interpret and give meaning to information we receive from the world around us.

There are some broad generalizations and statements we can make about a general culture of American policing, but in the interests of precision and accuracy it is more proper to speak of the cultures existing within individual agencies. Every police agency – every corporation, business and work environment, for that matter – has a unique culture. Within these cultures exist a unique set of relationships, interaction patterns, status systems, core values, and formal and informal vehicles for transmitting knowledge and information. Viewed in the broadest context, we can discern similar patterns or themes of culture throughout police agencies and cultures, but we must not lose sight of the fact that every police agency's organizational culture is unique, often vibrant, and more or less oriented toward the attainment of organizational goals.

It is misleading, though, to speak of a single culture within a particular police agency, since more often than not (and especially in larger and more complex organizations) there exist two cultures: a street cop culture and a management cop culture. According to Elizabeth Reuss-Ianni, who first challenged the idea of a single culture within police organizations in her 1982 examination of social interactions in the NYPD, the two cultures are characterized by competing and often conflicting perspectives on procedures, practices and goals.

Street Cops

Street cops believe that their experience, expertise, and deep involvement in the everyday activities of fighting crime, saving lives and providing police service gives them a truer and more realistic picture of police work, and they believe that distant headquarters bureaucrats have lost touch with the realities of contemporary policing. They believe that headquarters bureaucrats are predominantly concerned with their own self-serving interests, and that they cannot be trusted.

At some level of awareness, many police managers and executives are mindful of this dynamic, and they may attempt to ingratiate themselves with the troops by portraying themselves, both inside and outside the agency, as a "cop's cop." This may be particularly true when an agency hires an outsider as the new chief executive or when a new commander is assigned to a precinct, since cynical officers at every rank and position will surely scrutinize and evaluate the "new sheriff in town," with particular emphasis on his or her street experience. Again, cops' informal evaluation of the executive and of the degree to which the executive supports the ethos and values of the organization and of the street cop culture may be a crucial factor in the executive's ultimate success. Like the managers discussed above who pretend to qualifications or expertise to which they are not entitled, the manager or executive who does not seem authentic when voicing support for the street cop culture's values will be seen as weak or ineffective and will be quickly marginalized by the officers within his or her command.

Street cops distrust management cops and the decisions management cops make because, in their view, the managers and headquarters cops have abandoned the street for the physical safety and comfort of bankers' hours and headquarters desks, as well as for the power their rank affords them. Street cops believe that the important decisions that affect their lives, their work and their safety are being made by individuals with little knowledge of or appreciation for their problems. Bosses and headquarters types, in the street cops' view, have forsaken the world of the street cop in order to pursue personal advancement by adopting the role of the professional manager. In line with this view, management cops are seen as remote, distant, and unenlightened bureaucrats whose interests center around their own advancement through the career ladder. In many police agencies there is, unfortunately, much to be said for the accuracy of these street cop perceptions.

Management Cops

For their part, management cops also tend to see themselves as different from street cops. Management cops tend to have a broader and more encompassing view of the agency, its operations, and the political and social environments in which it operates, and they tend to be better educated and more politically savvy than the average street cop. Because they have achieved rank and the legitimate, coercive and reward power that goes along with it (or, for others, because they have access to the power of executives), they have also cast themselves in a different role that isolates them from the street cops.

The headquarters management cop culture is bureaucratically juxtaposed to the culture of the operational street cop, and has an entirely different set of values, goals and aspirations. The real or perceived incongruence in value systems, expectations and orientations is a source of great alienation for the street cop, and a source of great divisiveness within the organization. As this alienation increases, it becomes more and more difficult to achieve organizational goals through consensus and agreement, and executives must expend considerably more time, effort, and power to ensure that goals are accurately communicated throughout the department and to ensure that directives are being followed.

Managing a police organization, especially a large and complex police organization, is a much simpler task when every member understands and subscribes to the vision of the chief executive. At the same time, that task is made infinitely more difficult when the occupational culture (whether it is the street cop culture or the management cop culture, or both) operates to oppose the chief executive's vision.

Because the administrative career track often enhances the potential for promotion and advancement, top executives are often drawn from administrative units rather than from operational duties. It is the rare police manager or executive who can rise to the upper echelon of a large police agency and at the same time maintain the kind of credibility with the rank-and-file that results from preserving a connection with operational policing. The manager or executive who attains high rank and legitimate authority while amassing the power of expertise and knowledge and maintaining the respect and admiration of others is indeed powerful, and is capable of effecting great change in the organization.

Summary and Conclusions

We began this chapter by introducing one of the fundamental tenets of the Compstat paradigm and management philosophy: that police can and do make a difference. Although many criminologists may dispute how much of a difference (if any) the police can make, their reasoning and their perspective are based on faulty logic. They tend to simplistically assume that because the number of officers an agency deploys has historically made little difference in overall crime rates, the police as a whole have little impact. It's not the number of officers deployed, though, but *what they are doing* and *how they are deployed* that makes the difference. Although some police executives may try to have it both ways - arguing at one time that crime is up because of demographics and at another time that crime is down because of their leadership – the Compstat paradigm demands that the police leader take a clear stand on the matter. Specifically, it demands that he or she subscribe to the position that police can and do make a difference.

We also saw that there are five types of bases of power in police organizations, and saw how various combinations of power can enhance or diminish the executive's or manager's chances for achieving his or her goals. Although legitimate, reward and coercive power are automatically afforded to ranking police officials, they can maximize their power potential by accessing the referent and expert power that resides elsewhere in the agency. Finally, we saw that police culture is a powerful mediator of police performance and organizational change, and we saw how the culture is typically fragmented into separate and distinct street cop and management cop cultures. Managers and executives who can successfully win over, harness and use the street cop culture will have a much easier time in changing the organization than one who ignores or tries to fight the power of police culture.

Having set forth some of the theories, ideas and concepts of police management that help to explain the background for changes that took place in the NYPD, it is time to turn our attention to the more substantive and important (and probably more interesting) issues of what really took place in the agency. We will begin by examining the NYPD's history and the forces that shaped it.

Additional Recommended Readings

Niederhoffer, Arthur **Behind the Shield: The Police in Urban Society**, Garden City, NY: Doubleday, 1967. Niederhoffer's classic book on the sociology of policing seems as accurate and authentic today as when the research was first conducted. Many of the factors Niederhoffer identified as causing cynicism continue to exist in the contemporary police context, and others have changed only slightly.

Manning, Peter K. **Police Work: The Social Organization of Policing (2nd Edition),** Prospect Heights, IL: Waveland Press, 1997. This well-researched and updated edition of an important earlier work examines the symbolic and practical aspects of the police role in society. It examines police activities and police behaviors in terms of public expectations, organizational constraints, and the effect of various organizational models on police, as well as the dilemmas these internal and external forces create. Manning has an excellent grasp of the complexities of contemporary police work and the influence of historical trends on police organizations.

Brady, Thomas V. "Measuring What Matters, Part One: Measures of Crime, Fear and Disorder," Washington, DC: National Institute of Justice *Research in Action* series (NCJ#162205), December 1996. This brief publication reviews the major findings and recommendations that emerged from a November 1995 National Institute of Justice conference attended by a well-balanced array of criminologists, criminal justice researchers and police practitioners. In particular, it highlights discussions of the NYPD's strategic approach and the dramatic impact it has in reducing crime and improving quality of life.

Questions for Debate and Discussion

1. Cynicism's impact on police officers' personal and professional lives, as well as its impact on their performance, has been well understood and frequently discussed in the police management literature since Arthur Niederhoffer's classic **Behind the Shield** was first published. The cynical attitude develops early in the police career as officers are exposed to organizational and interpersonal factors that erode their sense of idealism and their belief in the legitimacy of the agency's stated purposed and goals. What steps can police executives take to prevent or decrease the negative impact of cynicism, and why haven't they taken them before?

2. How can Compstat be used to measure and hold managers accountable for the quality of interaction between citizens and the officers under their command? What quantifiable measures would you develop and use to assess the overall quality of these interactions?

3. Given human nature, and given the tremendous effort police executives have expended over the course of their careers in order to reach positions of power, is it reasonable to expect them to give that power away to others in the organization? Can they actually increase their own power by giving it away?

4. In addition to providing a basic framework of assumptions about human behavior and human motivation, (that is, a set of two competing paradigms), what implications does McGregor's Theory X and Theory Y model have for policing? Which theoretical position or paradigm tends to dominate the executive/middle management mindset in contemporary American policing?

5. Take a moment to think of the best boss – either a supervisor, a manager or an executive – you've ever worked for. What are the qualities and attributes that distinguish him/her as the best? Was he/she a Theory X or Theory Y manager? Now think about the *worst* boss you've ever worked for, and determine whether he/she was a Theory X or Theory Y manager. Which dimensions of power did the best boss possess and utilize? The worst boss? What conclusions and implications do you draw from this?

Chapter 3
The Legacy of the Professional Model

Introduction

This chapter will briefly recount some of the historic trends and driving forces that have shaped American policing as an institution, as well as their specific impact on the NYPD prior to the development of Compstat and the implementation of strategic policing practices at the beginning of the Giuliani/Bratton administration. Compstat and strategic policing were certainly not the NYPD's first attempt to introduce and manage problem solving at the agency-wide level, but the difficulties and organizational impediments outlined in this chapter effectively precluded the development and implementation of a highly refined management control system which could support effective problem-solving. The NYPD could not support effective problem solving because the dimensions of power, accountability and discretion were grossly misaligned – power was highly centralized at Headquarters and vested almost exclusively in the department's top brass, individuals at all levels of the organization were highly accountable but for all the wrong things, and successive generations of timid or indecisive administrators sought to limit and curtail any use of discretion that might put their careers at risk.

Without such a management control system, and without overcoming these difficulties and impediments, effective problem solving would probably never have become a viable reality in an agency as large and as decentralized as the NYPD. The discussion of the issues and difficulties faced by the NYPD is necessarily brief, since it would be impossible to fully enumerate or discuss the tremendous number and variety of organizational difficulties the agency faced within the format of this chapter.

It is important to understand the difficulties and impediments the NYPD faced at the beginning of the Giuliani/Bratton administration, not simply because they point up the prevailing spirit and general conditions affecting management in the agency but because they so closely resemble the type of problems that continue to face American policing as a whole. This description of the state of affairs in the NYPD puts the process of change in context by identifying the operations and functions which most needed to be transformed, and by providing a brief historical view of how these operations and functions became problematic in the first place. The problems enumerated here may not affect every police agency as profoundly as they did the NYPD, but because they are to large extent the unintended consequences of the so-called Professional Model they are symptomatic of American policing in general.

The NYPD is the nation's largest and arguably most complex police agency, and the problems it faces are correspondingly large and complicated. These problems are not exclusive to the NYPD, though. Rather, they seem to exist in one form or another in every police agency the author has ever encountered, whether in the United States or abroad. They exist in these agencies because they are part of the legacy of the Political Model, which dominated policing until the early decades of this century, and of the Professional Model, an ideology which shaped policing throughout most of the century. Although the Professional Model (or the Professional movement) was primarily an American policing phenomenon, its impact was also felt elsewhere. This chapter therefore seeks to outline in fairly broad terms the kind of general issues and impediments to effective strategic problem solving that operated in the NYPD prior to the Giuliani/Bratton administration and were common throughout American policing. Other issues and impediments that were more closely related to the peculiarities of the NYPD or were the result of particular historical events are discussed in the next chapter.

It should also be clearly stated that it is not the author's contention that the social impact of either the Political Model or the Professional Model was entirely negative. Both models had desirable and positive characteristics, and both reflected the political and management spirit of their times. It is also not the author's contention that the principles, policies and practices which comprised the Professional Model were, in themselves, inherently flawed or that the principles of Professionalism should not have been so widely adopted. On the contrary, at the time they were developed and first applied to policing they were at the cutting edge of management theory, and they were a tremendous advance over the management styles and practices which preceded them during the Political Era.

When any set of good and innovative management practices (including Compstat and strategic policing) are applied too rigidly or without continual adaptation to meet and respond to newly-evolved factors and forces in the internal or external environment, they can lead to unanticipated consequences. These consequences can easily have a negative impact on the organization, on the individuals who inhabit it, and on the society the police are mandated to protect and serve. The old adage about "too much of a good thing" certainly applies to the Political Model, the Professional Model, to Community Policing, and to the Compstat paradigm as well. Each of the models was (or, in the case of Community Policing, is) appropriate at the time of its introduction, but the risk always exists that when a successful model or idea takes hold it will endure beyond its logical point of usefulness. One of the Compstat paradigm's strengths in relation to the other models is the emphasis it places on continual evolution and continual adaptation to new ideas, problems and forces within the agency or in the external environment.

The history of American policing is generally divided into three distinct periods or eras, each with its own set of characteristic ideologies or guiding philosophies. These periods are generally known as the Political Era, the Reform or Professional Era, and the Community Policing Era. For policing as an institution as well as for individual agencies, the guiding philosophy of each in era defines overall missions and goals, determines the kind of policies and practices that are developed, and generally shapes the way departments are organized and managed. Thus specific organizational practices and management paradigms generally correspond to the ideology prevailing during a historic period. Like every other American police agency, the policies and practices of the NYPD were profoundly affected by the Professional Model.

As a new management ideology begins to develop and take hold, a transitional period of experimentation occurs across the spectrum of policing. In this transitional period, the relative merits of both the old and new systems are discussed and debated, and innovative programs based on the new model are implemented, evaluated and analyzed. A sort of power struggle or dialectic takes place as the upstart proponents of the new ideology challenge the stalwarts of the old order. The same type of transition and power struggle, albeit on a smaller scale, applies to any innovative program or policy implemented in an agency.

This gradual dialectical process of reconciling different ideas and practices usually results in a sort of compromise: agencies adopt some of the policies and practices the new philosophy prescribes, and some policies and practices remain the same. When and if the newly-adopted policies prove fruitful, the remaining policies come under scrutiny and are slowly adapted to fit the emerging philosophy. The success of initial pilot projects and programmatic efforts can permit police departments to evolve gradually into the new ideology, and change usually takes place incrementally. At the same time, the danger in pilot projects is that they are easily subverted or permitted to founder if top management is not committed to innovation, or if other forces and events intervene.

If an early pilot project fails because the innovator designed or implemented it poorly, the effect may be felt in subsequent pilot projects, or an early failure can even compromise the model's overall success in the agency. Rather than gradually building on the success of individual pilot projects as components of organizational transformation, the Compstat paradigm asserts that change should take place across the board – multiple targets for change should be identified and aggressively pursued simultaneously.

The pace and direction of change in an agency is impacted by a variety of internal and external forces. Externally, there must be support from the elected and appointed government officials who oversee the agency and control its budget and resources, and there must also be public support for any radical departure from previous practice. Internally, the champions of the new ideas must have sufficient power, authority and expertise to make the new practices work effectively as well as to resist the opposing efforts of the agency's stalwarts. As the new ideology develops, gains momentum, and proves its value, though, it becomes more and more difficult to return to previous practice.

Policing in the Political Era

The period from the mid-19th Century (when municipal governments first began establishing police forces) through the 1920s and 1930s is generally referred to as the Political Era. This era was followed by the Professional Era, and the Community Policing Era began to emerge and take hold in the early 1980s. These eras did not rise spontaneously in response to particular events or incidents, but instead they evolved over time as the law enforcement philosophies and practices of one period became anachronistic, as shortcomings became more and more apparent, as new ideas emerged, or as public dissatisfaction with police performance increased to critical proportions. It is difficult to pinpoint with any degree of accuracy when a particular model begins to evolve or when the influence of a particular model begins to decline.

Evolution and gradual change have always been a feature of American policing, and revolutions have been few. Because more and more police agencies are now embracing the Community Policing style and are beginning to experiment with new methods and practices that improve police effectiveness at the same time they ostensibly bring police closer to the communities they serve, American policing as a whole is currently involved in a shift away from the doctrines and practices that comprised the Professional Model. Whether the ideologies, practices and policies that characterize the Community Policing Model will ultimately dominate American policing or whether they will undergo substantial change and evolve in some other direction is uncertain, but whatever model evolves is sure to include vestigial features and characteristics of the Political and Professional Eras and the ideologies they entailed.

The Professional Model arose in response to widespread public dissatisfaction with the way police agencies and police officers conducted their business during the Political Era, and it was linked to the Reform movement in American politics. Its early direction was shaped by a handful of highly influential police chiefs and police theorists who challenged the prevailing notions of what policing could and should be. These early proponents of the model that came to be known as the Professional Model were themselves influenced by the current management theories and practices of their day, which promised greater efficiency, greater control and accountability of personnel, and greater cost-effectiveness. The Professional movement's leaders also placed great value on technology and they generally saw the police role as more concerned with fighting crime than with providing social services to the community.

During the Political Era, most American police departments (especially large municipal police departments) were dominated by political interests. Police agencies were highly decentralized during this period, and they were rife with corruption, misconduct, and mismanagement. Police agencies were so closely tied to the political organizations that ran municipal governments during this period that police historian Robert Fogelson (1977) characterized police agencies of the day as "adjuncts of the political machine." The political machine, which Fogelson (1977, p. 17) defines as a highly decentralized "association of loosely affiliated and largely autonomous ward organizations whose power depended on their ability to get the vote out on election day," had tremendous control over the delivery of all municipal services. Regardless of their political party, ward "bosses" operated in similar fashion throughout American urban areas.

In return for delivering the vote, ward bosses demanded and received tremendous influence over mayoral and city council policy making, as well as influence over the day-to-day operations of police and other city agencies. This power and influence translated into the power to grant lucrative contracts to their constituents, to appoint judges and other city officials, and the ability to demand or create jobs in city agencies, especially for recent immigrants. Ward bosses were the power brokers through whose offices these material inducements were exchanged for party loyalty. Because the police were an armed and somewhat well organized body who wielded tremendous power through their ability to invoke or ignore the criminal law as well as their ability to suppress and control the immigrant classes in teeming urban centers, they were an important asset to the political machine. A system of close interdependence developed.

Mandelbaum (1965) notes that the NYPD was created in 1844 with a force of 800 men, and that although the chief of police was selected by the Mayor, each member of that force was appointed annually through the nomination of his ward councilman. In cooperation with the politicians who had appointed him, each district captain was the law in his own district, and successive attempts to reform or alter this system were defeated by the entrenched political interests.

> Each reorganization of the force which attempted to break the hold
> of this localism ultimately failed. The police could not draw on a
> class of administrators with a tradition of disinterested action on the
> public behalf… Police administration was continually disrupted by
> party conflicts. The board could not control the corps. The captains
> were able without much interference to select the laws which were
> enforceable in their little kingdoms (Mandelbaum, 1965, p. 51-52).

Police commissioners were virtually powerless before the vested influence of the captains. Appointments, promotions and even tours of duty were secured through political influence. Within precincts, captains were absolute monarchs, preying on both the criminals and the poorer classes (Mandelbaum, 1965, p. 52-53). The disproportionate power of the captains and their political allies can be glimpsed in the commentary of an 1887 Harper's Magazine article about the NYPD:

> As it is at present, the Police Commissioners of New York know the
> abominable character of some men on the force, but cannot dismiss
> them, because the civil courts with their astounding technicalities
> will at once reinstate him. The thing has been tried, with this result.
> Thus the police captains may defy the Board of Commissioners, for
> they dare not remove him (Wheatley, 1887, p. 17).

Police agencies and police officers depended almost entirely upon local politicians for their legitimacy and their resources, and because civil service and other forms of job security were virtually unknown, officers of every rank were often beholden to politicians for their very jobs. The so-called "spoils system" of patronage proliferated in many or most municipalities, and elected politicians and party officials had almost absolute power to hire, fire and promote police officers.

Various arrangements existed in American cities to allot appointments to the police departments. In Los Angeles in the 1890s, for example, where three of the five Police Board seats were held by Republicans, the Republican members appointed three fifths of the force and the Democrats two fifths (Fogelson, 1977, p. 27). In some cities, Fogelson (1977, pp. 27-28) notes, politicians demanded a pay-off in return for a position in the police department – the going rate was $300 in New York and $400 in San Francisco in the 1890s – but in general the politician's primary interest was the individual's past or future service to the political machine.

The connection to politics was so great and the political machine's domination was so complete that in many cases police candidates applied not to the Police Commissioner or to the agency for employment, but directly to the local ward heeler or political boss (Fogelson, 1977). The candidate's education, intellect, background, level of physical fitness and integrity were often of little consequence, and other than political affiliation and connections there were few established criteria for hiring. While these payoffs were exorbitant in the economy of the day (New York City patrolmen earned an annual salary of from $1,000 to $1,200 in 1887), it should be recalled that in many places the position amounted to a veritable license to steal – graft and corruption were commonplace and endemic to the system.

Graft and corruption were extensive and closely linked to the political structure. New York City Mayor James "Gentleman Jim" Walker is said to have publicly commented that the police did not need a salary increase; any cop too stupid to figure out how to make more money, he said, was too stupid to be on the force.

This system facilitated and in some cases encouraged corruption and serious misconduct. The 1895 Lexow Commission in New York City, for example, detailed how deeply the police were involved in graft and corruption, as well as how poorly managed and politically dominated the agency was. The patterns opened up to public scrutiny by Lexow, though, were in place as early as the 1870s (Mandelbaum, 1965, p. 52).

The police mandate was extremely broad during the Political Era, and police agencies were involved in all sorts of activities and regulatory functions for which no other specific municipal agency existed. Examples include the fact that the NYPD was responsible for housing the homeless in police stations, and Wheatley (1887) reports that 72,832 males and 61,513 females were provided overnight accommodation in vacant precinct cells in 1887. As late as 1918, the NYPD was still responsible to inspect and test steam boilers in buildings throughout the city and to test and issue licenses for ice machine operators (NYPD Annual Report, 1918). The problems associated with this extremely broad mandate are especially well illustrated in the NYPD's early responsibility for street cleaning.

In 1872, in the face of mounting public pressure to address the unsanitary conditions in New York City, a special street cleaning bureau was created within the Police Department. The bureau's utter failure to adequately fulfill its mandate led to a Board of Alderman investigation in 1874, when it was determined that the police had completely failed to

> prevent garbage from being dumped in the streets. The bureau was infested with incompetent political employees. Supervisors were ignorant and disdainful of their duties and they levied assessments on their subordinates. The work force of the bureau, in its turn, demanded contributions from householders (Mandelbaum, 1965, pp. 166-67).

Interestingly, in 1878 the Police Board attempted to institute a system of block-by-block accountability for street cleaning, but the effort failed. According to an 1879 report, the failure of the accountability system and the overall mandate of the street cleaning bureau derived from the fact that the bureau was managed more in the interests of the political party than in the public interest (Mandelbaum, 1965, p. 167). The NYPD's responsibility for street cleaning continued well into the 1890s.

The primary focus of American municipal policing was clearly not on fighting crime during the Political Era – it was on serving the political machines and providing social services, especially to those individuals and groups who were aligned with the machine. It should be noted that there are more than a few similarities between Political Era policing and the ideals of the Community Policing Model, primarily in terms of decentralization, local control and the mandate that police officers become involved in either directly providing social services to the community or in providing access and referrals to those services. Although many treatises on Community Policing observe that American policing had its roots in social service provision, this observation may be somewhat disingenuous or ill-informed. One reason the police were involved in such matters was that municipal governments had few other mechanisms available to provide services, and many tasks were relegated to the police simply because they were the only municipal agency to operate on a 24-hour, seven-day basis.

Samuel Walker (1984), for one, has also pointed out that the romantic notions which support a great deal of Community Policing's ideology and rhetoric by evoking nostalgic feelings for a simpler past are just that – romantic notions and simplistic nostalgia. They have little or no basis in fact. The police of the Political Era were, all too often, brutal and uneducated thugs who acted in the interests of politicians rather than according to the rule of law. The police of the Political Era may have sheltered the homeless in police stations and fed the poor of their day, but they also licensed vice and thrived on the graft they were often induced to share with their political sponsors. While the police may have provided social services, there is little evidence pointing to the fact that the police did this effectively or well. In the absence of other governmental agencies or entities charged with these responsibilities, by default they were assigned to the police. Police control over the distribution of social services also equated with political control over their distribution: public resources could easily be allotted or denied on the basis of political favoritism.

Police Reform and the Emergence of Professionalism

It was against this highly politicized backdrop that American police reform was born. The Progressive Movement in early 20th Century politics "sought to shore up the position of the upper-middle and upper classes by reforming the courts, schools and other urban institutions. It attempted to reorganize their structure, upgrade their personnel, and redefine their function in ways that would once and for all destroy the system of machine politics (Fogelson, 1977, p. 44)." In terms of the police, early proponents of reform advocated a centralized and fairly autonomous bureaucratic agency structure which would be divorced from direct political control. The early champions of police Professionalism sought to insulate police from corruptive political influences and interference, and because other municipal agencies were being formed to provide social services, they focused instead on finding effective and efficient ways to fight crime. This focus on fighting

crime ultimately redefined the police role and the police identity. It later
became clearly apparent that in the 1990s the majority of NYPD officers, for
example, had greater affinity for the "crime fighter" role than for the "social
service provider" role.

Reformers, and police reformers in particular, also recognized that public
servants could not distance themselves from the winds and whims of political
change unless they possessed a degree of job tenure, and along with the
recognized need to raise hiring and promotion standards through the
imposition of valid selection criteria they advocated that civil service
protections be instituted. The police, they believed, should be devoted to the
rule of law and not to the pursuit of individual or partisan political interests,
and the attainment of this goal required that they have greater individual and
organizational independence. They recognized that greater centralization and
more clearly-defined lines of authority would enhance independence from
politics, and so they pushed for a more bureaucratic organizational structure.
Bureaucracies promised greater efficiency through the specialization of
functions, and they tended to ensure that the organization remained committed to its defined mission. Apolitical bureaucracies also tend to ensure
that the agency continues to fulfill its mission in times of political upheaval.
In line with their focus on efficient and effective crime fighting, the
reformers of the Professional movement also emphasized tighter and better
supervision of police personnel and they began to introduce specialized
training and education programs.

These reforms – insulation from undue political influence, corruption
control, bureaucratic structures and clearly delineated lines of authority, the
imposition of civil service hiring and promotion standards, effective and
efficient crime control, tighter supervision, and enhanced training and
education for police officers – became the goals and eventually the hallmarks
of the Professional Model. They were not achieved overnight, nor were they
achieved completely or evenly throughout American policing. Some agencies
were professionalized more rapidly and more thoroughly than others, and in
many cases the vestiges of undue political influence remained.

American police agencies are (and should be) politically accountable for
their activities, and civilian oversight of police is an absolutely essential
safeguard for the American system of liberal democracy. A great many of the
problems which led to the highly publicized 1991 Rodney King incident and
the April 1992 Los Angeles riots, for example, were laid at the doorstep of
the LAPD – an agency which became the very epitome of Professional
Model policing – and the fact that its chief executive was not functionally

accountable to the political structure. The Christopher Commission's (1991) scathing report on the Rodney King incident was as much a criticism of the Professional Model as of the LAPD's chief executive and his management style. It may be difficult in other settings, though, to distinguish the fine line where accountability and control ends and politicization and political domination begins.

Notwithstanding the advent and growth of Professionalism in American policing, controlling corruption and misconduct also continues to be an issue with which many agencies (including the NYPD) have struggled throughout this century. Civil service protections are still not universal in American policing, and even in those places where it has been adopted there continues to exist great variation in the specific methods and practices it involves. For the most part, though, the doctrines of the Professional ideology that began to take shape in the 1910s and 1920s spread in various forms and configurations throughout the century.

August Vollmer and O.W. Wilson were among the chief proponents of early police Professionalism, and they were perhaps the most influential figures in making it the dominant paradigm in American policing. As the Chief of Police in Berkeley California between 1905 and 1932, Vollmer introduced a variety of management techniques and policing strategies which were considered unique and revolutionary in their day. These innovations sought to enhance efficiency in a cost-effective way, and they included the first call box signal system which allowed beat police officers to be quickly contacted on their posts and informed of assignments, and the establishment of the nation's first training school or police academy in 1908. Under Vollmer's management, the Berkely police eventually became the first police agency to deploy its entire patrol force in automobiles, enabling officers to respond to reported crimes even more rapidly.

Vollmer understood that policing is a complex enterprise that demands intelligence, knowledge and social skills, and he was a staunch advocate of advanced training as well as higher education for police officers. Vollmer recruited college students from the University of California to serve as police officers in Berkeley, and he had a vision of policing in which every officer would have a college degree. He believed that advanced education held the key to transforming policing into a true profession, equal in status and stature to the legal and medical professions. For a variety of reasons, this vision was never fully achieved.

Vollmer played an important role in the 1929 National Commission on Law Observance and Enforcement (popularly known as the Wickersham Commission, after its chair, George Wickersham) which was the first comprehensive national study of the American criminal justice system. The Wickersham Commission was a potent force for the overall reform of the American criminal justice system, and the repeal of the Volstead Act and the end of Prohibition are credited to the strength of its findings and recommendations. The Wickersham Commission released a fourteen volume report, and two volumes - **Lawlessness in Law Enforcement** and **The Police** related directly to the problems and reform of American policing. Vollmer was the primary author of **The Police**, and in it he outlined the need for better recruitment and hiring practices, better pay, more training, and higher education for police officers. **The Police** also set forth many of the management principles Vollmer believed were necessary to reform American policing (Wickersham, 1931).

Vollmer was instrumental in creating the School of Criminology at the University of California's Berkeley campus, and both as a professor there and as a police chief he trained many students who went on to apply his progressive principles in the agencies they headed. In his many speeches and published works, Vollmer was a forceful voice espousing more effective, autonomous and centralized law enforcement (MacNamara, 1977).

O.W. Wilson was one of Vollmer's protégées in the Berkeley Police Department, and his contributions to the Professional movement include the early reform of the Wichita, Kansas Police Department, based on principles he learned under Vollmer. Wilson also conducted a study of the effectiveness of one-officer patrol cars, concluding that they were a more cost-effective means of deploying officers than simple foot patrol. Wilson's advocacy of increased cost-effectiveness through the adoption of new and emerging technology is reflective of the great value the Professional movement placed on technology. This central value resonated throughout the Professional movement, and police agencies began to implement automobile patrols, rudimentary radio dispatching, telephone systems, and call boxes so that foot patrol officers could respond quickly to events on their posts. Ultimately, this emphasis on technology as a means to faster response led to the development and implementation of 911 systems in departments across the nation.

In combination with the emphasis on technology and the focus on crime-fighting, rapid response (especially to calls for crimes in progress where the likelihood that a perpetrator would be apprehended was greatest) became a cherished value and sought-after ideal of the Professional Model. Indeed, it is difficult to underestimate the lasting impact the demand for rapid response had on police work and on police-community relations as more and more officers were reassigned from foot patrol to radio cars. For much of this century, response time has been a standard barometer by which agencies judged their own and other agencies' performance. Agency goals were (and in many cases, still are) formulated in terms of reducing response time, and response time became one of the few quantitative measures by which precinct commanders in the NYPD, for example, were evaluated.

The advent and implementation of 911 technology in the early 1970s contributed greatly to this emphasis on rapid response to crimes and calls for service, but along the way this goal became overriding. The quality of service provided by officers became subordinate, in the eyes of professional administrators, to the number of calls the officers handled and the speed with which they responded. Officers raced from call to call to take reports, and positive contact with the community declined in importance.

To keep response times down, cops were admonished to quickly complete their interactions with the public and return to service so that they could resume randomly patrolling the streets and again be ready to respond to the next call at a moment's notice. The rapid response mandate kept cops in cars and essentially prevented them from having a great deal of meaningful contact with citizens except while providing assistance on a call. Even then, the interactions were often strained because the contact took place around an emotionally-charged crisis situation. The police and the public lost touch with one another.

Compounding this estrangement from the community was the all-too-common prohibition against unnecessary conversation with the public. Banas and Trojanowitz (1985), for example, point out that as early as 1897 leading members of the International Association of Chiefs of Police (IACP) exhorted their fellow chiefs not to tolerate unnecessary conversations or other breeches of discipline on the part of patrol officers. Policies barring unnecessary conversation were adopted – and selectively enforced – in police agencies across America and overseas. These unnecessary conversations, in the Professionals' view, were an unseemly erosion of discipline, contributed nothing toward the attainment of agency goals, and distracted officers from their primary mission – fighting crime.

Even in the contemporary age of Community Policing, when rapidity of response is seen as less important than the quality of response and the effectiveness of the problem-solving activities officers employ, debates over response time are still regarded as an important measure of police performance. Response time issues continue to figure prominently at virtually every New York City Council hearing on the NYPD's performance, and the Mayor's Management Report continues to present response time comparisons and statistics.

The studies of automobile patrol by Wilson and other leaders of the Professional movement went far beyond merely demonstrating a useful and expedient strategy or encouraging the use of automobiles for patrol purposes, though, since they illustrated how agencies could conduct and use experiments and other forms of quantitative research to solve management problems and make their organizations function more effectively. On a broader scale, writers and researchers including Bruce Smith (1925; 1940), Sheldon Glueck (1926), and Raymond Fosdick (1929) conducted organizational studies and wrote compelling analyses and critiques of individual agencies and police systems, and their views on bureaucratic reform and other management issues were widely adopted.

One of Wilson's most powerful and lasting contributions was his book **Police Administration**, which was first published in 1950. This classic textbook was one of the earliest and most widely-read texts on police management and organization, and for many decades it was the standard textbook for college-level police studies courses as well as for promotional exams. Wilson's book embodied the principles and extolled the virtues of the Professional Model, and the organizational structures, policies and practices it prescribed shaped the ideas of several generations of police leadership in America. Lawrence Sherman (1974) points out that **Police Administration** was the "bible" of the Professional movement in a time when the academic world paid little or no attention to policing and few other sources were available. Based on Frederick Taylor's principles of "Scientific Management," this influential text emphasized efficiency, hierarchical structures, and bureaucracy as the means to effective management.

Wilson's **Police Administration** was first published in 1950 as part of a McGraw-Hill series in Political Science – until that time there was only a small market for police management texts, and the academic discipline of Criminal Justice had not yet emerged – and revised editions appeared in 1963, 1972 and 1977. Wilson also conducted and wrote research reports on police organizations, records systems and deployment practices in Witchita, Kansas and San Antonio, Texas in 1939; in Hartford, Connecticut in 1942; in San Antonio in 1951; in Detroit in 1952; and in Albany, California in 1953. In general, these reports advocated a management decision-making system in which statistical analysis of crimes and calls for service would determine how patrol officers should be geographically and temporally distributed. This method of statistical analysis would determine the size of patrol areas or sectors as well as how officers' working schedules could be coordinated with the times of peak demand, and the basic model continues to inform police deployment practices today. By basing these management decisions on quantifiable statistical analyses of work-load data, the kind of political considerations, pressures and influences that are inevitably involved in police deployment and precinct staffing decisions could be somewhat allayed.

Wilson held a somewhat cynical view of rank-and-file police officers, though, and this basic distrust was reflected in his writings and his personal management style. He favored a fairly rigid and highly directive system of rules and regulations as a means of curtailing officer's discretion, coupled with a strong disciplinary system. This preference for rigidly adhering to rules and regulations and imposing strict limitations on discretionary behaviors was fairly successful in terms of controlling corruption and misconduct, but overall it tended to have a negative impact on officers' morale.

Scientific Management

Many of the management principles emphasized and adopted by Wilson and the early Professionals were grounded in the "scientific management" principles articulated by Frederick Winslow Taylor, and the trend toward agency bureaucratization was also influenced by the writings of sociologist Max Weber. Taylor, an engineer by training, developed a system of management principles that had a profound effect on American business practices and ultimately upon police organizational theorists. Taylor conceived of management as a true science resting on clearly defined laws, rules and principles, and he said that these fundamental principles are applicable to virtually any kind of human organization, without regard to its size or complexity.

Scientific management took a highly mechanistic and fairly narrow view of organizational behavior, and Taylor's theories evinced a strong belief in the "one best way" – the idea that there was a single best way to perform any operation or task. On an assembly line, for example, the "one best way" was identified by breaking down every step, operation or task involved in making the product into its individual elements. These elements (as well as the workers performing them) could be observed and measured, and the time and effort required to complete each task could be measured, analyzed and improved. By eliminating unnecessary or repetitive steps and by streamlining processes, each task could be performed more efficiently and more economically. The effectiveness and efficiency of the organization as a whole could be vastly improved, Taylor said, by identifying the "one best way" to perform each and every task and by standardizing those practices throughout the organization. In a general sense, scientific management called for greater specialization of function and highly specific training for workers so that each could perform their particular job in the most efficient way. These principles were generally mirrored in the Professional ideology.

Scientific management also argued for a clear division of labor between workers, supervisors and managers, and for careful delineation of their respective duties and responsibilities. The worker's role was limited to performing the specific tasks he or she was trained to perform, and the supervisor's role was limited to overseeing and directing workers' activities. Managers were primarily charged with studying and analyzing the organization and its operations and with finding improvements which would result in even greater efficiency. According to scientific management doctrine, if every duty, responsibility and task involved in fulfilling the organization's mission was precisely defined and effectively carried out by the person specifically responsible for it, the organization would run like a well-oiled machine. So-called "efficiency experts" armed with stopwatches and clipboards became commonplace in American industry, and the "time and motion studies" they conducted became a mainstay of American manage-ment. Their influence and the influence of scientific management principles in general extended to American policing as well.

As Banas and Trojanowicz (1985) have pointed out, this spirit of efficiency and highly disciplined standardization influenced the early Professionals in their quest for a viable crime comparison system – a quest that ultimately led to the creation and implementation of the FBI's Uniform Crime Reports system.

The chiefs frequently conceptualized their mission as a business. Just as they borrowed their imagery from the rapidly industrializing private sector, so they defined their *raison d'etre* as efficiency. Efficiency became synonymous with disciplining the rank and file to the point that officers became viewed as passive entities possessing absolutely no discretion. The chiefs simultaneously invested themselves and their command officers with all the prerogatives of decision making. By centralizing discretion within the command structure, the chiefs sought an "objective" basis to exercise authority. The Uniform Crime Reports became an attractive measure for the chiefs, one through which they could communicate with both the public and the rank and file (Banas and Trojanowicz, 1985, p. 8).

In policing, scientific management doctrines and demands for standardization and specialization also prompted the development of myriad written policies and procedures, seemingly with the goal of creating a procedure to cover every task or function an officer could conceivably be required to perform. Each of these procedures, it seemed, had a corresponding specialized form or report to go with it.

Scientific management and the principles of Weberian bureaucracy shared a mechanistic view of organizations, emphasized efficiency and effectiveness, and provided practical management models for directing and controlling the activities of personnel. They held great appeal for police reformers, and ultimately shaped the structures of police agencies as well as the management styles of police executives.

Weberian Bureaucracy

The German sociologist Max Weber (1864-1920) certainly did not develop the idea of bureaucratic organizational structures, but his studies of how they functioned as social systems contributed greatly to their acceptance and implementation in the administration of businesses and government agencies. The bureaucracy is a type of organizational structure in which particular tasks and the authority to make decisions are compartmentalized according to functional area and then positioned throughout the organization. In theory as well as in fact, this streamlined structure avoids unnecessary repetition or duplication of effort and helps the organization function efficiently.

Fairchild (1970) succinctly describes the bureaucracy as a graded hierarchy of officials, each of whom is responsible to his or her superiors. The term is ordinarily applied to governmental organizations, but bureaucracies also exist in business, industry, commerce, labor unions, social institutions, churches and other forms of social organization. At their worst, bureaucracies have come to be characterized by adherence to routine, more or less inflexible rules, red tape, procrastination, an unwillingness to assume responsibility, and refusal to experiment (Fairchild, 1970, p. 29).

Because bureaucracies can often seem overly rigid or inflexible, and because they can engender great frustration among those who work in them as well as among outsiders who attempt to deal with them, the term bureaucracy often takes on negative or pejorative connotations. Notwithstanding their tremendous capacity to frustrate, though, bureaucracies *are* an essential part of the police organization and *can* be designed and structured to efficiently perform tasks and functions that are essential to the organization's overall mission.

Weber described bureaucracies as having particular characteristics that enhance their capacity to manage the organization effectively. As excerpted from Freund's (1969) and Bendix' (1962) descriptions of Weber's organizational theories as well as Gerth and Mills' (1946) translation of Weber's work, these characteristics can be summarized as follows:

1. Within the bureaucratic organization, there exist specific spheres of competence which are strictly defined by law or regulations, so that the decision-making powers of particular individuals, units or positions are clearly defined and apportioned. Every official is, in theory, given the amount of authority necessary to fulfill his or her function.

2. Specific regulations guarantee officials some protection and tenure, so that public service becomes the principal occupation.

3. The bureaucratic structure is hierarchical. Units and positions are organized according to the function they fulfill, and clear divisions can be distinguished between executive and subordinate positions. Higher offices and positions have the duty to supervise lower offices and positions, and to some extent those in lower positions have the right to appeal decisions from above. Weber pointed out that the terms and conditions of both supervision and appeal may vary greatly from organization to organization. Because of this hierarchical structure, bureaucracies demonstrate a tendency toward increased centralization of power and authority.

4. Bureaucracies tend to recruit their employees on the basis of competitive examinations, and they often require that employees undertake specialized training or meet specific educational criteria which equip them for the particular tasks and duties they perform.

5. Officials in bureaucracies tend to have fixed salaries and a pension upon retirement, and salaries are graded according to rank in the admini-

strative hierarchy as well as the amount of responsibility their work requires.

6. The superior has the legitimate right to regulate the work of his or her subordinates, if necessary through the imposition of discipline.

7. Promotional opportunities are on the basis of objective criteria rather than the subjective discretion of superiors.

8. There is a complete separation between the office and the incumbent: employees have no property rights with regard to either the position they hold or the resources necessary to conduct the organization's business. Neither the position or the authority that goes with it can be legitimately inherited, transferred or sold. Although employees may not own the organization's resources, they are accountable for their use. The bureaucracy distinguishes between and separates the employee's official business and his or her private affairs.

To some extent, large and complex organizations need bureaucracies in order to achieve their goals: as frustrating as they may be at times, bureaucracies fulfill essential functions in ways other organizational structures simply cannot. By assigning certain functions to specific units or offices, they streamline the flow of work and allow specialists to perform the duties they do best. Because they involve specialization, bureaucratic structures also facilitate the development of expertise in particular fields – individuals come to know the ins-and-outs of their respective jobs and the duties they perform.

Even if one conceives narrowly (and incorrectly) of the police bureaucracy as consisting solely of the agency's administrative and support functions, it is clear that many of these functions are best managed by a centralized and structured entity. Few would argue that these functions are unnecessary. By creating specialized areas in the administrative and support realms, bureaucracies free up personnel and other resources to pursue the agency's primary operational mission.

At the same time, there is a distinct tendency in American policing bureaucracies to deal with new or emerging problems by creating specialized units to address them. This practice, in itself, is less detrimental to the operations of the department than the related practice of formalizing the units within the bureaucratic structure. Once a unit is formed and a box is added to the organizational chart, it becomes difficult to eliminate even after the problem that led to its creation is solved. As these overly-specialized units proliferate, little boxes start to collect on the organizational chart. Anthony Bouza (1990) likens these specialized units to barnacles on the hull of a ship – they draw resources and attention from other important functions, and generally slow down the agency. They permit the development of small fiefdoms, and they unnecessarily diffuse power in the organization. To ensure a lean and streamlined bureaucratic structure, these barnacles must be scraped off or prevented from adhering in the first place. The problem is basically one of balancing the need to address a specific operational problem with the need to maintain a simple organizational structure. A far more cogent strategy, as discussed in subsequent chapters, is to assemble small *ad hoc* task forces designed to resolve a problem, at the same time refraining from giving them official status so that they can be easily disbanded and their personnel and resources redeployed when they have outlived their usefulness or fulfilled their mission.

Invariably, though, the problems of inflexibility and frustration do not usually lie within the bureaucratic structure itself, but with the personnel that inhabit and manage it. Inflexible and frustrating bureaucratic organizations are those in which personnel have limited autonomy and limited discretion to bend the rules, or whose in which personnel are so poorly managed or demoralized that they are incapable or fearful of using their discretion in this way. In the long run, the problem is not typically the bureaucracy itself, but how well it is designed and managed. Because bureaucracies are based in the centralization of power and authority, they tend to take on a narrowly-focused life of their own when they are poorly managed, and members of the bureaucracy can easily lose sight of the agency's larger overall goals.

Well managed bureaucracies give stability and order to organizations and encourage efficient operations, and are not necessarily inflexible. In the extreme, though, a poorly managed bureaucracy slips into paralysis and stagnation, compromising the efficiency they are designed to encourage.

In the context of Compstat paradigm management, an important part of managing the bureaucracy entails determining which functions, responsibilities, and decision-making processes should remain the province of the central bureaucracy and which should be decentralized. Certainly such functions as payroll, budget, procurement and purchasing, employee benefits, record keeping and other functions that are important but not closely and narrowly related to the fulfillment of the agency's core mission can be safely entrusted to the central bureaucracy. Other functions and decision-making processes that *are* crucial to fulfilling the core mission must be stripped off from the central bureaucracy and both decentralized and streamlined.

If some minor delays or administrative breakdowns occur in the budget process, for example, the result may be annoyance or some minor organizational discomfort but the repercussions will not be all that significant. In the operational sphere, though, a breakdown in communication or an attenuated decision-making process can easily translate into human tragedy – lives can literally be lost through bureaucratic lassitude and delays. Units and entities in the operational sphere remain part of the agency's organizational and bureaucratic structure, of course, but as we shall see in subsequent chapters they should not operate according to the same bureaucratic principles and policies as support and ancillary units.

Corruption Control

Controlling corruption and misconduct was another overriding concern of the Professional Model. Because corruption and misconduct are inevitably tied to the police officer's discretionary behaviors, the Professional Model sought to limit discretion through the imposition of tight supervision as well as rigid discipline for infractions of the rules and regulations. Police officers wield tremendous power in our society, and this makes the potential for corruption and misconduct an enduring and endemic feature of police work. The problem of corruption control is further complicated by the fact that despite the best efforts of police administrators to impose supervision and limit their discretion, police officers spend the vast majority of their time working without direct supervision. Whether they recognize and respond to them or not, police officers confront corruption hazards every day, and no amount of rule-making or supervision can ever truly eliminate these hazards. Corruption and misconduct can be controlled and brought within manageable limits in a well-run police agency, but the potential for corruption can never be completely removed. A police executive in any agency who claims he or she has entirely and permanently eliminated corruption is either a liar or a fool.

The difficulties involved in controlling corruption are well illustrated in the history of the NYPD, where corruption scandals have been said to recur on an approximate twenty-year cycle since the beginning of the century. This vaunted twenty-year cycle has been widely cited in the literature of police corruption, but in truth it is a simplistic interpretation of history based on an incomplete analysis of the forces and factors that operate within police agencies. These forces and factors do not cause corruption, *per se*, but they create an environment in which it can readily flourish. In reality, the twenty-year cycle of corruption and reform actually consists of a cycle involving corruption followed by reform and the imposition of effective corruption control strategies, followed by managerial and organizational apathy toward the problem and the easing-off of control mechanisms, and ultimately the emergence of new patterns and types of corrupt activities (see, for example, Henry, 1993; 1994).

A close analysis of the history of corruption in the NYPD reveals that the types and patterns of police corruption have changed dramatically over the years, and that specific strategies can be brought to bear to radically reduce or virtually eliminate them. The pervasive and well-organized system of payoffs (or "pads") that existed at the time of the Knapp Commission in 1972, for example, were virtually eliminated by the corruption control mechanisms put in place by Police Commissioner Patrick Murphy at that time. The types and patterns of corruption of the early 1990s, as described by the Mollen Commission in 1994, were of an entirely different kind from those identified by Knapp, and this demonstrates both the evolutionary nature of police corruption and its enduring potential: because the mechanisms to detect and prevent organized payoffs were effective, new forms or strains of corruption evolved that were resistant to the mechanisms.

Although new patterns of corruption began to evolve, by the 1980s the department's management had become complacent and it did little to amend or update its corruption control strategies. The corruption control strategies and mechanisms put in place in 1972 remained virtually unchanged until the new scandal occurred in 1992, and during that time management's posture deteriorated from one of aggressively and proactively seeking out and attacking corruption to one of passively responding to minor scandals. The fact that these minor scandals pointed to the evolution of new and more virulent (though nowhere near as widespread or pervasive) types and patterns of corruption was apparently lost on the complacent NYPD executives responsible for corruption control in the late 1980s (Henry, 1993; 1994). Once again, the failure of management to continually identify and adapt to new problems and new environmental factors eventually exacted a heavy toll on the police organization.

The corruption control mechanisms enacted by Patrick Murphy in the early 1970s merit some exploration, both because they had a profound effect on the NYPD and because they illustrate the kind of practices the Professional Model espoused. Patrick Murphy was appointed Police Commissioner as the scandal was unfolding, and he seized upon it as a means of changing the department's structure, policies and practices as well as its organizational culture. Scandal can be a powerful impetus for reform, since it focuses attention on a wide range of agency problems and usually permits executives to gain and apply additional resources to solve them. Murphy was a staunch advocate of the Professional ideology, and the reforms he implemented followed the Professional Model's prescriptions.

The organizational changes Murphy brought about were extensive. Although the changes go well beyond the scope of this chapter, they basically involved limiting officers' discretion and their contact with corruption hazards. Because the corruption of the day involved gambling and vice, for example, Murphy essentially forbade patrol officers from directly enforcing these laws. Patrol officers were told not to take summary action when they saw narcotics or vice violations taking place, but instead to pass the information along to specialized narcotics or vice units where the investigators were subject to extremely tight supervision. In time, the specialized (if possibly overburdened) units would get around to taking some enforcement action.

Officers were also prohibited from enforcing a variety of other statutes which would today be characterized as quality of life offenses, and they were prohibited simply because they presented a real or perceived corruption hazard. Cops in New York City were forbidden from entering a bar or licensed premise without a supervisor present, and the department virtually ceased conducting alcoholic beverage control enforcement because these activities had been a source of graft. Unlicensed bars and social clubs therefore proliferated, and they freely sold alcohol (many permitting or encouraging other illegal activities as well), secure in the knowledge that the police would not interfere. The same "hands-off" policy for patrol officers applied to street narcotics dealers, prostitutes and gamblers. The non-enforcement edicts gave illegal operators all the benefits of a pay-off system but cost them nothing.

Along with the prohibition on certain types of enforcement activities, Commissioner Patrick Murphy also instituted integrity testing, in which officers were purposely exposed to corruption hazards under carefully controlled and monitored conditions in order to see whether or not they would take the bait. Other corruption control strategies included the use of "field associates," in which officers were recruited to work in an undercover capacity among other officers but secretly report to Internal Affairs any corruption they observed. These strategies were effective in detecting and discouraging corruption, but they also affected morale and were a divisive force within the police culture. The messages cops received were clear and unequivocal: corruption control, not crime control, is management's preoccu-pation and top priority, and management does not trust cops.

"Hands-off"

Beyond the fact that the NYPD's "hands-off" policy toward drugs, vice, prostitution, illegal alcohol and other offenses tacitly encouraged their proliferation during the 1970s, 1980s and early 1990s, the policy had a powerful impact on morale and on the agency's organizational culture, as well as on public perceptions of the police. Consider, for example, the plight of a conscientious young Probationary Police Officer, recently graduated from the Police Academy and assigned to foot patrol on a tough Brooklyn beat. Imagine the young officer's sense of pride and purpose as he walks his post and greets people waiting for the bus or entering the subway for the morning trip to work, and the officer's secure belief that his uniformed presence makes these people and their neighborhood a truly safer place. He introduces himself and stands chatting with the grocer opening his awning, when from across the street the steerer's voice calls out "smoke, ganja." The grocer looks from the officer to the dealer and back to the officer, whose only officially approved recourse is to file an intelligence report and hope that the specialized narcotics unit will get around to making arrests on his post sometime soon. In the interim, the officer, the grocer, the dealer and everyone else on the post either know that the officer is impotent to act or they suspect that he is on the dealer's payroll. How can they be expected to place their trust in him when the police department seems not to trust him? The officer knows from the Police Academy that if he takes action and begins to make drug arrests, his supervisor or commanding officer will scrutinize his activities very carefully and may change his assignment. If the drug dealer complains and alleges misconduct, the officer will become the subject of an official corruption investigation. The scenario is not far-fetched. Thousands of New York City police officers during the 1970s, 1980s and early 1990s (including the author) felt their pride, their sense of commitment, and their belief in the legitimacy of their leaders diminish and fade as they were tacitly and overtly told to turn a blind eye to the kind of offenses that most concern the public.

One of the first messages articulated during the Giuliani/Bratton administration was that the "hands-off" policy – which had never actually been reduced to writing in a formal policy statement – was abandoned. Officers could once again use their discretion to fully enforce the law, and could effectively address the kind of quality of life problem the public complained of most. The real message though, was that the department and the administration trusted police officers to act with honesty and integrity in enforcing the law, unless and until officers gave them reason to believe otherwise. That articulation of trust gave a much-needed boost to police morale, self-image, and confidence in their leadership.

Most importantly, Murphy instituted a system of command account-ability in which supervisors and commanders were held strictly accountable for any corruption or serious misconduct taking place within their chain of command. The department's executive corps (those 180 or so members above the civil service rank of captain whom Murphy could promote or demote at will) were the key to implementing accountability and reform. Murphy articulated his message of command accountability shortly after taking office:

> If you are above the rank of captain, you serve at my pleasure and you won't be serving in that rank if I decide you are not vigorously pursuing the policies I'm laying down for going after the wrong-doing police officer and eliminating corruption in your command. I charge each of you – eliminate corruption in your command. No matter how honest you may be, you will be held responsible and you'll not keep your rank above captain (Janasoff, 1977, p. 8).

Murphy was determined to remove commanders who failed to act vigorously against corruption in order to make room for commanders who would. He concurrently announced his intention of reaching a 30% annual executive turnover rate, which, in fact, he achieved over his three year tenure (Jasanoff, 1977, p. 8; Murphy and Plate, 1977, p. 239). If corruption or serious misconduct was uncovered, the officers involved as well as their supervisors and commanding officer were held strictly accountable. Officers were prosecuted criminally for corruption and administratively for serious misconduct, but their superior officers and commanders were also subject to a range of sanctions including transfers, disciplinary action for failure to adequately supervise, or in the case of executives, the threat of demotion. Managers and executives quickly got Murphy's message: "'Ooh, new ball game! I advance my career by proving to these characters Murphy has around him that I'm really a corruption fighter. Watch me go.' And boy did they go" (Jasanoff, 1977, p. 10).

As each commander stepped (or was pushed) aside, another stepped up to fill his position, and the impact on the agency's management style was dramatic. In terms of transforming management and reducing corruption, the policy worked: newer, younger and more aggressive managers vigorously pursued corrupt officers, imposed unprecedented levels of supervision and accountability, and limited officers' exposure to corruption hazards. The new policy also introduced an unprecedented level of competition within middle management. In short order, corruption began to abate but with few exceptions the policy of command accountability was never expanded to include performance measures other than those related to corruption. This rapid turnover and ascendance of a new executive cadre scrupulously committed to strict discipline and corruption control, in fact, is cited by Reuss-Ianni (1983) as the single most influential factor contributing to the fragmentation of the NYPD's organizational culture into a "street cop culture" and a "management cop culture." We will revisit this fragmentation and its impact on the organization in subsequent chapters.

Disciplinary policies and procedures were revamped under Murphy, and discipline as a whole was significantly tightened. Murphy promulgated a new set of rules and regulations (the Department's Patrol Guide) which ostensibly provided procedures for almost every eventuality an officer might face, and within a few years the new Guide grew to over 800 pages – not including temporary orders and directives.

These and other fairly draconian corruption control strategies, which were reflective of the Professional Model's prevailing view of police management, had at least three immediate results: they reduced organized corruption significantly and brought it to within manageable limits, they created a rule-bound working environment characterized by a general reluctance to use discretion or to take police action, and they drove a wedge of distrust and antipathy between cops and bosses. Over time, and notwith-standing the natural tendency of police officers to take risks and act decisively, this sense of timidity or reluctance became part of the organizational culture but was particularly pronounced among members of the agency's executive corps. As will be discussed in subsequent chapters, the Compstat process became essential in weeding out these indecisive managers and replacing them with more dynamic leaders who were willing to trust their personnel and to take appropriate risks, and in at least partially healing the rift between cops and bosses.

Civil Service

The Professional movement also sought to improve the quality of policing through the development and implementation of appropriate selection and hiring criteria to screen police candidates, as well as the use of civil service examinations for hiring and promotion decisions. Police agencies developed physical, medical, psychological and background criteria to screen out unsuitable applicants, and the civil service system was seen as a vehicle to ensure that hiring and promotion was conducted fairly and without nepotism or political influence. The civil service concept was adopted widely in policing, and although the system may be administered differently in different agencies, it ultimately became a cornerstone of the Professional Model.

Part of civil service is the idea that the employee receives job tenure after a probationary period of satisfactory performance – tenure in position assures officers that their positions are protected from politics and from the arbitrary or capricious actions of supervisors and managers. In practice, tenure is generally granted unless the probationer engages in misconduct or exhibits extreme incompetence during the probationary period. Once granted, job tenure means that the officer cannot be fired without adequate cause. He or she cannot be fired or reduced in rank for taking a lawful action, even if that action displeases the chief executive or the political powers-that-be.

In the NYPD, the probationary period was not generally used to identify and terminate marginal or borderline performers – only those whose performance fell well below expected standards were terminated. Along with the civil service practice of paying a comparable salary to every individual within a particular job title regardless of the amount and quality of their work, tenure may in time lead to the development of the "civil service mentality" – the idea that it is best to do the minimal acceptable amount of work since the tangible rewards for outstanding work are few and far between.

The NYPD's promotional system differs from the system used in some other locales, and because promotional systems ultimately have a powerful impact on the characteristics of managers and upon the quality of management within an agency, the NYPD's hybrid promotional system merits some description.

Promotion to the civil service ranks of Sergeant, Lieutenant and Captain in the NYPD are based almost entirely upon the candidate' performance on multiple-choice examinations. In an ideal sense, the whole point of the civil service promotional system is to ensure that the best and most qualified candidates are promoted, but this aim is also balanced against the mandate for a fair, open and entirely objective testing system. To forestall the appearance or the reality of nepotism, favoritism or unfairness in the promotion process, the NYPD's system is supposed to be transparent – fair and objective multiple choice examinations are open to all candidates meeting the basic requirements, and the questions that comprise the examination are drawn from a reading list that is specified in advance and available to all candidates. In order to meet the goal of objectivity (and to withstand challenges that the test questions were ambiguous or open to interpretation), the questions themselves are supposed to be carefully written so that only one of the possible answers is correct.

The promotional examinations must also be job-related, so the reading list – the body of knowledge whose acquisition and mastery holds the key to advancement – typically consists of the NYPD's ponderous 800-plus page book of rules and procedures (the Patrol Guide), the department's numerous standing orders and temporary amendments to the Patrol Guide (called Interim Orders), the New York State Penal Law and Criminal Procedure Law, and selected Constitutional case law decisions governing police behavior (Legal Bureau Bulletins). Until the early 1980's, the reading lists often included a basic text on police management, such as Iannone's **Supervision of Police Personnel** or O.W. Wilson's **Police Administration** (both of which emphasized Professional Model themes and practices). Even the questions drawn from these management texts, though, must have clear and objective, right-or-wrong answers – subjective judgment questions are incompatible with the mandate for objectivity. This is, of course, paradoxical, since one would expect that the best and most effective police supervisor or manager is the one who can make good subjective judgments in ambiguous or equivocal situations. The realities of contemporary urban policing are not nearly as cut-and-dried as the civil service examination writers would have them.

Because the mandate is for purely objective testing, the examinations rarely incorporate any type of qualitative measures of supervisory or managerial aptitude. Personality factors, such as the candidate's inherent charisma, leadership ability or personal and professional integrity (which are potential sources of referent power) cannot be easily measured without resorting to subjective evaluations, so they are simply not considered in the NYPD's civil service promotional process. For the same reason, the process also neglects to consider the candidate's special experiences or expertise in particular fields, and his or her annual performance evaluations, sick record, and record of disciplinary complaints, and level of education (beyond a qualifying minimum) count for nothing.

Because the examinations are given infrequently and are administered to a large pool of candidates, they are extremely competitive. In order to narrow the field of candidates to those with the most detailed knowledge, the examinations often ask extremely specific and very narrow questions taken from fairly obscure procedures. For example, a long-standing procedure which required that all department forms be completed in blue or black ball-point pen (yes, the NYPD's rules and regulations even covered the color and type of pen officers are required to use) was altered shortly before a recent Sergeants exam. Blue ball-points were outlawed. An exam question was fashioned to determine whether candidates knew of this procedural altera-tion. Any possible connection between this arcane bit of procedural trivia and the characteristics of dynamic leadership is tenuous, at best. The irony of using such obscure questions lies not just in the fact that otherwise-qualified individuals with strong leadership and management skills could be excluded from further advancement (and the agency deprived of their skills and expertise) because they missed a few such esoteric questions, but in the fact that others will be promoted without regard to other qualifications because they *did* know them.

Unlike many smaller agencies, the NYPD has never used assessment centers for promotional purposes. In assessment center testing, a battery of tests designed to measure the candidate's expertise and skills, capacity to think creatively and mastery of other intellectual or interpersonal skills which are important indicators of supervisory or managerial potential are administered, and candidates are evaluated subjectively on the basis of these multiple measures. The agency can thus select the candidates who possess the experience, interpersonal and intellectual skills, and expertise the chief executives believe are most important to the agency's proper management. Although assessment centers and other qualitative measures of management potential are much more comprehensive than simple multiple-choice examinations, they also open up the possibility of favoritism and would be extremely difficult and expensive to administer in an agency the size of the NYPD, where more than 20,000 Police Officers may be eligible to sit for a Sergeants exam and more than 4,000 Sergeants may sit for a Lieutenants exam.

In a nutshell, the NYPD's highly competitive promotional system for the supervisory and middle-management ranks gives a distinct edge to those candidates who, through an innate capacity to amass detailed cognitive information or through the devotion of a tremendous number of hours to studying, can accrue the greatest and most detailed knowledge of the agency's rules, regulations, directives and orders. Interpersonal skills which might contribute to the prospective manager's referent power counts for nothing in this system, and the system also takes little account of the

candidate's expertise in any field, excepting his or her cognitive knowledge
of rules and regulations.

The testing and promotion process ensures that those on the "fast track"
have an exceedingly strong grasp of the ins-and-outs of police procedure and
an in-depth knowledge of the rules, but the process does absolutely nothing
to ensure that these people have the aptitude and skills to apply their
knowledge wisely. The process assumes that they can, but intuition,
experience, and observation shows that in many cases this assumption is
faulty. Some proportion of those promoted undoubtedly possess desirable
management traits, but they possess them independent of the process: the
testing does nothing to give these people a promotional edge or even to
ensure that the majority of those promoted have the desired attributes.

Civil service examinations are the sole determinant of promotion to the
ranks of Sergeant, Lieutenant and Captain in the NYPD, but once the rank of
Captain is attained, promotion to the higher executive-level ranks of Deputy
Inspector, Inspector, Deputy Chief, Assistant Chief and Chief is at the
discretion of the Police Commissioner. Only at that point do aptitude,
expertise, skills and previous performance begin to matter for promotional
purposes. At the same time it should be pointed out that members of the
executive corps serve at the pleasure of the Police Commissioner, subject to
certification by the Mayor. Because these are appointive positions, the
integrity of the advancement process could be subverted. The potential that
internal and external political considerations will affect the promotional
opportunities of managers and executives becomes viable, as does the
possibility that entirely inept executives with strong political connections
will, as in the days of the Political Era, soar to the heights of legitimate
power in the agency. The advantage, as George Kelling (1996, p. 81) points
out, is that

> the appointment and promotional system establishes clear account-
> ability to political leadership, so that elected officials can determine
> the overall policies of the police department through their power to
> appoint top management. The danger is that an unscrupulous mayor
> can reach into the department by appointing a political hack as
> commissioner and distribute appointments above captain on the basis
> of party loyalty.

Like many other pillars of the Professional Model, the civil service
promotion system in the NYPD has undergone few substantive changes since
it was introduced. With the exception of the educational requirements

introduced in the late 1980s as qualifiers for promotion – sixty college credits for promotion to sergeant, one hundred for lieutenant and a Bachelor's degree for captain – the promotion process has evolved little since it was introduced at the turn of the century.

Civil service, in the NYPD and elsewhere, affects the individual and the organization in both positive and negative ways. On the positive side, it sets a clear and objective path for promotion and it ensures that the opportunity for promotion to civil service ranks are equally available to every candidate. Political connections and nepotism have zero impact on civil service promotions. On the other hand, civil service impacts the organization negatively in at least four ways.

First, it virtually ensures mediocrity by lumping high, medium and low performers together in an identical and virtually unbreakable salary structure in which seniority is the usually sole determinant of pay increments above base salary. In failing to distinguish and financially reward high performers, and in failing to offer incentives for high performance, the system fails to get the most out of would-be high performers. It also ignores practically everything management and motivation theories tell us about the importance of tangible reward systems and their impact on performance.

Second, the system's failure to adequately reward high achievers in proportion to their contributions inevitably causes some of the best and brightest to become apathetic and disaffected. In many cases, those who have extremely marketable skills or expertise leave the agency to pursue more rewarding and more remunerative second careers in the private sector. Some – often those who were initially the most conscientious and idealistic performers – go beyond apathy to outright bitterness and antipathy toward the organization and its leadership. If these disenfranchised former high performers have a good deal of referent and/ or expert power, and especially if they have attained some legitimate power through advancement to at least a supervisory rank, they can exert a powerful debilitating influence over others and easily erode the best efforts of the executive corps. There is often far more power and influence in the sergeant's tone of voice as he or she reads the chief's directive to the assembled platoon than there is in the directive itself. Truly, there are few greater threats to the executive's authority than the tenured supervisor or respected senior officer who has lost his faith and has little to lose by challenging the executive's legitimacy and expertise.

Third, the civil service system in itself usually provides little or no motivation to individually pursue higher levels of skill, education or personal development. Quite aside from the civil service promotion system, though, it should be emphasized that especially in recent years the NYPD's twenty-year retirement system has indirectly encouraged such development. Any NYPD officer can retire with a half pay pension upon completing the twentieth year of service, and receive an incrementally greater pension for each additional year of service. Twenty year retirement encourages many officers to develop internally- and externally- marketable skills on their own time and at their own expense, in anticipation of a more lucrative or rewarding second career. Of course many of the most qualified officers leave the agency when they become eligible to retire (depriving it of their continued expertise), but in the interim the department is often able to make good use of their skills.

This dynamic is one reason why expert power tends to be concentrated among younger officers at the supervisory and middle management level, rather than in the executive corps. Officers with the most marketable skills and greatest expertise tend to have many options outside the agency, and many of the most talented leave to pursue these options as well as the generally higher salaries offered in the private sector. Officers with less valuable skills and fewer external options often remain in the agency and seek promotion through civil service.

Finally, if an organization lacks a genuine and proportional reward system or if its promotional system does not intrinsically link advancement to the skills, attitudes and areas of knowledge that are most essential to good management, it will never achieve its peak potential. The agency may perform tolerably well, it may fulfill the modest expectations of the public and the political officials to whom it is accountable, and it may even enhance its achievements dramatically by implementing other supplementary strategies to boost morale and performance, but it will never achieve its maximum possible level of achievement so long as the promotional system serves to de-motivate a significant number of its members.

The Professional Model and Crime Fighting

The Professional Model had a profound effect on American policing and policing in New York City . Perhaps the supreme irony of Professionalism, though, was that it failed miserably to address the very goals and issues it defined as most important and most appropriate for the police to pursue. Crime fighting was the soul and substance of the Professional movement, and yet nationwide levels of crime increased radically during the 1960s and 1970s – the decades in which Professionalism came to fullest flower and exerted its greatest influence. Total FBI Index statistics on criminal offenses reported to the police – a standardized crime measurement and comparison system created through the persistent efforts of early Professionals who sought a method of comparing crime within and between jurisdictions (see, for example, Banas and Trojanowicz, 1985) – show that the overall number of Index crimes reported to the police nationwide increased about 240% between 1960 and 1970, and by almost 400% between 1960 and 1980.

Violent crime increased even more dramatically during the heyday of Professionalism. The number of offenses in the FBI's Violent crimes category, consisting of murder and non-negligent homicide, forcible rape, robbery and aggravated assault, increased 256% during between 1960 and 1970, and by 466% between 1960 and 1980. By 1990, the number of violent crimes reported to police in the United States was 630% higher than it had been in 1960.

The national Index Crime rate – the number of Index crimes per 100,000 population – increased 224% between 1960 and 1970, and increased by 315% between 1960 and 1980. The violent crime rate per 100,000 population jumped 226% between 1960 and 1970, 371% by 1980, and 455% by 1990.

Equally dramatic changes took place in New York City's crime figures between 1970 and 1990. A total of 440,063 Index Crimes were recorded in New York City in 1970, and although the total number of Index Crimes fluctuated from year to year, it reached an all-time high of 607,461 in 1981 – an increase of more than 27 percent. With the exception of 1987, the total Crime Index in New York City did not drop much below one half million offenses in the period from 1979 to 1992. In 1989 and 1990 – the period in which the NYPD made its first real attempts to break with the Professional Model and implement Community Policing – reported crime was still increasing. Overall crime began to decrease after 1990, falling seven percent between 1991 and 1992 and about six percent between 1992 and 1993.

The first truly dramatic declines came about when Compstat was instituted in 1994: the UCR Crime Index dropped a precipitous 11.7 percent between 1993 and 1994, another sixteen percent between 1994 and 1995, and another fourteen percent between 1995 and 1996. Crime continued to decline through the decade, and an overall 49.88 percent decline in reported Index Crimes took place in the period between 1993 and 1999.

Clearly, the Professional Model did not live up to its self-proclaimed promise to reduce crime. One outgrowth of this failure to reduce crime during the heyday of the Professional Model was the growing perception, both inside and outside policing, that perhaps the police can have little real impact on crime after all. At the same time the Professional Model was having its greatest impact on agencies throughout the nation, the police and the public began to lose faith in it. Academic criminologists, for example, had always sought to explain crime in terms of various social and economic forces, and Professionalism's failure to produce its promised results certainly did nothing to allay criminologists' arguments that the police have little or no impact on crime.

A curious thing took place in policing, though, as this sentiment or rationalization gained currency. When crime figures rose, police chiefs often went before the media's cameras and microphones to protest that social forces beyond the control of the police – unemployment, drug addiction, the failure of our school system, etc. – were driving the increase. They evaded personal and organizational responsibility for rising crime by implying or professing that the police could do little about it. If crime dropped a point or two, though, the chief went before the cameras to tout his or her triumph in introducing a new program or policy or initiative that worked, and to take credit for the decline. In some jurisdictions and some administrations, this dynamic took an additional twist: the bad news of increasing crime was announced by the department's chief executive, but the good news of any decline was announced (and credit taken) by the mayor or city manager. Unfortunately for the mayors and city managers, the general upward trend in crime throughout the nation gave them few opportunities to take credit.

Summary and Conclusions

The forces and factors outlined in this chapter are only part of the Professional Model's legacy in American policing and the NYPD, and in the interests of fairness it must again be stated that Professionalism brought a great many benefits and was clearly a tremendous improvement from the state of affairs during the pre-reform Political Era. Professionalism did introduce an unambiguous and transparent (albeit imperfect) career path in which political connections or nepotism had little impact, and it did a great deal to eliminate the kind of corruption and criminality that, perhaps more than anything else, diminished public respect for the police and made the honest cop's job more difficult. Professionalism made police officers and agencies aware of technology's potential benefits, and gave cops enhanced training to help them better perform the increasingly difficult and complex tasks entailed in policing during the latter part of the century. The impact of the Professional Model can also be seen in the establishment of physical, medical, intellectual, and background standards for entry into policing. Although Vollmer's vision of a highly educated police officer, and of agencies in which the minimum educational qualification would be a college degree, proved as illusory in the NYPD as it did in many other police departments, many officers and managers were encouraged to seek higher education. The trend toward a more highly educated NYPD increased dramatically in the 1980s, as more and more recruits came to the job with college degrees and as others continued their education in order to meet the promotional requirements instituted toward the end of that decade. Overall, policing is far better off for the influence of the Professional Model. The main problem with the Professional Model of police management is a potential problem with any good thing – a good thing can be taken too far. Indeed, the caveat about taking a good thing too far applies to the Compstat paradigm as well.

In its essence, the Professional Model was all about controlling the police and directing their activities, and it fulfilled these expectations superbly. In the NYPD and elsewhere, though, it controlled officers to the point of stagnation and directed their activities so closely that it radically reduced officers' discretion as well as their motivation. Moreover, it often directed police activities into areas which did little to achieve the agency's primary mission. Young men and women of good impulse came into the department with hopes of making a difference and were soon stymied by a suspicious and overbearing management cadre, deprived of discretion by a rule-bound bureaucracy and a plethora of procedures and directives, and de-motivated by a system that placed little value on performance as a criteria for reward or advancement. Professionalism encouraged officers to respond quickly to the scenes of crimes and other incidents requiring police attention, to rapidly prepare the appropriate report, and return to random patrol while awaiting the next assignment. Their actions had little or no impact on the root causes of these incidents and did almost nothing to decrease the likelihood that they would have to respond again in the future to the same location to deal with the same or a similar issue. In each instance, the officers would take a report and move on. To a significant extent, NYPD patrol officers came to see themselves not as crime fighters or agents of social change, but as highly mobile report takers in uniform.

Also as the result of the Professional movement, cops lost touch with the community and the community lost touch with them. As importantly, cops lost touch with the reasons they first aspired to become police officers – to make a difference by fighting crime and improving the quality of peoples' lives. By the early 1990s, and notwithstanding the agency's first tentative steps toward introducing Community Policing and problem solving, the NYPD was to a large extent a demoralized, poorly motivated, highly centralized and overly-specialized department populated by apathetic officers and led by apathetic and timid administrators whose actions and inactions communicated a potent message throughout the organization: "don't take risks, don't take chances, don't get involved, and above all don't give me any trouble."

The following chapter delves more deeply into the climate of policing in New York City in the early 1990s and the organizational culture of the NYPD at that time.

Additional Recommended Readings

Fogelson, Robert M. **Big City Police**, Cambridge, MA: Massachusetts Institute of Technology Press, 1977. Fogelson traces the history and development of urban policing in the United States from its roots in Political Policing to the period immediately before the emergence of Community Policing and the demise of the Professional Model.

Wilson, O.W. and Roy C. McLaren **Police Administration (4th Edition)**, New York: McGraw-Hill, 1977. Wilson and McLaren's classic police management text provides unique insights into the practices as well as the underlying assumptions of the Professional Model.

Lardner, James and Thomas Reppetto **NYPD: A City and its Police**, New York: Henry Holt, 2000. This recent addition to the history of policing in New York parallels the history of the NYPD with significant trends and social changes taking place in New York City as a whole. As the authors unravel the NYPD's history they reveal how the agency influenced these trends and changes as well as how they influenced the agency.

Murphy, Patrick V. and Thomas Plate, **Commissioner: A View From the Top of American Law Enforcement**, New York: Simon and Schuster, 1977. Murphy's autobiography reveals a great deal about his philosophy of policing, its basis in the Professional Model, and the events of the Knapp Commission era that so dramatically changed the face of the NYPD for the next few decades. As Police Commissioner during the Knapp Commission and as chief architect of many of the corruption control policies and programs that followed it, Murphy had a profound effect upon the NYPD and its organizational culture.

Questions for Discussion and Debate

1. In what ways are the organizational structures, police activities and basic operating philosophies of police agencies during the Political Era similar to those in contemporary Community Policing? Do agencies practicing Community Policing take adequate measures to prevent the problems associated with Political Era policing from resurfacing? What measures do they take?

2. Can you think of an effective organizational design for a police agency that doesn't have elements of bureaucracy? Realistically, is the term "flexible bureaucracy" an oxymoron?

3. Controlling corruption by strictly limiting the types of activities officers could engage in became a preoccupation for NYPD managers and executives in the 1970s and 1980s, but along the way they either lost sight of or ignored the fact that the patterns of corruption were changing. How can Compstat principles be used to monitor the patterns and practices of corruption and misconduct throughout an agency as well as in individual commands? What type of empirical and qualitative data sources would you develop or collect in order to monitor and respond to corruption and misconduct?

4. Based upon what you know of Compstat thus far, would you say that it is really just a high-tech version of Taylor's Scientific Management paradigm? What are the important similarities and differences?

5. In terms of basic philosophy and practices, is the Compstat style of strategic, enforcement-based problem solving closer to the ideals of the Professional Model or to Community Policing?

Chapter 4
The History of Community Policing and Problem-Solving in the NYPD

Introduction

Compstat is a uniquely effective interactive management process that has proven to be highly successful in identifying and solving the type of crime and quality of life problems that contemporary police agencies confront, but it is by no means the first effort to introduce problem solving activities to the NYPD. Problem solving has, of course, been a part of modern policing since Sir Robert Peel established the London Metropolitan Police in 1829. Viewed in a broad context, Peel's creation of the Metropolitan Police was in fact an attempt to find a partial solution to the crime, quality of life and public disorder problems that plagued London and other urban areas during the social upheaval of the Industrial Revolution. Since that time, governments at the national, state and municipal levels in Western democracies have created police agencies or altered existing policing entities it order to deal more effectively with the crime and disorder problems they face.

Police officers and police agencies have always devoted some amount of their time and effort to solving problems, but they typically approached these problems in a haphazard way and often only after the problems reached critical proportions. The philosophy that police agencies should have a commitment to actively pursue problem-solving as an organizational goal, and the idea that police officers at the beat level should be engaged in using specific proactive techniques to identify and address low-level offenses as a means to prevent more serious crimes, are relatively new in policing.

Under the broad rubric of "Problem-Solving Policing" – an organizational style and a set of related prescriptive strategies championed by Herman Goldstein (1990), Eck, Spelman, Hill, Stephens, Steadman and Murphy (1987), Spelman and Eck (1987) and Vaughn (1993), among others – the principles of problem solving have been applied by many agencies to many diverse types of police activity. Police problem solving activities are certainly nowhere as refined, as focused, or as successful, as in the NYPD under the Compstat model. The Compstat paradigm, in essence and substance, is all about the energetic and innovative solution of crime and quality of life problems.

In this chapter, we will briefly review the NYPD's early attempts to introduce problem-solving tactics and strategies as part of Community Policing prior to the introduction of Compstat. Those efforts, though well-intentioned, were less than fully successful largely because they were instituted as programmatic efforts within an organizational culture and an organizational structure that otherwise remained relatively unchanged. They were unsuccessful because managers and executives played with them as they might play with other pet projects, but there was no organization-wide commitment to them and there were no adequate systems in place to effectively measure their results.

Even if they had been successfully promulgated throughout the agency, and even if they had received the kind of commitment and organizational support they needed in order to thrive, they probably would not have achieved the kind of results achieved under the Compstat paradigm. Again, unless all the agencies of the criminal justice enterprise and the other arms of government with which the police interact operate in a coordinated fashion (as they have come to operate in New York City), a police department cannot hope to achieve great results. A high-performance police department that is part of a lethargic and unconcerned municipal government will, like highly effective small units of cops and detectives in lethargic police agencies, be isolated and ultimately overwhelmed.

Problem Solving and Community Policing in the NYPD

The frailties and deficiencies of the Professional model (perhaps especially its failure to reduce crime) became more and more apparent as the 1970s drew to a close. The police and the public became estranged and distant from each other, and both political and public pressure for improved relations increased. Police leaders began to realize and in some cases admit that the strategies they had pursued under the Professional model were having little effect. Along with academic theorists who studied the police, police leaders began looking beyond the traditional Professional model for solutions. It became more and more obvious that American policing needed a fundamental re-evaluation and reformulation of its goals, strategies, practices, and interactions.

A new model of policing – the Community Policing model – began to emerge, and in many respects the NYPD was at the forefront of efforts to develop and implement it. Although Compstat and the strategic policing style practiced in New York City since 1994 have retained and refined the best elements of the Professional model, they have also profited immensely from the lessons learned as the agency struggled unsuccessfully to implement a particular vision of Community Policing during the late 1980s and early 1990s.

That vision of Community Policing generally failed to deliver what it so triumphantly promised. The failure to deliver – to reduce crime and fear of crime and to substantially improve the quality of life enjoyed by New Yorkers – was primarily the result of a failure by police executives and managers to adequately articulate the vision in a way that officers could understand and operationalize it, or to reconfigure the agency's structures to support it effectively. By the time improvements began to occur, it was almost too late. The public lost whatever faith they might have had in this vision of Community Policing, and because many or most members of the department never really bought into it in the first place, it withered on the vine. Crime and disorder continued without a substantial and politically significant decrease, and crime became a major issue in the mayoral election of 1993. As noted in the first chapter, Rudolph Giuliani's defeat of incumbent David Dinkins was, by any measure, attributable in part to Dinkins' failure to control crime, fear and disorder through Community Policing. Crime statistics may have declined a few percentage points, but public perceptions of crime and public fear of crime did not decrease. For David Dinkins, the statistical decline was a matter of 'too little, too late.'

The goals articulated by the Giuliani administration – to reduce crime, restore order and return a sense of civility to the city – were quite similar to the promises implied in the earlier vision of Community Policing, but the NYPD's approach to them in the latter administration differed from the earlier vision in significant ways. Most importantly, the Giuliani administration advanced a strategy based on Broken Windows concepts but involving aggressive enforcement of minor offenses, and the Mayor brought on William Bratton as Police Commissioner to see this new vision to fruition.

On the heels of its abortive and largely unsuccessful first attempt to introduce Community Policing, the NYPD found itself a deeply divided, demoralized and highly unfocused police agency. Perhaps more than any other reason, the failure of Community Policing strategies in the late 1980s and early 1990s can be attributed to managers' and executives' unwillingness or inability to shape the organization into one that would support the kind of changes necessary for Community Policing to take hold. The department as a whole never truly broke free of the organizational and structural constraints imposed by the Professional model, and the Professional policing ideology still dominated the management mindset.

In fairness, it must be said that modest declines in crime were achieved under Mayor David Dinkins in 1991, 1992, and 1993. Total Index Crimes in New York City respectively declined 4.4 percent, 7.8 percent, and 4.3 percent in those years, but little seemed to change in terms of public satisfaction with the police or in terms of public fear of crime. Too, in fairness it should be noted that crime in New York increased steadily from 1987 to 1990, when the number of murders reached an historic high of 2,262 and the number of auto thefts was also the highest on record. The number and rate of serious felony assaults hit their record highs in 1989. The city seemed to be under siege from the criminal element, and the modest crime declines of the early 1990s had little, if any, positive impact on the public's perception. The city was riven by public unrest in the aftermath of the Crown Heights and Washington Heights riots, and the Mollen Commission's public hearings and its report on police corruption did little to bolster public confidence in the police or to advance the goals of Community Policing. Although the Mollen Commission's fairly tepid report found that corruption existed in isolated pockets of small corrupt "crews" of dishonest cops rather than on a widespread or pervasive basis, that important finding was largely overlooked and the focus of public and media attention on the scandal did little to raise morale in the department. The undeniable fact was that the department failed in its responsibility to manage corruption control as it had failed in its responsibility to manage other essential police functions.

Some police executives and some politicians tried to cast the modest crime declines as evidence of Community Policing's success, but within the department there remained a deep and unsettling undercurrent of cynicism and a growing recognition that something was terribly wrong with the way the agency conducted its business. The prevailing sense was that the department had strayed too far afield of its core mission of fighting crime and disorder and there was a growing perception, especially among the rank and file officers, that the agency and its officers had been subsumed by a political agenda. Whether real or simply perceived, the idea that Community Policing had become a mechanism of politics was troubling for police officers.

Community Policing - A Critique

Community Policing remains a somewhat vague and amorphous concept. It appears, though, that the basic principles and practices of the Community Policing model are here to stay, and that it will continue to evolve as an organizational and philosophical model. It also appears that the tremendous results achieved through Compstat and the strategic policing principles developed by the NYPD will continue to have a crucial impact on the pace and direction of Community Policing's future development.

Community Policing is a problematic concept. At first, one might be tempted to summarize the problem with the concept by saying that the predicament is that no one knows what Community Policing means, but upon reflection it becomes clear that the real problem is that everyone *thinks* they know what it means. There is both a lack of conceptual clarity about what Community Policing is and is not, as well as a lack of consistency in the way the term has been applied to a host of programs, practices and policy initiatives.

Because everyone thinks they know what Community Policing is, there is a distinct trend in American policing to stick the Community Policing label on almost any new program or initiative that comes along. Conversely, there is also a tendency to retrospectively label traditional police practices as Community Policing. The term has been used in agencies across the nation to describe vastly different programs and practices that have few philosophical or operational similarities.

The version of Community Policing practiced in Flint, Michigan, for example, was called the Neighborhood Foot Patrol Program; in Houston, the Community Policing effort was called Neighborhood Oriented Policing (NOP). Baltimore called it COPE - Citizen Oriented Police Enforcement, and Newport News called it POP - Problem Oriented Policing. Even Los Angeles, the bastion of the Professional model, implemented a Community Mobilization Project (CMP). The NYPD initiated Neighborhood Police Teams (NPTs) in 1971 and the Community Patrol Officer Program (CPOP) in 1984. The Community Patrol Officer Program became the Community *Police* Officer Program, but precinct-based CPOP Units remained CPOP units until they became CPUs (Community Policing Units) in the early 1990s. Beyond the similarities in acronyms and catchy titles and a general focus on enhancing interaction with the public, these versions seem to have little in common.

The problem with Community Policing extends beyond the fact that the term is applied so broadly, though. The larger problem is that there seems to be so little agreement as to what Community Policing means in a practical and operational sense. Even Herman Goldstein, one of the ideology's earliest theorists and staunchest advocates, says that the term is often

> widely used without any regard for its substance. Political leaders and, unfortunately, many police leaders latch onto the label for the positive images it evokes but do not invest in the concept itself. Some police personnel resist Community Policing initiatives because of the belief that they constitute an effort to placate an overly demanding and critical segment of the community that is intent on exercising more control over police operations.

> Indeed, the popularity of the term has resulted in its being used to encompass practically all innovations in policing, from the most ambitious to the most mundane; from the most carefully thought through to the most casual (Goldstein, 1993, p. 1)

Peter K. Manning (1997), in summarizing his own 1984 critique of Community Policing, characterizes it as primarily a rhetorical device and a presentational strategy – a "rhetorical sponge" that soaks up all sorts of reform concepts and ideas. Community Policing, he says, is an ill-formed ideological vehicle that operates in service of police self-promotion and crudely deflects classic critiques of traditional police practices, and he asserts that there are no firm criteria with which to prove or disprove the claim that Community Policing is present or absent in an agency (p. 15). Manning (1997) also declines to call Community Policing a full-fledged philosophy since it has no broad theoretical grounding (p. 11), but this lack of grounding as well as it ambiguities, contradictions and lack of consistency are the very thing that makes people of such diverse ideologies and backgrounds come together around the idea (p. 13). If Community Policing had a clear, consistent meaning and a readily identifiable set of ideologies and practices, it might not have such broad appeal, Manning (1997) points out. In particular, it might not appeal to politicians and police executives intent on using Community Policing rhetoric to improve police-community relations or to deflate other forms of pressure from community groups.

The purpose of this critique is certainly not to bash Community Policing or its zealous adherents, but rather to point out that although the Community Policing model has many attractive points it remains too ambiguous and conceptually amorphous to be of much practical guidance to police officers, or to police executives for that matter. Because it lacks specificity, the Community Policing rubric can be (and has been) improperly applied to virtually any police activity that differs from the way things were done before. The term's misapplication can be the inadvertent or unintentional result of simple misunderstanding, or it can be used deliberately and mindfully to mislead both the police and the public that some positive change is taking place. In either event, there is no real consensus or agreement achieved as to what the term means in a practical sense. This was certainly the case when the NYPD tried to implement a particular vision of Community Policing during the early 1990s.

The inability to conceptualize and define Community Policing in the NYPD during the late 1980s and the early 1990s was a significant obstacle to its successful implementation. It seemed that every time NYPD police officers and supervisors asked for a clear operational definition of Community Policing or asked directions as to the specific kinds of action they should undertake, the agency's chief executive responded simply that Community Policing was a philosophy in which the police and community form a partnership to creatively solve community problems. No one, it seemed, could or would explain to NYPD cops what Community Policing meant in a practical sense or offer anything other than anecdotes to describe the practices it prescribed.

There are, however, several broad but consistent themes evident in the rhetoric of Community Policing. These include greater consultation with community residents about the crime and quality of life issues considered to be of greatest importance, organizational decentralization to support the empowerment of officers, an emphasis on solving problems rather than merely responding to repeated incidents, and an emphasis on addressing quality of life offenses as a means to reduce more serious crime. All of these themes are similarly features of the Compstat paradigm. Efforts to introduce Community Policing in New York City in the early 1990s placed far too much emphasis on the first two themes, and not enough emphasis on the latter two.

Problem-Oriented Policing

Two of the most important early influences on the development of Community Policing were a 1979 article by Herman Goldstein in the journal *Crime and Delinquency* and a March 1982 article by James Q. Wilson and George Kelling in *Atlantic Monthly*. Goldstein's work – later fleshed out more thoroughly in his 1990 book **Problem Oriented Policing** – contributed the important idea that the police can make a greater difference by addressing problems, not just responding to incidents. Under the Professional model and its demand for speedy efficiency, the police would typically respond to a call, deal superficially with the issue presented in the incident, and quickly return to service in order to patrol randomly while awaiting the next call. All too often, the next call brought the officers back to the same location to again deal superficially with the same frustrating issue. Police dealt with many incidents, but they rarely if ever got to the source of the problem. Incidents were treated as isolated and discrete events requiring a response, rather than as events that might indicate a deeper and more entrenched problem.

In a problem-oriented approach, the police go beyond simply handling incidents in a cursory way, recognizing that incidents are often merely the symptoms of the real problem. Police activities must go beyond simply responding to incidents and treating the symptoms – they must identify and address the underlying problem and its causes. In order to do so, Goldstein (1990, p. 33) says, the police must be able to first identify problems by recognizing relationships between incidents (i.e., similarities of behavior, location, the descriptions or identities of persons involved, etc.), and they must acquaint themselves with some of the conditions and factors that typically underlie the problems. By attacking the underlying problem, the number of subsequent incidents will be reduced.

Like Compstat, the problem solving ideal also assumes that officers are equipped with the proper skills and tools to combat the problem, but this was not necessarily the case during the NYPD's early attempts at Community Policing. Beat officers and radio patrol officers were still enjoined from aggressively attacking narcotics problems through enforcement action, for example. The fear of corruption remained pervasive among the agency's managers and executives, essentially depriving cops of the capacity to do much more than chase away street drug dealers. Instead, they still had to rely on specialized narcotics squads to do simple buy-and-bust operations. It seemed that as quickly as the dealers were arrested and whisked off to jail and court, others stepped up within hours to replace them. Street-level dealers were often released on recognizance after arraignment, and they were 'back on the set' within a few days of their arrest.

The same constellation of issues and constraints surrounded prostitution enforcement and many other quality of life crimes, but perhaps the most important outcome of the continuing 'hands-off' policy was that it communicated the agency's timidity and reluctance to aggressively engage criminals. It tacitly encouraged cops to turn a blind eye toward certain offenses. This attitude changed dramatically under the Giuliani/Bratton regime, when police executives first began articulating and reinforcing the policy that uniformed officers could take these and other formerly-proscribed enforcement actions. Part of the message communicated was that, unlike previous administrations, the new administration trusted officers to do their jobs honestly and to more fully engage in the fight against crime and criminals. It trusted them to do the job they signed up to do.

Broken Windows

In March 1982, the *Atlantic Monthly* published an article by James Q. Wilson and George Kelling entitled "Broken Windows: The Police and Neighborhood Safety." The article, which quickly became a classic in police management, articulated a set of principles and concepts that have come to be known as the Broken Windows Theory. Although Wilson and Kelling could probably have published their article in any criminology or police management journal they chose, they instead opted to reach the larger and more influential literary audience *Atlantic Monthly* caters to. In essence, the Broken Windows theory suggests that there is both a high correlation and a causal link between community disorder and more serious crime: when community disorder is permitted to flourish or when disorderly conditions or problems are left untended, they actually *cause* more serious crime. "Broken windows" are a metaphor for community disorder which, as Wilson and Kelling use the term, includes the violation of informal social norms for public behavior as well as quality of life offenses such as littering, graffiti, playing loud radios, aggressive panhandling, and vandalism. Wilson and Kelling cited studies showing that

> if a window in a building is broken *and is left unrepaired*, all the rest of the windows will soon be broken. This is as true in nice neighborhoods as in run-down ones. Window-breaking does not necessarily occur on a large scale because some areas are inhabited by determined window-breakers whereas others are populated by window-lovers; rather, unrepaired broken windows is a signal that no one cares, and so breaking more windows costs nothing... Untended property becomes fair game for people out for fun or plunder, and even for people who would not ordinarily dream of doing such things and who probably consider themselves law-abiding... We suggest that "untended" behavior also leads to the breakdown of community controls (Wilson and Kelling, 1982, p. 31. Emphasis in original).

According to the Broken Windows perspective, a downward spiral begins as community disorder and quality of life offenses increase. In essence, disorder and the disintegration of community that it signals breeds fear, and as people become more fearful in their own communities they tend to keep more and more to themselves. They tend to mind their own business and not to get involved when they see minor acts of incivility. The bonds of community and of the social fabric begin to unravel as community residents curtail their activities, and they interact less frequently with other community members and spend less time outside their homes. Their sense of "ownership" of the community begins to deteriorate. In effect, they are intimidated into giving up their communities to petty criminals when disorderly conditions are left unchecked, and as the disorderly conditions continue to escalate the seriousness of the criminal offenses also increases. When the community, the police and other social institutions fail to address minor quality of life conditions and other petty incivilities of modern urban life, they essentially give violators license to continue violating. When the untended quality of life problems proliferate, it gives the impression that "anything goes" – including more serious criminal offenses.

At some level of awareness, both the police and the public knew all along that the principles Wilson and Kelling articulated in the Broken Windows Theory were accurate. They knew, to paraphrase the old adage, that if little problems were taken care of they would not develop into big problems. Although the police knew this intellectually, they rarely acted upon it in a focused and strategic way. Here again, individual officers or units may have been effective at solving these problems from time to time, but on the whole police agencies were not geared up with a problem solving orientation.

The dominant paradigm of Professionalism still cast the police in the role of fighting more "serious" and "real" crimes such as murder, robbery, assault, burglary, rape and larceny, and police organizations were geared up to focus narrowly on addressing these crimes and not necessarily the problems that give rise to them. To a large extent they treated the symptoms and ignored the cause. Importantly, and once again as a reflection of the Professional ideology, the police also *saw* themselves as "serious crime" fighters, and police cultures generally minimized the importance of quality-of-life enforcement. A good robbery or burglary "collar" brought more status, more excitement and more rewards than one hundred littering summonses.

Broken Windows - A Practical Example

How does the application of Broken Windows theory and its emphasis on addressing untended quality of life offenses reduce more serious crime? Consider the following.

Almost every night for the past decade or more, groups of young men have congregated at a certain street corner to drink beer. They have a few beers, get rowdy, and generally annoy the folks who live on the nearby streets. At times, they harass the people walking home at the end of their day from a nearby bus stop or subway station, but even when they are not actually harassing anyone, their presence and their litter casts a pall of disorder over the neighborhood. Many people walk a block or two out of their way to avoid the drunks on the corner, whose offensive conduct also begins to include urinating in alleys or in the street. Most people on the block don't like to sit outside on their porches or stoops on a warm summer night because the drunks on the corner are just so annoying, and as a result they don't have much interaction with their neighbors. Perhaps they stay inside and watch television instead. The people who live on the street are also a bit reluctant to let their children play outside without supervision, and they certainly don't want their children to play on the corner where the drunks congregate each night. They are intimidated into having little sense of community. Four or five drunks on the corner basically intimidate the entire neighborhood and impinge upon residents' freedom to enjoy their neighborhoods and to live their lives without such annoyances. They reduce the quality of life to which every person is entitled.

The drunks on the corner come to think that they own the turf, largely because the police (who are occupied with randomly driving around seeking out more serious "real" crimes) have rarely if ever moved them along. Another group of drinkers pops up on the opposite corner, and before long all four corners are populated by beer-drinking rowdies who compound the neighborhood's problems. The drinkers feel secure in the neighborhood, and because they are such tough guys some of them begin to carry knives and guns. Now multiply this scenario across an entire city – drunks congregating and intimidating residents on perhaps hundreds of street corners.

How many drunken nights have to pass before a fight occurs? How many fights have to occur before the fight escalates from fists to knives, or from fists to guns? It's only a matter of time before drinking on the corner leads to a serious assault or a murder.

Let's change the scenario a bit once again. Instead of driving by, the police stop and issue summonses on one corner for consuming alcoholic beverages in public, for public urination, or for disorderly conduct – whatever quality of life offenses are being committed and are prohibited by state or local legislation. Although the police certainly have the legal authority to conduct warrant checks on the people to whom they issue summonses, they have rarely done it in the past. Now, though, they begin conduct the warrant checks, and they begin to arrest the drunks who have outstanding warrants. Perhaps the circumstances are such that the officers reasonably suspect that one of the drinkers is carrying a weapon – they have legal grounds to frisk him, and indeed they find a gun. In fifteen minutes, the officers have issued four summonses and effected one gun arrest as well as one arrest for an outstanding warrant.

What impact does this fifteen-minute intervention have on the street? The dozen or more drunks on the other corners see their friends summonsed or taken off to jail, one of them on a gun charge. If in fact they come back the next night, are they more likely to carry a gun or to leave it at home? If they do come back on another night and a fight occurs, is it likely to be a fist fight or a gunfight? The residents of the block have seen that the police are beginning to take the problem seriously, and perhaps in some measure their faith in police is restored a bit.

Let's assume that the police continue this type of summons enforcement for quality of life offenses for a sustained period, and continue to conduct warrant checks. How many summonses do they have to issue before one or more of the accused fails to appear in court, generating a warrant for their arrest? How many times do the police have to visit the corner, issuing summonses and effecting warrant arrests, before the drunks begin to modify their offensive behavior? How long do they have to continue issuing summonses and making warrant arrests before control and ownership of the street returns to its residents?

Sustained and targeted quality-of-life enforcement restores the balance of power in a neighborhood, permits a sense of community to thrive, and significantly reduces the likelihood that serious crimes will occur.

Although it took some convincing, NYPD cops in recent years have come to appreciate that quality-of-life enforcement can reduce more serious crime, and that sustained strategic enforcement is an effective crime fighting tool. This is not to say that NYPD officers no longer take pleasure in apprehending "real" criminals – there are few experiences as rewarding as a good robbery or gun arrest – but rather that their view of police work and of their own role has broadened considerably. The department did not abate its efforts to deal with these serious crimes – if anything they redoubled their efforts – but rather they attacked crime problems from both ends. Cops in New York also came to find that focused attention on quality of life problems could easily lead to the prevention or solution of more serious crimes. Examples abound, for example, of how a simple summons for unruly behavior can lead officers to develop information about a more serious crime.

As Police Commissioner Howard Safir pointed out in a January 1997 interview on the PBS *NewsHour* program, a particularly brutal sexual assault in Central Park and a related murder were solved (and a conviction achieved) because the suspect had been arrested earlier in the year for subway fare evasion. It was the defendant's first and only arrest, but his fingerprints were on file and available for computerized Automated Fingerprint Identification System matching (*NewsHour*, 1997).

Because both the enforcement of quality of life violations or other minor offenses *and* making good felony arrests have become are part of the NYPD officer's repertoire, the result has been substantial. NYPD cops take great personal and professional pride in the fact that they have cut crime by more than half in a few short years by pursuing both agendas with equal intensity.

One reason the Compstat paradigm has been so successful is its almost-immediate impact on crime and quality-of-life results. Compstat gets results, and it gets them quickly. This immediacy of results underscores a fundamental ideological difference distinguishing the NYPD's innovations from other "brands" of Community Policing. Champions of other Community Policing styles assure police officers and the public that change will *eventually* occur and that crime will *eventually* decrease. To achieve that decrease in crime and disorder, these other ideologies maintain that the police and the public must work together in the interim to build communities that are capable of policing themselves – communities that are strong and resilient and committed to community betterment.

While there is a great deal to be said for this optimistic ideology, we must also recognize several overriding political and organizational realities of contemporary policing: that programs, policies, and practices that do not achieve immediate results are easily dismissed as ineffective, opening up the possibility that they will be dismantled or subverted for some other political or organizational purpose. Programs or activities that have not shown results are, perhaps justifiably, usually the first to be eliminated when budgets shrink or when new priorities arise. If Community Policing activities promise results but do not deliver, they also risk losing the cooperation of the community members upon whom they are tremendously dependent. It is difficult for anyone to argue with a program, policy, or activity that shows immediate and positive results.

Another political reality may effect Community Policing programs whose results are less than immediate: if a community learns that a new style of management and a slightly different philosophy of policing have reduced another municipality's actual level of crime more in a year than their local agency has reduced crime in four or five years, they may demand that the present Community Policing program be shelved and the new management style adopted. Paradoxically, if the agency and its executives truly embrace and practice the Community Policing ideal, they will have to accede to the community's desires and change the agency's entire focus and direction.

The Father of Community Policing?

There is some disagreement over who first set forth the principles of problem-oriented policing and who first articulated the principles of the Broken Windows Theory. As described in the March 31, 1993 issue of *Law Enforcement News*, in December 1977 then-Captain Aaron Rosenthal of the NYPD's 6th Precinct wrote an article for a local newspaper in which he sketched out the problems of community frustration with the police department's failure to deal with what would now be called quality of life problems, as well as the criminogenic effect these problems have in leading to more serious crimes. As *LEN*'s editor noted, the article "addresses with surprising prescience the community-based and problem-oriented policing phenomena that are now gripping law enforcement…" In the 1977 article, Rosenthal said that his theory began to take shape shortly after his appointment as a patrolman seventeen years earlier: The article said, in part:

> I believe that the erosion of the quality of life in our town began
> when our "system" demonstrated its inability to cope – not with
> the murderers at the top of the scale, but with the petty violators

at the bottom. Once the word was out that the "system" could not and would not effectively deal with the graffiti artist, the drunk in the hallway, the aggressive panhandler, the neighbor with the blasting radio, the habitual peddler, the petty thief, the late-night noisemakers, the garbage picker, vandals, desecrators, public urinators, kids under 16, litterers, careless dog owners, and on and on… once that word was out, the seed was planted that has since blossomed into a full-grown disrespect for our laws.

"When the neophyte violator first encounters the criminal justice system, it is inevitably at the lowest levels on the scale of "criminality." What he takes away from this encounter is the realization that the expected awesome trinity of police, courts and jail is merely a paper tiger...

"In order to resurrect the quality of life that once existed in this city, we should begin at the bottom of the scale. We must create an atmosphere where the non-violator is discouraged from becoming a violator. We must have a solid foundation upon which to rebuild the respect for law that certainly did exist in our boroughs. We must indeed stoop to conquer..."

Rosenthal pointed out that citizens typically expect the police to function in much the same way as the Sanitation Department – "We are both expected to visit an area, observe the problem, confront it and then remove it." The Sanitation Department dumps its cargo at sea, though, and prepares to deal with the next shipment, but the police response is only the first step in a system that functions "as if only "high crimes and misdemeanors" had any import. Notwithstanding the hundreds upon hundreds of statutes, codes and laws, the Police Department is an isolated, almost impotent agency when it comes to dealing with the "low-level" annoyances that make life miserable… The criminal justice system approach to dealing with petty violators reminds me of the Wizard of Oz. Ostensibly an all-powerful, fire-breathing tower of strength, it is actually a tired, amplified old soul with unreal solutions to real problems."

"… As it now stands, summonses and desk appearance tickets are issued and often stockpiled until they are either disregarded or pleaded to *en masse* at a fraction of the penalty. In view of this, there is some likelihood that the summonsing process vis-à-vis petty violators is in fact costing the city money. We must re-examine our approach to crime and deterrence. Someone in the political structure must address the problem of the low-level, pernicious weeds that threaten to strangle our community and forever destroy the quality of life in our once-fair city.

At the time the *LEN* article appeared, Rosenthal was an Assistant Chief and commanding officer of the Community Policing Assessment Unit. While Rosenthal may have been the first to set his thoughts to paper, the treatises by Goldstein and by Wilson and Kelling certainly received broader attention. The main point here is that Community Policing or problem-solving policing were not "invented" by a single individual, but rather evolved as part of a larger trend in which both practitioners and theorists questioned the validity and effectiveness of police practices and sought imaginative alternatives to them.

Community Policing and Problem-Solving: Early Efforts

Compstat's strategic policing style differs from the Community Policing and Professional models in a number of important ways, at the same time it embraces the best elements of both. Although it shares with Community Policing, Problem-Solving Policing and Broken Windows Theory an emphasis on addressing low-level quality-of-life offenses that many police officers and agencies previously regarded as unimportant, it differs from the way Community Policing is practiced in most agencies because of its intensity and focus and because it has an almost-immediate impact on crime and quality-of-life issues problems. Along with Problem-Solving Policing, Compstat and strategic policing share an emphasis on identifying problems, gathering information, developing solutions, implementing them, and assessing the results, but Compstat does this much more rapidly and intensively. Under the Compstat paradigm's approach, traditional enforcement activity takes place within an organizational environment that has a highly focused and sustained strategic orientation, far surpassing the expectations of the Professional model.

Rather than having community members communicate their needs and expectations directly to beat officers who then autonomously develop and implement plans to address them, the primary lines of communication under the Compstat paradigm are to middle managers – specifically, Precinct Commanders. The beat cop or radio motor patrol officer is certainly not excluded from communicating with the community, but within the Compstat paradigm the Precinct Commander is accountable for developing and implementing coherent crime control plans and orchestrating the activities of his or her subordinates. As we shall see, placing this responsibility on the commander rather than the cop is in some respects an inversion of the Community Policing philosophy the NYPD tried to implement in the early 1990s.

The Early Days: NPT and CPOP

It is useful to briefly examine some of the NYPD's early attempts to introduce Community Policing practices, if only to see how these efforts failed and what the failures tell us about police management and the dynamics of police organizations. The NYPD's first effort to use patrol strategies to improve community relations as well as community conditions was the Neighborhood Police Team (NPT) concept introduced in the 77th Precinct in Brooklyn's Bedford-Stuyvesant in 1972. In this program, one sergeant and a handful of officers were regularly assigned to motorized patrol within specific sectors or beats. They were given fairly broad authority to devise and implement strategies to deal with crime and other community problems, and to a large extent they were relieved of the responsibility to respond to 911 calls. The NPT officers were assigned to the same area every day so that they would develop a deep understanding of the particular neighborhood as well as the people in it.

It should be emphasized that this was a programmatic effort and that other powerful trends in the department were at that time operating in opposition to it. The general trend in the early 1970s, for example, was to further increase the already substantial gulf between police and community as a means to prevent corruption, while the NPT concept sought to increase interaction. Officers in NPT were also asked to get out of their cars to interact with the community as part of the related "Park, Walk and Talk" community relations program, at the same time the general trend was to reduce the number of officers assigned to foot patrol. Finally, NPT officers were steadily assigned to the same patrol area so that they could develop a rapport with residents at the same time the Department was enhancing its efforts to rotate officers through assignments just so that the corruption hazards posed by such rapport would be reduced. The NPT program was nevertheless gradually expanded from precinct to precinct and, in 1973, detectives were even added to several teams. Neighborhood Police Teams were not introduced in every precinct, though, but rather were run as a series of pilot projects in selected precincts.

One problem with NPT, though, is a potential problem with any pilot project or programmatic effort: because it was a project of limited scope and was confined to certain areas of the city, it was easily eliminated. Because NPTs were an add-on and not an agency-wide practice with sufficient administrative, managerial and philosophical support systems in place, the entire project was easily and quickly closed down during the city's fiscal crisis of the mid-1970s. Regardless of how effective they might actually have been in terms of community relations, Neighborhood Police Teams were personnel-intensive and they demonstrated few tangible or measurable results. Because there were few tangible results, they became an easy target for elimination when resources got scarce, and they were never restored when the city's fiscal conditions improved.

The NYPD's next venture into programmatic Community Policing was the Community Patrol Officer Program (CPOP) implemented in 1984 in Brooklyn's 72nd Precinct and eventually expanded to all the agency's precincts. Initially composed of one sergeant and ten police officers assigned to steady foot patrol beats, CPOP units were expected to provide a full range of police services and to interact with community residents. The program's purpose was to increase community awareness of and involvement in crime prevention activities, to enlist community support in the effort to address neighborhood problems, and to improve community relations through the more positive interactions that typically accompany foot patrol.

Although the CPOP officers were given some elementary training in basic problem solving techniques, in practice their role and function differed from that of other foot patrol officers primarily in that they worked a steady beat and were given wide latitude in determining their own working hours and the type of calls to which they would respond. They *were* expected, though, to conform their tours of duty to the needs and conditions existing on their beats. Because the Community Policing philosophy suffered (and continues to suffer) from the lack of a clear operational definition, their activities were governed by few formal guidelines and they had broad discretion in choosing and applying the problem-solving methods they thought would be most effective. They also had broad discretion in selecting the particular problems they would address, and little supervisory oversight to ensure that the problems they chose were those the entire community was most concerned about.

The flexible hours also resulted in comparatively lax supervision and little accountability, factors which may have attracted less-motivated and less assertive officers to CPOP. These flexible tours of duty were thought to be an essential element of Community Policing's effectiveness, though, since it was believed that the rewards of Community Policing would so motivate police officers to act in the best interests of the community that they would work the days and tours of duty when the community needed them most, rather than the hours and days that fit best with their own interests. This might have been the case if, in the aggregate, more highly motivated officers were attracted to join the CPOP units. The program proved to be very popular with residents who relished the idea of seeing "their" cop on the same foot post each day, though, and who welcomed the opportunity for friendly interaction with the officers.

Although the CPOP program's impact on reducing crime remains questionable, the program was eventually expanded to include seven additional precincts in 1985, and CPOPs were in place in thirty-one precincts in 1986, and in each of the Department's seventy-five precincts in 1990. The precinct CPOP units were redesignated Community Policing Units (CPUs) in 1990, and after a comprehensive Staffing Analysis Report examined deployment practices in every unit, squad, precinct and command throughout the agency it was determined that the number of officers assigned to Community Policing duties would increase by 523% to nearly 4,000 officers (NYPD, October 1990, p. 7). The City's 360 square miles were to be divided into separate neighborhood beats (five years later, at the end of the Dinkins administration, the actual number of beats and their boundaries was still under discussion), and each was to have one or more officers assigned permanently to it.

Community Policing in the Early 1990s

The CPOP program was dramatically expanded in 1990, concurrent with the election of Mayor David Dinkins and his appointment of Police Commissioner Lee P. Brown. Brown, a leading proponent of Community Policing, previously introduced a Community Policing variant called Neighborhood Oriented Policing in Houston, Texas during his tenure there as Police Commissioner. Prior to holding the Commissioner's job in Houston, Brown served as Public Safety Director in Atlanta, as Sheriff of Multnomah County, Oregon, and taught at Portland State University after earning a Doctor of Criminology (D.Crim.) degree from the University of California at Berkeley in the early 1970s.

Brown faced a number of difficulties when he came to New York, not the least of which was the fact that he was an outsider who was unfamiliar with the organization's culture and complexity as well as the culture and complexity of the city as a whole. He was charged with the formidable task of re-shaping the agency's operations, structures and policies to support a new style or philosophy of policing, and these difficulties were further complicated by Brown's seeming inability to effectively communicate his vision to members of the agency, much less to convince many members (perhaps especially those highly tenured members with a great deal of export, referent and legitimate power who subscribed to professional model doctrine) that the vision had merit. As in so many other agencies, Community Policing in New York had already developed a reputation as "soft" policing. The poor reputation was exacerbated when so-called "real cops," who spent their tour of duty responding to crimes in progress and other emergency calls for service (and who faced a far greater potential for physical danger), saw their "social worker" colleagues chatting amiably and sharing coffee with community members while they raced to the next crime scene. In conjunction with other factors, a deep divisiveness eventually developed within the patrol force.

For the most part, NYPD cops also perceived themselves as action-oriented crime-fighters, not social workers. Many officers were initially attracted to policing and to the NYPD in particular because of the potential for action and excitement. This is not to say that officers were not also attracted by the possibilities police work offers for helping people and for making a difference – these and other altruistic possibilities are important if less frequently surfaced and articulated motivations – but that action, arrests, chases and danger were (and to some extent remain) central components of the NYPD police identity. In large measure, these components did not correspond to the image or reality of Community Policing. For a host of reasons, the fact of the matter is that NYPD street cop culture placed greater value and afforded greater status for "crime-fighter" behaviors than it did for "social worker" behaviors. Whether he recognized it or not, Lee Brown needed to quickly and permanently forge fundamental and permanent changes in the street cop culture if his vision of Community Policing was to take hold and flourish.

Nevertheless, officers assigned to radio motor patrol were told that they, too, were expected to practice Community Policing. In addition to their overall cynicism about the merits of Community Policing techniques, one of the more glaring problems with this idea was that they were still expected to respond rapidly to priority radio calls in a time when the overall number of 911 calls continued to increase. They simply had little time or inclination to play community beat officer. The Professional Model's demand for rapid response continued unabated, and to many radio patrol cops the demand seemed incompatible with the demand for effective Community Policing practices.

Brown's first major policy change took place within a few weeks of taking office in January 1990, when he implemented steady tours for the patrol force. The rotating "around the clock" work schedule for patrol officers was abolished, and precinct radio car officers were assigned to work steady tours of duty. Community Policing Unit officers retained the luxury of flexible tours. The rationale behind this change was that if radio car officers were to be effective at Community Policing they had to understand the needs of the community and to interact with the same community members every day, so that officers permanently assigned to the day shift would become experts in precinct conditions during the day shift, *et cetera*.

Brown's philosophy was that every officer should have broad discretion and authority to pursue problem solving, as well as the responsibility to provide virtually all police services on his or her beat. In the rhetoric of the day, each beat cop was to become the "chief" of his or her beat, and the 1990 **Staffing Needs Report** (NYPD, 1990) determined that a minimum of 3,795 officers would be assigned to beat policing duties. To this end, beat officers were cross-trained in a number of specialties with the idea that they would eventually take over most functions performed by specialists. Community Policing Unit officers were supposed to be trained to perform plainclothes anti-crime patrol if necessary, and many received training from the Street Narcotics Enforcement Units with the expectation that they would be called upon to assist or lead these teams in making drug arrests on their posts. The cross-training strategy consumed many precious man-hours that removed the beat cops from their posts. How often and how well they actually utilized the training is unknown, but it was given in case they ever needed it.

A representative example of the training bungle was fingerprint training. All beat cops were trained to lift latent fingerprints, and all were provided with a latent fingerprint development kit they could take with them to post. Aside from the huge training expense involved and the loss of manpower on the beats while thousands of officers took this and other courses, there were a number of other problems with the concept. One problem was simply that it was more cost-effective to continue to have one or two latent fingerprint officers (who may have also fulfilled other important specialist functions) assigned to each precinct than to have every beat officer lifting prints. The problem of whether officers were supposed to carry their latent fingerprint tool kit around with them on post every day or leave it at the precinct and retrieve it on the fairly rare occasion they were called upon to lift prints from a routine burglary scene was also never resolved, nor was the fact that the Crime Scene Unit was quite properly called to conduct the forensic investigation at specified serious crimes, so the Crime Scene Unit continued to respond. Certainly no one wanted a rather inexperienced and relatively untrained beat cop to either contaminate or fail to recognize evidence at the scene of a serious crime. The beat cops were relegated to collecting fingerprint evidence at routine burglaries which, in most cases, the detective squads never investigated. The public may have been fooled, but few cops were.

Another problem with this approach was the fact that despite their training, some beat officers simply didn't have the knack for this type of work, which requires a certain amount of physical dexterity as well as constant practice to retain one's skills. Perhaps contrary to public perception, identifiable fingerprint impressions are rarely recovered at burglary scenes, and even when partial prints are found it is extremely difficult to use them to identify a suspect. Most often they become important when a burglar is arrested and his or her prints are subsequently compared to those recovered at earlier crime scenes. Automated Fingerprint Identification System (AFIS) technology now permits latent prints to be checked against literally millions of individual prints on file, but AFIS still requires a clear, clean and unsmudged latent print image. As if the fingerprint training scheme wasn't enough, beat cops were also ostensibly trained and given responsibility for misdemeanor arrest warrant enforcement and the analysis of traffic safety conditions on their posts.

Like the cross-training strategy as a whole, the fingerprint scheme also seemed a threat to officers who worked long and hard to receive the reward of a specialized assignment they enjoyed and did well. The perception of the entire fingerprint project was emblematic of the perception of Community Policing as a whole: it had little substance but attempted to placate and convince the public that something would be done about their problem. It showed good intentions but delivered little.

The "chief of the beat" rhetoric was intended to elevate the status of Community Policing Unit officers, but again it was not supported by cogent management strategies. Further, if the "chief of the beat" analogy is carried to its logical end, what would become of the beat cops' supervisors, commanders, chiefs, and the members of specialized enforcement and investigative units? In Brown's schema, they would all be cast in a support role, applying their time, expertise and resources at the behest and direction of inexperienced rookie beat cops. This expectation was not only widely perceived as an affront to the legitimate authority of ranking officers and investigators and a complete inversion of the agency's rank and power structure, but it flew in the face of sound management theory.

The attempt to implement Community Policing as the agency's dominant philosophy was, however, supported by an extensive training program and by the assignment of all new Police Academy graduates to Community Policing Units. The training and assignment strategy was necessitated in part by the seeming reluctance of many tenured officers to join CPU units, as well as by the fact that it was easier to inculcate officers with Community Policing values and techniques at the beginning of their careers than to change the ingrained attitudes and practices of tenured cops. Given the agency's rapid growth at the time, the CPUs were soon populated by a cadre of comparatively young, idealistic, and entirely inexperienced officers. The overall plan, in essence, was to expand and refine the existing program with additional personnel and with organizational, structural and policy changes until the agency as a whole embraced the Community Policing ideal. There were, unfortunately, several important frailties in this plan.

First, the assignment of all new Police Academy graduates to CPUs created units comprised overwhelmingly of young and inexperienced officers. Although the Police Academy curriculum provided them with six months of basic police training that emphasized Community Policing philosophy and technique, there was some question about how well the new training protocol prepared them for police duties in areas other than the narrow Community Policing mode. A perception developed among more tenured patrol officers that the training had indoctrinated recruits to have disdain for the traditional response-based policing methods senior cops had been practicing for years. The narrowness of the training as well as the relative youth and inexperience of most CPU officers also compromised, to some extent, their ability to do effective police work outside the Community Policing sphere.

Well-conceived and well-delivered training can do a fine job of preparing officers with many of the basic skills they need to be proficient police officers, since it can give them knowledge of law, policies and procedures, rules and regulations and general patrol tactics, but the subtle interactive skills and bits of police knowledge that elevate cops from merely proficient to expert are primarily learned by observing and emulating the older and more experienced cops they work with (Bayley and Bittner, 1984). Unless rookie cops are exposed to expert mentors, they learn the important everyday skills of policing from other inexperienced rookies. The informal system for transmitting the agency's wisdom, experience, cultural values, normative behaviors and the "tricks of the trade" learned through years of experience breaks down without this kind of contact. As one might predict, there evolved a nascent but quite separate Community Policing culture in the NYPD.

As time went on, the perception of Community Policing officers as lazy and ineffective grew more concrete and the divisions between the groups became more pronounced. It became common for Community Policing Unit officers to respond to the jibes of patrol cops by retorting that the patrol cops were just angry that they couldn't get away with doing as little as the Community Policing cops did. By 1994, this divisiveness evolved into a deep animosity between patrol officers and Community Policing officers. Perhaps justifiably, officers assigned to radio motor patrol believed that they worked harder than Community Policing officers and that their work was also more dangerous. The patrol cops' view was that while they were busy fighting crime, the Community Policing officers occupied themselves by attending meetings and drinking coffee with shop owners. They resented the fact that Community Policing officers could not be utilized to back-fill motor patrol vacancies and that they were exempted from various duties that might take them off their posts. Senior radio patrol officers became angry that the rookie officers assigned to precinct Community Policing Units straight from the Police Academy could easily take the day off on holidays, but the senior cops had to work to fulfill minimum manning requirements. The Community Policing Unit cops were rarely if ever utilized at demonstrations, parades, or other events taking place outside the precinct, for example, but radio patrol cops frequently had to "fly" to these details. Clearly, there were two different sets of standards applied to Community Policing officers and radio patrol officers, and the two had very different jobs.

The escalation of frustration and animosity illuminated the fact that Community Policing, as put into practice by the NYPD during the early 1990s, was fundamentally flawed and was having a severely negative and divisive impact on the street cop culture as well as management culture. In extolling the supposed virtues of Community Policing and community beat officers, the department seemed to devalue and demean the good work and dedication of tenured and highly experienced radio motor patrol cops.

Because many managers and executives continued to publicly laud the virtues and enthusiastically exaggerate the impact of Community Policing, they lost legitimacy and credibility in the eyes of the cops who worked for them, and their expertise came into question. Cops felt that the bosses were either shamelessly currying favor with the chief executive and the political powers-that-be, or else they were hopelessly deluded as to what was really taking place on the street. Either way, it was difficult for cops to maintain respect for the bosses. When many of the same bosses trashed Community Policing in private, the shadow of doubt was cast on their personal integrity and their candor. The old fable of the Emperor's New Clothes took on a new life and a new meaning, since few in management had the courage to tell the truth: Community Policing was just not working. To many officers, both Community Policing and its ardent supporters lacked authenticity.

The steady tour concept fractionalized work groups and precinct cultures, leading to the emergence of small, tightly knit cliques in precincts. Officers came to have little knowledge of or regard for the officers assigned to other tours, and they felt no pressure to go out of their way or to make life easier for the strangers working on other tours. Many missed the informal locker room banter and camaraderie they once shared in larger work groups.

Another frailty of the plan was its demand that every operational unit develop and embrace Community Policing practices and techniques. Given the overall lack of commitment to Community Policing throughout the agency, many operational units gave little more than passing attention to this demand. Narcotics and Public Morals Units, for example, simply continued to conduct their enforcement activities as they had before. So long as the investigative supervisors and commanders attended the requisite community meetings, no one really seemed to care that they were not addressing the problems and locations that were of greatest concern to community members. Apparently no executives or senior managers followed up to see when, where and what kind of results they achieved so long as arrest activity remained fairly high. It mattered little when and where the arrests occurred, or whether they coincided with the times and locations the problems were taking place. If diligent beat cops were getting no cooperation or support from these specialized units (recall that the agency still frowned upon uniformed patrol officers becoming involved in narcotics or public morals enforcement) few executives seemed to know or care about it.

This vision of Community Policing certainly recognized the need for primary decision-makers to have access to detailed information about crime and quality of life conditions, but it went about gathering, memorializing and disseminating the information in all the wrong ways. First, it seemed to designate beat cops (in rhetoric, at least) as the agency's primary decision-makers. Second, the time they spent gathering and analyzing information was time spent away from providing police services to the community. This information was compiled in cumbersome "Beat Books" maintained for each of the approximately 2,500 beats in the city. The Beat Books contained detailed descriptions of the geographic and demographic characteristics of the beat, as well as information about beat residents and the crime and quality of life problems that occurred on them. Every meeting the beat cop attended was memorialized in the Beat Book,[5] and many beat cops spent several hours each day working on this community profile. Third, the vision assumed that the mass of information beat cops collected could and would be easily shared among officers – that radio motor patrol officers and officers assigned to other beats would remain familiar with the Beat Books and ensure that their problem-solving activities conformed to the Community Policing plan outlined by the 'chief of the beat.'

Even if this had taken place, another problem remained. The information was collected for a rather small and well-defined geographic area, and the criminals seemed not to pay any attention to beat boundaries. The plan might have worked if criminals respected the beat boundaries and committed all or most of their crimes within the same small neighborhood, but they just wouldn't cooperate. They seemed to commit crimes wherever and whenever the opportunity presented itself, so even if their criminal activity constituted a pattern the police might have been able to address, information about the pattern was spread throughout several Beat Books and could not easily be discerned. Beat cops were supposed to share this information, and "hot sheets" with information about other crimes were supposed to be posted and distributed. In addition to its 3,795 full-time "chiefs of the beat," its 3,795 part-time fingerprint experts, 3,795 part-time traffic safety analysts, and 3,795 part-time warrant enforcement officers, the NYPD found that it had 3,795 part-time crime analysts. Just as this vision of Community Policing sought to decentralize authority and discretion to the furthest extreme, so too it decentralized crime analysis to a ridiculously low level.

At the same time this supposed extreme decentralization and devolution of power, authority and discretion was taking place, the entire operation was still tightly controlled from Headquarters. Precinct commanders were not empowered or given significantly more discretionary control over their personnel and resources: Headquarters still decreed the number and percentage of officers assigned to the Community Policing Unit, the plainclothes Anti-Crime Unit, the Street Narcotics Unit, and to radio motor patrol on each tour.

---

5 Community Policing's performance evaluation criteria and its definitions were so vague and amorphous that virtually any contact with any person on one's beat could be classified as a meeting. The more frequently an officer dropped in to share coffee with a shop owner, for example, the more meetings he or she could report and have reflected in his or her performance evaluation.

For example, Headquarters decreed that the size of a precinct's Community Policing Unit would depend upon the precinct's size and demographic characteristics. The CPU would have either exactly forty, fifty-five or seventy officers – no more and no fewer. The commander had no discretion to increase or decrease this number, regardless of the particular kinds of crime and quality of life conditions existing in his or her precinct. The formal rules and regulations governing Community Policing activities – so important to rule-bound commanders who had been reared in the Professional model environment – were few and far between. There were no clear, objective and measurable indicators of whether or not Community Policing was working.

Indeed, when Lee Brown testified in November 1991 before the City Council's Public Safety Committee relative to evaluating Community Policing, he said that traditional quantitative measures such as crime incidence, response time, etc. were too narrow to be of much use. Many of these elements were, he said, far beyond the control of the police, and he cited education deficiencies, economic conditions, and family disintegration as some of crime's causative factors. Police officers, in other words, don't make much of a difference in terms of crime.

In addition, Brown said that because the police do not control the response of other elements and agencies in the criminal justice system, including judges, prosecutors and the correctional system, we should distinguish between the elements where police can have an impact and those that are beyond the control of police. He offered no guidance as to where that line might be drawn. Instead of focusing primarily on empirical performance data like crime, Brown suggested that Community Policing should be assessed on the basis of how well it reduces fear and restores a sense of order to communities.

Acknowledging that fear reduction and the public's sense of safety do not lend themselves to easy or accurate measurement, they were nevertheless the kind of thing that could be examined using citizen surveys and the qualitative observations of beat officers about conditions on their posts. Twenty-two months into his tenure as Police Commissioner, Brown promised to look at the issues and to develop pilot programs to determine the best way to measure the effectiveness of Community Policing (Brown, 1991). None of the pilot projects ever bore fruit: by the time the Giuliani administration came to City Hall in 1994, there was still no performance measurement system in place for Community Policing or Community Policing officers.

Operation Mood Ring

One ranking NYPD officer, a highly experienced and truly gifted (though somewhat cynical) organizational management analyst, came up with what might have been the perfect measurement for Community Policing during the Dinkins/Brown administration. The irascible analyst poked fun at the entire concept of actually measuring the results of Community Policing when management had only the vaguest idea of what results Community Policing were supposed to achieve, other than the fact that it contained no promise to reduce crime.

Remember mood rings – the fad of the 1970s that changed color according to changes in body temperature and skin conductivity ("happy, sexy, angry, sad")? Our insightful analyst suggested that Community Policing mood rings be distributed to everyone in New York City. At a certain time a police helicopter would fly over a beat and with a loudspeaker ask everyone to "show us your mood rings." A photograph would be taken and examined to determine the public's prevailing mood – the perfect barometer of effectiveness under that particular version of Community Policing. If people were happy, Community Policing was working.

The same analyst often told a story about a Community Policing Unit officer who carefully examined crime and quality of life conditions on his beat and determined that a robbery problem existed at a particular hot-spot. He further examined the problem and determined that the street lights near the hot-spot were broken, and that they might be contributing to the robbery problem. The officer called the Highway Department – the agency responsible for street lights – and managed to get them to repair the lights. The robbery problem subsided. When a cop calls the Highway Department and gets them to repair street lights, the cynical analyst said, you have a triumph of Community Policing. When you have 5,000 cops calling the Highway Department to get street lights repaired, you have a Highway Department that stops answering the telephone.

His point? That Community Policing cannot live up to its promise unless and until you have the committed support of every agency and mechanism of local government. To be effective, Community Policing cannot rely solely on the beat cop to change a community's crime and quality of life conditions; the police organization must develop cooperative relationships with other entities of local government, and those entities must be as responsive to community concerns as the police agency.

Brown was right in at least one respect, though: public opinion is a good measure of Community Policing's effectiveness. In November 1993, the public took its opinion to the polls and the Dinkins administration, as well as its particular vision of Community Policing, ended in defeat.

Without further belaboring the factors and forces that conspired to undermine the attempted implementation of this Community Policing variant, suffice it to say that a lack of genuine commitment to it existed at almost all levels of the agency and that the overall plan lacked adequate performance measures to ensure that it was achieving the desired results. This lack of commitment and focus came to light in a series of 1993 memoranda which criticized the Community Policing model's implementation in New York City.

The Failure of Brown's Vision

Many of the organization and management problems which plagued the implementation of the Community Policing philosophy were brought to light in a series of memoranda prepared in 1993 by Assistant Chief Aaron Rosenthal, Commanding Officer of the Community Policing Assessment Unit. Rosenthal, who would soon reach mandatory retirement age and who had managed to rise to the top of the organization's rank hierarchy despite his independent and contrarian ways, was selected by Police Commissioner Raymond Kelly[6] to assess the implementation and success of the Community Policing philosophy. Aaron Rosenthal was the perfect choice to give Commissioner Kelly a complete, thorough and unvarnished analysis of Community Policing's status. To his credit, Police Commissioner Raymond Kelly began to implement a host of changes in line with Rosenthal's sweeping findings and recommendations. He put the NYPD on a path away from the existing Community Policing vision and toward what would ultimately become the Compstat model.

---

6 Lee Brown resigned as Police Commissioner in August 1992, shortly after the Crown Heights and Washington Heights communities erupted in riots, and shortly after the appearance of media reports which would lead to the creation of the Mollen Commission to investigate police corruption and the deterioration of management of the internal affairs function. Brown left in order to care for his wife during a fatal illness, later becoming Director of the Office of National Drug Control Policy in the first Clinton administration. He is currently Mayor of Houston. Raymond Kelly went on to become Undersecretary of the Treasury in charge of law enforcement functions, and ultimately the US Customs Commissioner. Aaron Rosenthal is a professor at John Jay College of Criminal Justice, and a police consultant and commentator.

The series of analyses and memoranda Rosenthal prepared for Kelly eventually caused a great stir when, shortly after Rudolph Giuliani's January 1994 inauguration, the media became aware of them and their criticisms of Community Policing. The New York *Daily News* alleged that the memoranda found widespread "fudging" of CPU officers' daily activity reports and statistics about how much time they actually spent on their beats engaged in Community Policing activities, and other media outlets quickly followed suit with similar coverage of the scandal (see, for example, Krauss, 1994; Marzulli, 1994, 1994a; McKinley, 1994; McQuillan, 1994; Strong and Queen, 1994).

Alarmed at the incompetence and lax administration they seemed to detail as well as by the implication that officers of various ranks may have falsely reported performance data, Giuliani ordered his Department of Investigation (DOI) to review the memoranda and determine whether they contained evidence of criminal malfeasance or misconduct. The DOI report found no evidence of false reporting or other improper conduct, but it highlighted several important issues that have been discussed here, including apathy and lack of involvement, burdensome administrative tasks, insufficient resources, the difficulty in recruiting and retaining officers for CPUs, and the lack of cooperation from outside agencies.

Problem Solving?

One of the issues the NYPD faced in the early 1990s was how to communicate what community police and problem solving were all about. This was done largely through anecdotes. This is how Police Commissioner Lee Brown described a triumph of Community Policing before the City Council. It is a telling example of what was wrong with that vision of Community Policing.

> Community Police Officer Michael Smith of the 50th Precinct in the Bronx set out to address the problem of repeated 911 calls complaining of suspected drug dealing out of an apartment building on his beat. He organized a group of people who resided in his area into a Block Watchers group. He acquired a large sign with a big police emblem which warned that the street was under surveillance by block watchers. He had tenants of a particular building, working in pairs, man a table in the lobby of the building to challenge anyone they didn't recognize. They did this during the suspected dealer's peak hours of activity.

Officer Smith then had his own tour changed to correspond with volunteer duties of the Block Watcher teams, and with the hours of the suspected drug dealing. Officer Smith would also walk along the street with the suspected dealer every time he saw him on his beat. Our Narcotics Division was also notified, but as a result of Officer Smith's activities, the dealer moved away and 911 calls to the location subsided.

This does not seem to be a valid example of problem solving: the 911 calls subsided when the drug dealer moved away. Did the problem move with him? We don't know. Did he move because of Officer Smith and the pressure put upon him by the community, or because rents were more affordable downtown? We don't know. Brown's description seems more concerned with the problem of too many 911 calls than with the damage drug dealers do to the social fabric and to the lives of community members. The example also points out the tremendous time and effort Officer Smith and residents of his beat put into allegedly "solving" a quality of life problem. Wouldn't it have been simpler and better (if Officer Smith had been trusted by his department to do so) to arrest the dealer? Didn't Brown realize that with all the time and effort it took Smith to set up the Block Watchers to deal with this problem, a responsive Narcotics Division could probably have conducted a complete investigation of the suspected dealer and, if he was dealing, arrest him? In terms of Broken Windows theory, it seems far more cogent to publicly demonstrate civil society's intolerance for drug dealing by putting the dealer in jail than by walking around behind him in an effort to make him uncomfortable or by posting signs that boast of our intolerance for his behavior. Compare Brown's anecdote with the following Compstat paradigm success story described by Safir (1997).

Problem Solving!

An excerpt from a December 1997 article by Police Commissioner Howard Safir in *Police Chief* magazine provides a good example of how Community Policing and problem solving take place under the Compstat paradigm. The article contains a brief case study of the actions undertaken by Police Officer Michael Kelley, a beat cop in Harlem's tough 28th Precinct, to rid his post of a violent drug gang. Kelly is credited with playing a pivotal role in obtaining the arrests and indictments of 35 members of the gang on murder, conspiracy, narcotics, weapons and racketeering charges.

When Kelley was assigned to the post, he found that the "No Fear" gang, which earned up to $3 million annually in drug sales and used young children as couriers, practically controlled the neighborhood through violence and intimidation. Kelley's initial approach was to try to arrest the dealers one-by-one, but he soon found that the dealers were being replaced as quickly as he arrested them. Kelley approached his precinct commander, whose position, power, rank, and authority provided access to the kind of personnel and other resources necessary to effectively address the problem in its entirety:

> Kelley continued to spearhead the effort, painstakingly gathering essential information about the gang's activities and leaders and chipping away at the gang by arresting individual members. At the same time, a task force of uniformed and plain-clothes patrol officers, narcotics investigators, homicide detectives and personnel from the district attorney's office also brought their expertise and resources to bear.

> Patrol officers aggressively enforced quality-of-life violations and determined whether violators had outstanding warrants. Those who did were taken into custody. When low-level dealers were arrested, they were questioned about higher-ups in the organization. Confidential informants were developed and introduced, and controlled buys were made. Homicide detectives shared information with narcotics investigators, and patrol officers with close ties to the community and its residents also provided intelligence.

> As a result of this coordinated approach, the entire drug gang was taken out of the picture in a matter of months, and control of

the neighborhood returned to law-abiding residents. Just as importantly, members of the community saw the police taking decisive action against those who had violated their rights through fear and intimidation. A sense of order and optimism has been restored in that neighborhood (Safir, 1997, p. 38).

For example, Rosenthal and his staff studied the tours of duty performed by community police officers in nine randomly chosen patrol precincts. In a 1994 article, Rosenthal noted that during this two-week period

beat officers performed approximately 63 percent of their tours with the day platoon, 35 percent with the evening platoon, and 2 percent with the midnight platoon. Tuesdays, Wednesdays and Thursdays accounted for 61 percent of all tours performed. All indications are that officers were working those tours most conducive to their personal needs and not in response to identified community problems (Rosenthal, 1994, p. 8).

Noting that no other innovation in policing had ever received such wide acclaim or been so poorly defined, Rosenthal (1994) described how, within the NYPD, Community Policing had become "the politically correct panacea of the day." Ranking administrators, he said "know full well the importance of "getting on the train," so while the emperor may be naked, he'll not hear it from career-conscious commanders (p. 8)." Rosenthal noted that while Brown created a total concept of Community Policing that focused on the beat cop but was supposed to involve support from all branches of the department, his own management studies determined that the Detective Bureau merely paid lip service to the concept while the Organized Crime Control Bureau (including the Narcotics and Public Morals Divisions) also worked tours that were unresponsive to problems identified by beat officers. Perhaps resistant to having their prestige and status diminished by the prospect of being directed by inexperienced rookie police officers, many units simply continued to conduct business in the traditional way. They did, however, avail themselves of the opportunity to work flexible hours and have weekends off.

With regard to Brown's vision that Community Policing would become a choice assignment, Rosenthal (1994) cited a study of seven randomly selected Community Policing units [that] found a turnover rate of 40 percent for sergeants and 38 percent for police officers. Thirty percent of the police officers who departed left for other uniformed assignments. A good argument could be made, we felt, that the high turnover rates reflected a cynicism stemming from the department's failure to fulfill the heightened expectations that its own policy statements had created (p. 9).

Dial-a-Tour

In 1991, the author was newly assigned as a patrol Supervisor in a geographically large and very diverse precinct. One beautiful summer Saturday afternoon, the need arose to assign an officer to safeguard a building where a small fire had occurred until the owner arrived to secure it. Rather than take a radio car team out of service so that one officer could safeguard the building, it seemed natural to assign the CPU officer on whose beat the fire had occurred. A quick glance at the roll call, though, revealed that it was the beat cop's day off. In fact, it was a day off for the entire Community Policing Unit. Upon returning to the station house and examining roll calls for the entire weekend, a curious fact emerged: unless an officer decided to change his or her tour and come in to work (something they called "dial-a-tour"), there was not a single CPU officer scheduled to work between about 2:00 P.M. on Friday and 4:00 P.M. on Monday during the summer months. From a criminological perspective, this was intriguing: were there factors operating in this area that made it unnecessary for beat cops to work on weekends? If we could identify and extend those conditions, perhaps we could all go home early.

This curious fact became more intriguing on Monday, when informal inquiries made to CPU officers revealed that there were, in their estimation, absolutely no problem conditions on any beat in the entire precinct that needed to be addressed on weekends, especially in the summer. Each of the beat officers gave essentially the same story: they worked very early morning tours on Friday and evening tours on Mondays only because those were the times when beat conditions demanded they work. Every beat cop could articulate a reason why they worked those tours. Their sergeant backed them on this – there really was little reason for him to work weekends, either, since there would be no officers there for him to supervise.

The Department of Investigation's analysis concluded, as Rosenthal had, that the problems were attributable to extremely poor management rather than willful misconduct. The definitions and formulas used to compute how much time CPU cops spent on the beat were so faulty and so broadly constructed that the time they spent in the office preparing reports was considered a Community Policing activity. Even officers on restricted duty or limited capacity status (who could only perform clerical duties) could be counted in to inflate the apparent number of cops engaged in Community Policing. After receiving Rosenthal's reports, Police Commissioner Kelly had seen to it that new and more realistic reporting formulas were developed and implemented.

The DOI report (1994) concurred with Rosenthal's finding that the following lapses had taken place:

-   The Narcotics Division was essentially closed on weekends. Only two percent of their narcotics arrests were effected on Saturdays and Sundays, and only one third of the narcotics arrests were at the primary or secondary locations identified by beat cops for targeted enforcement;

-   The Public Morals Division also had weak coverage on week-ends, and prostitution enforcement activities did not coincide with the times and locations identified by beat officers;

-   The DOI echoed Rosenthal's findings about tours of duty and days off being out of synch with beat needs, highlighting his conclusion that supervisors gave CPU officers practically free rein in scheduling because it was so difficult to otherwise attract and retain experienced officers in the units;

-   Rosenthal found serious flaws in the department's Blockwatcher Program. Officers were expected to recruit community residents for this and other programs, and because they were not required to expunge old records the number of registered Blockwatchers grew and grew.[7]

The public airing of Rosenthal's detailed (and often dryly sardonic) explication of the problems and pitfalls of Community Policing in the NYPD effectively set the stage for the implementation of Compstat at the beginning

---

7 Rosenthal noted that one enterprising officer registered herself as the Blockwatcher for the precinct station house's street, and in another case a blind person was registered as a neighborhood Blockwatcher (Rosenthal, personal communication, 1997).

of the Giuliani administration and for the other organizational changes implemented by Police Commissioner Bratton.

In a 1994 article summarizing his earlier studies of Community Policing in New York City, Rosenthal again criticized what he called "the 'get on board' syndrome" – the tendency among managers and executives to demonstrate their affinity for Community Policing by bringing every new policy and procedure under the Community Policing umbrella and to herald commonplace police activities as extraordinary triumphs of Community Policing – and clearly linked it to police cynicism. Management, he said, tried to justify the investment of time, personnel and money paid to Community Policing by "awarding citations and issuing press releases for acts that department members know were long considered routine aspects of their daily duties" and which were now being heralded as examples of the "revolutionary" new concept. Pretty soon, he noted, the public gets wise to the chasm between Community Policing's sales pitch and the product their tax dollar really buys (Rosenthal, 1994, p. 8).

Rosenthal also pointed to the findings of a 1993 report by a committee of 72nd Precinct residents that after nine years of Community Policing in that precinct, cops and community members were still uncertain about the definition of Community Policing and their respective roles in it. After nine years of Community Policing, the NYPD still had no mechanism in place other than anecdotes to measure its effectiveness or the performance of officers assigned to it.

There seems little point in elaborating further on the ideological and organizational difficulties that plagued the NYPD's heralded agency-wide conversion to the Community Policing philosophy under the Dinkins/Brown administration. It may suffice to point out that the Dinkins/Brown model appears to have been premised on the spurious supposition that police officers as young as 20 years of age with the minimum educational level of a high school diploma were socially, emotionally, and intellectually equipped to solve a neighborhood's crime and quality of life problems by disentangling enormously complex and often deeply entrenched community problems. In the simplest of terms, the David Dinkins/Lee Brown model of Community Policing/Problem Solving policing failed (i.e., it did not substantially reduce crime or fear of crime and it did not significantly improve the quality of life experienced by neighborhood residents) because with few exceptions the individuals nominated to deliver its services lacked the skills, knowledge, authority and organizational power to assemble and deploy resources to solve resilient neighborhood crime and quality of life problems. Moreover, they were not adequately supported by the organization, its systems, or its managers and executives.

Managing "Squeegees"

For many years, the problem of "squeegees" – those individuals who approached motorists at intersections and offered to wash their windows for a fee – seemed a ubiquitous part of the New York City scene. The main problem was not simply that they impeded the flow of traffic, but that many "squeegees" were unruly characters who intimidated drivers into paying for a service they didn't want. In many cases, drivers paid them *not* to touch their windows. The squeegees' attitude and demeanor compounded the perception that the city was a disorderly and dangerous place, and they became symbolic of the incivility and the disorder problems existing in New York City. Perhaps because they were such a potent symbol of disorder, the "squeegees" became an issue of debate in the 1993 mayoral election campaign.

In the Fall of 1993, Dr. George Kelling, Deputy Chief Michael Julian and Sergeant Steven Miller of the NYPD confronted the "squeegee" issue and applied some common sense problem-solving to it. They studied the problem by unobtrusively observing squeegees, driving unmarked police cars through intersections where they worked, and by interviewing them as well as neighborhood police officers. They determined that the squeegees fell into three general groups: fairly competent window washers who did not overtly attempt to intimidate drivers; youths who tended to swarm around cars with the intention of intimidating drivers into giving them money; and casual hangers-on who generally seemed to suffer from substance abuse or mental health problems. About three quarters of the squeegee men were *not* homeless, about half had criminal records for serious felonies, and about half had criminal records for drug offenses. Although squeegeeing was prohibited by the City's Traffic Regulations and the obstruction of vehicle traffic was prohibited by the Penal Law's Disorderly Conduct statute, the laws were rarely enforced, and were never enforced in a consistent and focused way.

Under the supervision of Kelling, Julian and Miller, the NYPD commenced a sixty-day study and pilot project in eight precincts aimed at reducing the incidence of squeegeeing through an enforcement-based Broken Windows approach. Each precinct identified areas at which squeegeeing was an on-going problem, and precinct officers were asked to issue summonses for the Traffic Regulation offense or to arrest the squeegees for Disorderly Conduct if they obstructed traffic. Due to limited precinct resources, the enforcement activities were to be concentrated during two days each week, and officers remained free to use their discretion to warn offenders rather than arresting them. To evaluate the project's impact, the number of window-washers at each of the identified sites was counted regularly by members of the study team.

Over a sixty-day period, officers made 28 arrests and issued 21 summonses to 41 individuals, and ordered the squeegees to disperse 191 times. Three quarters of the arrests and summonses and about two thirds of the warnings to disperse took place in the project's first three weeks. By the end of the second week, the average number of window-washers observed at the locations dropped from 48 to 15 – a seventy percent decline across all eight precincts. These levels were maintained for the remainder of the eight weeks. The study concluded that consistent and firm policing by patrol officers was the key to managing this problem, and it recommended that the policy be expanded beyond the immediate pilot area.

The policy was, in fact, expanded and applied even more vigorously, and, in short order, the squeegees virtually disappeared. Although Mayor Giuliani and Police Commissioner Bratton received much credit for ridding the city of squeegees, the fact of the matter is that this took place during Police Commissioner Raymond Kelly's tenure. Bratton (1999) credited Kelly for this accomplishment.

In an example of how coordination between the various spheres of the Criminal Justice system can have dramatic and immediate impact, arrangements were made to notify precinct officers immediately when an arrest warrant was issued for one of the squeegees they had arrested. When a squeegee failed to appear in court to answer a summons (none of the 21 squeegees summonsed in the pilot project appeared in court), judges would automatically issue an arrest warrant. Because this fact was immediately communicated to the patrol officers who arrested them, the squeegees faced another arrest and additional time off the street. Squeegees are rarely seen in New York City these days, but when they do emerge they are treated like virtually every other quality of life or public order problem: they are quickly and rather easily addressed with a rapid, consistent and sustained enforcement approach.

Power, Authority and Discretion

Problem solving policing, no matter how well conceived or designed, cannot succeed unless the individual designated to take the lead in solving problems has the requisite knowledge, skills, authority and discretion to intelligently identify problems and construct viable tactical responses, as well as the organizational power to marshal and apply resources to address them.

It is quite clear that the organizational realities that determine the distribution of power in police organizations were antithetical to Brown's blurry vision of an agency whose priorities were to be determined and actualized by those at its lowest level. The officers who were expected to spearhead the Community Policing movement putatively had tremendous discretion and autonomy but they lacked the power, the experience, the insights, and in may cases the intellectual capacity to perform what are essentially (and quite properly) management functions. Because the necessary support was not forthcoming, this vision of Community Policing betrayed the officers who bought into it. Brown's ideology did not account for these and other organizational realities, and they collectively conspired to defeat it.

While the David Dinkins/Lee Brown model of Community Policing or Problem-Solving Policing had tremendous costs (both in financial and human terms) and little success in reducing crime or improving the quality of life enjoyed by New York City's residents, several important lessons can be gleaned from it. Just as an army led by its private soldiers is doomed to failure, no police agency can find success unless power, authority and discretion are vested in those individuals whose experience and position make them the best suited to lead. In a similar fashion, no war can be won unless the battlefield commanders have the authority and discretion to move troops and conduct tactical engagements without first asking for approval from rear-echelon bureaucrats.

If an agency is to successfully reduce crime and solve quality of life problems, most operational and deployment decisions must be made by commanders at the appropriate management level. In the NYPD (and presumably most other large decentralized police agencies), Precinct Commanders with a field perspective are in a far better position than Headquarters executives to appreciate and meet the particular needs of their communities and to direct the efforts of the 200 to 400 officers they manage. They are also in a better position than beat officers to understand and harmonize the agency's overall policies with the particular social dynamics operating within their geographic compass. To operationalize this, a host of NYPD policies were revised to empower precinct commanders and to significantly expand their authority, responsibility and discretion as well as the degree of control they exercise over personnel and other resources. To a large extent, the specific policies and procedures which required amendment or revision were identified and changed through a process of organizational reengineering.

In the next chapter, we will examine the characteristics of high performance organizations, describing in fairly general terms how police agencies can refocus their energies and achieve greater performance. We will then move on, in Chapter 6, to discuss how the NYPD's structures, policies and culture were altered in line with and in support of the Compstat paradigm's demand for enhanced middle-management discretion and accountability.

Additional Recommended Readings

Goldstein, Herman "Improving Policing: A Problem-oriented Approach," **Crime and Delinquency**, 25 (1979), pp. 236-58. Goldstein, Herman **Problem Oriented Policing**, New York: McGraw-Hill, 1990. Many consider Goldstein's works to be the foundations for Community Policing and Problem Solving Policing.

Eck, John E. and William Spelman with Diane Hill, Darrel W. Stephens, John Steadman and Gerard R. Murphy **Problem Solving: Problem Solving Policing in Newport News**, Washington, DC: Police Executive Research Forum, 1987. This book gives a practical overview of some early attempts at implementing the problem-solving model.

Trojanowicz, Robert and David Carter **The Philosophy and Role of Community Policing**, East Lansing, MI: National Foot Patrol Center Community Policing Monograph Series #13 (Michigan State University), 1988. This brief document provides a great deal of insight into two leading Community Policing theorists' philosophy and vision of Community Policing.

Rosenthal, Aaron "Problem Solving Policing: Now and Then," *Law Enforcement News*, 19, 377, March 31, 1993; pp. 8, 10. Rosenthal, Aaron "NYC's Trouble with Community Policing," *Law Enforcement News*, 20, 412, November 30, 1994; pp. 8, 10. Rosenthal's articles outline his experiences, the difficulties he faced, and the shortcomings he found while evaluating the NYPD's early attempt to implement Community Policing as the agency's dominant paradigm.

Questions for Further Discussion/Debate

1. Some commentators have characterized the NYPD's assertive enforcement-based approach to solving crime and quality-of-life problems as a "zero-tolerance" policy. The term "zero-tolerance" connotes a complete lack of discretion on the part of officers in the manner they enforce the law. It implies that the officer's judgment and discretion to decide when, where and how aggressively to enforce particular statutes has been taken away. Based on what you know of the Compstat paradigm so far, does it seem that NYPD officers' discretion has been expanded or narrowed by Compstat? How about middle managers? Is the term "zero-tolerance" a fair and accurate description of policing under the Compstat paradigm?

2. One of the problems with the NYPD's Community Policing vision of the early 1990s was that it seemed unable to develop and utilize quantifiable performance measures. How would you go about developing accurate measures of performance under Community Policing?

3. In terms of organizational culture and the informal rules of most police organizations, explain how and why the "steady tour" concept fragmented the NYPD in the early 1990s.

4. Given the tremendous number and range of problems the NYPD faced as the result of its attempt to implement Community Policing in the early 1990s, and the tremendous dissatisfaction that existed within the agency, do you think it was easy or difficult for the new administration to convince the rank-and-file that its philosophy would work where Community Policing had failed?

Chapter 5
The High-Performance
Police Organization

American policing stands poised at the cusp of an exciting new age. As police agencies and police officers throughout the nation move rapidly into the 21st Century, they face an unprecedented array of pressures, challenges and opportunities for organizational and individual growth. They face increasing public and political pressure to reduce crime and fear of crime and to restore order in our communities, and the old excuses and rationalizations that the police can have little impact on these problems no longer ring true. The tremendous success of the NYPD and the other agencies that have adopted Compstat paradigm practices have proven the pessimists and naysayers wrong. Police *can* make a difference. Police *do* make a difference. Police *must* make a difference.

If police officers and agencies choose to pursue these worthy goals and to fulfill the expectations of the public they are sworn to serve and protect, they must also embrace the daunting challenge of radically transforming their organizations and their organizational cultures.

The extent to which police executives and operational police officers create beneficial changes within their organizations to accommodate the evolving demands will not only determine the ultimate success or failure of policing as an institution, but will say a great deal about the quality and determination of police leadership in America. To accomplish these goals and to establish a solid foundation for the new relationships it will create, police officers and police executives will be required to draw upon the substantial resources that the academic, corporate, public and private sectors provide them. They must also draw upon the principles for successful strategic policing provided by the agencies that are most successfully reducing crime and fear of crime and improving the quality of life in their jurisdiction.

Particularly within the past few decades, police agencies have successfully drawn upon emerging and current research to create organizational change. Academic and social research into policing and police-related issues have flourished in recent years, and police organizations have demonstrated their enthusiasm to incorporate these findings into operational practices. The Kansas City Preventive Patrol Experiment (Kelling, Pate, Diekman and Brown, 1974), for example, caused police executives to question and ultimately modify their patrol deployment strategies. Despite the subsequent replications that challenged or altered its findings, the Minneapolis Domestic Violence Experiment (Sherman and Berk, 1984, 1984a) also had a profound effect on domestic violence enforcement policies, and the rapid adoption of the practices it endorsed also speaks to policing's greater willingness to utilize academic research. One of the most formidable forces in terms of policy change and practical impact on police operations has been the Broken Windows Theory (Wilson and Kelling, 1982). The list of research projects that have affected police practices and management policies goes on and on.

This appreciation for academic input speaks to the fact that the traditional gulf of distrust and mutual suspicion between "hard-headed cops" and "egg-headed academics" has been largely eroded and replaced by a new level of respect and a willingness to share expertise and knowledge. Indeed, the notions of Community Policing that so many police agencies now practice were first developed and refined in the academic sphere. These notions of Community Policing emerged from a relatively new and rather accurate body of research that debunked many of the common myths and misperceptions that tended to isolate the police and questioned the efficacy of many police practices.

As the traditional barriers between the police and the community continue to fall, and as new organizational models and practices (such as the Compstat paradigm) continue to decrease crime and fear of crime while improving public safety, the police will be under increased pressure to provide their services more economically, more effectively and more efficiently than at any time in the past. In light of these pressures, police executives will seek the means to transform their agencies from passive, reactive agencies to dynamic, high performance organizations. They would also do well to continue to look to the corporate sector for appropriate organizational models and strategies. With its emphasis on accountability, the rapid retrieval and use of critical information, and enhanced employee discretion, the Compstat paradigm uses principles that highly successful corporate entities have utilized for years.

It is only recently that any police agency began to operate like a private-sector corporation in a competitive market, and a great deal of the NYPD's success over the past several years is attributable to its use of corporate metaphors and successful corporate practices. In one sense, it is quite baffling that agencies have just recently begun to adopt current corporate practices, since this failure to stay abreast of emerging management practices has so impeded their opportunities for success. It is also baffling that the public did not demand the adoption of such practices.

Before Compstat and its strategic approach to policing, for example, it took the NYPD months to develop even rough crime and arrest figures – probably the simplest and most rudimentary measures of agency performance. Would any rational person buy stock or invest hard-earned money in a corporation that took several months to figure out its sales and production data? Certainly not – the company would be unable to respond to changing market or industry trends, and the competition would soon drive it out of business. Why, then, would any rational citizen trust his or her safety and that of his or her family to a police agency that lacks the capacity to immediately grasp its own performance data, much less use it to respond to changing crime trends? The Compstat paradigm and its emphasis on accountability, rapid retrieval and use of critical data, and employee discretion are principles that successful corporations have used for years.

Successful management techniques and business practices have been available to police executives for years, yet police executives have largely failed to make use of this knowledge. Models, plans, and designs that were readily adaptable to create more effective police management were available in innumerable management books written over the past few decades, but police executives seem to have made little use of them. This point is well illustrated in the book **In Search of Excellence: Lessons From America's Best-Run Companies**, a widely-read and very influential survey of American business management written by Thomas Peters and Robert Waterman in 1982. While the NYPD did not base its management transformation on the Peters and Waterman's template, *per se*, the principles they identified as characteristic of excellent companies are strikingly similar to the principles involved in the NYPD's transformation.

In Search of Excellence had a significant impact on American business theory, and although it was written in 1982 its organizational insights, its descriptions of successful companies, and the directions it suggests for transforming organizations and their management still have great currency. It seems that some good ideas and good designs never become outdated.

By surveying the American corporate sector and identifying forty-three large businesses that met their operational definition of "successful companies," Peters and Waterman distilled eight guiding principles or characteristics that distinguished the excellent from the mediocre organizations. While these two management consultants (who were affiliates of the highly respected McKinsey and Co. firm) dealt primarily with private sector, income producing corporations, their findings can be generalized to public sector institutions like policing. Despite the inherent differences between the public and private sector organizations (vis-à-vis the constraints engendered by public and political accountability the absence of a profit motive, and often the lack of clearly defined measures of productivity and "success'), the analysis draws upon theoretical constructs of human organizational behavior that appear to be, with some minor adjustment or modification, equally valid for almost all organizations. The validity of the theoretical constructs is proven by the success they engender within the excellent companies that embrace them. Although Peters' and Waterman's lessons were discussed in the police management literature (see, for example: Brown, 1988; Couper, 1988; Duke, 1985), and although the authors subsequently produced other successful management guides, the extent to which the lessons actually impacted policing is uncertain. Given the success of the Compstat paradigm and its role in transforming the NYPD into an agency resembling the corporate entities described by Peters and Waterman, these principles seem well worth revisiting.

Peters and Waterman defined successful companies in terms of six measures of long-term profitability and asset growth over a twenty year period from 1961 to 1980, as well as such less-discrete subjective measures as the continuous flow of innovative products and services and the general rapidity of the corporate response to the demands of changing markets and other external conditions. The forty-three large companies that emerged from the culling process led their respective industries, both in profitability and in innovation. It should be noted, particularly in light of this analysis, that the researchers specifically excluded large financial institutions, particularly banks, because they believed such corporations were too highly regulated to determine their own corporate destiny. Like policing and many other public sector endeavors, banks and financial institutions are somewhat constrained in their ability to function independent of superseding regulatory structures. The law of the marketplace, more than the rule of law, determined the success of the companies Peters and Waterman studied.

Peters and Waterman distilled eight characteristics held commonly by the forty-three companies. These findings are elevated from mere corporate platitudes or slogans by the intensity with which each company practiced them, and by the degree to which they inculcated the value structure of the corporate culture. Each of the companies studied had strong corporate cultures abounding in imagery and stories illustrating individual and organizational devotion to the principles of the corporate credo. The findings, therefore, should be viewed as interdependent characteristics and descriptions of a cohesive whole, rather than as discrete entities. The eight findings were, in effect, an integrated corporate *modus vivendi* in each of the successful organizations studied. The eight rather simple attributes of excellent and innovative companies that Peters and Waterman describe are:

1. A bias for action;
2. Close to the customer;
3. Autonomy and entrepreneurship;
4. Productivity through people;
5. Hands-on, value driven;
6. Stick to the knitting;
7. Simple form, lean staff; and
8. Simultaneous loose-tight properties.

The following sections will expand upon each of these corporate attributes, and upon their implications for policing.

1. A bias for action.

In each of the excellent companies, Peters and Waterman found a palpable excitement for getting things done. The companies had an action orientation, and by design they were unencumbered by the stifling strictures of bureaucracy. The companies were not besieged with complex interlocking sets of committees and lethargic task forces that endlessly review and analyze and wring the life out of ideas: the companies utilize

> distinctly individual techniques that counter the normal tendency toward conformity and inertia. Their mechanism comprises a wide range of action devices, especially in the area of management systems, organizational fluidity, and experiments - devices that simplify their systems and foster a restless organizational stance... (p. 121).

This bias for action is accompanied and empowered by a vast network of informal, open communications systems and an insistence on informality. These patterns are saved from chaos by the frequency of contact between individuals and by their quasi-competitive (peer versus peer) nature. Internal communications are facilitated by an insistence upon open-door policies and a commitment to small informal task forces that are, by definition, short-lived and action oriented. These small *ad hoc* task forces are a remarkably effective multifunctional problem solving tool, but they lose their effectiveness and viability when they expand beyond ten members or they become an appendage to the rigid system they are meant to avoid. Task forces are successful when they are comprised primarily of volunteers, when they concentrate upon the generation of ideas and solutions rather than the generation of formal documentation, and when their members have the authority to make binding commitments and to act swiftly to implement their findings.

Management is highly visible in these companies, and "Management-by-Walking-Around" is a corporate practice used effectively to foster and maintain informal communication at every level of the organization. Managers did not stay behind the doors of their offices – they were highly visible and interacted with employees at every level of the organization. Further, the management cadre within excellent companies were characterized by a willingness to seek out new ideas and to experiment with them. Much of their personal and corporate success derived from their ability to quickly leap from an idea to a plan to production to the marketplace, and from their ability to create an environment and a set of attitudes that encourage experimentation. Experimentation and prototype development also allows individuals (workers, designers, managers and end-product users) to think more creatively and more abstractly about the product and to further develop and refine it. Management was also flexible enough to tolerate experiments that fail.

Implications for Policing

Perhaps more than other public sector endeavors, the business of policing (especially the street cop culture) has an inherent and fundamental action orientation. The organizational culture of policing places great value upon decisive action, both at the management and operational levels, and police officers gain official reward (in terms of promotion, overtime compensation and departmental recognition) as well as status and peer approbation through the decisive actions they undertake. This emphasis on action may, however, be somewhat a double-edged sword, insofar as spectacular acts of police derring-do will typically have greater appeal to the public, as well as to the police, than the less heroic day-to-day triumphs of the neighborhood cop on the beat. The agency's public image and its cultural mythology can be shaped as much by it's media portrayal as by individual contact between officer and citizen. The media should therefore be enlisted for the support it can lend to the agency, its mission, and the positive changes it seeks to accomplish.

To a large extent, both the police organization and the public expect operational police officers to respond fairly quickly to the rapidly changing and often ambiguous demands placed upon them, and both the organization and the individual officer must be capable of flexibility in their modes of response. A great deal of operational police work occurs in response to unpredictable crises occurring within the community, and police management is often similarly besieged with changing priorities in a politically volatile environment. A bias toward action is an indivisible feature of police work.

Unlike the organizations studied by Peters and Waterman, however, the police agency is bound by strict controls at both the management and operational levels. The nature of police work and the tremendous legal and social powers police officers wield makes accountability and control an entirely necessary feature of the police organization. The vast majority of police decisions (arguably, the most important decisions) are made in a difficult and unpredictable field environment by patrol officers who have enormous legal authority and great discretion to invoke or ignore their authority, and whose decisions are usually not subject to the scrutiny and review of direct supervision. The decisions made by field officers involve a clientele who are typically in crisis and who are frequently anti-social or violent, and inappropriate use of police authority or discretion can have extensive individual and organizational consequences. Each of these factors militate for imposition of limits and structures.

As discussed in Chapter 3, such commentators on police work as O.W. Wilson (1941; 1950; 1952), Bruce Smith (1940), Raymond Fosdick (1920), and the authors of the Wickersham Commission Report (1931) stressed the need for more and better training for police officers, greater availability and application of technology, a tight and centralized organization that clearly delineated responsibilities and duties, and extensive use of internal control mechanisms and discipline to ensure rank-and-file compliance to management directives. Police operational effectiveness, it was believed, would flow from standardizing operational procedures and from organizational and administrative efficiency. Their analyses, while an important developmental aspect of the Professional Model of policing, did not fully account for the realities and vagaries of operational police work, particularly the difficulty of imposing control over police behavior in highly ambiguous circumstances. The Professional Model still exerts a strong influence upon police management and practices.

Lawrence Sherman (1974) notes that the next generation of police researchers, including Egon Bittner (1967), Arthur Niederhoffer (1967),

James Q. Wilson (1968), and William Westley (1970), delved into the practical realities of street policing to develop an expanded and more realistic sociological perspective on the police. Concurrently, the late 1960s and early 1970s saw tremendous public and political pressure placed upon police organizations, and an emerging criticism of police behavior. The National Advisory Commission on Civil Disorders (Kerner *et. al.,* 1968), convened in the aftermath of the civil strife and riots that engulfed so many urban areas during the 1960s, detailed police insularity and their estrangement from the public as well as the impact this estrangement had upon police-community relations in general and urban unrest in particular. The President's Commission on Law Enforcement and the Administration of Justice also dealt generally with these issues in its main report, **The Challenge of Crime in a Free Society** (1967), and more specifically in its **Task Force Report: The Police** (1967). These and other critiques of police and police behavior were a powerful external force for reform, and the educational opportunities provided to police officers at that time by the Law Enforcement Assistance Administration exposed a tremendous number of officers (including future managers and executives) to these critiques. The LEAA's higher education programs and research initiatives gave the academic discipline of Criminal Justice a "jump start" that sensitized many police officers to a host of important issues and concerns (in policing, in other spheres of the criminal justice enterprise, and in the external political and social environments) they might never have considered. This exposure and sensitization created the basis for an internal force for reform.

Much of the research conducted up to that point resulted from the various movements to reform corrupt police agencies and to limit the intrusive influence of partisan politics within the police agency (Fogelson, 1977), but the civil disturbance and public dissatisfaction of the 1960s highlighted the failure of police management to adequately or properly control police behavior, despite their fetish for accountability, efficiency and bureaucratic streamlining. The police management policy of the day was simply insufficient to the task of flexibly controlling and directing police behavior in accord with the needs and desires of the public.

Goldstein (1990) argues that the research of the 1970s and 1980s questioned the practical value of standardizing procedures and demonstrated that as an institution

> the police erred in doggedly investing so much of police resources in a limited number of practices, based, in retrospect, on some rather naive and simplistic concepts of the police task. They sought to deal

in a generic way with a wide variety of quite different tasks for which the police are responsible (p. 13).

The leading principles of the Compstat management style are in general harmony with the Problem-Solving model espoused by Goldstein (1979; 1990), and they also seem to fit well with the management practices described by Peters and Waterman (1982). Broadly speaking, Goldstein's (1979; 1990) problem-solving model calls upon the police to recognize that the incidents they encounter are often symptomatic of a much larger and more complex problem, and calls upon them to utilize the resources available within the community and within the police organization to treat the underlying problem as well as to provide immediate remedy for the incident. This is a radical departure from the traditionally held concepts of the Professional Model because it requires the officer and the organization to go beyond "taking satisfaction in the smooth operation of their organization; it requires that they extend their concern for dealing effectively with the problems that justify creating a police agency in the first place (Goldstein, 1990, p. 35)." Viewed in this manner, the "problem," rather than the "incident" becomes the basic unit of police work.

The Compstat paradigm and the strategic policing practices it subsumes refine Goldstein's concepts and provide identifiable goals and measures of success (i.e., crime reduction and quality of life improvement) as well as practical and effective operational strategies to achieve them. The Broken Windows theory provides the theoretical underpinnings or conceptual basis for the strategies and the techniques.

Informed by the success of the Compstat-based policing initiatives in New York City and other jurisdictions, American police leaders have the opportunity to take on the formidable task of transforming their agencies to bring them in line with current management theory and with the Problem Solving model. This change involves abandoning the traditional de-personalized view of management as a sterile and distant process of planning, leading, organizing and controlling, in favor of a more enlightened, holistic and humanistic approach concerned primarily with the management of people. Police executives are recognizing that the analogy to business is apt: in the industry of policing, the public is the customer, and police service is the product. Agencies that provide the best, most innovative and most effective product will be the most successful.

The small, fluid and committed task forces described by Peters and Waterman are more than merely amenable to the emerging style of problem-solving policing: they are an integral feature of it. As the Compstat paradigm continues to be adapted and refined in New York City and elsewhere, the formation of these task forces becomes inevitable. Small, fluid and flexible task forces were used throughout the NYPD's transformation, from the re-engineering committees to the task forces that developed each crime strategy to the focus groups and policy advisory groups that defined and offered suggestions for the problems facing the agency. In the operational sphere, innumerable small, fluid and committed task forces were established to deal with problems that spanned precinct or patrol borough borders, and rapid mobilizations to deal with an immediate crisis or situation are certainly little more than a temporary and informal task force. While task forces can be a powerful management or operational tool, they also entail a number of caveats that must be addressed to ensure their success and the success of the organization.

Anthony Bouza (1990) describes the tendency within American policing to respond to public and political pressure for action on a particular issue by creating task forces. These task forces are often a viable strategy to address a specific short-term issue or situation, and their creation serves as a dramatic demonstration of the police chief's commitment to resolving the issue, but they become problematic when they outlive their usefulness or when officers remain assigned to them long after the problem has been remedied. These task forces, which Bouza calls "barnacles," accumulate on the organizational superstructure like parasites, depleting the personnel resources of the agency. In order to avoid the formation of such "barnacles," police task forces must, by design, be short-lived, goal oriented and mandated to cease once the desired remedy has been achieved.

The success of the Compstat paradigm shows that police organizations must cede some of the restrictive behavioral controls over their members which inhibit creativity, in favor of enhanced individual discretion and the opportunity for individual action. Under the Professional Model, police management "stifled many attributes of the rank-and-file that, if allowed the opportunity to develop, would contribute enormously to the quality of police service. Policing is denied the benefits of their constructive thinking, creativity and resourcefulness (Goldstein, 1990, p. 28)." In other words, Goldstein is saying that agencies must stop depreciating their officers and start elevating experience and expertise as organizational values. Street cop cultures already place great value on experience and expertise, and it is about time that management cultures recognize their own inadequacies. Police agencies must draw upon and develop the innate qualities, capabilities, and expertise of their operational, supervisory and executive personnel, not only to accomplish the goals of problem solving but also to provide a very potent form of motivation. The value of autonomy, peer recognition, self-actualization and other intangible reward systems have been emphasized by many organizational and management theorists since Abraham Maslow (1968) first enunciated them, and it is virtually impossible to underestimate their importance in police organizations. The Compstat model of police management provides ample opportunities for the enhancement of police officer discretion, autonomy, and peer recognition, especially in the process of experimenting with new tactics and strategies.

As Peters and Waterman describe, successful organizations place great emphasis upon experimentation, and are highly tolerant of experiments that fail. Just as officers must be encouraged to experiment with innovative new strategies to reduce crime and solve community problems, the police agency as well as the community must learn to tolerate, accept and learn from attempts that are well-intentioned but not ultimately successful. Obviously, strategies and tactics that work are likely to gain the most attention and are likely to be copied elsewhere, but agencies must also create mechanisms to inform their members about activities that *did not* prove effective at the same time they ensure that no one is implicitly or overtly blamed for the failure unless negligence or mismanagement were contributing factors. Executives who insist that every initiative must be successful create an environment in which taking risks is a career-threatening gambit.

Another vestige of the Professional Model (indeed, of the military influence that has always dominated American policing) is the highly formalized rank structure within the police bureaucracy and its impact upon the flow of communication between and among ranks. The police bureaucracy's rigid reliance upon specific chains of command and formal lines of communication erects barriers that must be removed or amended to foster the free flow of information and ideas. It would be foolish to advocate that ranks, chains of command, or formal lines of communication be entirely abolished – this would surely lead to chaos and undermine the overall effectiveness and discipline of the agency – but a more collegial management style permits these artificial structures to be circumvented or sidestepped under appropriate circumstances. Agencies usually permit them to be circumvented in "appropriate situations" (usually in a crisis or when a compelling need to bypass them exists), but the goal should be to expand our definition of "appropriate situations" and communicate this throughout the organization in order to facilitate the flow of information and ideas.

Even within a creative and innovative police organization devoted to the solution of problems, attempts to excessively flatten or "bend the granite" of the rank structure are problematic and are unlikely to succeed (Guyot, 1979). A more viable alternative is to encourage greater communication between existing ranks by making management both more approachable and more visible to the operational police officer, in the context of "Management-by-Walking-Around." Efforts must be made to bridge the gulf between management cops and street cops, groups that, Reuss-Ianni (1983) has argued, comprise two disparate and dissimilar occupational subcultures possessed of entirely different value systems and perceptions of the police role.

2.   *Close to the customer*

Peters and Waterman state emphatically that excellent companies consistently have an obsession for customer satisfaction. They stay close to the customer, they are aware of customer needs, and they anticipate customer desires. This unfailing external focus exists to such profound extent that it may at times be a "seemingly unjustifiable over-commitment to some form of quality, reliability or service (p. 157)." Nevertheless, these companies recognize that this rather simple dictum of customer service is inextricably linked to the most important determiner of corporate success: revenue generation. In many companies, customer service is valued more highly than profit: they recognize that profit (read: success) will naturally follow service.

Customer satisfaction is, of course, a goal of all business organizations, but the excellent companies are again distinguished by the fervor with which they embrace the ideal. Excellent companies use a variety of management devices to make sure that they stay in close touch with the customer, including customer satisfaction surveys, employee attitude surveys, and incentive compensation plans. In excellent companies, top management provides a role model for corporate employees by becoming personally and regularly involved in the company's dealings with individual customers. At Walt Disney Productions, for example, every executive spends one week per year working at a Disney theme park taking tickets, operating rides or selling hot dogs, and generally interacting with both employees and customers (Peters and Waterman, 1982, p. 167). No matter their industry, the excellent companies all define themselves as service businesses, and obsessively pursue customer service.

Peters and Waterman (1982) cite research that identified three principal themes in an effective service organization:

a. intensive, active involvement on the part of senior management;
b. a remarkable people orientation; and
c. a high intensity of measurement and feedback (p. 165).

Compstat meetings are nothing if they are not a mechanism for active and intensive involvement by senior management with a profound emphasis on measurement and feedback, and notwithstanding the competitive and potentially adversarial nature of the meetings, they are also highly focused on people. In particular, the feedback obtained at the meetings permits executives to ensure that management positions are held by people who have the skills and abilities specific positions demand.

The top managers in top companies treat service problems as "real time" issues that require their personalized and immediate attention, and they often skirt the ordinary chain of command to intervene directly in decisions about the provision of service. By paying attention to customer details, executives communicate a sense of personal accountability to all employees at all levels of the corporation. This degree of involvement also allows the manager to gather potent, reliable and firsthand feedback about the quality of service the organization provides.

The top companies recognize the motivational need for employee enthusiasm about the company and its products, and utilize a variety of methods to increase employees' involvement in both the production and management processes. As they manage by walking around, top executives converse with and compliment employees, instilling them with their own enthusiasm for the company and its product, as well as gathering valuable management information. Such strategies as quality circles and focus groups are also used to great effect. As a result, employees are motivated and infused with organizational pride and commitment.

Implications for Policing

Staying close to the customer (i.e., members of the public) is a central theme in contemporary police management, especially in light of Community Policing doctrine. Police agencies that stay close to the community, are aware of community needs, and anticipate community desires will be successful, but the agencies that obsessively pursue this closeness and awareness will be outstanding. Unlike the corporate world, however, police departments cannot measure success by a simple glance at the corporate balance sheet: the "bottom line" in policing does not translate into dollars and cents, just as it does not translate solely into decreasing crime rates. Rather, an agency's "bottom line" must incorporate measures of public satisfaction, crime reduction, quality of life improvements, and any other demands or expectations the public may place upon them.

A variety of strategies can be employed to redirect the predominantly internal focus of policing under the Professional Model toward the external focus necessary to achieve excellence, including the kind of "customer satisfaction" and employee satisfaction surveys mentioned by Peters and Waterman. "Customer satisfaction" becomes a complex concept in policing due to multiple and often conflicting public expectations, but it is certainly addressed in the Compstat meetings and in the accountability placed on commanders to reduce civilian complaints about police behavior. Commanders also gather important qualitative information about public satisfaction with police activities in their informal interactions with community members and in meetings with community groups. Internally, the department made great use of focus groups, policy advisory groups and surveys on officers' attitudes and operational needs. In smaller communities and smaller agencies (specifically those in which managers and executives are personally acquainted with all their officers and many community members), surveys and focus groups may be helpful but not entirely necessary. In whatever form it takes, the key to remaining close to the customer lies in actively seeking out and remaining continually attuned to their suggestions and requests as well as to their complaints.

In terms of motivating employees, it must be recognized that although incentive compensation plans for police often fall within a problematic area and often conflict with collective bargaining arrangements, they are nevertheless worthy of further consideration and study. Peters and Waterman note that one of the simplest, least expensive and most effective forms of recognizing employee excellence consists of managers wandering around giving individual compliments for exemplary service (p. 176). Employee recognition costs little but generates tremendous organizational benefits in terms of productivity and morale-building, particularly when recognition is coupled with ceremony. Such simple and inexpensive awards as certificates, plaques, and medals provide employees with tangible rewards for service and they are made even more powerful when they are presented in ceremonies attended by peers and superior officers. The guiding principle should be to have an array of rewards available and to know which specific types of reward motivate the individual employee. One should never assume that every reward holds the same attraction for every employee.

Motivation, Compstat Style

Early on in the Compstat meeting's evolution, some precinct commanders began to realize the meeting's potential as a motivational tool for operational police officers as well as commanders. Precinct commanders began to bring along an officer or two who made an exceptional or particularly "smart" arrest, who effectively employed an innovative tactic, or who in some other way acted in a manner deserving of special recognition (see, for example, Kelling, 1995). Consider the following hypothetical exchange and the important symbolic and practical impact it could have.

At the end of his or her presentation to the executive staff, the Precinct Commander asks for a few minutes to recognize some outstanding police work by some outstanding officers. The officers are asked to step up to the podium alongside the commander, and they are introduced by name to those present at the Compstat meeting. The Commander addresses the meeting:

"Last Thursday evening, Officers Smith and Jones stopped a car to summons the driver for passing a stop sign. Officer Smith was writing the summons, and he noticed scratches on one of the rivets holding the Vehicle Identification Number to the dash. Even though it matched the registration papers and even though a radio check listed the car as properly registered, the officer took the extra step. His partner, Officer Jones, recently took the Auto Crime Course and he climbed under the car with a flashlight and found the engine VIN. He determined that it didn't match the dashboard VIN, and they arrested the driver for the "tag job." The detectives debriefed the driver, and he wanted to trade time for giving up a neighborhood guy who sells guns. The detectives got the District Attorney to get them a search warrant – over the telephone – for the guns based on the driver's sworn statement. When they hit the place they got four guns and made two arrests. The gun dealer's friend is on parole and wanted to trade, too, so he gave up a homicide. The detectives made the collar yesterday, and one of the guns ties in to another homicide in the Bronx. Bronx Homicide is running line-ups this morning. Auto Crime is following up on the registration angle. The whole thing brought us four, maybe five good felony collars – two of them homicides – and took four guns off the street, and its all because these officers took the extra step. Commissioner, I think these officers deserve a hand."

The Police Commissioner, three or four Deputy Commissioners, the Chief of Department, the Chief of Patrol, the Chief of Detectives, the

Borough Commander, seven or eight Precinct Commanders and about fifty other ranking members of the department get on their feet and applaud the officers, and the Police Commissioner and all the chiefs step up to congratulate them and shake their hands. It is a moment the officers will remember for the rest of their lives, and it is a story they will tell other cops in their command and other precincts. This simple and impromptu form of recognition cost absolutely nothing, but will have a powerful impact on these and other officers, and will clearly communicate the agency's values and management's respect for those who exemplify them.

Policing also lends itself to the high visibility, "hands-on" style of management that Peters and Waterman describe. Operational officers who see managers taking an active role in the provision of police services at the beat level will not only be impressed with the importance of their own work, but will be exposed to suitable role models whose actions communicate organizational values. As always, managers must resist the temptation to become meddlers, and avoid actions that may be interpreted as interference when a situation is being handled well. Managers have the opportunity to demonstrate the personal and organizational value they place upon improving neighborhood or precinct conditions, as well as to monitor the officer's effectiveness and gain feedback about the agency's progress toward its goals. Greater communication and sharing of information between the ranks must be one of those goals.

Peters and Waterman describe how high performing organizations use "quality circles" to facilitate the greater flow of ideas and information, and this concept of employee participation in management decision-making has successfully been adapted to policing. Through quality circles, policy advisory groups or focus groups employees identify organizational problems and goals, propose viable and practical solutions based on their knowledge and expertise, and monitor the results of the solutions they implement. Advisory groups give the operational police officer a stake in the agency's management, and they also serve as an important interface between management and line officers. Not only do these committees yield the benefits of the members' experience and insights and increase communication between officers and management, but the agency's positive response to the concerns of employees tangibly demonstrates the organization's concern for the welfare of the officer and its respect for his or her opinions. Through such committees, officers are encouraged to assume "ownership" of the programs, policies and goals they suggest. This tends to ensure their cooperation in bringing the policies to fruition, and the overall process is even more powerful when the officers selected as participants have both expertise and referent power. Operational officers with high referent power who have a stake in seeing the policy actualized can serve as management's informal emissaries and are likely to use their powers to persuade others that the policy has merit.

3. Autonomy and Entrepreneurship

Creativity and innovation are central realities in excellent organizations, according to Peters and Waterman. The organizations initially become successful and ultimately maintain their success in highly competitive markets by fostering employee autonomy and entrepreneurship traits and by providing the necessary formal and informal support systems through which their employees can excel. Peters and Waterman refer to creative innovators as "champions," and relate that these individuals are, almost without exception, zealous volunteers whose fanaticism challenges tradition. The champion is not necessarily "a blue sky dreamer, or an intellectual giant. The champion might even be an idea thief. But, above all, he's the pragmatic one who grabs onto someone else's theoretical construct if necessary and bullheadedly pushes it to fruition (Peters and Waterman, 1982, p. 207)."

Peters and Waterman propose a typology of champions in excellent organizations, based upon the three primary roles they fulfill. The *product champion* is the zealot or fanatic within the ranks of the organization whose staunch belief in a specific product or concept may create conflict between him/herself and the organization. The *executive champion* is invariably an ex-product champion who has successfully been through the lengthy and demanding process of guiding ideas through the organization's bureaucracy, and who acts to protect the product champion and push the innovative concept forward. The executive champion is a sort of mentor who encourages, supports and assists product champions. The *godfather* is the senior executive role model for championing, who shapes and creates the crucial and convincing organizational mythology that fosters the idea that risk taking and innovation lead to individual and corporate success (p. 208-09).

Excellent organizations recognize that successful and sustained innovation is a function of repeatedly and speculatively attempting to implement new and innovative ideas. In Peters' and Waterman's analogy, innovation is a "numbers game" in which innovative organizations increase their number of "hits" by increasing their number of "at bats:" the more oil wells a company drills, the greater its chances of striking oil (p. 209-211).

They differ from other organizations in that they do not ascribe to the conservative "home runs only" mentality that proceeds from "a misplaced belief in planning, a misunderstanding of the disorderly innovation process, a misguided trust in large scale, and an inability to comprehend the management of organized chaos and lots of base hits (p. 211)."

Excellent companies provide structured support for their champions and for their prospective champions, in part through the open internal communications systems that they create. The five attributes of communications systems that seem to foster innovation are informality, extraordinary intensity, physical support, "forcing devices," and the remarkably tight informal control system that results from the previous four attributes. Because everyone is involved in the communication system, peer review, oversight and accountability are fostered.

Implications for Policing

The tremendous emphasis contemporary policing places upon problem solving ties in neatly to the themes of autonomy and entrepreneurship. Police officers on the beat require a significant degree of individual autonomy if they are to identify and seek solutions to the crime and quality of life problems they confront, and the same certainly applies to Precinct Commanders and other managers. Members throughout the agency must be encouraged to be creative and innovative in their problem solving. As discussed above, this is accomplished in part by eliminating the perception that negative consequences will follow a well-intentioned experiment that ultimately fails to produce results. It is also accomplished when the executive articulates and continually communicates his or her commitment to innovation and experimentation.

Peters' and Waterman's notion of the "champion" is particularly amenable to the context of policing, given the tendency within the police subculture and within the organization to define some members as heroes and to reward them with subcultural status or with more tangible rewards, such as the detective designation. In many respects, this tendency to confer status on heroes is quite similar to the process of creating referent power. Heroic figures are replete throughout the history and the mythology of modern policing (Repetto, 1978), and indeed the exploits that earned the heroes their status as legendary figures comprise a unique and informative window through which to view the values of the subculture, the organization and the institution of policing. In their most salient form, mythological "war stories" provide an important means of socializing the recruit officer and bringing him or her to an understanding of the formal and informal roles, responsibilities and social norms they will be expected to uphold and practice.

"War stories" are a type of informal and personalized organizational history within which important characters, events, places and relations can be located and understood. These symbolic depictions often take the form of cautionary tales that illuminate the culture's shared meanings and interpretations of events, affirm the occupational culture's belief systems and values, and serve as an important medium of police socialization (see, generally, Manning, 1977). "War stories" illustrating the cultural and organizational values are implicitly motivating: the young officer learns that status and reward are gained by emulating and modeling the valued behaviors.

The dilemma facing the police organization, though, arises from the difficulty in transforming the "war story," with all its attendant connotations, to the "success story" or the "innovation story." Several inter-related transformation strategies might be employed to bring about the desired change in an agency's culture. First, the agency must provide tangible and intangible reward systems for officers and managers who demonstrate the willingness to take prudent risks as well as proficiency in achieving the desired results. At first glance, this observation may seem trite and axiomatic since most police agencies already have some sort of reward system in place. Typically, though, reward systems only operate when a successful outcome is achieved, not when best efforts are made. Even when the tangible rewards available to a manager or executive are few, officers who continually and conscientiously test innovative tactics and ideas deserve to be recognized. This is especially true during the early stages of an effort to transform a risk-averse agency. Creating a new reward system can be a risky business with many pitfalls, though, and managers should carefully weigh their options and their goals before they radically alter the existing system.

As discussed above, though, one of the key elements is ensuring that managers have a variety of rewards in their repertoire, but another key element is the intensity and the integrity with which managers apply these motivational tools. Those who are familiar with police agencies will recognize that regardless of their rank or position or the size and configuration of their agencies, police officers seem to universally disparage the integrity of their agency's reward system. The depth of these feelings and the frequency with which they are expressed suggest that police agencies and executives need to take a long, hard look at the inadequacies of their reward systems. Many executives seem to assume (naively, at best) that the rewards they personally respond to will motivate others equally well. Because the power to reward is such a jealously guarded function of management, officers who see a lack of integrity in the system (or in reward decisions in general) will perceive an overall lack of integrity among managers and executives as a whole.

To transform the agency, to retain and enhance the respect they get from officers, and to achieve organizational goals, executives must absolutely ensure that rewards and promotions are awarded solely on the basis of performance rather than interpersonal or organizational politics. The executive who practices politics through the formal reward system may accrue short-term benefits, but in the long run he or she loses credibility. He or she also loses referent power and legitimacy in the eyes of the rank-and-file. In particular, such an executive risks alienating and disaffecting the very officers whose high performance and whose affinity for the organization's goals make them most deserving of the rewards that are given to less-qualified officers. Additionally, the executive loses some amount of coercive and reward power because the potency and desirability of the formal rewards, as well as the status they confer, is eroded.

Reference Groups and Reward Systems

In 1949, sociologist Samuel Stouffer wrote a multi-volume report, entitled **The American Soldier**, summarizing the extensive research he conducted on America's servicemen and why they fought in WWII. Among the many important motivational insights gained from Stouffer's classic work was the connection between motivation, morale and the perceived integrity of the promotional reward system. Stouffer's insights about the motivations of soldiers seem to be quite applicable in contemporary policing as well.

Stouffer discovered that it was the perceived equity and integrity of the reward system, rather than the number or value of the rewards handed out, that determined morale and how motivated soldiers were by the reward system. Specifically, he found that morale within a unit was based on the individual's subjective perception of his own opportunity for promotion and reward relative to other similarly-situated individuals within a "reference group." In Military Police units, for example, where promotions were few but truly based on merit and performance, morale and belief in the fairness of the reward system was higher than in the Air Corps, where promotional rewards were much more frequent. In the Air Corps units, soldiers were far more likely to receive rewards but because they saw that some less-qualified and less-competent (i.e., undeserving) members of their immediate reference group inevitably managed to get promoted, morale and confidence in the promotional reward system as a whole was eroded. They were less motivated to work for the promotion and reward. Stouffer concluded that morale, the potency of the reward system, and confidence in the reward system are primarily determined within an immediate reference group of individuals we know and with whom we interact regularly, not within the organization as a whole. The Military Police did not know or care about promotional opportunities in the Air Corps, nor did the Air Corps members know or care about promotional opportunities in the Military Police. We only compare ourselves to similarly situated individuals with whom we are acquainted in one way or another.

Similarly, the number and value of tangible rewards distributed in one unit or precinct does relatively little to motivate an officer in another precinct or unit. This puts the onus for a fair and objectively equitable reward system clearly on the unit's commander. If he or she administers that reward system based solely on merit and performance and without political influence, the members of the unit (i.e., the reference group) will have respect for the integrity of the system (and will likely be motivated by it) regardless of how the system functions elsewhere.

Another often-overlooked vehicle for providing rewards and shaping perceptions is the media. The police agency should make every effort to communicate its successes (i.e., to market its product) through the media, and to use the news media to create and reward champions in the organization. By publicizing the positive actions and efforts of individual champions, the agency can emphasize the champion's contributions and harness an additional source of police motivation. Realistically, the tendency among many news organizations to prefer the more sensational and spectacular aspects of police work may somewhat constrain the agency's ability to shape its image, but some inroads can undoubtedly be made by appealing to the "personal interest" or "slice of life" side of the news. A story or feature article highlighting a champion conveys an important message about the agency's values to the public and to members of the department. Further, many of the larger police organizations utilize internal magazines or newsletters to keep their members abreast of agency affairs, and a variety of journals and periodicals that pertain to policing have wide circulation among police officers. Executives often miss the motivational boat, though, when they either permit or cause the internal newsletters to focus too closely on a handful of ranking officers. By focusing upon the chief executive and his or her top managers, the opportunity to communicate values and to motivate line officers is often lost. Although many executives may not recognize it, most line officers are not at all interested in the executive's exploits: they'd much rather read about those in their own reference group, and they may well perceive such articles as part and parcel of an executive ego trip. Articles featuring officers and middle managers who developed, implemented or participated in successful initiatives can do a great deal to raise the esteem and status of the ordinary patrol officer. Executives can also facilitate the creation of champions within the agency and within the mythology of the police occupational culture when they publicly award credit where credit is due.

The police agency must actively exploit the possibilities made available to them through heroes, who can influence others in a way that mission statements, policy statements, and the lines and boxes of an organizational chart simply cannot. Indeed, the police executive must realize that in many cases the actions and attitudes of a few heroes can have greater positive or negative impact on the day to day activities and attitudes of officers than the executives themselves. The executive must do everything in his or her power to develop and create heroes who exemplify the values he or she is trying to communicate. As Deal and Kennedy (1982) comment,

> It is time American industry recognized the potential of heroes. If companies would treat people like heroes even for a short time, they might end up being heroes. Employee motivation is a complex science, but its foundations rest on the simple recognition that we all need to feel important in some phase of our lives. Heroes, as they epitomize the best that people can be, are the stuff and hope of culture (p. 57).

The evolution of "executive champions" who support and mentor the development of innovative police officers as champions can similarly be hastened within the police agency, particularly when the agency's chief executive assumes the benevolent and visionary guiding role of "godfather.'

The police chief or commissioner who desires to inculcate new values and foster the development of champions within the organization might do well to emulate the basic principle of holding managers accountable for creating and nurturing innovative strategies and methods. Agency heads have at their disposal a variety of discretionary tools to influence supervisors' and managers' practices, including promotions and transfers. By utilizing

Compstat principles to hold managers accountable for fostering innovation and by convincingly casting themselves in the "godfather" champion role, police executives can fundamentally change the dimensions of innovation within their agency.

4. Productivity Through People

Peters and Waterman contend that one key to a successful organization is the degree of trust with which the organization invests its employees. Although the notion of trusting employees may at first glance seem simplistic and axiomatic, Peters and Waterman found that there was

> hardly a more pervasive theme in the excellent companies than *respect for the individual.* That basic belief and assumption were omnipresent. But like so much else we've talked about, it's not any one thing - one assumption, belief, statement, goal, value, system, or program - that makes the theme come to life. What makes it live at these companies is a plethora of structural devices, systems, styles and values, all reinforcing one another so that the companies are truly unusual in their ability to achieve extraordinary results through ordinary people (pp. 238-39).

The level of trust is tied directly to motivation: excellent companies give employees a high degree of control over their own destinies, treating them as professional adults and both allowing and encouraging them to become winners. Peters and Waterman are quick to note that the excellent companies do not mollycoddle their employees, but rather they have a tough-minded respect for the individual, setting attainable goals and granting the autonomy to achieve those goals. Unlike the less-than-successful companies that give mere lip service to their people orientation, but in point of fact rarely extend any perceptible level of trust or positive regard toward the employee, the excellent companies persistently demonstrate an ingrained corporate belief that people are their most valued asset.

Peters and Waterman note that many of the "lip service" companies fall prey to "the gimmicks trap (p. 241)." They depend upon a few faddish programs (such as quality circles, job enrichment strategies, or team building exercises) to create a smoke-screen behind which management continues to avoid real people involvement. Despite the potential effectiveness of these programs, they become worthless gimmicks because true management concern, and true management enthusiasm for the employee, are lacking.

Successful companies provide an array of incentives to their employees to boost morale, empathy for the corporation and individual employee productivity. The excellent companies rely extensively upon positive reinforcement, actively seeking out and pursuing excuses to give out rewards. In an analogy that seems particularly salient within policing, Peters and Waterman stress the importance of non-monetary rewards by citing the fact that Napoleon was a compulsive medal-granter, and they quote a former WW II infantryman: "A man won't sell his life to you, but he will give it to you for a piece of colored ribbon (p. 268)."

Implications for Policing

The strategies and philosophy of the Compstat paradigm are wholly consistent with Peters' and Waterman's notion of "productivity through people," although police executives are faced with a range of difficulties in translating the idealized concepts of trusting and encouraging employees into credible management practices. All too often, the organizational requirements of accountability and control of police discretionary behavior is interpreted by the officer as an unnecessary and meddlesome intrusion upon his or her judgment and professional acumen, and as an inappropriate negation of their legitimate discretionary power. Reduced to its simplest form, many officers feel that although the realities of their job calls for a high level of sensitivity, decision-making skills and courage, the police organization does not treat them as mature adults capable of making such judgments.

This dynamic poses a central dilemma for the police manager, since the perplexity of maintaining adequate accountability and control while encouraging discretion, innovation, prudent risk-taking and professional excellence is not easily resolved. One possible solution lies in training the supervisor and middle manager to be a more effective, more empathetic and more flexible manager of people. Rather than simply depending upon training, though, a more cogent strategy might be to amend civil service promotional criteria to include additional and more varied measures of latent managerial and leadership potential.

Like the excellent companies whose concern for employees and whose regard for them as responsible adults capable of making tough decisions ran throughout every fiber of the organization, police agencies must continue to develop supervisory and management personnel who can communicate, through example and through words, their respect for the officer on the beat and for his or her functional autonomy. The relationship of mutual respect between the officer and the agency can be facilitated through Employee

Assistance Programs, expanded health care programs, etc., but the most effective means of fostering the sense of concern is through the interaction of officers with managers who care. Such interaction is, in itself, a powerful motivator.

With few exceptions, the system of rewards and incentives found within police agencies are limited by the requirements of rigid civil service systems and by the demands of police unions that all members be treated uniformly. Unlike the private sector organizations studied by Peters and Waterman, where executives are relatively unencumbered by these constraints, police chiefs in many larger agencies generally have little discretionary ability to offer monetary incentives or promotion even to exceptional performers. Admittedly, the application of civil service laws to police agencies occurred as a reaction against many of the abuses, including nepotism and undue political influence, that characterized some of the promotional policies existing in police agencies earlier in this century (Fogelson, 1977), but modern police executives are nonetheless fettered in their capacity to adequately reward deserving employees through monetary incentives.

While police executives may be deprived of the ability to reward officers financially, a variety of incentives, some of which were mentioned above, are available to them. Peer recognition and the approbation of superior officers, particularly when accompanied by ceremony, are proven incentives. Deal and Kennedy (1982) comment upon the role of ceremony within occupational cultures, noting that ceremonies help the organization celebrate its heroes, myths and values, and keep the heroes, myths and values uppermost in the employees' hearts and minds (p. 63). Awards and recognition are a viable management strategy, but many police managers fail to maximize the potential benefits they present.

Tremendous diversity exists in the ways these awards are assigned: in some agencies or commands, police officers must prepare their own requests for recognition, and they receive the award at a much later date, typically without ceremony. In other venues, a commanding officer or a peer review panel will prepare and submit the request forms and will present the award in the presence of the officer's peers. Further, these medals and awards are typically available only for heroics or for arrest activity, rather than for community service or innovation, and this is to the detriment of the service-oriented officer as well as the innovator.

5.   *Hands-On, Value-Driven*

When asked to provide a single piece of all-purpose advice for management in any corporate endeavor, Peters and Waterman note, they are tempted to reply, "Figure out your value system. Decide what your company *stands for*. What does your enterprise do that gives everyone the most pride?" In the excellent companies they studied, Peters and Waterman were struck by the amount and the extent of personal attention that leaders paid to corporate values and by the way leaders create exciting working environments through their own personal attention, persistence and direct intervention at all levels or phases of the operation (p. 279).

Each of the excellent companies clearly defined its value system, and each seriously embraced the process of shaping and communicating those values. Almost all companies had objectives and goals, but only the most successful companies had a coherent, integrated and well articulated set of corporate values. These values are stated in qualitative, rather than quantitative, terms; they are as inspiring and as relevant to the people at the very bottom of the organization as to the people at the top.

Effective and inspiring leaders who refuse to compromise on matters of corporate values are the key to the success of this value system. When a conflict arises, for example, between the corporate value of producing a product of the highest quality and the realistic prospect of rising production costs (and reduced profitability), the value-driven executive of an excellent company does not hesitate to support quality at the expense of profit. These value-shaping leaders understand that they are responsible for communicating abstract ideals through their own enthusiasm and through their own deeds, and they understand intrinsically that by steadfastly upholding the corporate credo through their own actions, they will develop the employee's allegiance and pride. The most effective way to demonstrate the corporate values is through personal attention and interaction.

The hands-on, value-driven managers constantly interact with customers and with employees, becoming involved in even the most mundane aspects of corporate operations. Management-by-Walking-Around yields at least three immediate benefits, Peters and Waterman claim: employees realize that the manager is accessible, approachable, and more than willing to listen to them; employees are kept informed about activities within the company; and finally, walking around interacting with people is just plain fun (p. 289).

In excellent companies, the entire executive leadership team is involved in the hands-on style of management. They become the role models, heroes and champions of the workforce as they wander about interacting, and they infuse the workforce with their own values and their own enthusiasm for the corporation. In excellent companies, the executives' personal values are identical to the corporate values, and their commitment to the values are borne out through their actions and deeds.

Implications for Policing

Even a cursory survey of current trends among police agencies evince a recent tendency to formally articulate mission statements, codes of ethics and statements of organizational values. The formulation and promulgation of such written codes are related to efforts to elevate the occupation of law enforcement to the status of a profession. To the extent that the traditional professions are at least partially distinguished by their adherence to a code of ethical conduct, such codes are emblematic of police professionalization.

Value statements and codes of ethics *per se* should not be viewed as a panacea, however. Even the most comprehensive and well-articulated value statements or ethics codes are ultimately deficient, in that they cannot hope to encompass the tremendous range and variety of ambiguous situations and ethically problematic circumstances the operational police officer encounters. The codes are flawed because although they do forbid certain practices and generally encourage others, they simply do not exhaust the legitimate moral possibilities the officer encounters.

Mere publication of a police agency's statement of values will never ensure the compliance of its members, but when agency executives and managers maintain a high profile and persistently communicate the philosophy they represent, all levels of the organization are infused with and inspired by those values. Perhaps the most compelling demonstration of an executive's commitment to the values he or she espouses comes when the executive incurs some personal cost or penalty rather than compromise the agency's values. A hands-on, value-driven executive corps that articulates and lives up to the same set of values held by the rank-and-file will also tend to reduce the dysfunctional perception held by many "street cops" that the "management cops" are out of touch with the realities and demands of operational police work.

6. *Stick to the Knitting*

Excellent companies are characterized by a reluctance to diversify into technologies, products or services that are far afield of their basic orientation. These organizations, according to research Peters and Waterman cite, "have strategies of entering only those businesses that build on, draw strength from, and enlarge some central strength or competence. While such firms frequently develop new products and enter new businesses, they are loath to invest in areas that are unfamiliar to management (p. 294)." The companies that branch out somewhat, yet still stick very close to their central skill, outperform all others.

Neither large corporations nor huge conglomerates are averse to acquiring new companies, but the acquisitions made by excellent conglomerates are carefully calculated to compliment the primary business interests. They buy up small companies that are readily assimilated without changing the basic character of the parent organization.

Peters and Waterman also warn that the excellent companies risk losing the strong corporate cultures that led them to superior performance when they extend beyond their reasonably narrow business competencies (p. 301). The merger of disparate and often incongruous cultures create confusion and disorder in both the parent company and the company that it acquires.

Implications for Policing

Peters' and Waterman's findings (as well as the experience of the NYPD in the early 1990s) clearly indicate that police agencies should not attempt to venture too far from the provision of police services, despite the pressures put upon them by some Community Policing ideologies. Police agencies must recognize that their proper and legitimate role is the protection of life and property under the law, the maintenance of order in the community, and the reduction of crime and the fear of crime. These mandates do not specifically exclude involvement in providing social services, but a delicate balance between these mandates and the seductive lure of becoming a full-blown social services agency must be struck. The police agency that takes on the broad Community Policing role may, in fact, find itself involved in a wide array of social services, but it should confine itself to facilitating public access to the legitimately established agencies and programs. It must define and remain within its own sphere of competence, or it risks diluting the organizational core.

The requirement to "stick to the knitting" in an era of Compstat management makes obvious the profound need to develop and articulate precise operational definitions of the agency's goals, strategies and practices, and to communicate these definitions through the ranks. Even within the law enforcement community, there exists tremendous divergence of opinion as to precisely what the Compstat paradigm means. Many police executives outside New York City and many academic criminologists, for example, appear to confuse the Compstat paradigm with strategic policing practices: they erroneously believe that Compstat is no more or no less than a high tech meeting and that strategic policing is no more or no less than aggressive enforcement. They do not grasp the fact that the paradigm entails establishing a fundamentally different set of relationships between executives, managers and members of the rank-and-file inside the department and between the department and the community. Without clear operational definitions and the understanding they provide, though, the Compstat paradigm becomes a mere rhetorical overlay to business as usual.

One challenge for police leadership is the need to define, as concretely and as precisely as possible, what this paradigm means for their particular agency. The definition must include the substance and the limits of community involvement, and must include realistic and quantifiable measures of productivity as well as customer satisfaction. The leaders must also construct realistic policies that lead these conceptual definitions to effective practices at the operational level, and they must educate middle managers, supervisors and patrol officers to ensure that they understand and embrace the concept and comply with the policies.

One factor militating against the development and implementation of realistic and effective operational policies derives from the patterns and directions of communication generally found within police agencies. As in many hierarchical bureaucratic organizations, the flow of information within policing tends to be downward, since the systems are simply not structured to efficiently transmit information (other than basic productivity data) and intelligence upward from the product-delivery level to the executive decision-making level. This dynamic accounts, in part, for the actual or perceived gulf between "street cops" and "management cops" (Reuss-Ianni, 1982). Cynical street cops, who carry out the policies and practices created by management cops, may denigrate the managers as ivory tower bureaucrats who are hopelessly out of touch with the reality of the street, and subtly resist their policies. The veracity of the perception is, again, almost immaterial - in the street cop subculture, the perception is accepted as reality.

Police-Management-by-Walking-Around tends to ameliorate this divisiveness by facilitating the upward flow of qualitative operational information and by providing the high-profile executives with the operational intelligence they need to make sound decisions. Management-by-Walking-Around allows for the establishment of a necessary and beneficial feedback loop.

7. *Simple Form, Lean Staff*

The large companies Peters and Waterman studied tended to avoid the organizational complexity that size often brings by maintaining flat, stream-lined structures. They note that overly complex structures automatically dilute a company's priorities because they imply that every endeavor and function, and every box on the table of organization, is of equal importance (p. 307). This complexity prevents a flexible and fluid response to rapidly changing conditions in the market environment (p. 308). Simplicity of organizational design also allows for the distribution of autonomy and authority closer to the bottom of the hierarchy, creates better and less rigid channels of communication, and focuses attention upon the delivery of products or services.

Staffing at the excellent companies was especially lean at the executive level, in part because the simple structure requires fewer people to make it work correctly (p. 311), so members of the executive staff can devote their attentions to solving problems in the field. In excellent companies, almost all functions, including purchasing, finance, personnel, and even strategic planning are decentralized to the division level. To ensure that all managers have a thorough working knowledge of all the various functions of the organization, many excellent companies adhere to a strict policy of rotation for corporate staff. Peters and Waterman note that staff rotation policies have an additional benefit: home office personnel are unlikely to create over-bearing bureaucracies when they may be transferred and called upon to deal with those bureaucracies themselves (pp. 312-13).

Unembellished, uncomplicated organizational structures that are populated by relatively few staff personnel characterize the excellent companies, allowing the corporations to respond quickly to new demands and to maintain the unifying values of the corporate culture. Decentralization of power, authority, autonomy, and staff resources are key elements to their success. In Peters' and Waterman's schema, small is better.

Implications for Policing

Although the prospect of flattening the rank structure of police agencies through elimination of specific ranks may be problematic (Guyot, 1977), many agencies can simplify their organizational tables in other ways. Early on in its process of transformation, the NYPD eliminated an entire level of bureaucracy. Prior to 1994, a command level known as the Division level was interposed between precincts and patrol boroughs. There were twenty-three Divisions throughout the city, each comprised of from two to four precincts, and in retrospect they were an entirely unnecessary part of the organizational structure. Division commanders held the rank of full Inspector but had few substantive responsibilities or formally prescribed duties other than a host of administrative tasks, and their elimination was achieved with scarcely a ripple in the agency's operations. Some of the Division Commander's operational responsibilities were subsumed by the Borough Commander, and others were relegated to the Precinct Commander, and because most of their administrative tasks were redundant or duplicative anyway, they were simply eliminated. The elimination of this level of bureaucracy and supposed supervision clarified the blurry dimensions of accountability and discretion, freed up a significant number of ranking personnel for deployment elsewhere, and put Precinct Commanders under the direct supervision of Patrol Borough Commanders.

In the context of the Compstat paradigm, adaptation of Peters' and Waterman's call for simplicity and for focusing attention upon the customer requires that local police managers (i.e., precinct commanders) are invested with enhanced authority and freed from the constraints of a stifling headquarters bureaucracy. If an agency were to reconfigure itself upon Peters' and Waterman's model, headquarters personnel would play a limited role and would be confined to the coordinating, planning and support functions. Overwhelming and intimidating bureaucracies would be deconstructed and their personnel dispersed to the field, where they would be in close proximity to actual operations, as well as to the consumers of police services.

Admittedly, the question of how centralized or decentralized an agency's coordination, support and planning functions should be is not easily resolved. It makes little sense in an agency as large and complex as the NYPD to have seventy-six autonomous planning units or seventy-six auto pounds, but it makes just as little sense to have no one at the precinct level responsible for planning or no space for the short-term storage of impounded vehicles. In a smaller or more geographically dispersed agency, it might make sense to completely decentralize these and other functions. As a general rule, though, the simpler the organizational structure the better.

8.   Simultaneous Loose-Tight Properties

In its essence, the apparently contradictory term "simultaneous loose-tight properties' means "the co-existence of firm central direction and maximum individual autonomy (p. 318):" rigid managerial control is balanced against an insistence upon autonomy, innovation, and entrepreneurship among the rank and file. This balance is accomplished in excellent companies primarily through culturally derived value systems that management uphold and exemplify. By providing appropriate reinforcement and rewards for volunteer champions, by fostering a bias for action, by maximizing autonomy, by insisting that management stay in touch with customers and with the company's essential business, and by keeping the structure tight and the staff lean, the executives of excellent companies shape, mold and maintain the occupational culture. The companies rise to excellence because the people who inhabit them are inspired, disciplined and motivated by the potent force of corporate culture. When peer pressure demands excellence, employees rise to the occasion.

Peters and Waterman found that the excellent companies

are simultaneously externally focused and internally focused - external in that they are driven by their desire to provide service, quality, and innovative problem solving in support of their customers; internally in that quality control, for example, is put on the back of the individual line worker, not primarily in the lap of the quality control department. Service standards are likewise substantially self-monitored. The organization thrives on internal competition. And it thrives on intense communication, on the family feeling, on open door policies, on informality, on fluidity and flexibility, on nonpolitical shifts of resources. This constitutes the crucial internal focus: the focus on people (p. 323).

Implications for Policing

Peters' and Waterman's final point can be seen as a summation and integration of their previous seven points: productivity is accomplished through people, and organizations that cherish and nurture their employees will reap benefits far in excess of costs. Their orientation is that people want to work and want to excel, and that the role of management should be to facilitate the excellence inherent in every employee through management of the corporate culture. This orientation is decidedly more Theory Y than Theory X.

As noted throughout this analysis, the police occupational culture is a vibrant and viable determinant of the agency's success in realizing its goals. Police officers, as individuals and as a group, are special people, by dint of their dedication to the work they do in spite of the myriad demoralizing circumstances they often encounter. More importantly, they *believe* they are special people involved in an occupation that rarely recognizes their specialness. Many police officers, in fact, were initially motivated to take the job because they believed in a particular set of values and beliefs, but as Niederhoffer (1967) described so well, their values, ideals and dedication are rather quickly eroded through frustration with the negative features of police work and through their frustrations with the organization they inhabit. Skilled executives and managers can harness the police occupational culture and use it to transform management practice, but in order to do so they must recognize the culture's strengths and the positive attitudes it upholds, and they must reward the personnel who possess and best exemplify them.

The younger and less cynical cadre of officers hold the greatest hope for police agencies that seek to achieve lasting excellence. To a large extent, younger and less tenured officers tend to be among the most energetic, enthusiastic and conscientious members of the agency. Managers and executives can have a powerful long-term impact on the agency's culture and its success if they act vigorously to preserve, protect, and develop the most desirable and admirable attributes of the culture's members. This is especially important among the younger officers, since their attitudes and attributes will one day come to define the culture.

Perhaps the simplest and most effective way the executive or manager can nurture the desired attributes is to recognize and commend those who possess them. Executives and managers who actively try to give away credit for the agency's accomplishments, for example – pushing credit as far down the organizational pyramid as is reasonable and practicable – may find that they have creates a host of heroes within the ranks. These heroes are not only likely to be fiercely loyal to the manager or executive (increasing the boss' quotient of referent power and his or her capacity to access and mobilize expertise), but are likely to have great influence over the actions and attitudes of their peers. Recognizing the officer's contributions and his or her commitment is a potent weapon against cynicism.

To abate the debilitating effect of cynicism upon police performance and upon the police occupational culture, agencies should act immediately to adopt the Compstat paradigm and the lessons of excellence Peters and Waterman advocate. The currently evolving concepts and notions of the Compstat paradigm provide police managers and executives with a fertile ground in which to bring about a fundamental change in the nature of police management, and a fundamental change in the nature of the police occupational culture. Only through reshaping and transforming the culture by unifying or bringing to closer alignment the separate street cop and management cop cultures can police agencies realistically aspire to high performance and excellence.

Additional Recommended Readings

Peters, Thomas J and Robert H. Waterman, Jr. **In Search of Excellence: Lessons From America's Best-Run Companies**, New York: Warner Books, 1982.

Peters, Tom **The Circle of Innovation**, New York: Alfred A. Knopf, 1997.

Peters, Tom **Thriving on Chaos: Handbook for a Management Revolution**, New York: Alfred A. Knopf, 1987.

Bennis, Warren and Patricia Ward Biederman **Organizing Genius: The Secrets of Creative Collaboration,** Reading, MA: Addison-Wesley, 1996.

Deal, Terrence E. and Allen A. Kennedy **Corporate Cultures: The Rites and Rituals of Corporate Life**, New York: Addison-Wesley, 1982.

Questions for Discussion and Debate

1. In this chapter we discussed how some organizational and management principles from successful private-sector businesses can be adapted and applied in policing. Keeping in mind our caveat about "cookie cutter management," and "cargo cult" and the inherent dangers of trying to impose practices from one agency upon another, can you think of other specific business practices that might be adaptable to policing?

2. When the Compstat paradigm was beginning to take shape, the NYPD's managers and executives frequently used business metaphors to describe the organizational change they were bringing about, and they often looked to the business world for appropriate organizational models. The NYPD learned a great deal from the business world, but what can the business world learn from Compstat?

3. If you were the CEO of a major corporation in a competitive market, could you fulfill your responsibilities to your Board of Directors, to your stockholders, or to your employees if the decisions you made were based on sales and productivity data that was several months old? Why do you think that police executives were (and in many cases, still are) able to get away with using out-of-date crime and quality of life data?

4. What are the major differences between private-sector organizations and police organizations that police executives and managers should consider as they try to adopt successful business practices in their agencies?

Chapter 6
The Mechanics of Change –
Organizational Diagnosis, Reengineering
and Crime Control Strategies

A point of continued emphasis throughout this book is the notion that the implementation of Compstat-type technology and Compstat-type accountability systems, absent other fundamental organizational and cultural changes to support them, is likely to cripple the agency's effectiveness in a relatively short time. To pursue this course of action is akin to taking an old clunker of a car out on the highway for a long, high-speed trip: you may get it to perform for a while, but if you haven't tightened the belts, checked the fluids and topped off the oil, one of the sub-systems is sure to fail. You may go fast, but you certainly won't go far.

The same analogy applies to the police organization. Like any other complex system – whether human, mechanical or a combination of both – a police agency is highly susceptible to breakdown if the executive does not take the time to feed and nurture it and to regularly perform essential preventive maintenance. Critical resources must be put back into the organization if it is to continue to thrive. How does the executive determine, though, what critical resources are most necessary and where they most need to be applied?

This chapter is about reengineering – the process of making the fundamental changes necessary to support the Compstat paradigm and to keep it from burning out the people who inhabit the organization and make it work. The reengineering process does not merely tune-up an agency's operations and culture – in many ways it radically transforms them. Reengineering, in essence, involves a complete and thorough redesign of the organization – it asks the question, "how would we design an agency to accomplish what we expect to accomplish if we were starting at the beginning?," and then sets about actualizing that design. Reengineering addresses the structure and operations of the agency as well as its organizational culture.

The first steps in the reengineering process are assessing the current state of the organization and its culture, diagnosing problems, and prescribing solutions. While some police managers may feel comfortable with their own subjective capacity to intuitively diagnose the agency's problems, a far more rational, objective, and beneficial approach is to incorporate the leadership team's insights with a thorough and systematic analysis of the agency using focus groups in tandem with organizational surveys.

The Compstat paradigm is also supported by specific crime control and quality of life strategies that set out the basic operational plans and tactical approaches the entire agency takes to achieve results and reduce crime. Crime control and quality of life strategies are quite similar to business plans – by specifying the direction the organization intends to take and by laying out the organization's goals and objectives, the strategies tend to ensure that every member of the department is "reading from the same page of music." The NYPD developed ten specific plans it called Crime Control and Quality of Life Strategies, but other agencies may require more or fewer strategies depending upon the goals they intend to pursue. As in the case of re-engineering, the development of truly effective crime control and quality of life strategies requires that the participants in this process are experts drawn from every level of the police organization – the critical insights and information they bring to the table must come from throughout the organiza-tion. The strategy development process reviews the policies, operational activities and tactics the agency uses to achieve its goals and completely reworks them. The agency's operating problems and shortcomings are identified, and a comprehensive, coherent and integrated prescriptive plan is developed and implemented. Once again, executives who bring the agency's personnel into the management process and capitalize on their insights and expertise are practically assured that the participants, as well as many other members of the department, will buy into and support the transformation process.

In this chapter, we will first examine the process of diagnosing the agency's problems, then consider the organizational reengineering process, and finally turn our attention to using diagnosis and policy reengineering to develop and implement effective crime control and quality of life strategies. As in other sections of this book, it should be pointed out that the methods and procedures outlined in this chapter should not be considered separate and discrete steps to be followed rigidly in series. While this chapter outlines a general process that should be followed, it is neither necessary or desirable for one element to be completely finished before beginning the next step. It should also be pointed out that the problems and pitfalls of cookie cutter management and cargo cult management apply to these processes: agencies that simply superimpose the strategies developed by the NYPD (or any other agency) or try to simply restructure their organization based on another agency's model are almost certainly headed for disaster.

The Cultural Diagnostic

Early in 1994, the NYPD began conducting a series of focus groups and surveys to identify the agency's most pressing organizational problems as well as the issues of greatest concern to its members. This information gathering and analysis process, which consultant John Linder called a "cultural diagnostic," ultimately informed a great many management decisions about the department's transformation and pointed out the directions the transformation should take. It also recognized the important role police culture plays in determining the attitudes, behaviors and activities of the agency's members and, by extension, the success the agency can hope to achieve in meeting its goals (Mollen, 1994; NYPD, June 1995).

By convening focus groups involving representative stratified samples (i.e., the number, ranks and functional assignments of officers taking part in the groups are roughly proportionate to their representation in the agency as a whole) of patrol officers, detectives, supervisors and managers from virtually all the agency's geographic and functional areas of responsibility, a concerted effort was made to identify and quantify impediments to performance and to discern their specific impact on officers and operations. Information obtained in the focus groups led to the development of a fairly comprehensive survey questionnaire that was distributed throughout the agency, and the results of that survey informed both the reengineering process and the development of crime control and quality of life improvement strategies.

The whole point of this exercise is to determine which organizational structures and policies and what cultural features need to be changed to bring the organization into conformity with the executive's vision for it. Although members of the rank-and-file fully participate, it is the executive who ultimately decides what changes are necessary as well as the best and most effective way to implement them. Beyond the immediate benefits of identifying problematic structures and policies, there is probably no more effective or efficient way for the executive to tap into the expertise and experience of the agency's members. The process also permits the executive to identify and elevate experts – to bring practical expertise to the executive level where it is often so critically needed.

The process of cultural diagnosis follows a traditional route of social science research that has also been widely applied in business and industry. Focus groups are a specific research methodology which, when properly conducted, yield a wealth of highly valid qualitative data – they provide a broad understanding of the way people feel about particular issues. Focus groups, which are often called quality circles when the same members meet on a regular basis, are widely used in American business and industry to develop and improve products and services, to streamline administrative procedures, and to gather important information from employees and consumers.

In the marketing field, for example, many companies use focus groups to explore what consumers like and dislike about their products (as well as their competitors' products), and to identify the kind of product features that are most attractive and most important to potential buyers. A manufacturer of bicycle helmets, for example, might conduct focus groups with potential buyers to determine whether consumers are most likely to buy a bike helmet on the basis of comfort, appearance, or the level of safety it provides. The focus groups might reveal, for example, that appearance and comfort are most important when an adult purchases a helmet for personal use, but that the level of safety is paramount when they purchase a helmet for their child. This information gives marketers an idea how to advertise and package their product, and it may influence how new products are developed and packaged.

Advertising agencies use focus groups to fine-tune commercials and ad campaigns in order to make them more attractive to consumers, and Hollywood studios have been known to film several endings to the same movie and to use the footage that focus group test audiences like best. Focus group methods are often adapted by business and industry in the form of ongoing "quality circles" and the kind of short-lived *ad hoc* task forces described by Peters and Waterman (1982).

The noted sociologist Robert Merton first developed the focus group as a research method in order to probe the practical impact of wartime domestic propaganda efforts upon public behavior, and research methodologist Earl Babbie points out that they are a flexible and relatively inexpensive way to capture real-life data about attitudes and social behavior (Babbie, 1992, p. 255). In addition to their wide use in business, advertising, and marketing, they have also been used successfully in policing – both as a research method and as a way to identify and find solutions for organizational problems (Melancon, 1984; Hatry, 1986; Brown, 1993; Mollen, 1994; NYPD, June 1994).

What, more specifically, are focus groups? They are highly interactive directed interviews of small groups of people who generally come from a similar background or share some common attribute, aimed at developing information and reaching conclusions about other individuals with similar backgrounds. The attitudes, perceptions and points of view observed within the focus group are assumed to be generally representative of the attitudes, perceptions and views of others with similar backgrounds. Because we are generalizing this information from small groups to a much larger population, we have to be very careful about the assumptions we make and the kinds of questions we ask. It is also usually a good bet to convene several focus groups as a means of raising the level of confidence we have for the conclusions drawn from the groups.

One of the key methodological issues involved in focus groups is that of selecting participants. If the issues involved are fairly broad and the level of inquiry is not particularly deep, a randomized sample of the agency's officers should suffice[8]. In other cases, as when we have developed our initial data and seek to probe it more deeply to test and refine our initial ideas and conclusions, it is advisable to select officers who have a particular know-ledge or point of view about the issue under study. Care must be taken (especially in demoralized or highly cynical agencies) that the focus groups do not deteriorate into mere gripe sessions or that the goal of the entire endeavor – improving the agency and the work environments of its members – does not get lost. A well-trained focus group facilitator can usually keep the discussions on track.

Care must also be taken when we attempt to generalize the findings from a few focus groups to an entire agency. Focus groups provide highly valid data about the participants' ideas, beliefs and attitudes, but they are not truly suited to the collection of hard empirical data. As methodologist David Morgan (1988) points out, the empirical issue of concern in large organizations is sample bias, not generalizability, since a relatively small sample of officers will never be perfectly representative of a large population. This fact argues against attempts to use focus groups to test specific hypotheses or to gather hard quantitative data. The goal of focus groups is to learn generally about others' experiences and perspectives, and any attempt to use this methodology to completely survey or to precisely

---

8 The terms "random" and "randomized" are used in a methodological sense. In research, the concept of random selection does not equate with haphazard selection. Randomization has a precise meaning and connotes that every member of the defined population has an equal probability of being selected for the sample. A variety of randomization strategies and techniques can be used to ensure that the sample is random, and therefore presumed to be representative of the population as a whole.

define the entire range of experiences and perspectives in a large and diverse agency can be a fool's errand (Morgan, 1988, pp. 44-45). As we shall see, there are other methodologies better suited to this purpose.

As a general rule, determining the appropriate size and number of focus groups to conduct involves a trade-off: smaller groups provide greater depth of information and insight, but because small groups require a greater number of sessions they tend to be more costly. Morgan (1988, pp. 43-44) recommends that the number of participants generally not exceed twelve, and Greenbaum (1993, p. 3) recommends that the groups range in size from eight to ten participants. One useful strategy in focus group research may be to conduct an initial round of focus groups with randomly chosen participants in order to generate a broad understanding of the issues and attitudes existing in the agency, followed by a second round (often involving participants with a particular expertise or depth of knowledge) to further probe and refine the information obtained. Each successive round of focus groups (if conducted) can focus in more narrowly on the issues involved, and also serve as a validity check for the information previously obtained.

As a general rule, officers and supervisors should not be combined in the same group – the groups should be as homogeneous as possible since the rank consciousness that is so pervasive in policing often tends to inhibit the free expression of opinions and observations. Also, it is usually a good idea that a "neutral" member of the agency (one who has high credibility in the organization and is not seen as implicitly allied with management, if such an individual is available and capable of moderating the groups) or an outside facilitator with a knowledge of police work and police culture be employed to conduct the actual focus groups. One need not be a highly trained researcher to conduct an effective focus group, but certain well-developed interactive skills and a general knowledge of the methodology's potentials and pitfalls is necessary.

Because executives need hard and accurate data to inform their decisions, the cultural diagnostic process involves gathering nebulous or generalized qualitative data through focus groups and interviews and ultimately transforming it into more specific and more useful quantitative information. This is accomplished through empirical surveys. The surveys ultimately yield a host of additional insights into the organization, its culture and its practices. As a whole, the diagnostic process helps to identify the constellation of attitudes and belief systems that constitute the agency's core organizational culture and defines where particular attitudes and beliefs reside and are most strongly held.

When properly conducted, focus groups can identify the issues of greatest concern to the agency's members and can provide executives with a good sense of how strongly these attitudes are held. This kind of qualitative information usually provides excellent insight into the culture and is often highly nuanced, but the information is also highly subjective. In conjunction with other data and other observations about the agency's operations and culture, focus group data can lead the executive to a series of tentative hypotheses about the sources and dimensions of the attitudes, experiences, values and beliefs that comprise the agency's core culture. The data may also point out subtle differences in the attitudes, experiences, values and beliefs of different subcultures (i.e., the patrol cop culture, the detective culture, and the supervisory/management culture) within the agency as a whole. Beyond these essential cultural issues, the focus group data can also lead the executive toward tentative hypotheses about the agency's other compelling problems in terms of management practices, structure and organization, training, personnel, equipment, community relations, crime reduction and a host of other functions.

These tentative hypotheses, in turn, can be empirically tested for accuracy by constructing an appropriate anonymous survey instrument that is distributed throughout the organization. Again, it is desirable that the person or persons who develop the survey have a certain degree of training in research methods, since developing a valid and useful questionnaire can sometimes be a tricky business. The more experience and training the survey developer has, the more accurate and useful the results are likely to be. To ensure a maximum rate of return, the survey instrument should be anonymous, although it will be necessary to include optional questions about each respondent's demographic background – his or her rank, assignment, gender, age range, and any other factors deemed important.

Generally speaking, it is an exercise in futility to conduct survey research if you ask police officers to directly identify themselves, but experience shows that many or most will provide their demographic characteristics if the items are characterized as optional and no request is made for the officer's name or any uniquely identifying information. It is also generally a good idea to pose the demographic questions at the end of the survey instrument, since experience shows that fewer officers will respond to a questionnaire that assures them of anonymity but immediately begins collecting information on their background. Beyond the issue of the survey's credibility, once people get into the flow of responding to questionnaire items they are more likely to complete the entire instrument.

When analyzed, the data resulting from a well-conceived and well-designed survey questionnaire can determine, with a great deal of precision, the contours and "topography" of the culture's belief systems. A well-written and well-executed survey can also identify even relatively minor differences in attitudes among different groups or categories of officers.

For example, a well-executed survey developed from accurate and valid focus group data can reveal a great deal about officers' perceptions of their immediate supervisors as well as supervisors and managers in general. The survey might reveal, for example, that patrol officers as a group are cynical about the leadership capabilities of upper management but have fairly high regard for the capabilities of their immediate supervisors. At the same time, the data might reveal that this perception is particularly strong among the more tenured officers (i.e., those who typically have a great deal of potential influence over the attitudes of younger cops) and that detectives as a group seemed *not* to disparage the leadership qualities of either their immediate supervisors or the agency's top managers. These hypothetical data tell the executive that he or she may have a problem (whether real or perceived, a lack of faith in the leadership abilities of supervisors or managers is *always* a critical problem) within the patrol function that does not seem to exist within the investigative function. Efforts to enhance management's credibility should therefore (in this example) target the patrol force, and especially the more tenured officers within the patrol force. Since detectives already tend to have confidence in the agency's top management, there is a less compelling need to devote the executive's time and resources to convincing them. Other data from this hypothetical survey may indicate whether the problem is best addressed through training, a change in promotional policy, or some other means. In any case, the executive is now aware of a problem that may or may not have been apparent before, and he or she has the opportunity and the mandate to address it before it reaches critical proportions.

Executives should be well advised, however, that conducting focus groups and surveys implicitly conveys a personal commitment to changing the organization in consultation with lower-ranking members of the agency. The executive must treat cultural diagnostic and reengineering activities as real-time issues that demand a great deal of his or her personal attention if they are to be effective. If executives have the focus groups and surveys conducted but shy away from confronting issues or implementing at least some of the necessary changes the process identifies, their legitimate and referent power will be diminished and they will likely increase the level of cynicism in the agency. The executive's referent and legitimate power can be enhanced, though, if he or she openly disseminates the survey results throughout the agency, thereby demonstrating his or her commitment to honestly acknowledging problems as well as symbolically affirming that all members of the agency have an interest and role in changing the organization. This feedback loop is absolutely essential if true participative management is to take place.

The fact that the executive must implement at least some of the changes identified by consensus of the agency's members should not be interpreted as meaning that the executive simply rubber-stamps their recommendations or that he or she turns control of the agency over to the rank-and-file. Indeed, some of the recommendations members make may be impossible to enact because they conflict too significantly with other policies, or due to legal, budgetary, political or other reasons. If these reasons are communicated to agency members, they will understand; but if they get no feedback and see no change or if recommendations are simply shelved without further action, they will feel they have been deceived by the executive and will be unlikely to give him or her their support in the future. The point here is that once the executive takes the agency down the reengineering path or engages in any kind of participative management program, he or she establishes a certain set of expectations and had better fulfill at least some of those expectations. Unless some of the expectations are fulfilled, the executive's power will diminish and he or she will be seen as inept or as lacking respect for the intelligence of the rank-and-file. Cynicism, resentment and bad feeling will result.

If it is properly conducted, of course, the diagnostic process of focus groups and surveys will not reveal just one or two problem – it will probably lay out an entire agenda for change. Can an astute executive develop this agenda for change without resorting to this kind of process? Possibly. But he or she will never be entirely certain that the changes implemented are the most essential to the continued health and viability of the organization and its culture or that his or her subjective evaluation of the agency's troubles is sufficiently comprehensive. Moreover, the executive also loses the important opportunity to gain referent power by demonstrating that he or she values the expertise of others in the agency. Simply taking the time and trouble to ask for members' input confers a degree of expert power upon them, and acting upon their suggestion further affirms the executive's respect for the individual and collective opinions of the agency's members. That affirmation is implicitly rewarding, and it permits line officers to participate meaningfully in the management process as well as to take vicarious "ownership" of the changes taking place throughout their department. The exchange certainly costs the executive nothing in terms of diminishing his or her own expert power, it provides a free or low-cost vehicle to spread a potent kind of reward throughout the agency, and it potentially expands the executive's referent power as well as the respect and loyalty he or she receives from officers.

Why should focus groups and surveys be used in tandem? For one thing, because each has strengths that compensate for the deficiencies of the other. One *could* simply conduct focus groups and use the information to chart a course for organizational change, but as pointed out above one could not be entirely certain that the perceptions and observations perceptions they raise are entirely accurate or free of bias. Surveys provide evidence to confirm that assumptions about the organization and its culture are accurate, and they pinpoint where the agency's problems are most entrenched and where its strengths are most pronounced.

Similarly, one *could* simply develop and distribute a survey whose questions were developed from an intuitive sense of the agency and its culture, but once again this is a highly subjective exercise. One could justifiably dispute the survey's objectivity and validity as a measure of the organization, its culture and its problems. Who developed the questions? Are they based solely on the executive's perception of what the rank and file need and want? As we've noted earlier, in many cases executives have a skewed perception of the rank and file's belief systems. If the survey does not ask questions about the issues that truly concern the rank-and-file, the executive opens himself or herself to potential ridicule and to the perception that he or she is entirely out of touch with the street cop's reality.

Additionally, unless the chief executive or a staff member has a fairly strong background in research and research methodology, it is probably advisable to contract the diagnostic process out to a private consultant who is familiar with transforming police agencies, or at the very least to seek advice and guidance from a methodologist at a local college or university. An outside consultant may also be able give a much more honest and objective appraisal of the department than an insider who may be concerned with the career repercussions of offending the chief executive.

In all cases, though, the executive must resist the simple and expedient temptation to borrow and use a survey instrument that another agency has used. Why? Cookie cutter management! The problems and issues this cultural diagnostic process seeks to identify are *not* simply generic problems – they may in fact be common to many agencies, but they take specific forms and specific features in different departments and organizational cultures.

Their causes and their solutions are as unique as the agency in which they occur. The whole point of the process is to achieve a comprehensive and objective understanding of the subtleties and nuances of how these problems affect that particular agency. Once that understanding is achieved, viable solutions are more readily identified. Moreover, if the executive just borrows and distributes a survey he or she loses out on the tremendous potential this process holds for bringing the rank-and-file into the management process – for encouraging them to take ownership of their department, their work, and their work environment. He or she also fails to take advantage of a powerful system for tapping into the expertise residing in the agency, for distributing rewards and power throughout the agency, and for consolidating and enhancing his or her own power.

The NYPD's Cultural Diagnostic

The early focus groups conducted in the NYPD probed officers' attitudes toward the organization and its management as well as toward the public, examining the factors that motivated and de-motivated them. Subsequent rounds of focus groups refined and probed more deeply into the foundations of these performance obstacles and cultural issues, as well as the specific types of impact they had on police performance throughout the organization. The initial set of focus groups were thus used to develop information from diverse sources in order to identify and "triangulate in"[9] on the broad range of issues and obstacles to effectiveness that officers faced. A comprehensive survey instrument was developed from these preliminary qualitative data and distributed to every sworn member of the department in the rank of sergeant and below.

The survey transformed qualitative impressions about the attitudes prevailing in the culture into quantifiable and measurable dimensions. The analyzed survey results were able to reveal, for example, whether officers in one kind of assignment had appreciably different opinions about a particular issue than officers working in other functions. The survey and focus groups plumbed the depths of the NYPD's culture, defining its dimensions and identifying strongly-held perceptions about the agency's problems. Because the process moved from qualitative impressions to empirical data and involved a huge pool of subjects, it provided a highly detailed and subtly

---

9 The term triangulation refers to the methodological practice of using several types of questions or several different research methods to explore the same issue. If we approach an issue from several angles and get generally consistent results, we can have greater confidence that our observations and conclusions are accurate and objective.

nuanced depiction of the landscape of attitudes and perceptions throughout the agency. About 7,000 of the completed surveys were returned and analyzed, and in conjunction with the focus groups they provided a rich source of statistically significant quantitative data (the margin of error at the 95% confidence level was 1.3%) on the policies and practices line officers and line supervisors believed were interfering with their effectiveness (NYPD, June 1994; Mollen, 1994).

As it did in the NYPD, this type of data can inform and shape a host of management decisions in agencies that survey their members. The survey can also tell executives whether anticipated policies are likely to be easily accepted and adopted by the rank and file, and this knowledge can help executives decide how to "market" its policies. If executives develop and propose a policy or program that is likely to meet with some resistance, executives know that a training and communication strategy will have to be undertaken to convince officers of its merits. On the other hand, if the survey results indicate it is likely to be easily accepted, less marketing is needed. The overall idea quite similar to that used by successful and pragmatic business leaders: the more accurate and detailed the information managers and executives have about their organization and its culture, about their product and how it is produced, and about the product's consumers, the more successful the executives and managers are likely to be.

Just as importantly, perhaps, the focus groups and survey can send a powerful message throughout the organization: the administration values the expert opinions expressed by the agency's members, and it is willing not only to listen to those opinions but to base policy on them. In the NYPD, the cultural diagnostic process brought the rank-and-file into the management's decision-making process in a way that had never taken place under previous administrations. The symbolism of the process was not lost on the rank-and-file, who suddenly recognized that the current administration valued them, their expertise, and their experience. The process was intrinsically rewarding because it showed appreciation for them and their opinions, and as a result they were more likely to work with management to achieve mutual goals.

The idea of using surveys and focus groups to measure the dimensions of the police culture and to gather information about the agency's problems was certainly not a new idea, and the cultural diagnostic did not represent the first time focus groups or surveys had been used in the NYPD. The author, for example, began conducting limited focus groups and surveys in the department as early as 1987. What differed, though, was both the scope of the cultural diagnostic process and the intensity with which these research tools were used. Police Commissioner Raymond Kelly was a proponent of focus groups as a management tool, and in 1993 he established a network of Policy Advisory Groups comprised of officers in practically every operational command in the agency to advise him on matters of concern to cops. The Policy Advisory groups met regularly in focus group sessions with Chief Michael Julian, a particularly astute and insightful young executive who would eventually become the department's Chief of Personnel, and from time to time they met with Commissioner Kelly himself. These interactive sessions served as an important communications interface between the agency's top executive and its rank-and-file. The ideas, perceptions and opinions of the rank-and-file were transmitted upward directly to the Police Commissioner, bypassing the usual lines of communication and the filters and barriers they impose, and the Commissioner was also able to directly communicate his message and his vision to line officers.

Because the Policy Advisory Group members were nominated by their peers, most already had a fairly high degree of referent and expert power in their units or work-groups; their "direct line" to the Police Commissioner served to enhance this power at the same time it provided the Commissioner with a cadre of credible liaison officers or spokespersons who could accurately communicate his message throughout the organization.

In the aftermath of the corruption scandal that gave rise to the Mollen Commission, in 1993 Kelly ordered that a series of focus groups be convened to develop a knowledge base about officers' attitudes toward corruption and misconduct. The focus groups involved several hundred officers and continued well into the Bratton administration. The information developed in that extensive series of focus groups shed a new light on officers' attitudes toward integrity issues, and the information was utilized to develop the policies, practices and structures of the revitalized Internal Affairs Bureau. The Mollen Commission also availed itself of the conclusions drawn from the focus group series, and the findings were cited in its 1994 Report to support many of its recommendations (Mollen, 1994; NYPD June 1994).

Importantly, the integrity focus groups revealed that the department's executives had been operating on dated assumptions about police officers' belief systems – no real research about NYPD officers' attitudes toward corruption had been conducted since the early 1970s, and the attitudes had changed significantly over the years. Before these focus groups, the agency's executive corps had never truly engaged the rank-and-file in an honest, meaningful, and sustained dialogue about integrity issues. For that matter, they had rarely engaged the rank and file in honest and meaningful dialogue about almost any important issue – it simply was not the prevailing management style to consult with cops. The focus group process and the reports they generated permitted policy-makers to make well-informed, cogent decisions about the most effective ways to combat corruption.

For example, prior to the focus groups it was uncertain how officers would react to the prospect of integrity tests and increased rates of random drug testing. When these corruption control practices were respectively introduced in the 1970s and 1980s, they encountered a great deal of resistance among officers (Montgomery, 1973; Henry, 1990). The focus groups revealed, though, that the vast majority of NYPD officers of the 1990s were generally *not* opposed to these practices: because the overwhelming majority are honest and do not use drugs, they believed they personally had nothing to lose so long as the tests were conducted fairly. In their opinion the goal of identifying and terminating corrupt or drug-abusing officers made the ideas worthwhile (Mollen, 1994; NYPD, June 1994). This example illustrates not only how faulty impressions can effect management decisions, but how enhanced communication and greater depth of knowledge permits executives to forge ahead to rapidly design and implement cogent and effective strategies. The NYPD commenced integrity testing and increased the number and rate of random drug tests with few cultural repercussions.

The fact that executives were misinformed about the prevailing attitudes among officers not only illustrates the value and importance of regularly measuring attitudes and opinions – taking the agency's temperature, so to speak – but it highlights the degree of estrangement and overall lack of communication that often characterize relations between an agency's executive decision-makers and its rank-and-file cops. This chasm again points to the existence of the "two cultures of policing" phenomena discussed in Chapter 2 and throughout this book.

The tremendous disparity between the attitudes, beliefs, aspirations and perspectives of street cops and those of management cops was perhaps nowhere as dramatically illustrated as in the results of the 1994 survey mentioned above. As subsequently described in the NYPD's Integrity Strategy document, at one point the survey presented officers with a list of twenty-two police functions or activities and asked them to select and rank the ten functions or activities they thought were the most important to the department's *managers and executives*. Later in the survey, they were presented with the same list of items and asked to select and rank the ten functions or activities *they personally* felt were most important to achieving the agency's mission.

The huge disparity between line officers' stated objectives and goals and those they perceived in the agency's managers and executives is perhaps nowhere as easily discerned as in the responses to these two survey items. Indeed, the disparity between the responses to these two items probably provides more insight into the most compelling problem the NYPD faced, as well as the scope and magnitude of that problem, than any other single piece of information developed in the focus group and survey process. As described in the NYPD's Integrity Strategy, the seven most frequent responses to these questions are as follows:

Officers consider most important to Department's management	Officers consider most important to themselves
1. Write tickets	1. Reduce crime, disorder and fear
2. Hold down overtime	2. Make gun arrests
3. Stay out of trouble	3. Provide police services to those requesting them
4. Respond quickly to radio calls	4. Gain public confidence in police integrity
5. Report police corruption	5. Arrest drug dealers
6. Treat supervisors with deference	6. Correct quality-of-life conditions
7. Reduce crime, disorder and fear	7. Stay out of trouble

The activities officers personally considered most important were much more closely aligned with the agency's stated mission and mandate – and with the core role of policing – than the activities they saw as important to management. The finding illuminates the prevailing sense among operational police officers that management lacked authenticity and legitimacy.

In conjunction with other data developed through this process, the huge disparity in the types of activities officers consider important to themselves versus those they consider important to the agency's executives and managers depicts an organizational culture of line officers dedicated to aggressively fighting crime but held in check by a real or perceived culture of managers motivated to avoid scandal and to maintain the status quo (NYPD, June 1995).

These data and the conclusions drawn from them, along with other survey data, also lend empirical support to Elizabeth Reuss-Ianni's (1983) observations about the ideological gulf separating the two cultures of policing: "street cops" and "management cops," each motivated and constrained by conflicting sets of belief systems, objectives and practices. On a more practical plane, these data also reflected the compelling need for the NYPD's executives to dispel, through communication and by effecting real change, the widespread perception that the agency was more concerned with maintaining the status quo and avoiding trouble and conflict than with reducing crime and improving the quality of life experienced by New Yorkers.

Commissioner Bratton, who was quite familiar with the NYPD's culture from his days as Chief of the Transit Authority Police Department, was well aware of this dynamic (Henry, 2000). His experience in revitalizing the Transit Police and the other agencies he headed in Boston also equipped him with the wherewithal to change the NYPD and its culture, and the survey data gave him and his staff a more precise and refined knowledge of the specific steps and strategies necessary to turn the NYPD around.

The agency's primary problem was clear: there was no lack of talented and dedicated officers who wanted to perform to the best of their considerable abilities, but the department's overbearing insistence upon strict conformity to the rules and regulations, coupled with management's overall timidity and lack of focus, created an atmosphere that blocked officers' creativity and suppressed their desire to do effective police work. The overbearing rules and blind insistence on tight managerial control systems that stifled the best impulses of police officers made it more difficult and more emotionally costly for cops to do good police work. The remnants of the Professional Model and decades of timid management ultimately created a cynical and demoralized agency in which the "street cop" culture was pitted against the "management cop culture." Unnecessarily restrictive rules and regulations prevented good cops from doing the job they sincerely aspired to do, and it should be no surprise that they strongly resented managers and executives for it.

Whether or not the perceptions were accurate (most evidence points to the fact that they generally were), the agency's structure, policies and command staff required a major overhaul. If the structure and policies were reconstructed in such a way as to support and encourage good police work (i.e., to support what was supposed to be the department's mission), attitudes would also change and at least some of the divisiveness would end. To change this perception and reality, an entirely new management team was needed. The new management team faced a daunting task, and team members would need all the organizational power they could muster. In selecting his management team, Bratton reached down into the agency to elevate assertive managers with a proven track record of achievement and expertise who could garner the respect and esteem of the rank-and-file.

To their great credit, the NYPD's new management team took these data and the harsh criticisms they implied to heart. They recognized the need to transform management and, rather than passing the buck or attempting to allay responsibility, they began to articulate an entirely new kind of message to the rank-and-file: the department's problems were primarily the problems of poor managers, not necessarily poor cops. Indeed, an attentive reading of the eight Crime Control and Quality of Life Strategy documents issued during the Bratton administration reveals how carefully the language was crafted to recognize management's overall shortcomings. Management's message, in the words of the cartoon character Pogo, was 'we have met the enemy, and he is us.'

In many respects this was an entirely new and unfamiliar kind of message to officers, and it got their attention and won their support for the kind of changes it proposed. Under previous administrations, when blame was to be fixed the executive corps always seemed to try to diffuse it and push it as far down the chain of command as possible – an exceedingly common dynamic in all sorts of organizations – but this administration seemed to be taking responsibility for the agency's problems and seemed to be making a commitment to eliminate those problems. This administration also seemed to be saying that it valued the opinions and the dedication of line officers, and seemed to mean it.

The administration tacitly admitted that executives had previously worked to suppress good cops' best instincts and to prevent them from putting their best effort into doing the kind of police work they initially signed up to do. The administration appreciated good assertive police work, encouraged reasonable and intelligent risk-taking, and had no tolerance for corrupt or brutal cops. Could it be that this administrations was actually 'on the level?'

Simply by taking responsibility, by honestly acknowledging the contributions of line officers, and by articulating the message that it trusted cops to do their jobs until individual officers proved that this trust was misplaced, the administration began to bridge the gulf between street cops and management cops. That gulf was further bridged as the executive corps took affirmative steps to re-configure the agency's shape and to systematically change the policies and procedures that determined how the agency went about its business.

An absolutely essential element in achieving the new administration's reforms was communicating the message. The new administration utilized every available avenue to foster communication throughout the agency. An interesting and informative "FYI" (For Your Information) newsletter was initiated, and rapid distribution meant new ideas could be broached or "floated" for discussion, short- and long-term policy objectives could be introduced, and noteworthy acts that exemplified the newly articulated mission could be clearly transmitted throughout the agency in a matter of days. The FYI newsletter also addressed current rumors, either confirming or refuting them. Bratton, a personable and engaging speaker, took the lead in personalizing the new management approach by regularly appearing in prefatory messages in the weekly training videos shown to operational cops, and he also maintained a high media profile in which he continually reinforced his message. The new administration articulated and communicated its vision and its reinvigorating message with an unprecedented intensity and clarity.

It is important to recognize that the process of surveying the agency and analyzing its problems can easily get bogged in details, and the tendency to over-analyze the data must be avoided. Given its public mandate to vigorously address crime and quality of life issues and to effect change rapidly, the Bratton administration did not wait for the surveys and focus groups to provide direction. On the contrary, the direction the agency had to pursue was clear, and the surveys and focus groups were used to refine rather than to determine the approach the NYPD would take. Bratton and his new management team had a good intuitive grasp of the department's problems, and they immediately seized the opportunity to move forward and gain momentum. The new management team had a basic blueprint for changing the agency, and the survey and focus groups helped them to tweak the process and make it even more effective.

Reengineering

Having obtained a highly descriptive, accurate and useful set of qualitative and quantitative data which illuminated many of the organization's problems (and which served as a baseline or benchmark against which the impact of its problem-solving initiatives could be measured), the NYPD's new management team began to formulate an array of strategies and tactics designed to address the issues. Further analysis of the focus group and survey data as well as other sources of information revealed that at least twelve problematic functional or operational areas existed within the agency, and that these areas required fundamental change if the performance barriers were to be overcome and crime was to be reduced. The department borrowed and utilized the corporate process of reengineering, a method or practice that has been used quite effectively in the private sector to improve organizational performance, to essentially redesign the agency from the ground up.

Typically, police agencies set about the process of change by charting a path of short term goals or milestones that eventually lead to the desired goal. Change is typically slow, mechanistic and incremental in police agencies, even when the need for rapid change is compelling. In the case of the NYPD, though, incremental change was simply insufficient. What was needed was a rapid, radical and immediate reordering of priorities and practices. The NYPD needed a complete reengineering.

Stated simply, reengineering is a process in which an organization looks at itself and essentially says, "if we were going to start over, from the ground up, to build an effective organization to achieve our goals, how would we design it?" Once that vision is defined, it becomes largely a matter of building the new structure, integrating it coherently and cohesively into other structures that are working effectively, and embracing the new practices. Reengineering also involves throwing out many of the obsolete ideas the agency previously embraced.

Michael Hammer describes the essence of reengineering in this way:

At the heart of reengineering is the notion of discontinuous thinking – of recognizing and breaking away from the outdated rules and fundamental assertions that underlie operations. Unless we change these rules, we are merely rearranging the deck chairs on the Titanic. We cannot achieve breakthroughs in performance by cutting fat or automating processes. Rather, we must challenge old assumptions and shed the rules that made the business underperform in the first place (Hammer, 1990, p. 107).

Hall, Rosenthal and Wade (1993) studied the reengineering processes used by over one hundred companies to reengineer, and found that two characteristics – breadth and depth – were critical if the process was to have a real impact on their operations. The overall process, they said, must be broadly defined in order to improve performance across the entire spectrum of the business' activities and functions, and the redesign must penetrate deeply to the organizational core to fundamentally change six crucial organizational elements. These crucial elements, which Hall, Rosenthal and Wade (1993, p. 119) call *depth levers*, are:

- roles and responsibilities;
- measurements and incentives;
- organizational structure;
- information technology,
- shared values; and
- skills.

They also found that corporate reengineering projects produced lasting change only when senior executives invested considerable quantities of their own time and energy to the process, in addition to extraordinary efforts by personnel at all levels of the organization. Without strong leadership from top management, the psychological and political disruptions that accompany such radical change can sabotage the project. Inevitably, managers and employees may feel that their turf, jobs and organizational equilibrium are under attack. But opposition to the new design can be overcome if top-level managers approach reengineering as a painful but necessary disruption of the *status quo* (Hall, Rosenthal and Wade, 1993, p. 119-20).

In order to achieve the kind of permanent change that is possible when the reengineering process has the committed support of executives, a broad compass and penetration to the six depth levers, the organization has to take a clean-slate approach. The new infrastructure must include long-term and

> comprehensive training and skill-development plans...
> performance measurement systems that track how well the
> organization is meeting its target and how employees should
> be rewarded based on those objectives; communication
> programs that help employees understand why and how their
> behavior must change; (Information Technology) develop-
> ment plans that capture the benefits of new technology at a
> minimal investment while, at the same time, long-term
> structural changes are being made; and, finally, pilots that
> test and refine the redesign as well as its implementation
> (Hall, Rosenthal and Wade, 1993, p. 123-24).

Reengineering the NYPD

After identifying the twelve functional areas or clusters of NYPD procedures and policies which required significant alteration, a dozen re-engineering teams were created and tasked with the responsibility to study and report on the problems and issues in each area. They were also tasked with recommending practicable changes within these organizational components. To ensure that reengineering did not degenerate into a top-down management process, the teams were comprised of ranking executives, field commanders, supervisors, line officers, and outside experts who volunteered their time and their expertise in managing large organizations. Thus the teams had tremendous depth, and they drew upon a wide range of expertise and experience in the selected areas as well as in the organization's management as a whole. Every member of every team was carefully chosen – not because of rank or title but because he or she was an acknowledged expert in his or her area.

Over the two-month period they met (from May to July 1994), each team gathered and assessed information from diverse sources (including additional focus groups, surveys, and other forms of input from the field) and used that information to develop practical remedies to the problems they faced.

Two months may seem an unusually short period, but time was of the essence if momentum was to be gained and sustained. It should also be recalled that many of those selected to participate in the reengineering process were, after years of frustration at organizational inertia and bureaucratic malaise, well aware of the type of changes necessary. This brief period also ensured that the tendency to analyze and study issues to death – a tendency that can potentially cripple progress – was avoided. Each team submitted a comprehensive report detailing the specific problems they identified, the methods they used to study the problems, the results they obtained and the recommendations they offered. Each team also presented their findings at Executive Staff briefings attended by the agency's top managers and executives.

The twelve problematic functional areas identified for reengineering were:

- Geographic versus Functional Organizational Structure;
- Building Community Partnerships;
- Precinct Organization;
- Supervisory Training;

- In-Service Training;
- Productivity;
- Paperwork Reduction;
- Integrity;
- Rewards and Career Paths;
- Discipline;
- Equipment and Uniforms; and
- Technology.

The twelve reports yielded over 600 specific recommendations, which were collated, further analyzed and shaped into a final Plan of Action during the summer of 1994. The recommendations had to be weighed, of course, against a variety of internal and external constraints including available budgets and collective bargaining agreements. Some of the recommendations were not solely within the power of the Police Commissioner to unilaterally implement, but rather they required the approval and endorsement of other entities outside the department, the allocation of funding, or the enactment of specific enabling legislation. The reengineering report on rewards and career paths, for example, set forth an array of rewards that might have been quite effective in motivating officers and might have been very well received by the rank-and-file, but the police unions generally opposed the idea of merit pay that rewarded some members and not others. In addition, the department's existing budget would probably not been able to bear the financial cost of these rewards. In other cases (and as might be expected), recommendations in one reengineering team report either conflicted with or essentially mirrored recommendations cited in another. The Plan of Action group addressed these conflicts in synthesizing its final report, which contained about 400 recommendations.

Certainly not every reengineering recommendation was implemented, but the vast majority were. As importantly, the kind of changes that were being made were clearly and repeatedly communicated through the organizational structure. Due to the unprecedented level of communication, officers at every level of the agency had a good grasp of what management was doing and why. Because they were so well informed and because their opinions were being asked about the directions and the activities the agency should pursue, they felt as if they were working with management to create change, not as if management was merely trying to change them.

By December 1994, the Plan of Action Committee co-chaired by Chief of Personnel Michael Julian and Assistant Chief Patrick Kelleher finalized its comprehensive Implementation Plan. The Plan of Action document became the blueprint for many of the organizational changes which followed, and a subsequent Plan of Action Committee was formed to monitor the implementation of each of the 400 or so recommendations. Although the individual impact of each recommendation is extremely difficult to measure, their cumulative and overall impact is quite clear: they re-shaped the organization into a leaner, more aggressive and ultimately more effective agency in terms of addressing its core mission to reduce crime and improve the quality of life enjoyed by the communities it serves.

The overall success of the NYPD's reengineering process and the lasting impact it has had – in terms of streamlining administrative structures and removing impediments to performance – illustrates how committed police managers can transform their agencies. At least part of the success, it seems, can be attributed to the fact that the NYPD process mirrored the kinds of reengineering processes used by successful corporations. As Hall, Rosenthal and Wade (1993, pp. 128-128) point out, there are five keys to a successful organizational reengineering and four ways to encourage reengineering's failure. The five keys to success are:

1. Set an aggressive reengineering performance target;
2. Commit 20% to 50% of the chief executive's time to the project;
3. Conduct a comprehensive review of customer needs, economic leverage points, and market trends;
4. Assign an additional senior executive to be responsible for implementation; and
5. Conduct a comprehensive pilot of the new design (p. 128).

The four ways to undermine the process are:

1. Assign average performers;
2. Measure only the plan;
3. Settle for the status quo; and
4. Overlook communication (p. 129).

The specific findings and recommendations offered by the twelve NYPD teams are almost beside the point, especially in light of what we know about cookie cutter and cargo cult management. Most of them addressed specific problems, issues and policy inconsistencies that were unique to the agency, while others were of the more universal and abiding type discussed throughout this book as symptomatic of American policing as a whole. What is more important than the specific findings and changes accomplished through reengineering is the process and method used to reach the findings and recommendations and the administration's commitment to implementing them. Both the goal and the result of reengineering the NYPD was to make the agency operate as one that supported and empowered line officers and precinct commanders rather than restrain them.

It is far beyond the scope of this chapter (indeed, beyond the scope of this book) to describe in detail all of the issues identified through the reengineering process and the steps the department took to remedy them. Nevertheless, some examples of the kind of changes instituted through the reengineering process are provided below. The examples were specifically chosen from the array of issues identified and addressed in reengineering because they reflect some of the major themes and police management problems we have mentioned in other chapters.

Geographic v. Functional Organizational Structure

The Geographic versus Functional Reengineering Committee was tasked with changing the fundamental structure of the agency to allow easier deployment of resources and personnel across organizational lines. The basic idea behind this objective was that the majority of police operations should be geographically-based – that grouping units according to their function, rather than according to the "turf" in which they operated, created unnecessary and often repetitive lines of supervision and communication. Precinct Detective Squads, for example, investigated crimes in each of the department's 76 precincts but they ultimately reported to the Chief of Detectives through a Detective Bureau command structure rather than through the Precinct Commander. Although relations with Precinct Commanders were generally positive, in a technical sense they were not under the command and control of ranking patrol personnel responsible for other police functions in that area. The same arrangement applied to the Narcotics District and Vice Enforcement District commands, which reported to the Chief of Organized Crime Control through their own organizational structure, and to most other specialized operational units.

The move to geographic policing facilitated the agency's overall decentralization and the empowerment of middle managers. The key to the success of the geographic model was that it placed some (but not all) specialized units and functions under the control of local commanders. Some specialized investigative and support units (like the Crime Scene Unit, the Emergency Services Unit, and various joint inter-agency task forces investigating bank robberies, terrorism and other specific types of crime) had less to do with everyday precinct operations and were more effectively utilized in a central structure. In some cases, decentralized specialty units were merged in order to enhance efficiency and reduce unnecessary duplication of effort. The Detective Bureau and Organized Crime Control Bureau, for example, each had a technical services unit devoted to electronic surveillance and other high-tech wizardry, and the units were united under a single command that would provide services to both bureaus. Greater efficiency and a significant cost reduction was also achieved by consolidating precinct-based K-9 teams within the Special Operations Division's Canine Team.

One outcome of the Committee's work was the creation of a pilot Strategic and Tactical Command (SATCOM) in Patrol Borough Brooklyn North. In the SATCOM model, precinct detectives, narcotics and vice detectives, and just about every other operational and investigative unit in the Patrol Borough (including precincts) were placed under the operational control of the SATCOM Brooklyn North Commander. With fewer organizational lines and barriers to cross, operations became more integrated and were under the direct control of the individual with responsibility for the "turf." The Borough Commander could be more immediately responsive to emerging crime and quality of life problems and could deploy a wider variety of resources without first obtaining the consent of other commanders. The new arrangement in SATCOM Brooklyn North facilitated the implementation of a major borough-wide initiative focusing on drug crime and had almost-immediate results: crime there dropped more precipitously in the following year than in any other borough.

Precinct Organization

The Reengineering Committee on Precinct Organization was an integral part of changing the accountability of Precinct Commanders as well as the discretion and latitude they enjoyed to deploy resources as they saw fit. As the senior problem-solvers in the command, Precinct Commanders were given greater authority to adapt the approaches they used to reduce crime and address quality of life issues. In contrast to the earlier administration's approach to Community Policing, for example, where the number of officers assigned to each precinct unit was determined by Headquarters according to a rigid and invariable formula, Precinct Commanders were given the discretion to decide how many officers to assign to the plainclothes Anti-Crime Unit, the Community Policing Unit, and the Street Narcotics Enforcement Unit. They could tailor the staffing of precinct units to fit the particular crime, quality of life and community issues within their geographic area of responsibility. They were also permitted to deploy units and officers in almost any way they saw fit – a marked contrast to earlier administrations where the duties and responsibilities of precinct specialty units were carefully defined and circumscribed. In order to make the Precinct Detective Squads outside SATCOM more responsive, Precinct Commanders also began to participate in the evaluation of Detective Squad commanders.

Another outcome was the delineation of a clear career path for Precinct Commanders. The agency's seventy-six precincts were designated as "A," "B," or "C" commands on the basis of their geographic size, levels of crime and disorder, and other indicators of the complexity and difficulty involved in managing them – not, as had once been the practice, solely on the basis of the precinct's crime rate. A Captain's first precinct command would generally be in a less-complex "C house" or precinct. If the Captain managed the command well, he or she might be promoted to Deputy Inspector and assigned to a "B" precinct, and ultimately to a difficult or highly complex "A" command as a full Inspector. In addition to creating a clear career track, this designation scheme also tends to ensure that rank (and the legitimate power it carries) is matched to the complexity of the management task the commander faces.

After reviewing the recommendations contained in the report of the Reengineering Committee on Precinct Organization and other committees, and in light of the historic difficulties that had plagued the "steady tours" concept since it was first implemented, the Plan of Action Committee called for the abolition of steady tours as the primary duty assignment schedule in patrol precincts. Instead, a so-called "scooter chart" – five day tours followed by two days off, followed by five evening tours with three days off – was phased in over the course of several months. The phase-in was aimed at minimizing disruption to police officers' established schedules. Almost all patrol personnel in the ranks of Police Officer, Sergeant and Lieutenant were placed in the scooter chart, with the midnight tour remaining a steady assignment tour. Precinct Commanders retained the discretion to assign other officers to steady tours for specialized functions or operations to address specific problems, and they were also given the discretion to create a steady "fourth platoon" tour that did not necessarily conform to the other tours. In some precincts, for example, the peak hours for crime and calls for service are between 6:00 P.M. and 2:00 A.M., so a fourth platoon assigned to work those hours might be established on a permanent basis.

We should also note that in addition to the operational difficulties the steady tours concept involved, the focus groups and survey revealed that many officers (particularly tenured cops) were dissatisfied with the arrangement. Although they enjoyed the regularity of a predictable schedule,

their immediate work group was rather small and they missed the camaraderie and variety of working different hours with a larger pool of cops. They
felt that steady tours fractionalized each precinct and led to the formation of
tour-based cliques: cops who worked the day tour were not well acquainted
with those who worked the four-to-twelve or midnight shift, for example, and
the same was true for each of the other platoons. This led to insularity and
conflict.

Productivity

Among the various issues considered by this committee was staffing at
large parades, demonstrations and other public events. Due to New York
City's size and the number of parades and demonstrations that take place
there, these public events often represent a significant drain on police
department resources – it is not unusual to have crowds approaching or ex-
ceeding one million people attending larger events and demonstrations. The
annual Saint Patrick's Day Parade, for example, frequently draws a crowd of
about one half million spectators, requiring deployment of at least 5,000
police officers along the parade route's several miles. The vast majority of
these officers are removed from precinct patrol or other operational duties for
the day.

One way the NYPD enhanced its productivity and reduced the drain on
scarce personnel resources was to dramatically alter the way it planned for
these events and deployed personnel at them. The simple expedient of using
plastic mesh barriers instead of wooden sawhorse barriers, for example,
dramatically reduced the number of officers needed to man crowd control
barriers and permitted the number of officers assigned to events to be pared
down. The agency also began to use Police Academy recruits and Police
Cadets for directing traffic and many other non-enforcement duties at parades
and large public events – a good training tool – and it implemented more
efficient scheduling processes to reduce overtime expense. Officer who were
on modified assignment or restricted duty status and could not, for a variety
of reasons, perform enforcement duties, were also utilized for many
assignments that full-duty officers performed. The overall result was that
more officers remained on duty in patrol precincts, where they were needed.

Some of the most important streamlining actions recommended by the
Committee and incorporated into the Plan of Action concerned the overall
flattening of the organizational structure through the elimination of redundant
overhead commands. It is unnecessary for the purposes of this chapter to
describe all of the specific units and functions affected, since the issues and

problems involved were specific to the NYPD. It should suffice to say that many centralized units were dispersed to Patrol Boroughs, in some cases with concomitant reductions in staffing. As a general rule, the dispersal of these units also consolidated their administrative tasks, which were rather easily absorbed by the new overhead commands.

Integrity

The recommendations of the Integrity Reengineering Committee effected dramatic changes in the way the NYPD approached the problems of corruption and misconduct. In the aftermath of the scandal that gave rise to the Mollen Commission, the Internal Affairs Division was radically transformed and its resources were significantly expanded. To reflect the importance of the internal investigative function and its increased size, the Internal Affairs Division was re-designated the Internal Affairs Bureau. The Bureau remained under the central command of a Deputy Commissioner for Internal Investigations (later, a Bureau Chief), but geographic-based investigative groups were established to investigate corruption complaints in each Patrol Borough. The changes went well beyond the structural and cosmetic, though.

Among the Integrity Reengineering Team's more important results was a redefinition of the kinds of misconduct Internal Affairs would investigate. The integrity focus groups had determined that Internal Affairs was widely regarded as aggressively pursuing so-called "white socks" misconduct – such minor offenses as wearing white socks in uniform – while it ignored or bungled more important criminal corruption investigations. This practice engendered significant resentment among the rank-and-file, and it drastically limited the Bureau's corruption-fighting capability: many cops had little faith in Internal Affairs' ability to conduct fair, complete and thorough investigations that would either identify the corrupt or exonerate the innocent.

The department clearly established that the central Internal Affairs Bureau would only investigate allegations of very serious misconduct and criminal activity and that less-serious misconduct complaints would be investigated by Inspections Units under the Patrol Borough structure. Moreover, the Committee clearly defined and distinguished between corruption and misconduct and between the investigative responsibilities of the various entities. Allegations of low-level misconduct and disciplinary infractions (i.e., "white socks" complaints) were simply referred to the Precinct Commander for his or her action. In keeping with the theme of empowerment, local commanders were given broad discretion in how they investigated the complaints and what kind of discipline they imposed, and they were not required to report back to IAB with the results of their investigation.

Another important element in reengineering the Internal Affairs function was developing a cadre of qualified and experienced investigators. Under previous administrations, the department neglected the Internal Affairs function and the quality of its investigators deteriorated. To generate a pool of top-notch investigators and to dilute some of the negative images most officers had of Internal Affairs personnel, a new policy changed the investigative career track and established a review board to screen applicants for all supervisory investigative positions in the agency.

As in many other agencies, an Internal Affairs assignment had fairly low status – the preferred investigative assignment was in the Detective Bureau or the Organized Crime Control Bureau's Narcotics or Vice squads. Under the new policy all Sergeants and Lieutenants who desired a transfer to any investigative supervisory assignment were interviewed by a screening board comprised of ranking officers from Internal Affairs, the Detective Bureau and the Organized Crime Control Bureau. Internal Affairs had first choice among the applicants: if the applicant turned down the offer from Internal Affairs, he or she was precluded from transferring to other units. If the applicant joined Internal Affairs, he or she served a two-year "hitch" and upon its completion was given preference for assignment in either of the other two investigative entities.

The new policy ameliorated much of the resistance and residual stigma that accompanied an Internal Affairs assignment, and brought the best and most productive investigative supervisors into the Bureau. The two year "hitch" in IAB was seen as a means to a highly desirable end, and few officers could fault another for following the stipulated career path. Confidence in the Internal Affairs function was bolstered because cops knew it had some of the agency's most expert investigators, and because cops trusted them to conduct fair, impartial and thorough investigations.

A new "policy of inclusion" was also instituted, and Internal Affairs began to inform Precinct Commanders of most internal investigations taking place in their area of responsibility. This policy was implemented in recognition of at least two realities: it was patently unfair to hold commanders accountable for corruption and serious misconduct if Internal Affairs kept them in the dark about it, and Precinct Commanders can often be of great assistance to internal investigators. If the commanders were doing their jobs properly, they should be able to provide Internal Affairs with

insights and information about officers who were the subject of an investigation. The basic premise behind the philosophy of inclusion was that if the
agency could not trust its carefully selected commanders with confidential
information about corruption and misconduct, no one could be trusted
(Henry, 2000).

The "policy of inclusion" and the notion that integrity is every member
of the agency's business was also extended by the creation of an unrecorded
"hotline" number officers could call to anonymously report information
concerning corruption or serious misconduct. Previously, the agency demanded that officers report corruption – failure to report corruption is itself
deemed an act of corruption or serious misconduct – but it had also required
that officers identify themselves. The focus groups on integrity pointed up
the fact that many officers remained distrustful of internal investigators and
were reluctant to identify themselves, reducing the amount and quality of
information available to Internal Affairs. The new policy was eminently
practical – it allowed officers who provided information anonymously to be
assigned a confidential code number the caller could subsequently use, if
necessary, to prove that he or she had fulfilled the responsibility to report
corruption.

In line with the findings of the focus groups on integrity, the agency also
increased the number and percentage of officers who are randomly tested for
illegal drugs each year, and in addition to urinalysis it implemented radio-
immunassay testing of hair. Procedures and criteria used in "for cause" drug
tests were also simplified. It should be noted that despite a dramatic increase
in the number and (because of the hair testing) the accuracy of its random
drug testing program, the percentage of positive drug "hits" in the department
declined substantially.

Disciplinary System

The Disciplinary Reengineering Committee introduced sweeping
changes to the agency's disciplinary process – both in terms of its structure
and its philosophy. Most notably, perhaps, it greatly decentralized the
disciplinary process by giving commanders a greater role in adjudicating
complaints. Under the previous system, the more serious disciplinary
offenses were adjudicated in administrative hearings conducted by the
Department Advocate in the agency's Trial Room, while less serious
offenses were handled by local commanders as Command Disciplines. The
old Command Discipline procedure enumerated specific schedules of

offenses and the disciplinary sanctions a commander had to impose if the officer was judged guilty. Commanders had little discretion – the rigid penalty schedules took little account of the circumstances under which the offense occurred, and the officer's previous disciplinary record or performance over the course of his or her career had little bearing on the penalty assessed. A Command Discipline carrying a set penalty was mandatory if an officer lost his or her shield or identification card, for example. A high-performing officer with an exemplary record and no disciplinary history whose shield or ID was taken from his or her home in a burglary, for example, faced almost the identical penalty as an officer with a poor history who lost the shield or ID through negligence. Under the new system, the commander could decide whether or not a Command Discipline was appropriate under the circumstances, and the range of penalties available to the commander were broadened.

The newly reengineered system significantly expanded the scope of the disciplinary offenses a commander could adjudicate and significantly expanded his or her discretion in determining appropriate penalties. Precinct Commanders were also permitted to delegate the responsibility for adjudicating minor disciplinary matters to their Executive Officers. Overall, and in conjunction with other changes in the disciplinary system, the new decentralized process expanded commanders' discretion and disciplinary power, permitting them to administer discipline more fairly and to use the disciplinary process more effectively as a management tool.

In-Service Training

As Hall, Rosenthal and Wade (1993) note, a reengineering process that is not supported by adequate long-term training is likely to fail, and this fact made the role of the In-Service Training Reengineering Committee (as well as the Supervisory Training committee) particularly important. Although the team did not develop specific training protocols to advance the department's goals, it examined the entire in-service training system and brought about significant changes in it.

Recognizing that operational police officers saw a distinct need for more and better tactical training, for example, the department instituted a TOP COPS tactical training course whose instructors were experienced operational officers temporarily assigned as instructors. The course consisted of various tactical role play scenarios that changed frequently and closely reflected the realities of the street. The fact that experienced officers were carefully chosen from patrol precincts to instruct their peers again recognized the value the administration placed on its "top cops," and it raised their status considerably. The training was also more effective and better received by precinct personnel because the instructors were "real cops" rather than Police Academy staff.

The department also got serious about the testing it conducted at the conclusion of various courses. In many cases, officers could attend an in-service training session or training course and, if an examination was given, fail it but still receive credit for taking the course. This absurdity was changed, and meaningful testing was implemented. Situations like these had done little to promote the idea that the department took training seriously, and indeed a fairly common perception was that many sessions or courses were given simply to abate the department's liability in the event that a lawsuit resulted from an officer's actions.

The In-Service Training Committee took a hard look at the training function and recommended a host of other improvements and enhancements to improve the entire training function. The final Plan of Action Committee called for increasing the Police Academy's academic and testing standards for recruit training, and the minimum passing grade for the recruit training course was raised from a 70 percent overall average to a 75 percent average, with a minimum grade of 70 percent in each subject. For the first time in many years, the percentage of recruits separated from the agency's employment for academic performance began to increase. The Plan of Action committee also recognized the clear and present need to increase the level of maturity and life experience among entry-level police officers, and the minimum qualifications for appointment as a police officer were revised – a police recruit had to be at least 22 years of age, with either 60 college credits completed or an honorable discharge from military service.

Supervisory Training

Supervisory training and supervisory leadership skills were among the areas of deficiency noted in the focus groups and survey process, and the Supervisory Training Reengineering Committee was tasked with developing a training model that would prepare supervisors with the leadership skills they needed. The Committee's perspective on supervisory training was, given the history of training in the agency, somewhat unique: it recognized that training should do more than simply provide the supervisor with the skills and knowledge necessary to perform the duties of a particular rank. What had long been missing in the training function was a sense of generativity – the idea that management is responsible to prepare the individual for the particular rank or position he or she holds as well as for future ranks and positions he or she might hold.

The idea of generativity recognizes that policing is much more than meeting a series of short-term goals, and that the abilities and qualities of supervisory and middle-management personnel today has a direct impact upon the quality and viability of tomorrow's executive corps. For a host of reasons, this sense of concern and regard for the agency's future, as well as for those who would eventually rise to the top of the organization, had been conspicuously absent. There was little concern among police executives to ensure that their successors had the requisite experience and the ability to function adequately in a more responsible role. This lack of generativity was not attributable solely to the need to protect one's own position in a threatening career environment: it appears to have been as significant among those executives whose positions were assured as among those whose positions were tenuous. Nevertheless, the absence of a sense of generativity and the long-standing failure to adequately prepare most supervisors for the managerial and executive positions they might ultimately achieve was in itself a reason for the agency's historically indifferent management style and its adherence to rigid structures.

One outcome of the Supervisory Training Committee's efforts was a complete reworking of the Basic Management Orientation Course provided to newly-promoted Sergeants as well as the Lieutenants Orientation Course. The new courses were geared toward equipping Sergeants and Lieutenants with the skills and the attitudes that make good leaders, with less emphasis on nuts-and-bolts paperwork and other procedural duties earlier courses had stressed. For a variety of reasons, both of these courses had been regarded with derision by those who had taken them over the years. As was the case in many in-service training courses, one could sit through the course but fail the examination without the slightest career repercussions. Of all the department's courses, BMOC was foremost in fostering the view that the department cared little about its supervisors or in adequately preparing them for their new responsibilities (see, for example, Henry and Grennan, 1989).

These courses were not only renamed and entirely revised in terms of content as the result of the Committee's recommendations, but they were made *pre*-promotional, and the actual promotion to the new rank became incumbent upon completing the course and receiving a passing grade. Because the earlier courses were *post*-promotional, the trainees had less reason to pay attention to the course material. The new curricula was leadership-oriented, and to an unprecedented extent it incorporated role-playing, interactive scenarios and other attitude-shaping exercises.

Rewards and Career Path

The Rewards and Career Path team's recommendations were geared toward establishing the primacy of patrol in the agency's overall operations by rewarding high performers who chose to stay in the patrol function. This committee was given one of the more difficult tasks, since the agency had struggled for years to find ways to bestow adequate rewards to outstanding patrol officers. As in many or most police agencies, and notwithstanding the enduring rhetoric that "patrol is the backbone of the department," few officers wanted to stay on patrol if the opportunity for an investigative or plainclothes assignment was available to them. Others sought assignment to specialized, administrative or support functions where they could more fully utilize special talents or abilities. Finally, the police unions in New York City have historically opposed giving performance rewards to some officers but not to others – in their view, rewards should be distributed equally among all the union's members.

Although a number of financial reward systems the team recommended were ultimately not implemented due to conflicts with collective bargaining arrangements, budget problems and difficulties in convincing union leaders of the reward system's merits, additional points for future promotional examinations were awarded to officers performing patrol duties.

Building Partnerships with the Community

As the result of the Reengineering Committee on Building Partnerships with the Community, a variety of organizational and structural changes were instituted in the agency's Community Affairs function. These included an expansion of the Police Youth Academy, a summer program designed to familiarize young men and women with police work and to encourage some to consider a career in policing.

Paperwork for Information and Accountability

The Paperwork for Information and Accountability Team faced a daunting task: eliminate the kind of unnecessary paperwork upon which bureaucracies thrive. Their initial research into the size and scope of the agency's paperwork problems revealed that the department utilized almost

750 official forms and about 1,350 unofficial forms, and that precincts submitted an average of fifty required written reports to overhead commands each month. On average, Precinct Commanders received from seven hundred to 1,000 written communications each year, and about half of them required a written response. The department budgeted about $3.5 million per year for in-house printing expenses, a cost which did not include the hardware and printing machinery involved. The overall cost of the paperwork burden, including the time spent in preparing, reviewing, and filing forms and reports, is almost beyond computation. The Committee also determined that precinct commands were required to maintain almost one hundred separate logs that recorded a host of information. The ostensible goal of all this paperwork, which had accumulated to a seemingly unbearable burden over the years, was to ensure accountability. The problem, though, was that much of the data these forms and logs collected were never analyzed in any meaningful way or used for any real purpose.

An example of how this paperwork problem impacted the agency can be glimpsed in the case of precinct logs. In addition to a main blotter or Command Log maintained at the Precinct Desk, each precinct was required to maintain a separate Dormitory Log (recording when officers stayed overnight in the precinct dormitory for a court appearance, for example), an Arrest Log (that captured arrest-related information identical to that recorded in the Command Log), a Bullet Resistant Vest Utilization Log (used on the rare occasion that an officer needed to borrow a vest from the precinct's supply), a Subway Token Log (subway tokens might be provided when an on-duty civilian employee was required to report to another command), and about ninety other bound logbooks. Despite the fact that many logs were rarely used, they had to be regularly inspected – a Desk Officer's nightmare – so a Log Log was used to ensure accountability of the log inspections. The true absurdity, though, was the fact that the information contained in all these logs was almost never used for any real purpose: they were a matter of accountability for accountability's sake. Ultimately, many of these logs were eliminated, and if the entries in them are still required they are simply put in the main Command Log.

The Paperwork Reduction Committee examined many of Department forms, eliminating some outright and condensing others. They changed procedures that easily permitted commands to develop and use their own data collection forms, and they launched several long-term programs to continually chip away at paperwork. The committee significantly reduced the department's paperwork burden, establishing systems that, with due management diligence and attention over time, will continue to reduce paperwork without sacrificing accountability.

Equipment and Uniforms

One unique element of the Equipment and Uniforms reengineering committee's work was that it asked officers' opinions about how to improve the uniforms they wore and the equipment they used. This was a marked departure from the agency's previous practice, when such decisions were made by a Uniform Committee comprised largely of ranking officers. The uniform and equipment reengineering process can truly be traced to the focus groups and survey process, when officers were asked a variety of questions about these issues. Among the results of the committee's work was a dramatic change in the patrol uniform: in line with the suggestions obtained from the survey results, the department abandoned its light blue uniform shirt and adopted a navy blue shirt. For many years, a prevailing media image of the New York City cop was one of a slovenly, overweight doughnut-muncher. Although many cops were personally offended by that image, in other cases it fit: some cops *were* slovenly, overweight doughnut-munchers with little pride in their appearance, but the uniform itself did little to project an aura of authority and efficiency.

At first glance, this change in the color of the uniform shirt may seem simplistic, but it had an important symbolic content that fit well with other agency goals. Beyond the fact that the new uniform's appearance was preferred to the old by those who wore it, and beyond the fact that the tailored dark blue shirt did project an entirely different and more assertive image than the powder blue "Mr. Goodwrench" shirts, the department was concurrently planning a merger with the Transit Police Department and the Housing Authority Police Department. Although the uniforms worn by members of those agencies were essentially similar to the NYPD uniform, the merger of the three forces required a new and unified image. Each of the agencies had a history of proud traditions, and members of each were proud of the uniforms they wore, but a clear need existed to establish new and unifying symbol systems to represent both the merger and the new approach to policing that this administration was taking. If the agency had simply required the Transit and Housing Police officers to wear the NYPD uniform after the mergers, it might subtly betray a lack of appreciation for the officers and for the agency traditions their uniform symbolized. Instead, a new and different uniform permitted members of all three agencies to symbolically break with the past and proceed into the future without threatening or diminishing the symbols of the past.

Another important symbol was the inclusion of hash marks on the uniform's sleeves to denote the officer's years of service – again, a symbol of the importance the agency placed on experience as well as the status other officers afforded to experienced cops. Hash marks representing tenure and experience had an additional but quite subtle significance. For many cops, worn-out uniform items (especially unpolished holsters and leather gear) were an informal symbol or credential of their street experience. While rookies' uniforms were noticeably newer and had more of a spit-and-polish look, some veterans took a kind of pride in the fact that their uniform and equipment looked a little shabby or showed signs of long use. Worn-out leather and other uniform items were incompatible with the image the NYPD was trying to portray, but some executives on the new management team were astute enough to recognize the importance of symbols as well as the fact that one should never take away an important symbol without providing another. In this regard, hash marks were a positive and viable substitute for worn leather and ratty uniforms. They conveyed status, experience and length of service without compromising appearance.

Taken collectively, the subtle uniform changes had a powerful impact on the agency's public image as well as individual officers' self-image. The new look also coincided with the NYPD's one hundred fiftieth anniversary, and a series of events celebrating the history of policing in New York City took place. Like the new uniform, these celebrations tied the officers psychologically to the past as well as to the future: it subtly conveyed that every member of the department was part of something much larger and much more important than the individual.

Technology

The work of the Technology Reengineering committee had impact on many other reengineering recommendations. One of the most significant problems facing the agency was an aging and often outmoded technology infrastructure that limited the department's capacity to respond effectively to the challenges of contemporary policing. To a great extent, the paperwork reduction initiatives, the crime data collection and analysis functions, and the productivity of individual officers depended upon developing and implementing new or emerging technology systems.

In order to reduce much of the paperwork burden associated with recording crime and arrest data, the committee endorsed the continued implementation of a computerized On-Line Complaint System. The OLCS, once fully operational and fully networked, would tremendously reduce the number of hard-copy crime complaints produced in the agency. Rather than a five-part snap-out form whose copies were distributed to various files and units, a computerized database would provide rapid access to the information currently recorded in the paper-based system. The system would also permit greater simplicity and accuracy in crime analysis functions, including the kind of automated electronic pin-mapping used in Compstat, and it would also eventually integrate vehicle accident reports.

The department began installing Mobile Data Terminals (MDTs) in every marked radio car, making arrest warrant, drivers license and vehicle registration information directly available to officers in the field to assist them in enforcement activities. The MDTs also cut down on a great deal of radio traffic, since requests for information could be conducted via the terminals. The department consolidated its Communications Division and Management Information Systems Division into a single Office of Technology and Systems Development, and in doing so it reduced the organizational boundaries between these closely inter-related functions and achieved greater efficiency in both.

Reengineering Summary

The reengineering process made a tremendous impact on the NYPD. Most importantly, reengineering lifted many of the barriers to effectiveness that had long frustrated good cops and prevented them from doing their best work. Reengineering streamlined or eliminated a host of administrative activities that unnecessarily consumed time and other vital resources that could have been better applied toward achieving the agency's primary mission, and it refocused members' attention on the agency's most important goals and objectives. Because the reengineering process utilized the knowledge and expertise of officers throughout the department, the blueprints for change that resulted were both practical and practicable. The fact that the individual committees had great depth in terms of members' ranks and assignments was also a powerful motivator: it rewarded and gave status to experts at every level of the organization. Reengineering scraped away many of the organizational barnacles that had accreted on the NYPD's superstructure, permitting it to move more rapidly and smoothly toward its mission.

Crime Control Strategies

To fully invigorate the NYPD and maximize its latent potential for reducing crime and improving the quality of life in New York City, it was not enough to simply conduct an organizational diagnosis that identified the agency's problems or to address those problems by reengineering the agency's policies, structures and administrative practices. Those efforts were certainly essential, but they could not in themselves guarantee results. They could not ensure that the NYPD's members would take a unified, coherent and comprehensive approach to the city's enduring crime and quality of life problems. In addition to cultural diagnosis and organizational reengineering, the NYPD needed a variety of fairly specific and highly effective crime control and quality of life improvement strategies that would provide cops, supervisors and commanders with the kind of tactics and strategies they needed to address these problems.

The NYPD therefore developed a series of ten Crime Control and Quality of Life Strategies, each focusing on a specific type of crime or quality of life issue. Each strategy was developed using the same general process that supported the cultural diagnosis and reengineering initiatives, and each strategy was communicated and disseminated through the department in the form of descriptive policy documents. Two types of strategy document were prepared – a small, pocket-sized outline booklet summarizing the major points of the larger document was distributed to the rank-and-file and their supervisors, and the comprehensive full-sized strategy document was distributed to middle managers and executives.

Each strategy document began by analyzing the size and scope of the problem, the current policies, strategies and tactical approaches used to address the problem, and the reasons the current policy was less than fully effective. The documents then outlined a broad strategy to remedy the problem, including the policy changes management would institute and the kind of overall strategies and specific tactics enforcement personnel should follow. The strategy documents were carefully crafted to be flexible and adaptable to the particular kinds of problems precinct commanders might face in their unique commands – the documents and the strategies they described had, in other words, the kind of "simultaneous loose-tight properties' Peters and Waterman (1982) described.

By remaining flexible and adaptable, the strategies avoided the pitfalls of too-rigid direction and control that had plagued the implementation of Community Policing several years earlier. For the most part the strategies did not mandate that the precinct commander utilize a particular set of tactics, nor did they mandate a specific number of officers be assigned to a given enforcement function. Rather, the documents outlined a comprehensive array of tactics and strategies that had proven effective in the past, allowing Precinct Commanders to tailor them to the uniquely individual problems the command faced.

Many or most of the tactics and strategies that comprised the documents had been used by effective cops for years, while other equally effective tactics and strategies had long been officially proscribed by the department. In terms of the tactics and practices good cops had always followed, it was clear that these cops had the answers management needed but never requested: management had never before engaged in a systematic effort to identify, analyze, write-up and disseminate "best practice" guidelines based on practical police experience. The proscriptions that were lifted included those on uniformed officers making narcotics or vice arrests. In both cases, the department's executives communicated that they had respect for their cops' skills and expertise as well as trust in their capacity to enforce the law without falling prey to the temptations of petty corruption. In both cases, the recognition was highly rewarding.

The first strategy document, for example, was entitled **Getting Guns off the Streets of New York**, and it was developed in consultation with expert cops who made an unusually high number of quality arrests for illegal gun possession. Some cops just seem to have a knack or innate ability to spot concealed weapons, but the truth of the matter is that they use learnable observation skills other cops do not use. They actively look for suspicious bulges in waistbands, for example, and they perceive the subtle differences in gait and the other behavioral cues that often indicate someone is carrying a concealed weapon. The *ad hoc* team that put the strategy document together identified and interviewed cops who made an inordinate number of high quality "gun collars," asking them about the specific skills they used as well as their ideas about improving the department's overall approach to gun crime. Their insights, observations and suggestions were incorporated into department policy, into the strategy document, and into the training programs developed to support the strategy. The same basic process – quite similar to the above-described process that informed the cultural diagnosis and reengineering – was used to develop each of the eight Crime Control and Quality of Life Strategies implemented during the Bratton administration.

The NYPD's ten Crime Control and Quality of Life Strategies are very briefly described below. Once again, the realities of cookie cutter management and cargo cult management make it both unnecessary and undesirable to describe each strategy in great depth. The details and specifics of each strategy were tailored to meet the specific needs of the NYPD, and the details are far less important than the process by which they were developed and implemented. The strategies are:

1. ***Getting Guns off the Streets of New York***. After exploring why the agency's earlier efforts to apprehend and jail gun criminals were largely unsuccessful, this strategy outlined the kind of training officers would receive as well as the resources that would be devoted to investigating and identifying gun traffickers and those using guns in the commission of violent crimes.

2. ***Curbing Youth Violence in the Schools and on the Streets*** required that every Precinct Commander develop individualized School Safety Plans for every public school within the precinct, increased the number of Youth Officers assigned to precincts, and focused patrol resources on locating truants and returning them to school. Although many cops had known for years of the relationship between truancy and delinquency – a huge percentage of daytime robberies and other crimes in New York City were known to be committed by truants – the agency never had a comprehensive plan to deal with truancy.

3. ***Driving Drug Dealers Out of New York*** authorized uniformed officers to get back into the business of enforcing narcotics laws. In addition, the strategy reallocated personnel and resources to better investigate the operations of mid-level and high-level drug dealers, and it revised agency policies and structures to facilitate the civil forfeiture of drug dealers' assets.

4. ***Breaking the Cycle of Domestic Violence*** created designated precinct-based teams of patrol officers and investigators who utilize databases to track complaints of domestic violence and intervene proactively. The strategy emphasizes coordinated investigations, the arrest of abusers, and the provision of appropriate social services resources for victims.

5. ***Reclaiming the Public Spaces of New York City*** was based in the Broken Windows principle that untended disorder becomes criminogenic, and it contained specific tactics to address more than a dozen types of disorder. The strategy emphasized the use of

various public order statutes to restore a sense or civility to public spaces, including statutes prohibiting unreasonable noise, squeegee window washers, and other public nuisances. The sound meters necessary to enforce the unreasonable noise statute, for example, were for the first time purchased and distributed to precincts under this strategy.

6. ***Reducing Auto-Related Crime in New York*** dramatically expanded the role precinct officers, detectives and commanders played in reducing auto theft. For the first time, Precinct Commanders were empowered to authorize their personnel to conduct stings operations at "chop shops" that dismantle stolen cars, and precinct detectives were required to interview and debrief every person arrested for auto theft to gather intelligence information and seek linkages to auto theft rings as well as unsolved crimes. Training was significantly expanded and the capacity of Auto Crime Division's expert investigators to respond to field requests was greatly increased. The number of patrol cars with Mobile Digital Terminals capable of accessing license, vehicle registration and stolen auto databases was also increased.

7. ***Rooting Out Corruption; Building Organizational Integrity in the New York City Police Department*** articulated one of the agency's most important and powerful policies against corruption: the policy of inclusion. While in previous administrations the NYPD had resisted providing commanders with any knowledge of corruption complaints arising from their commands, the policy of inclusion sought to empower commanders by giving them this information and by utilizing their knowledge and sources of information to combat corruption. The strategy outlined the steps taken to restructure the Internal Affairs Bureau and described, in very frank terms, the failures of the previous structural model. The strategy also outlined the department's plans to implement integrity testing and other tactics designed to prevent or detect corruption and serious misconduct.

8. ***Reclaiming the Roads of New York*** dealt with the issue of traffic congestion and the quality of life problems it creates for New Yorkers. A Traffic Control Division was established under this strategy to manage various traffic enforcement functions, to quickly gather and analyze information about traffic accidents and other

emerging situations that can snarl traffic, and to quickly deploy personnel to address traffic conditions.

9. The ***Courtesy, Professionalism, and Respect*** strategy, developed and implemented during Commissioner Howard Safir's tenure after Police Commissioner Bratton left office, was intended to ensure positive relations between the police and the community. This strategy attempted to set performance goals to measure how well the principles of courtesy, professionalism and respect were practiced in the NYPD, to introduce new training, and to educate the public about the positive aspects of policing.

10. The NYPD's final Crime Control strategy, ***Bringing Fugitives to Justice***, was intended to facilitate the apprehension of individuals who have been arrested or summonsed but failed to appear in court. This strategy restructured the fugitive apprehension function by strengthening patrol officers' and investigators' capacity to track down warrant violators.

Summary and Conclusion

The transformative processes outlined in this chapter played an integral role in the NYPD's ability to reduce crime and improve the quality of life in New York City because they fundamentally reshaped the department's organizational structure, its policies and programs, and the strategic approaches it took to solve problems. These transformations were absolutely essential to the success of Compstat and to the evolution of the Compstat paradigm. As we saw in earlier chapters, a great deal of the NYPD's organizational dysfunction resulted from inadequate, half-hearted or antiquated structures, policies and practices. These structures, policies and practices were the vestiges of outmoded ways of looking at police work, and they severely hampered the organization and its members from maximizing their potential. They were often not in synch with the realities of the agency or of contemporary urban policing. In order for the new paradigm and the more contemporary view of policing it espouses to flourish, these outdated organizational artifacts had to be swept out in order that new structures, policies and practices that reflected Compstat principles could be instituted.

The process of organizational diagnosis – of assessing the current state of the police agency and its culture, identifying problems and developing solutions – is the basis for redesigning the agency's structures and policies as well as for developing new strategic practices that support the Compstat paradigm. One thing that strategy development, the organizational diagnostic, and the reengineering process have in common is the emphasis they place on identifying and mobilizing police expertise. Another thing they have in common is the way they collect information: in all three cases executives begin with a general idea of the goals or results they hope to achieve and develop those ideas as new information comes to light. They proceed from a set of generic observations based on qualitative impressions of an issue, moving steadily toward more refined and empirical quantitative data that can be used to generate policy. They consult with experts inside (and often outside) the department, gather a range of opinions and points of view, weigh those opinions and points of view against known facts, and ask more refined and cogent questions. Because executives ultimately obtain "hard" and objective information, they can be confident that decisions based on that information are sound.

Recommended Readings

The following books and articles describe the art of focus group and / or survey research in very practical terms, providing a host of suggestions and pointers to maximize the potential of these methodologies.

Babbie, Earl **Survey Research Methods (Second Edition)**, Belmont, CA: Wadsworth, 1990.

Greenbaum, Thomas L. **The Handbook for Focus Group Research (Revised and Expanded Edition)**, New York: Lexington Books, 1993.

Jick, Todd D. "Mixing Qualitative and Quantitative Methods: Triangulation in Action," in John van Maanen (Ed.), **Qualitative Methodology**, Newbury Park, CA: Sage, 1983. pp. 135-48.

Kreuger, Richard A. **Focus Groups: A Practical Guide for Applied Research**, Newbury Park, CA: Sage (*Qualitative Research Methods Series*), 1993.

Morgan, David L. **Focus Groups as Qualitative Research**, Newbury Park, CA: Sage *(Qualitative Research Methods Series)*, 1988.

The following books and articles provide a basic understanding of the reengineering process, and the principles they set forth are fairly easily transferred to the reengineering of police agencies.

Champy, James **Reengineering Management: The Mandate for New Leadership**, New York: HarperBusiness, 1996.

Hall, Gene, Jim Rosenthal and Judy Wade "How to Make Reengineering Really Work," *Harvard Business Review*, (November-December 1993), pp. 119-121.

Hammer, Michael "Reengineering Work: Don't Automate, Obliterate," *Harvard Business Review*, (July-August 1990), pp. 104-112.

Hammer, Michael and James Champy **Reengineering the Corporation: A Manifesto for Business Revolution**, New York: HarperBusiness, 1996.

Questions for Debate or Discussion

1. In describing the cultural diagnostic process, it was noted that it may be worthwhile for the police agency to retain an expert consultant with experience in transforming police departments to conduct the diagnostic, to report his or her findings to the chief executive, and to guide the overall project to completion. At the same time, an argument could be made that the agency should utilize the skills and abilities of its own members to conduct this analysis and see the project to fruition. In your opinion, do most police agencies have personnel qualified to conduct this type of research? If not, what should these agencies be doing to ensure they develop this capacity?

2. As we described in this chapter, there are a number of great opportunities to be realized if the police chief executive decides to perform a cultural diagnostic and / or to reengineering the department. There are also a number of substantial organizational and / or career risks involved. What are those risks, and are they worth taking? What steps can the chief executive take to maximize the potential opportunities and limit the potential risks?

3. The processes described in this chapter require that the police chief executive be receptive to the critiques and criticisms of the agency's members. Are police chief executives generally receptive to criticism from within the department? Can the processes succeed if the chief is not receptive?

4. We briefly noted that during the Bratton administration the NYPD used small teams of experts drawn from throughout the agency to research and develop the Crime Control Strategies. As was the case with the reengineering teams, these small work groups had the great breadth and depth they needed to bring about results, and they drew upon the expertise of experienced cops to construct viable structures, policies and practices. In many ways the work done by these short-lived project task forces reflect principles Peters and Waterman (1982) found in the nation's best-run private-sector companies. What other principles identified by Peters and Waterman (1982) and discussed in Chapter 5 are applicable to the processes the NYPD used?

5. Throughout this book we've discussed the five bases of power that operate within the police organization – coercive, legitimate, expert,

referent and reward power. How does conducting a cultural diagnostic enhance a police chief's organizational power in each of these spheres, almost regardless of the diagnostic's findings and outcome?

6. We briefly mentioned the NYPD's "policy of inclusion" as it pertains to internal investigations, noting that precinct and unit commanders were informed about corruption and misconduct allegations and investigations taking place within their area of responsibility. This new policy contrasts sharply with earlier policies that seemed based in a distrust of police commanders' capacity to participate in corruption investigations without compromising them. What are the logical limits of a "policy of inclusion" with regard to corruption and misconduct? Should such a policy be expanded to include police supervisors (such as sergeants and lieutenants) below command rank? How about those in the police officer and detective ranks?

7. In this chapter we very briefly reviewed some of the issues addressed by the NYPD's Reenginering teams and a few of the solutions they prescribed. Given your knowledge of the many organizational and cultural problems the agency faced at the beginning of the Bratton administration, examine the list of twelve reengineering committees. Does the list seem sufficiently comprehensive? Are there any significant problems that do not seem to fall within an area addressed by a reengineering committee? What are those problems?

NOTES

Chapter 7
The Compstat Process:
Communication, Information,
Accountability and Results

s we have seen in earlier chapters, prior to the advent of the Compstat process and the Compstat meetings in early 1994 the NYPD faced a host of organizational problems that inhibited it from maximizing the potential of its personnel. Some of these problems were common to many or most American police departments and some were particular to the agency itself, but in either case the NYPD was not operating anywhere near its maximum efficiency. A rigid bureaucratic structure inhibited free and open communication, there were deep divides between management cops and street cops, and many in the department – perhaps especially those in positions of legitimate power and authority – seemed unconvinced that police could really make much of a difference in terms of reducing crime. There was insufficient political will or political support for aggressively fighting crime, and the agency was beset by an organizational malaise.

As importantly, the statistics and other data we've reviewed also confirm that the NYPD was doing a rather poor job at controlling and/or reducing crime and improving the quality of life enjoyed by those who visited, lived or worked in New York City. Crime began to decline and quality of life began to improve as the NYPD started to embrace and practice the Broken Windows theory during Raymond Kelly's tenure as Police Commissioner, and we will never know how successful those methods and strategies would have been. It is certain, though, that Compstat dramatically accelerated New York City's crime decline and quality of life improvement, that it radically reshaped communication and communication systems within the department, and that it introduced a much-needed affirmation that police can and do make a difference.

The crime problems facing the NYPD were not primarily the result of a lack of interest or commitment on the part of the rank and file or even among supervisors and middle managers, but rather they emanated from the organizational tone set by an executive and middle management cadre that was largely unwilling to take risks or trust cops to do their jobs fully and effectively. Concerns about corruption, misconduct and the potential for scandal, along with other vestiges of the Professional Model's emphasis on centralized bureaucratic control and centralized decision-making, created a management mindset that to a large extent devalued even prudent risk-taking. For the same reasons, the prevailing mindset was also quite wary of expanding the quantity or quality of discretion available to middle managers, supervisors and rank-and-file cops. The subtle message this mindset communicated was that cops, supervisors and middle managers couldn't be trusted to use their judgement and discretion wisely or honestly.

As we've seen, there certainly were quite a few disaffected cops, supervisors and middle managers within the agency, but the ultimate responsibility for their indifference and for the fact that so many had become indifferent rested with the agency's leadership. Over an extended period of time, leadership had failed to assume its responsibility to prevent or address these issues, essentially granting them license to flourish. Attempts to implement a particular vision of Community Policing were hampered by the same set of organizational factors. The NYPD was to a large extent an agency adrift, and by 1994 significant and rapid changes were necessary if the department was to live up to its potential, carry out its mission, and fulfill its responsibility to the public.

In this chapter, we will see how the Compstat process and the Compstat meetings evolved, and how they address many of the organizational shortcomings we identified earlier. We will see how the Compstat process facilitates the interactions taking place between executives and middle managers at Compstat meetings, how these meetings create new lines of communication that disseminate critical crime intelligence and quality of life information, how they serve as forums for the development and implementation of effective strategies, how they support the rapid deployment of personnel and resources, and how they allow for relentless follow-up to ensure that crime and quality of life problems are actually solved. Compstat meetings also serve as a forum in which effective crime control strategies (along with the individuals who champion them) can be identified, empowered, and promoted.

The meetings lead to the attainment of the agency's goals primarily by enhancing management accountability and management discretion, by devolving discretion from the executive level to middle management, by sharing effective crime-fighting strategies throughout the agency, by equipping executives and middle managers with the information they need to make critical decisions, and by fostering transparency in managerial and executive decision-making. Ultimately this enhanced accountability, expanded discretion and more accurate crime intelligence percolated through the department to the rank-and-file. By understanding how the Compstat process and Compstat meetings operate, we can glimpse the entire Compstat paradigm in microcosm, and we can see how it improves performance at every level of police work.

Compstat also involves technology, and in this chapter we'll see how that technology was developed and implemented, as well as how it currently functions to support the entire process. Technology is an important part of Compstat, but it is by no means the only part or even the most important part; rather, technology is interwoven in the fabric of both the Compstat process and the Compstat meetings in order to make the whole enterprise operate more effectively. Without Compstat meetings and the kind of interactions they foster, the technology would be of little value; by the same token, without Compstat technology the meetings would be an almost-futile exercise since participants would have little to talk about. Many casual observers believe, erroneously, that Compstat involves very expensive, highly complex cutting-edge technology. It doesn't. As we'll see, the Compstat technology used today by the NYPD and some other agencies evolved from some very basic technology that was, even by 1994 standards, already antiquated. Even with that antiquated technology, Compstat had an immediate impact on crime and quality of life, on communications patterns, and on the NYPD's mindset.

1994's Mandate for Change

Before we begin looking at Compstat's evolution, it is important to once again emphasize the need for rapid and dramatic organizational change at the beginning of the William Bratton's tenure as Police Commissioner. Rudolph Giuliani was elected with the mandate to control crime, and that mandate necessitated a host of changes to the NYPD's organization, its structure, its culture and its style of management. Time was of the essence, and although newly-appointed Police Commission Bratton and the management team he assembled certainly appreciated the value of employee surveys, reengineering teams and the strategy development process – indeed, the new team would soon come to use these tools to great advantage – they did not have the immediate luxury of conducting the kind of rigorous and detailed organizational studies previous commissioners had. They could not, for example, begin the administration (as Lee Brown had) by conducting a thorough and

exhaustive needs analysis before effecting substantial positive change. They
had to act quickly and decisively to seize and exploit the opportunities available to them at that time. Surveys and studies were important, and they would
certainly be conducted within a few months, but a more pressing issue was
that of taking the initiative to immediately show results by reducing crime.

Fortunately, Bratton knew a great deal about the NYPD and its problems
from his time as Chief of the Transit Authority Police Department (which
was, until it merged with the NYPD in 1995, a separate agency), and he had
a great deal of experience reinvigorating the Transit Police as well as the
various police departments he headed in Boston (Bratton, 1999). Bratton was
also fortunate that within the NYPD he had a substantial cadre of
experienced and insightful potential leaders and a great many experts within
the ranks to assist him in transforming the department. A significant
impediment to progress, though, was that these assertive and aggressive
leaders were not necessarily at the ranks that would afford them the
legitimate power to fundamentally shape the agency.

One of Bratton's first acts as Police Commissioner was to reconfigure the
agency's top management. He requested (and received) the undated resignations of the department's top chiefs, replacing five of the six 'superchiefs'
within a few weeks of taking office (Bratton, 1999; Silverman, 1998; Buntin,
1999). Many other executives, recognizing the direction the new administration was taking and the difficulties they would face, opted to retire. These
retirements and vacancies facilitated the movement of Bratton's team into the
appointive upper ranks. The new management team members he selected for
the top positions were highly experienced experts, they were decisive
managers, they were enthusiastic and optimistic about the agency's capacity
to substantially reduce crime, and to a large extent they shared Bratton's
vision for a reinvigorated NYPD. Bratton quickly crafted a new management
coalition of energetic, experienced, well educated and highly competent
leaders.

One of the key questions Bratton asked when interviewing candidates for
these top executive positions was their estimate of how substantially crime
could be reduced in New York City within the coming year. Those who
responded with pessimistic estimates were not seriously considered for
promotion. Bratton's rationale was that if the executives did not believe they
could substantially reduce crime, they almost certainly wouldn't (Bratton,
1999). In many cases, the executives he promoted were 'jumped' two or three
ranks – an almost unheard-of practice in the tradition-bound NYPD – and
this reinforced the message that performance and initiative, rather than

tenure, would be the prime determinant of promotional opportunities in the new administration.

In the new administration's first year, almost three quarters of the agency's precinct commanders were transferred, promoted or reassigned to positions better suited to their particular strengths and skills. This proportion of transfers, promotions and reassignments exceeded the number of executives moved by Commissioner Patrick Murphy in his first year in office, but in both cases the house-cleaning was essential to the agency's reform. Many of those transferred or reassigned to less prominent commands recognized the difficulties they would face in achieving promotion or further advancement and opted to retire, but no one was demoted or coerced into retirement. This movement in the upper ranks was undertaken in order to rapidly replace underachievers with more motivated and aggressive leaders who proved themselves successful at achieving the agency's goals. No commanding officer was removed simply because crime went up in his or her precinct or because the crime declines they achieved were insufficient; they were replaced when they repeatedly displayed poor leadership or repeatedly failed in their responsibility to develop and implement effective new tactics and strategies. As we'll see, the Compstat meetings were (and continue to be) an important venue for identifying middle managers for promotion or lateral reassignment.

The management coalition Bratton assembled, though, was not comprised entirely of high-ranking officers – he reached down into the middle-management and supervisory ranks as well as the rank-and-file to identify experts and include them in his inner circle of advisors. Unlike the managers and executives above the civil service rank of captain, who could be promoted (or demoted) at the Police Commissioner's discretion, the constraints of the civil service system meant that Bratton could not unilaterally promote expert police officers, detectives, sergeants or lieutenants to positions of higher rank that afforded greater legitimate power. Instead, by bringing these experts into his inner circle as informal advisors, he made them *de facto* members of the management team, often rewarding them with the status and salary increment of a "special assignment" designation.[10] The fact that they worked closely with the Police Commissioner and/or his top executives, like the fact that their opinions and expertise were highly valued, gave these individuals a quantity of organizational power well beyond their legitimate rank. As important, though, was the fact that Bratton listened to what these and other officers had to say, and their experience and expertise informed his management decisions.

Bratton's penchant for engaging cops and supervisors in informal dialogue was an important and effective element of his management style as well as a very pragmatic source of organizational power. During his days as the Transit Police Chief, Bratton developed a reputation for riding the subways alone at night (if Transit cops patrolled the subways alone, why should their Chief require security and an entourage?) and stopping at various stations to buy cops a cup of coffee and chat with them about police work and about organizational problems or issues. He continued this practice during late-night walks around the city as Police Commissioner. With the exception of Theodore Roosevelt (who was in many ways a role model for Bratton), no other Police Commissioner gained as powerful a reputation for walking the streets (or riding under them) to interact with cops and discuss their perceptions and experiences, much less to value their opinions. For the most part cops genuinely liked and respected Bratton because, unlike Commissioners who have maintained an austere and distant – even disdainful – demeanor (some have appeared to be positively contemptuous of cops), his image was that of a very approachable 'regular guy' who loved police work as much as they did. As importantly, he showed them the genuine respect of

---

10 The NYPD's rigid civil service regulations permit the Police Commissioner to promote a limited number of Police Officers to the rank of Detective Specialist, and a limited number of supervisors in the ranks below captain as 'special assignment' or, for investigators, 'detective squad commanders.' The designation carries an additional salary stipend and considerable status. Of the approximately 5,000 sergeants in the NYPD, for example, about 100 hold the 'special assignment' or 'detective squad commander' designation. Previously, these promotions were heavily influenced by internal (and in some cases, external) politics, but Bratton's insistence that only top performers be selected deflected a great deal of cynicism about the role of politics in his administration. The three individuals who had perhaps the greatest hands-on role in developing Compstat's technology – Sergeants John Yohe and Gene Whyte and Lieutenant Bill Gorta – were among the first group of 'special assignment' designees in the new administration.

listening to what they had to say, asking their opinions and advice, and often following that advice.[11] This individualized contact enhanced Bratton's referent power in several ways: it humanized him and personalized his administration, it illuminate his grasp of issues that were of concern to cops, and it demonstrated the value the administration placed on cops' expertise and experience. These contacts also permitted Bratton to directly articulate his message of organizational change to members of his target audience and get their feedback.

It is somewhat paradoxical that many of the individuals who emerged to play important roles in the NYPD's transformation were so enthusiastic about change simply because they felt so confined under earlier administrations. These individuals had retained an idealistic vision of what the NYPD could realistically become, they knew that they and the agency had the capacity to make a tremendous difference, and they were extremely frustrated by the lethargy that characterized many earlier administrations. Given the opportunities and the motivation Bratton provided them, they rose to the occasion, rediscovered their idealism, and found tremendous personal and professional fulfillment in creating a new NYPD – they were able to do the job they always believed they could, but had never been permitted to do. This sense of renewed commitment was not limited to members of the new management team, though: men and women of every rank and position recaptured their energy, initiative and willingness to engage in the effort to reduce crime and improve quality of life. One of the policies the new administration articulated, for example, was that uniformed patrol officers would play a much more significant role in narcotics and vice enforcement; they were no longer prohibited from aggressively pursuing street-corner drug dealers.

The sense of idealism and revitalized commitment was refreshing and contagious, and others quickly got on board with the new administration's agenda for change. This idealism and sense of renewed commitment to police

---

11   The overall intent of this informal and unstructured practice seems virtually identical to the intent behind Raymond Kelly's more organized process of focus groups and formal advisory groups: furnish the agency's top decision-maker with useful information about the attitudes, ideas and opinions circulating within the street cop culture. Bratton's informal process reinforced his referent power through face-to-face and one-on-one contact with a fairly limited number of cops, but the information he obtained in this way did not necessarily represent the full range of opinions; Kelly's group meetings with representatives of the rank-and-file could not capture the same intimacy of personal contact, but his structured process gave him access to a much broader and empirically more valid cross-section of ideas and information.

work spread fairly quickly throughout the agency, and it soon reached a kind of critical mass or tipping point at which the enthusiasm began to resemble an epidemic. More and more, cops at all levels of the organization began to buy in to the agenda for change and to fight crime more aggressively, effectively aligning themselves with the new management coalition.

One of the most important challenges Bratton and his new management team faced was communicating the administration's goals and expectations. They needed to immediately and clearly communicate that the new administration would reduce crime and improve quality of life through accountability, professional responsibility, and strategic utilization of resources. In both his actions and his rhetoric, Bratton communicated this message to the public and to members of the agency. Press accounts of the administration's early days resonate with the message and with the public pledge that the NYPD would commit itself to reducing crime and restoring order to the city, and in his public statements Bratton convincingly articulated the notion that the department's members would aggressively fight crime "block by block, house by house" if necessary. Bratton was a highly skilled, charismatic and polished communicator who used the media as well as a highly focused internal communications initiative to put out this message, and his pledge rang true with the public as well as with members of the agency. Although this message served to focus attention on the new agenda for change, and although it helped to motivate and recapture the latent idealism of many cops, it could never in itself be sufficient to bring about the agency's reinvigoration or achieve results in terms of substantive crime reduction or quality of life improvement.

The new management coalition needed effective support systems that would give it the wherewithal to fundamentally impact crime and disorder. It needed, first and foremost, a system or process that would provide every member of the agency with the kind of timely and accurate intelligence information about when, where, and ultimately how crimes were taking place. It needed a mechanism to facilitate the rapid deployment of personnel and other resources to fight crime when and where it was taking place, and it needed highly effective crime control strategies and tactics. It needed a process that would allow members of the agency to monitor their effectiveness against crime on a continuing basis and to relentlessly follow-up to ensure that crime and quality of life problems were actually solved rather than merely suppressed or displaced. Finally, it needed a system or process that would enhance discretion at the same time it maximized accountability, disseminating essential management information quickly throughout the organization. If the NYPD was to effectively engage the problems of crime and disorder, it needed the kind of surveillance system or radar the vastly outnumbered RAF used so effectively in the Battle of Britain. It needed Compstat.

Enter Compstat: Evolution of a Revolution

The highly visible Compstat meetings and the behind-the-scenes Compstat process were major management breakthroughs that have certainly revolutionized policing in New York and other jurisdictions where they have been applied, but like the Compstat paradigm itself they did not result from a sudden discovery or invention. For some time there had existed an unsettling sense throughout the agency that the prevailing style of management was faulty and that new methods and strategies were needed to address the problems of crime and disorder, but despite the energetic vision the new administration brought to the NYPD, no one woke up one morning with a clear vision of Compstat and a plan to bring it to fruition. Rather, the Compstat revolution was the cumulative sum of numerous small incremental revolutions that took place at the margins or boundaries of the existing management paradigm prior to or during the early days of the Bratton administration. An array of forces and factors came together at a particular time and place, ultimately leading to an erosion and ultimately a collapse of the prevailing management paradigm. Essential to this collapse was the recognition that the prevailing paradigm was no longer adequate to address the needs, problems and issues the NYPD faced.

The Compstat process and the Compstat meetings developed and took shape fairly quickly under the new regime, however, as experts and visionaries within the department saw the possibilities these small advances entailed, collaborated with each other to maximize their potentials, and pushed harder against the borders of earlier management theory and practice. The insurgents, the iconoclasts and the frustrated within the NYPD began to have a voice. The new management coalition listened to these voices and incorporated their collective wisdom into policy and practice.

One of the new administration's top priorities was to develop a systematic mechanism that would provide the Police Commissioner and the executive staff with the timely and accurate crime data they needed. Bratton, a student of successful corporate management systems, had long recognized the importance of timely and accurate information in the decision-making process. As Chief of the Transit Police, he began work each day with a briefing on all the significant crimes taking place within the rapid transit system over the previous twenty-four hours as well as any other developments that could conceivably require his attention, and he wanted an analogous system to operate within the NYPD (Bratton, 1999). As a student of business management, Bratton knew that no corporate executive could run a successful business or fulfill his or her responsibility to shareholders, to customers or to employees without accurate and up-to-date sales and productivity figures. In the rapidly changing business environment of a competitive marketplace, no corporation could survive if the chief executive lacked real-time data that would allow him or her to identify and quickly respond to changing business conditions and trends. As importantly, Bratton knew that shareholders, customers and employees would never tolerate a private-sector chief executive who failed to meet their expectations for running a successful business.

Jack Maple, the iconoclastic former Transit Police Detective Lieutenant who Bratton appointed Deputy Commissioner of Crime Control Strategies for his expertise in making police operations more effective and efficient, was a student of military history and he understood that every successful military campaign throughout history had been successful in part because the winning general had more timely and more accurate intelligence about the enemy's strength, movements and intentions than the enemy had about his. Jack Maple knew that successful crime-fighting is based on knowing who the criminals are and when, where and how they operate. Without this kind of timely and accurate crime intelligence, and without the ability to identify and respond to emerging crime trends, no police agency can hope to fulfill its responsibilities to society, to crime victims, or to its officers and employees. In a rapidly changing social and political environment, no agency can successfully reduce crime and improve quality of life if the chief executive lacks real-time data that allows him or her to identify and quickly respond to changing crime conditions and trends.

Perhaps more than any other figure in the NYPD's recent history, Jack Maple embodied the management principle of identifying experts and elevating them to positions of legitimate power. As a detective supervisor in the Transit Police, Maple began collecting detailed information about crimes taking place within the subway system and symbolically depicting this crime intelligence on large schematic maps. These "charts of the future," as Maple called them, consisted of twenty- to thirty-foot long sheets of paper he hung in the corridors outside his detective squad office. By analyzing the charts' symbols, he could discern when, where and what kind of crime was taking place at every station and on every subway line throughout the rapid transit system.

Maple used this basic crime intelligence system – a more sophisticated version of the pin maps police agencies have long used to depict the ecology and spatial distribution of crime – in conjunction with effective strategies and tactics. If the pattern analysis of the A train, for example, showed that robbery gangs (called 'wolfpacks') were victimizing sleepy businessmen returning home after midnight following lengthy business dinners, Maple's Decoy Squad would be deployed on A trains around midnight. The decoy cops would be dressed in suits while the back-ups dressed in other disguises, ready to move as soon as the wolfpacks struck the 'victim.' Similarly, if elderly women were especially prone to purse snatchings in the afternoon in another part of the system, Maples detectives would be there with undercover cops dressed as old ladies (Daly, 1985; Maple and Mitchell, 1999).

The 'bad guys,' as Maple called them, were usually apprehended at the scene so there were few legal problems associated with identification and few of the problems associated with complainants and witnesses who failed to show up in court. Further, Maple's detectives always followed up these arrests by debriefing the perpetrators in order to identify accomplices and to obtain information leading to the solution of other crimes. While this should have been standard operating procedure in all detective squads, the reality was that it was not. Policies in the Transit Police as well as the NYPD permitted cases to be closed 'by arrest' if only one of the perpetrators was arrested; identifying and arresting accomplices who had not been apprehended at the scene was good police work, but it did nothing to enhance the agency's case closure rate. It did, however, create additional paperwork for bosses and often led to additional overtime for the detectives. To say the least, Maple's methods frequently put him in conflict with his superiors (Maple and Mitchell, 1999).

Once again, we see that many of the principles and practices of good policing that came to be part of Compstat had long been in the repertoire of effective cops; they were simply not the agency norm in the Transit Police or the NYPD. Indeed, the fact that so many of Jack Maple's ideas and practices were not typical made them appear unorthodox, and this also put him in conflict with higher-ups in the Transit Police. Maple's methods – both those described above and many others he implemented – were certainly effective, but within a conservatively managed and fairly risk-averse agency that valued uniformity and order over innovation and performance, he and his unorthodox methods were viewed as troublesome. Maple, though, was undeterred: he continued to push the boundaries.

Maple came to Bratton's attention shortly after Bratton became Chief of the Transit Police, when he sent Bratton a memo outlining his plan for fighting crime in the rapid transit system. Bratton, recognizing Maple's genius and the tremendous value of his vision, brought Lieutenant Maple into his inner circle and relied upon him for ideas and strategies. Maple's nuts-and-bolts knowledge of the Transit Police – especially its problems and frailties – made him an invaluable part of the agency's reinvigoration as well as the tremendous declines in crime the agency achieved in the subways. Maple retired and joined Bratton when Bratton left the Transit Police to become Boston's Police Commissioner, and he was named Deputy Commissioner of Crime Control Strategies when Bratton returned to New York as Police Commissioner in 1994.

During the new administration's first few days, Maple began making the rounds at One Police Plaza (the NYPD's headquarters) asking all the units that collected crime statistics – there were several – how quickly they could compile the kind of accurate and fairly detailed crime figures he, Bratton and other executives needed to manage the agency and reduce crime in New York City. Without belaboring the point, none of the units Maple visited – including the Office of Management Analysis and Planning's Crime Analysis Section, which was responsible for capturing and reporting the FBI Uniform Crime Report statistics – could give him the kind of data he needed in a reasonable time frame. In every unit he visited, Maple heard essentially the same excuses: this is the way we've always done it; we can't release the numbers until they've been verified and double-checked; our data collection system was never designed for producing crime statistics quickly. Crime Analysis Section, for example, argued that with the current system it would take at least six months to produce accurate counts for the seven major FBI Index crimes, and they could not link individual crimes to the time, date and location each offense occurred. The statistics the unit could produce were, in terms of management's crime-fighting needs, virtually useless. Just as no military commander worth his salt would conceive of launching a campaign if his latest intelligence on the opposing force's strength, location and intentions was six months old, the NYPD's commanders were essentially precluded from mounting an effective offensive against crime.

Finally, Maple walked into the Office of the Chief of Patrol and encountered Lieutenant Bill Gorta and Sergeant John Yohe, who ran the Chief's computer system. Both were experienced street cops, both were self-taught 'computer guys,' both were exceptionally bright and well educated, both were 'out of the box' thinkers, and both were fairly new to Headquarters. Like so many others in the department, Bill Gorta and John

Yohe felt the tremendous disappointment of the dedicated street cop who wants to make even more of a difference. Both were frustrated, iconoclastic insurgents with a host of good ideas and a latent idealism about what policing could and should be, and both were waiting for their voices to be heard.

Gorta and Yohe were intrigued when Maple explained what he was looking for, but they were not equipped to help. There was no mechanism in place to report crime data in the real-time format Maple needed, and their unit had never been tasked with collecting crime statistics. Maple went on his way, but fortunately, serendipity intervened to ensure the birth of Compstat.

Serendipity, or the unanticipated discovery of some new phenomena or the occurrence of an unexpected beneficial event, often plays a role in the emergence of new paradigms. Often, two seemingly disparate events take place at or around the same time and the connection between the two leads to the discovery of something new, or the events set into motion a chain of other events that leads to some sort of discovery. Serendipity can't be planned for or anticipated, and managers certainly shouldn't rely on the hope that some fortunate event will come along and bring tremendous benefits, but good managers recognize the good fortune of serendipity and use it to their advantage.

In the case of Compstat, the serendipitous event was a blizzard that closed the Long Island Railroad and left John Yohe stranded overnight at the office. As he sat in the empty office thinking about the intriguing problem Maple had spoken of earlier in the day, the inkling of a solution began to take shape. Yohe began flowcharting, writing and pecking away at his computer terminal. After several hours, exhausted, Yohe closed the rudimentary database file he had created in the antiquated software program the NYPD used. Because his computer was an old DOS-based 386 system (yes, the NYPD's Office of the Chief of Patrol still used DOS-based systems and applications in 1994), file names were limited to eight characters and a file extension. Yohe closed the file, naming it COMPSTAT – an abbreviation for Compare Statistics. Yohe did not know it at that time, but the rudimentary program he developed and casually named late one night in an empty office during a blizzard would eventually revolutionize American policing.

The primitive design of flowcharts and a database that John Yohe sketched out remains the basis of the Compstat process today. It has certainly been improved upon, and somewhat more sophisticated hardware and software systems are now used to collect, process and analyze the basic crime statistics, but that early system reflected the essential elements of any Compstat technology system. It permitted management to rapidly collect accurate crime statistics and to analyze the data in a useful and meaningful way so that informed decisions could be made about the deployment of resources and the type of strategies that would be most effective in reducing crime. It also permitted management to quickly identify fluctuations and changes in crime statistics, to rapidly assess the effectiveness of these decisions and strategies, and to monitor crime conditions to ensure that the strategies work. If the strategies employed to reduce robberies in a particular area or sector are effective, reported crimes in that area will decline, and the comparison of crime statistics from week to week, month to month and year to year will therefore indicate how well the strategy is working.

The Basic Compstat Technology Package: Collecting the Data

The primary data component of Compstat is a database that contains daily crime counts, by precinct, for each of the seven major crimes (murder, rape, robbery, felonious assault, burglary, grand larceny and grand larceny-auto) that comprise the FBI's UCR Index.[12] In addition, the database contains daily counts of such statistics as the number of shooting incidents and the number of shooting victims (again, by precinct) as well as daily summons tallies. The databases the NYPD and other Compstat-driven agencies use are not proprietary software developed entirely by in-house programmers or special consultants. Instead, they are off-the-shelf software packages any agency can purchase and use. Similarly, Compstat technology does not require highly sophisticated hardware. A couple of basic stand-alone PCS or a small networked LAN system can generally run even the largest agency's Compstat initiative.

Prior to the advent of Compstat, the data referred to above was simply not available on anywhere near a real-time basis. Under the crime and arrest reporting system that existed at that time, officers prepared handwritten

---

12   It should be noted that the NYPD's Compstat system does not use the FBI's UCR definitions *per se*, but rather each offense's associated definition from the New York State Penal Law. Because the New York State Penal Law applies in New York City, and because any criminal charges that will ultimately be filed will be based on the Penal Law, NYPD crime complaint reports (known as UF 61s) capture the Penal Law offense that was violated. Although there are slight differences between the UCR definitions and the NYSPL definitions of the seven major crimes, the differences are negligible. For example, in practice the UCR offense of 'Murder and Non-Negligent Manslaughter' conforms very closely to the NYSPL definition of "Murder," and the UCR's "Vehicle Theft" is practically the same as the NYSPL category of Grand Larceny – Auto.

'scratch copies' of crime complaint reports (known as 'UF61s') that were typed by precinct clerical personnel on snap-out forms and reviewed by supervisors. The snap-out forms were broken down at the precinct and distributed, with one copy forwarded to headquarters for manual keypunch entry into a mainframe computer database. Importantly, not every item listed on the complaint report was entered into the database – the precise address or location of the crime, for example, was not entered. Eventually, the resulting mainframe dataset would be 'cleaned' (that is, the data would be audited for keypunch errors and necessary revisions to the original crime classification would be added) and eventually it would be statistically analyzed.

This attenuated process led to the delivery of statistical reports and analyses up to several months after the crimes had occurred, making them virtually useless as deployment and strategy tools. As we've noted, the structure of the database and the limited number of data fields it contained allowed only a very rudimentary statistical analysis – essentially, it permitted managers to know how many offenses occurred within a given precinct during a given month, but managers could not tell the precise time, date or location these offenses were occurring. They certainly could not use the months-old analyses to predict or respond to immediate crime trends.

To make Compstat effective – to utilize real-time data – required a new approach. The development of a new crime data collection system would be a difficult and time consuming process, and the NYPD's new management team did not have the luxury of time. Rather than wait for state-of-the-art computers and a multi-million dollar online information system, Maple, Yohe, Gorta and the others involved in the initial effort utilized existing resources in new ways. Faced with the fact that most precincts were still equipped with nothing more than bare-boned 386 DOS-based PCS (as well as the fairly limited computer skills many cops had), a simple database pro-gram was written that would allow each command to enter a daily tally of the seven major crimes and corresponding arrests occurring within its jurisdiction. During Compstat's first year, each precinct was also directed to research its paper files to determine the number of Index offenses (and arrests for those offenses) reported during the previous year's corresponding period, thus creating a dataset that would enable immediate comparison of the current period's crime and arrest figures to those of the same period in the previous year. Each week, every precinct copied the current week's data onto a floppy disk and delivered it to the Compstat Unit at Headquarters, where the individual precinct files were up-loaded and appended to a city-wide database. In just a few weeks, sufficient data was collected to begin printing a simple report comparing the weekly, monthly and year-to-date changes in crime rates on a precinct-by-precinct and a city-wide basis.

The numbers included in the Compstat report were, and still are, preliminary counts. The Compstat figures were never intended to replace the UCR figures, which undergo a lengthy review to ensure their accuracy. Rather, the Compstat figures were intended to give managers and executives a close approximation of actual crime statistics, but to give that approximation as quickly as possible. The arguments various NYPD units raised in claiming that rapid delivery of crime statistics was impossible – that the statistics should not be used until their complete accuracy was ensured and that it would take at least several months to provide them – were proven wrong.

The Compstat report is intended as an early warning system that alerts police managers and executives to rapidly changing conditions and allows them to deploy and re-allocate resources in response to those conditions, and for this reason the report does not require extremely precise statistics. Although there is always some degree of slippage between the number of crimes captured by the weekly Compstat report and the final annual tally of reported UCR crimes, the slippage is so minuscule it does not effect Compstat's ability to identify and predict real-time crime trends. In terms of an early warning system, it matters little whether an apparent five percent increase in robberies from one week to the next is in actuality a four-point-eight percent increase or a five-point-two percent increase: managers and executives still know they have an emerging spike in crime that requires immediate attention.

Although the Compstat data collection process has undergone many refinements and improvement over time, the basic concept of collecting daily tallies of reported crimes and arrests and submitting them each week remains the same. These data are still compiled into a city-wide database each Monday morning, subjected to computer analysis, and used to prepare the Compstat Report. Sufficient copies of the Compstat Report are printed and delivered to all designated recipients by Tuesday morning, and the data this report contains is current through Sunday midnight. By the time the first Compstat meeting of the week is convened (usually on Wednesday morning at 7:00 A.M.), all the participants have had time to review the report and to learn how well each precinct is performing.

The Compstat Report

The weekly Compstat Report is printed on legal-sized paper and is about an inch thick. It contains a page for each precinct, Housing PSA and Transit District, as well as a page for each Patrol Borough and a City-wide page. Each of these pages follows a standard format with columns detailing the crime and arrest statistics (both the actual number in each category and the percentage increase or decrease) for the past week, the past month, and the year-to-date period. Although the initial Compstat Reports of 1994 only permitted comparisons to the corresponding 1993 periods, current NYPD Compstat Reports recapitulate these statistics from 1993 to the present. Thus short- and long-term trends and changes in reported crime and arrests can easily be discerned. Examples of Compstat Report pages (albeit with arrest, shooting and summons activity figures redacted) can be found on the NYPD website (www.ci.nyc.ny.us/nypd.html) and current crime trend data can also be obtained at John Yohe's Compstat website (www.compstat.com).

The Report does not contain sophisticated statistics or difficult formulas; the report was designed to be simple, straightforward, and user-friendly. There are a number of good reasons to keep the Compstat Report pages as simple as possible. First, experience shows that the more complicated the report, the fewer the people who will actually read and understand it. Second, although the report is an essential part of New York's crime-fighting efforts, most police executives simply do not have a great deal of time on their hands to spend deciphering complicated statistical reports. Third, the basic statistics provided in the Compstat Report (i.e., the actual number of crimes reported and arrests effected and the percentage increase or decrease for each) are easily interpreted and sufficient to understand whether a trend is taking place, while more complex statistical analyses are often beyond the average police manager's level of comprehension.

The weekly Compstat Report also includes pages that rank, in descending order, all patrol commands by the number of crimes committed and arrests effected. Separate pages are prepared for each of the seven major crimes as well as for overall crime, and they permit users to easily determine which commands lead the city in reported crimes and arrests. Every commander therefore knows exactly where his or her command stands in relation to all others, and as importantly every executive knows where his or her peers (and competitors) commands stand in relation to each other. By ranking commands in this way, everyone knows precisely which precincts have the highest levels of crime.

These ranked lists might not be as important in municipalities that have only one or a few precincts, but the main point is that the Compstat database permits an agency to develop simple statistical reports that suit their particular needs. The NYPD's Compstat database captures reported crimes and arrests for major offenses (among other data) and the Compstat Report ranks precincts according to crime and arrest activity, but smaller agencies might want to rank patrol car sectors or foot patrol beats according to the number of crimes committed, the number of arrests made, the average response time to calls for service, the number of summonses issued, or any other type of performance indicator. It is important that executives, managers and supervisors know who is doing the most work so that high performers can be identified and rewarded and so that low performers can be identified and motivated. The number and type of performance indicators in the database and in the report should be determined by the specific needs of the individual agency.

Let's say that a smaller agency with just one precinct or police station places great emphasis on Driving While Intoxicated (DWI) enforcement. In that agency, the data collection system and the database could be constructed to include the capture of statistics on DWI enforcement. According to the chief executive's needs, this data could be analyzed and processed to provide a ranked list (by shift) of every officer according to the number of DWI arrests he or she has made. Do a handful of officers make the majority of DWI arrests, while others make few or none? If this is the case, is it because some officers are less aggressively pursuing the agency's goals than others, or is their time being devoted to other activities? What, exactly, are these officers doing while others are making DWI arrests? Is it because those with a low DWI 'batting average' are legitimately concentrating on other enforcement or quality of life issues? Are the cops who make the most DWI arrests taking a different (and more effective) strategic approach than others?

The Compstat Report may not provide the answers to these and other questions, but this information should raise questions executives, managers and supervisors need to ask. The various reports a Compstat database can provide are as important for the information they provide as for the questions they raise. The chief executive needs to know these things and ask these questions if he or she is to properly manage the agency.

The NYPD Compstat Report provides executives with data in a variety of formats, including pie charts, bar charts and tables that summarize and visually depict performance data. The simplicity and versatility of many off-the-shelf software packages available today make databasing and report generating a simple matter that does not require exceptional computer skills. These software programs make the basic concept of the Compstat process – collecting data that is important to manage the agency and achieve its goals, statistically analyzing the data in a way that will quickly identify new trends and patterns, and presenting this data in a format managers and executives can easily understand – a relatively simple task.

The Commander Profile Report

An important adjunct to the weekly Compstat Report is the Commander Profile. This report, developed as a refinement to the Compstat process and intended to be used as a reference for executives during the Compstat meeting, provides detailed information on patrol and investigative commands as well as their Commanding Officers. In smaller agencies, it might provide data on shift supervisors or specialized units. By consolidating various data in a single report, the Commander Profile permits top executives as well as other middle managers to be generally familiar with conditions and issues in every unit and command, and it also serves as a kind of 'report card' for the way commanders manage non-crime management issues. As a document with wide circulation in the NYPD, the monthly Commander Profile (like the weekly Compstat Report) enhances the transparency of the agency's management: almost everyone knows exactly how well they are performing in relation to others.

Like the Compstat Report, the concise Commander Profile report contains a page for each precinct, Housing Bureau PSA, Transit Bureau District and Patrol Bureau, as well as for each detective squad and specialized investigative entity. Pages for patrol commands provide information on the command's population and demographics, the number and ranks of personnel assigned, the number and categorized type of civilian complaints made against officers, the number of vehicle accidents involving Department vehicles, and a host of other information by which the commander and the state of his or her command can be assessed. These include sick rates, the number of line-of-duty injuries suffered by officers, response time to various types of calls for service, overtime expenditures, and the number of calls for domestic violence. Patrol Borough and city-wide averages are also provided for comparative purposes. These data give executives important insights into the state of a command, and because commanders are expected to manage each of these issues the statistics are important indicators of the manager's abilities. While the NYPD uses its own specific criteria in assessing managers, other agencies can easily substitute other variables they deem important to managing the agency and achieving its overall goals.

The Commander Profiles were initially developed for patrol commands, but were subsequently expanded to encompass investigative units as well. These profiles are tailored to the specific kinds of issues and problems investigative commanders are expected to manage, and so they include statistics on case clearance rates, the number of search and arrest warrants executed, and other criteria of investigative quality. Whether they are for investigative or patrol commands, every profile also includes a photo of the commander and such bibliographic and career information as his or her dates of the appointment and promotion, previous commands, level of education, and any advanced or specialized training undertaken. In an agency as large and complex as the NYPD, this information helps executives to become familiar with the qualifications and career potentials of key middle managers.

Because they have such wide scope and so much information, the profiles also provide good insight into morale conditions within a precinct or unit. Occasionally, commands are identified in which the average sick rate is well above the city-wide average, the response time to calls for service is significantly lower, and a high percentage of radio calls are reported back as unfounded, for example. These indicators are typically accompanied by lackluster reductions in crime, but in any case they tend to raise questions at the Compstat meetings. Just as commanders can expect to be queried about their performance in the area of crime control and quality of life improvement, they can expect questions about the state of their command. While none of these performance indicators, in themselves, offer conclusive proof of a manager's abilities or the state of morale within the command, they nevertheless serve an early warning function. If morale or leadership problems become apparent, executives can make further inquiries leading to informed decisions regarding necessary operational or personnel changes, and they can make these decisions before conditions worsen. Similarly, commanders of precincts and units that appear to have few morale, discipline or personnel problems can be more easily identified, and they may be questioned about the personnel strategies and tactics they use to maintain a highly motivated workforce. Like other elements of the Compstat process, the Commander Profile serves as an information source for decision-making as well as an early warning system for emerging problems and for effective practices.

The specific performance indicators enumerated in the NYPD version of the Commander Profile are almost immaterial – for our purposes, the important thing is that the Commander Profile gives managers and executives the opportunity to glimpse what is going on behind the scenes within a unit. In conjunction with other sources of information, the indicators reveal how well the commander is managing the personnel and other resources entrusted to him or her, and because the information is widely disseminated it can create a positive peer pressure for commanders to improve the command's morale and working conditions. As is the case with the Compstat Report, agencies can include virtually any behavioral performance measure they deem essential to good management, and as long as the commander has the capacity and resources to control, manage or influence the behavior he or she can be held accountable for it. As we will see, the Compstat meeting is the perfect venue for this accountability to begin.

Crime Mapping

The Compstat Report's statistical summaries provide executives and middle managers with considerable information about the number of crimes, arrests and other enforcement actions taking place within a given geographic area (i.e., a precinct, Patrol Borough or the city as a whole), but it says nothing about *where* or *when* those crimes are taking place. We recall from earlier discussions of effective early warning systems and effective police tactics that this kind of aggregated information it important, but it is also insufficient if we are to strategically deploy resources to address crime. Following the analogy of the RAF and its use of radar, we can easily see that simply knowing *how many* planes were taking off from enemy airfields would not permit us to interdict them before they could strike a target. As is the case in any strategic intelligence system, we certainly need to know the enemy's strength, but we also need to know where he will be and what he will be doing at a given time. Compstat uses crime mapping technology to determine and geographically depict the time and location crimes are most likely to take place.

Like many police agencies, the NYPD had long employed pin maps to ascertain where crime had taken place, and almost every precinct had some form of pin maps depicting the spatial distribution of various crimes over time. These traditional maps required constant attention to ensure they were up-to-date and accurate, but because there was no standardization of mapping or updating throughout the department, they provided a fairly limited view of crime's temporal dimension. That is, a pin map of robberies might depict the spatial distribution of these crimes over the previous month, but gave no insight into robberies occurring the previous month or over the course of the previous year. One precinct might update its maps each month, while another updated the maps every six weeks. The lack of standardization meant that every precinct might not have a separate map for each crime – robberies, burglaries and car thefts could conceivably be depicted on the same map. Different colored pins were typically used to denote different types of crime (or, if separate maps were prepared for each of the major crimes, for different times of day), but especially in high crime precincts the range of colors could be confusing. Without belaboring the issue, the scope, quality and accuracy of the existing pin map system were more or less dependent upon the individual interests and abilities of seventy-six Precinct Commanders and their crime analysts. In any event, the traditional push-pin maps were rarely used for any strategic purpose.

Other drawbacks to traditional pin maps are that they rarely do more than portray a two-dimensional depiction of crime and that they do not lend themselves to experimentation and exploration. One map may be devoted to robberies, for example, while another is devoted to assaults or car thefts, but although these maps are informational they do not explore the potential relationships between seemingly disparate crimes, locations and conditions. Members of a plainclothes Anti-Crime team may look at the robbery map and see only robberies, and detectives may look at another map and see a pattern of shootings or assaults, but it is only when these maps are placed atop each other and overlaid with a map of known narcotics sales locations, for example, that the true relationship between these seemingly disparate criminal events emerges. The maps, viewed separately, cannot convey the fact that there is a spatial (and perhaps a causal) relationship between drug sales, shootings, and robberies within the precinct. Further exploration and analysis may reveal that the individuals being robbed and assaulted are often customers at the drug spots. If this is the case, the strategy developed to address the robbery and assault problem should include highly focused narcotics enforcement. Further analysis of the same crime maps by the time of day each crime occurs may point out the specific times enforcement resources should be used in order to have the greatest impact. These analyses are not particularly sophisticated, but they are virtually impossible using traditional multicolored push-pin maps.

The first crime maps used at the early Compstat meetings were the conventional kind: commanders were instructed to bring large precinct maps with clear acetate overlays depicting the distribution of major crimes. The maps, about two feet by three feet in size, were set up on easels. Color-coded dots on the acetates indicated the location of individual crimes, and by placing several acetates atop the precinct map the areas of highest crime could be identified and some spatial relationships between crimes could be discerned. Still, it was time-consuming, labor intensive and somewhat cumbersome for precinct staff to prepare the overlays, various precinct landmarks and facilities were not depicted, and temporal relationships could not be identified.

These problems were largely overcome when, in the summer of 1994, the Compstat Unit began using an off-the-shelf mapping program that generated computer-based maps of every precinct in the city. These computerized maps, which could be viewed on a computer screen or printed out on paper, were capable of interfacing with the Compstat database and generating layers to depict each of the seven major crimes. They could also depict those crimes by time of day or day of the week – all that was required was expanding the existing Compstat database to include information fields for the address, time of occurrence and day of the week. All this information was readily available to the precinct personnel who compiled the weekly crime recapitulation from paper crime reports.

Eventually, computerized layers were developed to include a wide range of related map information such as the locations of schools, parks or playgrounds, transit facilities, houses of worship, banks, automated teller machines (ATMs), and past and current drug arrests – all locations or facilities that could conceivably impact the crime equation. With these maps and layers, members of the Compstat Unit could easily explore relationships between crime, time and place. They could immediately identify 'hot-spot' crime clusters and, as importantly, executives could question Precinct Commanders about these hot spots at Compstat meetings. As a result, commanders were forced to become intimately familiar with individual crime conditions in their precincts. Instead of merely discussing statistical upswings or decreases in aggregate crime at the Compstat meetings, the introduction of computerized mapping required commanders to develop an in-depth knowledge of specific criminal events and crime locations: if Deputy Commissioner Maple, Chief of Patrol Louis Anemone and their Patrol Borough Commander knew about a cluster of five early-morning robberies near the 14th Street subway exit, the precinct commander had better know about them too. The commander had also better have a plan or strategy in place to address the robberies.

The flexibility and ease of analysis afforded by mapping software facilitated an in-depth examination of the causes of crime: the kind of exploratory analysis of the relationship between shootings, robberies and drug sale locations mentioned above, for example, – an analysis that was scarcely possible with conventional push-pin maps – became a simple matter through technology. Commanders could also explore whether certain locations or facilities were attracting crime at particular times and develop effective strategies to prevent the offenses. A precinct map that depicted the locations of schools as well as robberies, for example, might not reveal crime clusters unless the robberies were filtered to include only those robberies taking place during school hours – between 9:00 A.M. and 3:00 P.M. In this example, it would be worth exploring whether many of the robbery victims and / or robbery perpetrators were teens. If they were in fact teens, the appropriate way to address the robbery problem might be through enhanced truancy enforcement that would alter the crime equation by reducing the number of victims and perpetrators on the street. Simply posting an officer outside the schools during these hours and devoting a team of uniformed officers to pick up and return truants to school authorities without formally arresting them (a legally-permissible tactic under New York law) might solve or significantly reduce this particular crime problem.

The mapping technology also made it a relatively simple matter to focus enforcement efforts when and where crime was actually taking place. By plotting the locations where crimes were being committed and superimposing the locations where arrests for the same crimes were being effected, commanders could ensure that their personnel were properly deployed and working effectively to have the greatest immediate impact. In the case cited above (the morning robbery pattern near the subway station), the commander might need to adjust the tours of his or her plainclothes Anti-Crime team and have them mingle with the crowd to apprehend the robbers, or he might simply assign a foot patrol officer to a special robbery post to deter them. The specific strategy is often less important than the fact that something is being done to remedy the problem, and no effective remedy can be prescribed unless the specific symptoms are known.

The Compstat Unit continued to evolve and improve its use of crime mapping software and technology. Computer-generated map images were displayed on video monitors at the Compstat meetings, and eventually they were projected on large-screen monitors. Because the mapping software was (and still is) provided to Precinct Commanders as an in-house crime analysis tool, they were better prepared to understand the geography of crime and better equipped to develop and implement immediate responses to crime before the Compstat meeting. They were also better equipped to answer the questions asked of them at Compstat meetings. By giving commanders almost the same capability to analyze crime as the Compstat Unit at

Headquarters, executives leveled the playing field and fostered transparency
– it would be patently unfair to hold commanders accountable if only the top
brass were able to analyze crime in their precincts.

The depth and quality of crime analysis – both by members of the
Compstat Unit and at the precinct level – was vastly improved as additional
geocoded layers were developed and put to use. Layers depicting parolee
residences were created, for example, and on several occasions viable
suspects were identified for investigators when a layer of parolees convicted
of burglary were superimposed on a map of burglaries: on more than one
occasion, convicted burglars on parole lived in the middle of a burglary
cluster. While this information is not, in itself, indicative of guilt, it is
certainly a useful investigative lead worth pursuing.

Summary: The Compstat Technology Package

The technology that makes Compstat possible is not terribly complicated,
but its impact on the agency has been formidable. The ability to quickly
gather, process and analyze large amounts of crime information created many
new opportunities for examining crime and crime trends, for developing
effective strategies to reduce crime and improve quality of life, and for
focusing personnel deployment and enforcement activities. Although the
statistics that comprise the agency-wide Compstat Report are compiled once
each week and the Commander Profiles are prepared monthly, every precinct
command can compile its own statistics and generate its own maps as often
as the commander deems necessary. This provides the capacity to analyze
events on practically a real-time basis, and permits a wealth of crime intelligence to be rapidly disseminated throughout and individual command or the
department as a whole. Collectively and individually, these technological
advancements dramatically altered the way the NYPD deals with crime.

In the NYPD and elsewhere, crime was traditionally analyzed in an
'incident-based' format: the agency counted the number of reported crimes
and calculated the number of cases cleared. This approach did not and cannot
adequately deal with the complexities of actually reducing crime. With the
introduction of computerized pin mapping and time of day / day of week
analysis, this began to change. Managers and executives began to view crime
in a more accurate multi-dimensional framework that included temporal and
spatial relationships between certain offenses as well as relationships
between offenses and the enforcement actions undertaken to reduce them.
Deployment strategies were refined and carefully focused, and members of

the department began to see how detailed information about crime patterns could point to appropriate crime reduction strategies. Personnel at every level of the organization also began to see how detailed analysis could be used to test how well various crime reduction strategies worked under specific conditions. In other words, the technology utilized in Compstat began to impact the way members of the NYPD thought about crime, crime control, and strategic policing.

In this section, we saw that although many elements of Compstat technology developed gradually as new enhancements were added or modified in response to changing conditions, they brought about organizational changes fairly rapidly. No time was spent on detailed analyses, studies and pilot testing, but instead the entire department was immediately put on notice that the new administration expected accountability, responsibility and strategic utilization of resources. Within a few months, this new technology and the information it made available began to have an immediate and lasting impact on the agency, its perspective on crime and crime management, and the way it conducted its business. In conjunction with the Compstat meetings, the new developments laid a solid foundation to ensure that this organizational growth and transformation would continue into the future.

The Compstat Meeting

Like all the other technological and organizational elements of the Compstat process and the Compstat paradigm, the Compstat meetings developed and changed as part of a rapid evolutionary process. The NYPD, like many other American police agencies, faced a serious problem of information flow, and a clear need existed for a method that would ensure more timely communication of ideas, information, policies and directives throughout the agency. The new administration's compelling need to get off to a running start and to immediately address the crime and quality of life problems it promised to resolve made the communications gap even more critical an issue.

Meetings and presentations are the traditional method for disseminating ideas, information, policies and directives, and the NYPD's executive cadre was certainly well-practiced at holding and attending meetings. One problem with the kind of high-level meetings police executives typically hold, though, is that in terms of communication they often resemble presentations: the majority of the information imparted typically flows downward rather upward, with rather little real interaction or exchange of information and ideas taking place. Rank-conscious (and promotion-conscious) middle managers and supervisors in a quasi-military organization may not feel comfortable raising questions, requesting clarification or volunteering information, and they may be somewhat reluctant to interact candidly with executives in such formal settings. This is particularly true when meetings have a large number of attendees.

Clearly, better and more effective communication (and better and more interactive meetings) were necessary if the new administration was to achieve its goals. Especially in the administration's early days, those goals included sharing information about effective crime control strategies as well as identifying competent leaders and aggressive crime fighters with the potential for promotion to higher rank and greater responsibility. Candid interaction and the exchange (rather than the mere transmission) of information would be a key element in the new administration's success.

Prior to the advent of Compstat, the NYPD's only institutionalized crime meetings were the relatively small monthly robbery meetings chaired by Patrol Borough commanders and attended by Precinct Commanders and the separate monthly meeting attended by each of the seven Borough commanders and chaired by the Chief of Patrol. Neither the Chief of Patrol nor any other Bureau Chiefs (the so-called 'superchiefs') or Deputy Commissioners usually attended the meetings chaired by the Patrol Borough commander. The agency's highest executives never met formally to discuss crime statistics or crime control directly with the 76 precinct commanders, and therefore had little opportunity to interact with them or to determine their leadership and crime-fighting credentials. For the most part, these *pro forma* robbery meetings were a review of basic robbery statistics and summons activity.

Statistics on robbery, the bellwether crime, were viewed in the aggregate, with precincts and Patrol Boroughs assessed on a loosely defined and highly informal concept of 'acceptable losses:' each precinct and Borough had its own informal threshold, and as long as the threshold wasn't exceeded there would be few repercussions. Precinct Commanders were not so much challenged to reduce crime as to ensure their crime increases were not as substantial as other commanders' increases – an informal mindset that the Compstat paradigm would invert. The upshot of this informal mindset was that mediocrity was tacitly authorized – the emphasis was not on reducing or eliminating crime, but rather at maintaining crime at tolerable levels that would not cause the department and its executives too much trouble. Because few believed that crime could actually be dramatically reduced, and because few were unwilling to 'rock the boat' and actively pursue crime fighting tactics that might cause trouble, crime reduction was not really an issue of tremendous concern and discussion.

Further exacerbating this problem was the fact that the statistics examined during the monthly robbery meetings were not particularly current. Depending upon the date of the meeting and other factors, the aggregated statistics might be thirty to sixty days old. There were no indications of robbery's frequency, location or areas of concentration communicated to personnel at the executive level. Moreover, the aggregated statistics did not permit commanders to focus on individual robbery incidents – at best, commanders could discuss robbery patterns. There was little real accountability in this process, but the accountability that existed was also placed too high: the Chief of Patrol did not (and could not) reasonably expect a Patrol Borough commander to be conversant with the details of individual robberies taking place over such a large geographic area and such a broad time frame, so these questions rarely arose. Any questions the Chief of Patrol might have had about a particular robbery pattern would often have to be tabled until the next meeting so that the questions could go down the chain of command (usually in writing) to the precinct commander and back up the chain of command (usually in writing) to the Patrol Borough commander.

This protracted process of responding to inquiries complicated any real efforts to combat crime, essentially removing any sense of urgency and absolving precinct commanders from the responsibility to be intimately familiar with ongoing crime conditions. Moreover, the meetings primarily addressed robberies and summons activity – other crimes and quality of life conditions were not typically items on the agenda.

At that time the NYPD's structure and chain of command also included an additional and largely unnecessary layer of bureaucracy that complicated communications and obscured the lines of responsibility and accountability. Geographic groupings of three or four precincts within a Patrol Borough were called Divisions, and in some matters Precinct Commanders reported to Division Commanders who usually held the rank of full Inspector. In other matters they reported to the Borough Commander, so the Division Commander's responsibilities and accountability were rather fuzzy. Because the Division Commanders were an intermediary level of supervision between the Precinct Commander and the Patrol Borough Commander, this structure further extended both the lines of communication and the time it took for information to flow between the Precinct and Patrol Borough Commanders. In order to flatten the bureaucratic structure, improve communication, enhance discretion, and open up budgeted positions for promotions, Division Commanders were eliminated early in the Bratton administration. This created an excess in budgeted positions in the rank of Inspector, and Bratton used this excess to put full Inspectors (rather than Deputy Inspectors or Captains) in command of the department's busiest and most challenging precincts. That is, he redistributed legitimate power in the organization as a way of empowering and rewarding top performers and as a way of creating a clearer career path to promotion: Captains who performed well in less-challenging precincts were given busier and more challenging commands and promoted to Deputy Inspector, and those who did an outstanding job at managing these precincts were assigned to the busiest and most challenging precincts as full Inspector. The strategy better aligned legitimate power with the responsibilities involved in a given command. As we've noted, Compstat meetings were an integral part of identifying commanders for promotion and additional responsibility.

Crime Control Strategy Meetings

The host of problems that plagued the robbery meetings began to change with the first Crime Control Strategy Meetings – the formal name for what have come to be known as Compstat Meetings. Armed with current statistics, a great deal of crime-fighting experience and an unequivocal mandate to reduce crime – Bratton clearly stated one of his goals was to reduce crime ten percent in 1994 – the new administration avoided many of the pitfalls that traditionally confounded efforts to direct police activity. Unlike the vague and subjective assessment standards of leadership and crime-fighting ability that previously existed, Compstat put extremely objective standards in place, basing them on clear goals that effective and energetic managers could reasonably achieve.

The first Compstat meetings were rather simple when compared with their current format, but they were a tremendous improvement over the earlier robbery meetings insofar as they brought the Chief of Patrol, the Deputy Commissioner for Crime Control Strategies (this position was filled by Jack Maple during Bratton's term in office and retitled Deputy Commissioner for Operations after Maple and Bratton left in April 1996), a Patrol Borough Commander and all the precinct commanders from the Patrol Borough together in the same room at the same time. Everyone at the meeting is armed with the same basic information and statistics (i.e., the Compstat Report) and specific questions regarding crime can be directed to the person with the immediate responsibility for controlling crime in the precinct – its commander. The commander can respond directly and publicly to the executive asking the question, and an atmosphere of transparency and fairness is created because everyone in the room is privy to the same information and everyone is held to the same standard. As we'll see, this arrangement altered the ineffective traditional system of hierarchical communication (that is, communication up and down the established linear channels of a traditional organizational chart), transforming it to a communications model that resembled what Bratton has called a "seamless web" (Henry, 2000) rather than a pyramid. Moreover, as commanders respond to questions they also have the opportunity to educate executives about the specific crime and quality of life conditions existing at particular locations or within particular neighborhoods; executives thus gain a deeper knowledge of the precinct as well as of the city and all its neighborhoods.

The communication methods employed at the early Compstat meetings were unusual for a police agency, and they immediately attracted attention within the department as well as outside it. A *New York Times* article noted that

> such meetings, which are much like those regularly held by major corporations, may seem a little thing, but they are new to the New York City Police Department and they are rare among departments around the country … Perhaps more than any other single thing the department is doing, the meetings reflect the Commissioner's intent to mobilize the tools of corporate management as he searches for "creative ways to reduce crime and the fear of crime" (Treaster, 1994, p. B3).

The early Crime Control Strategy meetings were held in the relatively small Press Room at Police Headquarters. The room did not offer any of the amenities or technology that would later be associated with Compstat meetings, but it did offer the opportunity for an unprecedented level of interaction between the agency's top leadership and its middle managers. From the beginning, the meetings permitted executives to communicate ideas and objectives directly to the people responsible for implementing them. Similarly, Precinct Commanders had a forum to communicate their accomplishments directly to the people who determined their promotion and advancement.

Precinct commanders also had the unprecedented opportunity to openly and directly address the 'superchiefs' and commissioners regarding crime and quality of life conditions as well as the organizational obstacles they faced in their command – again, directly to the people who had the resources to help resolve these issues. Finally, the meetings provided a forum for commanders to communicate their accomplishments and reveal their failures to their peers. By introducing a transparent peer-to-peer (or, in other terms, competitor-to-competitor) system of transmitting information, Compstat meetings put additional pressure to perform on commanders. Some precinct commanders were initially reticent to speak candidly to the top brass or in front of their peers and competitors, but in time their reluctance generally eroded and they took the opportunity to communicate openly.

The administration's newly constituted executive staff also benefited immensely from the new arrangement. Instead of just seeing Precinct Commanders at review boards, promotional ceremonies or occasional social events, the agency's top leadership was able to formally and informally assess each middle manager's knowledge, presentation and leadership ability. Further, they were able to conduct this assessment on a monthly basis and to monitor the individual's career progress as additional challenges and responsibilities were taken on. As each Precinct Commander responded to questions or addressed the group, it became apparent which ones had natural leadership talent, who showed promise as motivators and problem solvers, and who presented himself or herself as a competent manager capable of moving the department forward to achieve its goals. In this sense, the meetings served as a showcase for new talent, and to further mine this pool of talent precinct Executive Officers were eventually asked to attend and make the presentation instead of the Precinct Commander. Later, when the Transit and Housing Police Departments merged with the NYPD, the Compstat meetings would again serve as a forum for scores of new and lesser-known commanders to come to the attention of the Police Commissioner and to facilitate their acceptance by their NYPD peers.

The Crime Control Strategy meetings were (and still are) convened twice each week from 7 A.M. to 10 A.M. The Press Room quickly proved inadequate as the meetings grew and the technology evolved, and to accommodate the increased attendance and make use of the technology they were soon moved to the Command and Control Center, a high tech conference facility that has often been compared to the Pentagon's War Room. The top executives attending the Compstat meetings typically include the First

Deputy Commissioner, the Deputy Commissioner for Operations,[13] the Deputy Commissioner for Policy and Planning, the Chief of Detectives, Chief of Patrol, Chief of Organized Crime Control, and often by the Police Commissioner. The Borough Commander responsible for the precincts whose performance will be scrutinized attends, as do the precinct commanders (or, occasionally, the precinct Executive Officers) and the heads of various investigative and enforcement units deployed within these precincts.

The Compstat meeting's primary participants are seated around conference tables set up in a horseshoe arrangement, with microphones placed every few feet. At the top of the table, executives sit at a kind of dais, while precinct and investigative unit commanders sit along the sides of the horseshoe. Facing the executives at the open end is a podium, and mounted high on the wall behind the podium is a large video projection screen measuring perhaps ten feet by thirty feet. Additional video monitors and projection screens are arranged nearby. Other meeting participants – including visitors and representatives from support and ancillary units – sit on folding chairs in a gallery behind the executives.

One by one, precinct commanders and the heads of investigative units operating within the precinct's jurisdiction are called to step up to the podium and brief the assembled group on current crime and quality of life conditions as well as the activities and strategies being used to address those conditions. There is no set format to the briefing in terms of its content or the specific issues discussed, but the commanders are expected to present a candid and fairly detailed overview of the state of the command, the priority crime and quality of life conditions it faces, and the strategies and tactics being employed to manage those conditions. Commanders typically review the changes in crime and quality of life conditions as well as arrest and enforcement statistics since their last Compstat appearance, and they usually brief the group on current major cases and initiatives. Commanders can have statistical data from the Compstat Report (as well as prepared charts and tables depicting various crime analyses) projected on the screens to bolster the various points they make. The briefing is intended to be a comprehensive and informative recapitulation of criminal activity and police activity within the command, showcasing what the commander is doing to identify and solve

---

13   When William Bratton resigned in April 1996, Jack Maple left the department with him. Edward Norris (currently Baltimore's Police Commissioner) assumed many of Maple's responsibilities and the Deputy Commissioner for Crime Control Strategies position was re-titled Deputy Commissioner for Operations.

problems. It is also important to note that executives may interrupt and direct the presenter to focus more closely on a particular issue, or they may interrupt to focus on a particular case. The overall process of interaction is fluid and flexible, with few fixed rules.

This briefing is the commander's opportunity to draw attention to emerging crime and quality of life problems, to explain what strategies and tactics are being pursued to address them, to demonstrate a thorough grasp of the issues facing the command, and to communicate the overall state of the command's management. The briefing is, in other words, the commander's chance to impress executives and other personnel present at the meeting with his or her knowledge, leadership talents, crime-fighting abilities, and overall career potential. This is the commander's chance to bring problems and issues (especially those concerning the adequacy of resources and crime patterns that cross precinct boundaries) to the attention of the executive staff – in essence to publicly communicate their needs and, in doing so, to place some of the responsibility and some of the accountability on the executives. It is also the commander's chance to impress his or her peers, and the motivational power of peer pressure is an important dynamic in Compstat. Many commanders say that their fear of appearing foolish or unprepared in front of their peers is more intimidating than their fear of appearing foolish or incompetent in front of executives, and this motivates them to work especially hard at making a good presentation. In other words, commanders feel accountable to their peers as well as to the executive corps.

Following this state-of-command briefing, the meeting usually heats up a bit as executives begin questioning the commander. Although virtually any issue related to the command's management is fair game for the executives' inquiries, crime reduction and quality of life improvement issues are usually given the highest priority. Based on their earlier review of the Compstat Report, the Chiefs and Deputy Commissioners are likely to have questions about statistical upticks in any crime category.

Although every Precinct Commander attending the meeting must be prepared to present, in practice not every commander is called to the podium. Each Patrol Borough has an average of ten precincts, and time simply does not permit a thorough review of every commander's performance. Executives determine which commanders will be questioned, and the length of time spent reviewing their performance varies according to the amount of information exchanged. While every commander may not be called upon at a given meeting, each must be fully conversant with the command's crime and quality of life activities and be fully prepared to answer questions, or be prepared to face the consequences.

Interactions at the Compstat Meeting

The give-and-take between Precinct Commanders and executives at Compstat meetings can at times become adversarial, but when the meetings are conducted correctly (that is, in line with the precepts of the Compstat paradigm) they also emphasize executive approval and public commendation for high-performers. Discussions may become quite heated as commanders try to justify their activities and demonstrate their knowledge of crime problems, but astute executives who understand the overall Compstat paradigm and put it to practice are as generous in lavishing praise as they are in censure. George Kelling (1995) described the type of interaction that takes place at the sessions when they are conducted properly:

> Another commander steps to the podium. "You had eight rapes this month, four above last year," Maple says, "What's going on?" The commander begins disaggregating: "Four rapes involved friends and family, one was a date rape, and three were stranger rapes Two of those appear to be the work of one person." Maple turns to the detective lieutenant assigned to the precinct and standing beside the commander. "Tell me about the investigation." The lieutenant moves to the podium and describes the investigation. Maple interrupts and addresses another precinct commander seated at the table: "You had a similar problem a couple of months ago, didn't you? How did you handle it?" Later in the presentation, while discussing auto theft, the commander asks if its legal to stop tow trucks towing cars (a common method of theft). Several people call out a jumble of opinions. Maple cuts them off. Nodding to the head of the legal department, he guarantees the captain a quick response: "We're not sure. Legal will get back to you with an answer by the end of the day." (Kelling, 1995, p. 44)

Kelling goes on to note how the precinct commander finishes his presentation by introducing two patrol officers brought with him to the meeting. He describes how the officers' initiative led to the solution of a series of robberies occurring across two patrol boroughs as well as within the jurisdiction of a suburban police agency outside the city. "Along with the rest of the participants and the audience, chiefs, *super-chiefs*, rise and applaud - applaud patrol officers. The officers have been assigned to a month of special duty in the detective unit, a career-enhancing honor (Kelling, 1995, p. 44; emphasis in original)."

Kelling's (1995) brief description of Compstat meeting interactions is certainly accurate, but in order to gain a more sweeping understanding of the interactions and dynamics, as well as to tie together some of the paradigm's themes, we would do well to examine these interactions in greater depth. Perhaps the best way to understand the interactions and dynamics that take place at a Compstat meeting is to examine a fictionalized account of a typical meeting. In this fictionalized account we can glimpse how technology, statistics, accountability, enhanced communications and all the other elements of the Compstat paradigm come together cohesively in the real-world setting of a Compstat meeting.

Let's say that one of the precincts selected to present has recorded a dozen burglaries in the past week, leading to statistical increases of ten percent from last week, three percent from last month, and five percent from this week last year. When the commander steps to the podium he or she will almost certainly be asked to explain the reason for the increase and the steps he or she is taking to do something about it.

As the commander explains the precinct's burglary problem, a map of the precinct with a series of twelve blue dots representing the recent burglaries appears on the projection screen. Six of the dots appear as a cluster in Sector Charlie, with the remainder spread fairly evenly through the precinct. The questions begin. Are these residential or commercial burglaries? What time of day are they taking place? Are they concentrated in any particular area? Is there an apparent pattern involved, or do these appear to be unrelated crimes? Which of the twelve burglaries reported in the past week are part of the pattern?

The projected map changes to show all the reported burglaries over the past month, and Sector Charlie has a disproportionate number of blue dots. Is this sector traditionally a hot spot for burglaries? The commander explains that Sector Charlie is primarily a residential area bordered on the east by a commercial district and on the south by an industrial district, so residential burglaries are unlikely to occur as frequently in the surrounding area. Have patrol officers and the precinct's plainclothes Anti-Crime team been apprised of the burglary pattern and directed to give special attention to the area? Are the Anti-Crime cops on-duty on the days and times this pattern is taking place? Is the precinct detective squad investigating?

At this point, the Precinct Detective Squad commander will probably be asked to step up to the podium to speak about the burglaries. Have detectives canvassed the surrounding neighborhood or residents of other apartments in the buildings? What have the canvasses revealed? Did the detectives interview the letter carrier assigned to the postal route to ascertain whether he or she saw anything? Is there a bus route through the area, and were bus drivers interviewed? Does information and investigation indicate a single burglar or a burglary team? Are these any suspects, or have descriptions of the perpetrators been developed? The detective commander explains that as the result of a tip the initial investigation focused on three potential suspects, but the evidence against them is not particularly strong and the investigation is ongoing. The Chief asks whether information about the burglary pattern and photos of the three tentative suspects have been provided to every uniformed officer in the command.

Everyone has been briefed at roll call, the squad boss says, but photographs have not been distributed. The precinct's digital image system printer has been down for two weeks, and repeated calls to Management Information Systems Division for repair or replacement have had no result. The Chief of Department turns to the gallery. "Where is the MISD representative?" "Here, Chief." "When will this problem be corrected?" "Today, sir." "What time today?" "By noon, Chief." "Thank you." Turning back to the squad commander, the Chief asks what time the suspect photos will be distributed to patrol cops, obtains a promise that the cops will have the photos by 1:00 P.M., and returns to his questions. What type of items are being taken in the burglaries? Have detectives visited area pawnshops to look for stolen property? What parolees live in the area, and have detectives spoken to parole officers to determine if there are potential informants among them? Following the Chief's nod, the Compstat Unit computer operator begins typing at his keyboard, preparing to superimpose another layer on the projected map.

The detective boss hesitates and glances nervously at the screen. "No, Chief. We haven't done that." The new map pops up, and three green triangles appear in the middle of the burglary pattern; one dot appears to be on the same block – perhaps even in the same building – as one of the blue burglary dots. "We'll get right on that, Chief." "Good. Another question, Lieutenant: since this pattern may or may not cross into the adjoining precinct, have your detectives conferred with the squad there?"

The detective boss swallows hard, and the Chief of Department begins thumbing through the Commander Profile Report to find the Lieutenant's page. "I'm not sure, Chief. I'll have to get back to you on that." "Well, let's find out now. Where is the squad boss from the Ninety-Ninth Precinct?" "Here, Chief. We'll get together on this right after the meeting." "That's good. And we'll talk about *your* burglaries in a few minutes; you're up next. Before we return to our discussion of this burglary pattern, Lieutenant, I notice that your squad's case closure rate is quite a bit lower than the citywide average…"

"Yes, Chief, I'm aware of that. As you may know, we've been rather shorthanded recently. Two of my most seasoned detectives retired suddenly and two others have been out sick on long-term line-of-duty injuries. We managed to borrow two newly-promoted detectives but they're still learning the ropes. Our closure rate has actually improved four percent from last month, and the two injured detectives are scheduled to come back to work in the next two weeks. I'm confident we'll be back on track within a month and back above the city-wide average within six weeks. We've consistently been about six points above the average over the past eighteen months, and this is a short-term problem." "Sounds good, Loo. We'll see how you're doing next month." The Chief nods to his aide, who makes a note to raise the issue the next time this precinct appears at Compstat.

The Deputy Commissioner of Operations refocuses the discussion. "Regarding these burglaries, Captain, can you tell us what your Anti-Crime team has been doing?" "Commissioner, my Anti-Crime sergeant is trying something we learned from an operation in one of the Bronx precincts last year. We've deployed two cops in plainclothes on bicycles with another two in an observation post in a high-rise building. The OP guys are in radio contact with the bicycle guys, and when they spot someone who may be checking out a house to burglarize they let the bike cops know and they cruise by. This time of year there are a lot of people out on bikes, and they're much less conspicuous than they would be in an unmarked car. We also have a plainclothes team working the area in an unmarked car. We've only been doing this for two days, but I think it has a good chance of working."

The Chief, nodding once again to the aide recording action notes, says "Okay, Captain, it sounds good to me. We'll talk about this again but in the meanwhile I'd like you to coordinate with the detective squad and with the CO of the Ninety-Ninth. I suspect he may also want to take a hard look at the burglaries around the precinct border and put something together with your people. Now lets talk about your street narcotics conditions…"

The meeting continues as the Precinct Commander discusses the strategies he is pursuing to eradicate drug sales, the deployment of his Street Narcotics Enforcement Unit team and their coordination with Narcotics Division investigators, and the overall success he is having in solving this deeply entrenched problem. A projected map shows that drug arrests (as indicated by green dots) are being effected throughout the precinct, but especially in the area with the greatest concentration of known drug locations (as indicated by purple triangles). The commander of the Narcotics Division investigative module assigned to the precinct joins the Precinct Commander, and they describe how a highly focused joint investigation/enforcement operation by has had success in 'buying-up' into a local drug gang. Search and arrest warrant applications have been prepared, and a major take-down of the gang's leadership is planned the following day. Two of the major players in the drug gang are uncooperative witnesses to a murder in another Borough, and detectives from the precinct concerned have been notified. The homicide detectives will be present to question the two, and with the District Attorney's consent they will offer the witnesses a deal: the DA will consider a reduction in the drug charges if they cooperate with the homicide investigation.

As the commander speaks, the video projection screen behind him depicts a map of the area the drug gang controls, and, using a laser pointer to highlight various locations, he explains the relationship between the gang's drug sales and robberies in the area. Photographs of a *bodega*, a florist shop and an apartment house the gang uses to deal drugs appear on the smaller video monitor, and as the Commander describes these drug spots, he points out their location on the projected map. Many of the robbery victims are suburban teens who come into the neighborhood by car to buy drugs. The commander notes that once the take-down occurs, the area will be saturated with uniformed officers from the precinct and the Patrol Borough Task Force. The uniformed officers will conduct intensive parking, traffic and quality of life enforcement to deter drug buyers from coming into the area ("Mommie and Daddy will want to know why Johnnie got a parking ticket on *their* car in *this* neighborhood"), to stabilize the area, and to prevent other drug dealers from moving in. The commander concludes by thanking the commanders of the various units taking part in the operation for their assistance and manpower, noting that a similar 'buy-up' operation targeting another drug sales hotspot is underway (he indicates the area on the projected pin map), and the take-down in that operation is expected to take place within the month.

The Chiefs and Deputy Commissioners ask a few questions about the investigation, but they are satisfied and impressed: the plan seems to have merit, and if properly executed it should have a dramatic impact on crime. The meeting has been going on for almost forty-five minutes, and the Chief of Department says that after a five minute break the meeting will resume. The Ninety-Ninth Precinct is up next.

Summary and Conclusion

The weekly Compstat Crime Control Strategy Meetings are but one facet of the comprehensive system by which the NYPD monitors and evaluates the performance of individual commanders and the agency as a whole. As the Compstat meetings and the Compstat paradigm developed, flourished and achieved results, similar or related evaluation systems and processes were instituted at all levels of the organization. These systems and processes include the pre-Compstat briefings at which Precinct Commanders make their presentations to their Patrol Borough Commander in preparation for the Headquarters meeting and the precinct-based Compstat meetings convened by Precinct Commanders to ensure the performance and accountability of the line supervisors who report to them. Each of these structures follows the general outline and process of the Compstat Crime Control Strategy Meetings.

The unprecedented reductions in crime achieved by the New York City Police Department since 1993 as well as the tremendous improvement in the quality of life experienced by New Yorkers are largely attributable to the innovative and dynamic management processes described in this chapter and throughout this book. These comprehensive processes integrate the four principles of crime reduction (timely and accurate intelligence; rapid deployment; effective strategies and tactics; and relentless follow-up) into virtually every function and activity undertaken by the Department and its members, and they work in synergy with other mechanisms to realign accountability, responsibility and discretion. The process permits personnel at all levels of the agency to access the information they need to identify problems and to develop tactics to effectively address them, as well as to rapidly deploy resources and assess their impact upon problems.

Weekly Compstat meetings are an essential element of this overall process, in that they are a viable feedback mechanism to ensure that local commanders remain accountable for the way they utilize the enhanced resources and discretion they have been given. Concurrently, the Compstat process and Compstat meetings give executives the capacity to remain fully conversant with the specific problems their commanders face. They are a forum at which commanders can communicate with executives and peers concerning their crime and quality of life problems and the specific tactics they use to address them, at the same time they are a means for the agency's executive cadre to intensively assess commanders' management strengths and weaknesses and their capacity to develop and implement effective crime reduction tactics.

This process differs from the management and problem-solving processes which have traditionally been used in American police agencies, and perhaps the principal difference lies in its intensity and the extent to which it focuses upon the uncompromising fulfillment of the agency's core mission. The process truly represents a revolution in the way police agencies are managed. Although this has become a revolutionary process, it continues to evolve insofar as it is sufficiently flexible to permit continual adjustment, refinement and enhancement in order to effectively respond to changing demands.

Recommended Readings

Eli Silverman, a Professor at John Jay College of Criminal Justice, has written an insightful management study of the NYPD that focuses on the impact of Compstat and strategic policing. In it, he provides a detailed description of how Compstat meetings, the Compstat process, and the strategic initiatives precinct commanders use to reduce crime were developed and implemented.

Silverman, Eli B. **NYPD Fights Crime: Innovative Strategies in Policing**, Boston, MA: Northeastern University Press, 1999.

Valuable insight into the Compstat's linkage to the "Broken Windows" theory and to strategic policing can be gained from reading Kelling and Coles' (1999) **Fixing Broken Windows: Restoring Order and Reducing Crime in Our Communities**. Importantly, Kelling and Coles describe how the principles that have become part of the Compstat paradigm were first tested and implemented in the Transit Police during Bratton's tenure there. Kelling's *City Journal* article also discusses the development of Compstat as a management tool.

Kelling, George L. and Catherine M. Coles **Fixing Broken Windows: Restoring Order and Reducing Crime in Our Communities**, New York: Touchstone (Simon & Schuster), 1996.

Kelling, George L. "How to Run a Police Department," *City Journal*, 5, 4 (Autumn, 1995), pp. 34-45.

Paul O'Connell, a professor at Iona College, has conducted extensive studies of the Compstat management model in connection with his doctoral studies at John Jay College of Criminal Justice. His monograph on Compstat is well worth reading.

O'Connell, Paul E. "Using Performance Data for Accountability: The New York City Police Department's Compstat Model of Police Management," Arlington, VA: Price Waterhouse Coopers Endowment for the Business of Government *Managing for Results* series, August 2001.

Questions for Debate or Discussion

1. Discuss the practice of crafting a new management coalition in terms of Gladwell's (1999) 'tipping point' perspective. Specifically, how did the accelerated movement of highly motivated leaders and expert crime fighters into the upper ranks of the NYPD help tip the balance of the agency's management philosophy? Would such dramatic changes and dramatic results have be possible in another agency without substantially altering the management philosophy through the infusion of new blood and new ideas?

2. Although the crime and quality of life data contained in the NYPD's Compstat Report is collected and compiled on a weekly basis, it would be possible to collect this data and prepare a daily Compstat Report. Is there any advantage to having a daily Compstat Report as opposed to a weekly Compstat report?

3. How could the concepts behind the Compstat Crime Control Strategy Meetings be applied to areas of police work other than enforcement and crime control? For example, how could Compstat be applied to manage a Police Academy and hold instructors accountable for recruits' performance?

4. Imagine that you are the chief of a medium-sized police department of about 120 sworn personnel. The agency has nine sergeants who serve as shift supervisors, and one of your goals is to hold them more accountable for the overall performance of officers they supervise. To increase their accountability and at the same time enhance their discretion, you devise a Shift Commander Profile Report. What kind of data should the Report contain, and how often should it be updated?

Prepared July 9, 2001

Weekly Crime and Arrest Comparison
Week of July 2 through July 8, 2001

Crime Complaints

	WTD 2001	WTD 2000	% Change	30-day 2001	30-day 2000	% Change	YTD 2001	YTD 2000	% Change	YTD 1999	2yr % Change
MURDER	XX	XX	XX.XX	XX	XX	XX.XX	XX	XX	XX.XX	XX	XX.XX
RAPE	XXX	XXX	XX.XX	XXX	XXX	XX.XX	XXX	XXX	XX.XX	XXX	XX.XX
ROBBERY	XXX	XXX	XX.XX	XXX	XXX	XX.XX	XXX	XXX	XX.XX	XXX	XX.XX
FEL. ASSLT	XXX	XXX	XX.XX	XXX	XXX	XX.XX	XXX	XXX	XX.XX	XXX	XX.XX
BURGLARY	XXXX	XXXX	XX.XX	XXXX	XXXX	XX.XX	XXXX	XXXX	XX.XX	XXXX	XX.XX
GR. LARCENY	XXXX	XXXX	XX.XX	XXXX	XXXX	XX.XX	XXXX	XXXX	XX.XX	XXXX	XX.XX
GLA	XXXX	XXXX	XX.XX	XXXX	XXXX	XX.XX	XXXX	XXXX	XX.XX	XXXX	XX.XX
Total	XXXXX	XXXXX	XX.XX	XXXXX	XXXXX	XX.XX	XXXXX	XXXXX	XX.XX	XXXXX	XX.XX
Shooting Victims	XX	XX	XX.XX	XX	XX	XX.XX	XX	XX	XX.XX	XX	XX.XX
Shooting Incidents	XX	XX	XX.XX	XX	XX	XX.XX	XX	XX	XX.XX	XX	XX.XX

Arrest Statistics

	WTD 2001	WTD 2000	% Change	30-day 2001	30-day 2000	% Change	YTD 2001	YTD 2000	% Change	YTD 1999	2yr % Change
MURDER	XX	XX	XX.XX	XX	XX	XX.XX	XX	XX	XX.XX	XX	XX.XX
RAPE	XXX	XXX	XX.XX	XXX	XXX	XX.XX	XXX	XXX	XX.XX	XXX	XX.XX
ROBBERY	XXX	XXX	XX.XX	XXX	XXX	XX.XX	XXX	XXX	XX.XX	XXX	XX.XX
FEL. ASSLT	XXX	XXX	XX.XX	XXX	XXX	XX.XX	XXX	XXX	XX.XX	XXX	XX.XX
BURGLARY	XXXX	XXXX	XX.XX	XXXX	XXXX	XX.XX	XXXX	XXXX	XX.XX	XXXX	XX.XX
GR. LARCENY	XXXX	XXXX	XX.XX	XXXX	XXXX	XX.XX	XXXX	XXXX	XX.XX	XXXX	XX.XX
GLA	XXXX	XXXX	XX.XX	XXXX	XXXX	XX.XX	XXXX	XXXX	XX.XX	XXXX	XX.XX
Total	XXXXX	XXXXX	XX.XX	XXXXX	XXXXX	XX.XX	XXXXX	XXXXX	XX.XX	XXXXX	XX.XX
Gun Arrests	XX	XX	XX.XX	XX	XX	XX.XX	XX	XX	XX.XX	XX	XX.XX
Narcotics Arrests	XX	XX	XX.XX	XX	XX	XX.XX	XX	XX	XX.XX	XX	XX.XX

Summons Activity

	WTD 2001	WTD 2000	% Change	30-day 2001	30-day 2000	% Change	YTD 2001	YTD 2000	% Change	YTD 1999	2yr % Change
Parking	XX	XX	XX.XX	XX	XX	XX.XX	XX	XX	XX.XX	XX	XX.XX
Moving	XX	XX	XX.XX	XX	XX	XX.XX	XX	XX	XX.XX	XX	XX.XX
Criminal	XX	XX	XX.XX	XX	XX	XX.XX	XX	XX	XX.XX	XX	XX.XX

SAMPLE COMPSTAT REPORT PAGE

NOTES

Chapter 8
Beyond Policing:
Applying Compstat in
Security Management

T hroughout this book, allusions have been made to the fact that the principles of the Compstat paradigm, as well as the Compstat process and meetings, have applicability beyond their current use in policing geographically large and densely populated urban environments like New York, New Orleans, Philadelphia and Baltimore. It is true that the paradigm developed in a large police agency in an urban environment and continues to work exceptionally well in big cities, but the principles and practices of Compstat and the strategic approach to problem solving it makes possible can be utilized as effectively in policing smaller urban areas as well as in suburban or rural environments.

Other chapters have also alluded to the fact that the effectiveness of Compstat principles and practices is not limited just to policing. The New York City Department of Sanitation, for example, uses Compstat principles and a Compstat-type meeting to ensure the cleanliness of the city's streets and sidewalks, sending inspection teams out throughout the city to measure various indicators of cleanliness: they count the number of cigarette butts and other items of trash on streets and sidewalks and determine how many trash baskets in a given area need to be emptied. The supervisors or managers of each sanitation district are responsible for these and other performance criteria, and they attend a Compstat-type meeting at which these issues and performance criteria are discussed. The meetings use these data to determine performance, to identify areas where problems recur or are particularly entrenched, and to demand accountability of the sanitation district supervisors and managers.

Similarly, the City's Department of Housing Preservation and Development adapted Compstat principles to the management of multi-unit residential properties. Known informally as "Boiler-stat," Housing Preservation and Development uses the process to keep track of broken boilers, plumbing problems, broken elevators, literal broken windows, and other maintenance problems in its real estate properties across the city. The process allows the agency to respond quickly to its problems, to identify properties requiring major renovations, and to ensure the accountability of property managers. In New York City's Department of Correction, a Compstat-type process identifies and tracks problem incidents, inmates and locations and a host of other corrections-related issues (see, for example, O'Connell and Straub, 1999).

In Baltimore, efforts are underway to manage the entire city through the Citistat process, in which virtually every municipal agency operates in a Compstat-based system. Moreover, in an important step toward public accountability, data from each of these municipal agencies (as well as a great deal of other information about the Citistat process) is posted on Baltimore's Internet site (www.baltimorecity.gov).

The point here is not just that Compstat-type meetings and the almost-immediate use of current performance data help to keep the streets cleaner in more ways than one, but that management according to the Compstat paradigm works in areas, organizations and endeavors beyond policing. In fact, Compstat paradigm management is directly applicable to virtually any organization or activity where managers need to be immediately aware of emerging trends or patterns of incidents or events in order to respond to them quickly and effectively. By attending to these small problems, larger problems are usually avoided. Compstat paradigm management also works in virtually any area or organizational structure in which performance indicators that contribute to the overall aims of the organization can be defined, captured, measured, and analyzed. Despite what some police executives may say, we need not rely only on anecdotal evidence or an intuitive sense of how well an organization (or individual) is performing. An honest and imaginative executive can develop real measurable performance indicators for any organization's activities. If we understand and can articulate what the organization is supposed to be and is supposed to do, we are at least half way to defining specific performance measures and goals. Accurate measurement of performance is the key to accountability.

In this chapter, we will focus on the use of Compstat principles and practices in private security. For a variety of reasons, private security is an appropriate area for applying this management paradigm and an appropriate area for discussing the expansion of Compstat principles to the private sector. These reasons include the overall similarity of the methods and mandates of public policing and private security, the organizational and operational similarities between many private security forces and the police, and the fact that many of the distinctions that once separated policing and security are beginning to blur. Certainly the private security industry is still primarily concerned with protecting privately-held corporate or individual assets while police are more oriented toward protecting the safety of the general public, but their missions and concerns do overlap in many areas. Further, over the past few years both policing and private security have increasingly recognized the benefits of cooperation and a synergistic coordination of activities to achieve mutual goals.

The sense of antipathy and condescension that once characterized the prevailing police attitude toward private security and toward private security personnel has begun to abate, and a great many retired police officers, managers and executives have taken upper-level positions in the security field. Many police managers and executives – some of the best and most skilled, in fact – have been lured away from policing by the prospect of greater earning power, more substantial challenges and other attractive rewards presented by the corporate security world. In contrast to policing's rigid civil service promotional system, private sector security executives often find a more flexible and more openly competitive labor market in which performance determines one's prospects for advancement. As evidenced by the fact that many colleges and universities now offer undergraduate and graduate degrees in the specialized field of Security Management, security is fast becoming a specialized sub-field of business management. The American Society for Industrial Security (ASIS) is among the groups or associations leading the effort to professionalize the security management field by developing relevant standards of practice, and the Certified Protection Professional (CPP) credential awarded by ASIS is fast becoming a prerequisite for executive-level employment in the security management field. The old image of security as a matter of a few elderly night watchmen rattling doorknobs on their rounds is largely a thing of the past.

Private security is a rapidly growing and rather dynamic field. According to the 1990 update of the Hallcrest Report on private security (a comprehensive study of the private security industry sponsored by the National Institute of Justice), annual spending for private security ($52 billion) exceeded annual spending for public police ($30 billion), and with about one and one half million employees the private security industry employs at least two and one half times the number of people employed in public policing. Both the initial 1985 Hallcrest Report (*Hallcrest I*) and its 1990 update (*Hallcrest II*) also forecast that this trend toward expansion of private security will continue for at least another decade (Cunningham and Taylor, 1985; Cunningham, Strauchs, and Van Meter, 1991).

An important contemporary trend in private security is the creation of security associations through which private security entities share information. An association of department store security managers, for example, may share such information as its surveillance photos, names, addresses, dates of birth and other pedigree data of apprehended shoplifters. The association may also circulate alerts about credit card scams, counterfeit currency passers, or virtually any other activity that threatens its members' assets. Unlike public police, who are often bound by a host of strong legal proscriptions against collecting or disseminating information about citizens who have not been arrested and formally charged with a crime, generally speaking these security associations can collect and share all kinds of information among their members.

Another important security management trend is toward enhanced interaction between police and private security through the creation of collaborative assistance programs, including specific cooperative partnerships. The 1990 Hallcrest Report, for example,

> revealed few collaborative efforts between police and private security groups, with the exception of crime prevention programs. Public law enforcement officials described their relationship with private security managers as fair to good at best. Few police chiefs even had lists of the names of security managers at area companies or contract security firms (Cunningham, Strauchs and Van Meter, 1991, p. 2).

Substantial progress has been made since *Hallcrest I* reported that over two-thirds of local law enforcement executives surveyed had no cooperative relationships with private security, and that where such arrangements did exist they were primarily limited to crime prevention programs (Cunningham, Taylor and Ford, 1985, p. 49). These once-strained relationships are beginning to improve as more and more interaction takes place. Because a great many security managers or security executives today are former police officials, their management style is typically influenced by their police experience. They also bring their contacts and relationships within policing, and are often able to offer assistance and resources to public police agencies. In summarizing the relationship and the compelling need for additional cooperation, Nemeth (1997) points out that "in the final analysis, the evidence demonstrates that the police/private security division is more an exercise in human prejudice than in logic or knowledge. Public/private cooperation would be an intelligent exercise of combined resources to combat criminality in American society (p. 291)."

Rather than seeing police and private security as separate entities with separate goals and agendas, each sector is better viewed as complementary elements in the range of choices available for the protection of life and property and as parts of a larger "community service network" of protective services. Because "private security is primarily concerned with *loss* protection, while law enforcement is primarily concerned with *crime* prevention, the relationship between the two can be depicted as the congruence of two overlapping spheres (Cunningham, Taylor and Ford, 1985, p. 41)."

Some private security companies and security associations partnerships recognize that public and private interests often overlap, and they are forging specific cooperative partnerships with police agencies. Police agencies often provide training and other assistance to the security industry, which may reciprocate by sharing facilities or other resources. It is becoming increasingly common for private security entities to provide police agencies with office space so that officers in the field can prepare paperwork or make necessary telephone calls. Some police-security partnership organizations hold regular meetings to share information about crime trends and to coordinate the activities of police and private security.

The trend is also not limited to the American scene, as evidenced by the New South Wales Institute of Security Executives' innovative "Precinct 2000" project in Sydney, Australia, which created a joint partnership between security personnel and police assigned to four Sydney police stations. Like the program it is modeled after, the NYPD's Area Police Private Security Liaison (APPL) project, the project involves regularly-scheduled meetings between security executives and police officials, sharing information, a network to facilitate the distribution of alerts and other important information, and the provision of specialized training by police to security personnel. Where these cooperative arrangements exist, Compstat can enhance and improve the way information is shared and resources are focused to solve problems facing both entities. Where these arrangements have yet to be established, Compstat may be the perfect vehicle for creating and nurturing the partnerships.

Despite these similarities and the emerging sense of cooperation between police and private security entities, there do not currently seem to be any concerted efforts by private security companies to incorporate Compstat technology or Compstat-type management. This is unfortunate, since the private security industry faces fewer bureaucratic constraints and often has greater resources available to it, and can therefore move even more rapidly toward this management style. Because private security companies are generally free of these encumbrances and are already part of an increasingly competitive industry, the companies that adopt Compstat principles can reap tremendous benefits and their success will lead to a larger share of the market. Not only will the companies offer improved service (i.e., better protection of assets), but they will operate more effectively and with greater profitability.

Business Improvement Districts

One of the more intriguing, promising and apparently best-managed areas in the private security industry today is the security component of the Business Improvement Districts that have flourished across the nation, especially in the past decade. Business Improvement Districts (BIDs) are cooperative business entities that improve public safety and other conditions that affect business and commerce within a commercial area. Generally speaking, property owners in a defined commercial area band together to create a BID – a management company or specially-created non-profit corporation operating under the terms of local legislation. Under the authority of this legislation, the BID's management company is granted limited taxing authority within the specified geographic area. All property owners in the geographic area are assessed a small additional tax (which is usually collected by the municipal finance and taxation agency and given directly to the operating company), and the revenue stream is used to fund increased or additional services beyond what the municipality provides. In essence, BID property owners pay slightly higher taxes but receive services in an amount and quality that their neighbors do not (Brooke, 1996). They also enjoy the benefits of having direct corporate control over how these services and resources are applied. There are currently over one thousand BIDs operating in municipalities across the United States, with thirty-nine in New York City alone.

In summarizing the impact of BIDs, Houstoun (1997) asserts that they represent

> a latter day counterweight to the American tendency to ignore, devalue, and often denigrate our city and town centers, despite their irreplaceable cultural attractions and entertainment offerings and their continued significance as centers of commerce. It is noteworthy that BIDs are primarily the creatures of businesses and property owners who share the belief that they can achieve greater profitability through cooperation than any of them can accomplish alone. The means to profitability include many investments in

intangibles - pleasant street vistas, a sense of security in walking after dark, the pleasures of convenient shopping, and diverse options for dining. All are important, and corporate assessees find all to be good for the bottom line.

The Grand Central Partnership in New York City, for example, consists of over six thousand businesses with about 51 million square feet of commercial space – an area roughly equivalent to the entire downtown Los Angeles area. The 12.5 cents per square foot supplementary tax BID property owners pay annually creates a $6,375,000 annual revenue stream for the operating company. In addition to providing uniformed and plainclothes security guards, the funds are used to hire private street sweeping and trash collection services, to maintain decorative flower boxes and street lights, to fund "drop-in" centers to feed the homeless, and even to hire multi-lingual tour guides to escort tourists and provide guided tours of the area's history. All of the security supervisors are retired NYPD officers, a credential that facilitates the generally amicable relationship with active police officers. The police and BID security share a substation and meet monthly to discuss crime trends (Carlson, 1995).

Recognizing that real and perceived public safety are key factors in an area's commercial viability, many or most BIDS devote a substantial portion of their budgets to maintaining private security forces. From a business management standpoint, these security forces present advantages that public policing does not. BID security personnel, for example, can be assigned to specific locations and, unlike police officers, are not called away to answer other calls. Private security guards give business owners as well as the public more control over their own safety. Also, because they can perform many tasks and roles that police perform (giving directions, handling minor disputes, and dealing with low-level quality of life conditions, for example), the police are freed up to attend to matters that demand law enforcement powers. Used intelligently, private security personnel can be an efficient means to maintain public order while reducing the burden on police services (Carlson, 1995). As importantly, BID security officers (like security officers in many other areas) have frequent contact with the public and can act as corporate good will ambassadors – indeed, the security officers in a downtown Stamford, Connecticut BID are actually called Ambassadors in recognition of their function.

In general, BID security officers are more concerned with preventing crime than with enforcement, and this also affects their relationship with the public. Many of the incidents they handle informally might otherwise require police attention. Of the almost 7,000 incidents Grand Central BID security officers responded to in 1994, for example, only 624 required police assistance and only 122 resulted in arrests. In the month of January 1994 alone, security guards told 144 unlicensed peddlers to leave the area, and only six refused. The police responded to these six incidents, but only two peddlers had to be arrested (Carlson, 1995). BID security officers also deal with quality-of-life problems like aggressive panhandling, unlicensed street peddlers and graffiti, and security personnel in a Buffalo, New York BID have been granted the power to write parking tickets as well (Houstoun, 1997).

Business Improvement Districts are at the leading edge in redefining the dimensions of cooperative police-private security interaction. Philadelphia's Center City District is a good example, since police precinct boundaries there were reconfigured to make them coterminous with the district. In an example of resource-sharing, police and private security there also share a joint operations center. The police work closely with BID management and BID security to address the kind of problems that mutually concern them.

Situations like this are tailor-made for Compstat paradigm management. Indeed, Carlson (1995) notes that the Grand Central BID's security manager, a retired NYPD detective, utilizes old-fashioned push-pin maps to track the location and movement of crime in the area. An up-to-date computerized pin mapping system could track crime and a host of other security concerns throughout the BID area with much greater accuracy, efficiency and effectiveness.

Other areas suitable for Compstat-based security or problem-solving practices include the kind of gated communities that have been springing up across the nation since the early 1980s. These communities include retirement villages, condominium complexes and affluent single family housing, and as Blakely and Snyder (1997) point out, security is a central concern of their residents. Indeed, these communities exist largely because their residents, who are predominantly affluent, want to reduce or escape from the impact of crime that exists in other places. Blakely and Snyder (1997) estimate there are as many as 20,000 gated communities in the United States, with more than three million housing units in them. They cite a leading real estate developer who estimates that eighty percent of new urban housing units are in gated communities.

The Compstat style is highly amenable to running a BID or gated community security force, or for that matter any security force, and this is especially true if the security manager's goals include facilitating a cooperative partnership with the local police. A police agency and a BID security force using parallel management practices and parallel data collection methods can more easily coordinate their activities and more rapidly respond to emerging trends or problems. The police agency and private security force can not only share data and intelligence about the times and locations crime and other street conditions occur, but if they essentially "speak the same Compstat language" they can more easily work together to coordinate and apply the resources at their disposal. When both police and private security are apprized of the spatial and temporal distribution of crime and quality of life issues, and when both work together to address them, the public benefits.

The police and the private security force share "ownership" of much of the same geography – the streets and public areas they both patrol – but often the police have little or no idea what kind of conditions and problems prevail in the private spaces of office or apartment buildings unless they are called to respond there. Even then, the information they receive is often limited. It is quite possible that the sharing of information could be the basis of joint projects to address the problems. The possibilities for cooperation and assistance seem limitless, but they all depend on sharing information, recognizing the mutuality of interests, and putting aside petty differences.

As importantly, private security often has insufficient knowledge of the number, type and location of crimes that come to the attention of the police: a common refrain throughout the security industry is that the police simply do not want to share this information. If they were armed with this knowledge about crime in commonly-patrolled areas, though, security managers could probably be of great assistance to the police by, for example, adjusting the deployment patterns of their patrol personnel or by instructing them to attend to particular situations or conditions. Private security personnel can bolster police efforts by serving as additional "eyes and ears" in the community, but only if they know what to look and listen for.

Until and unless police and private security forces begin sharing crime and quality-of-life intelligence and begin developing coordinated strategies to deal with them, neither will reach its full potential for effectiveness, and neither the public nor the private interests will be best served. This is not to suggest that the police completely "open the books" or make every detail of every police record available to non-sworn security personnel (this may, in fact, be prohibited by law in many jurisdictions). Nor is it suggested that publicly-employed police officers should be regularly deployed on private property to deal with matters that could as easily be handled by private security.

There are important legal and philosophical distinctions between police and private security, and police managers in particular have an ethical responsibility to ensure that police powers – bestowed by the public to serve the public interest – are not misused for purely private interests. It is suggested, though, that there exists a tremendous need for greater cooperation between the police and private security, and that cooperative partnerships will never reach their full potential until Compstat-like information systems and management styles are introduced.

Another very practical reason Compstat fits so well in the private security industry is the fact that so many corporations still tend to lump their security, grounds-keeping, custodial services and physical plant maintenance departments under one umbrella on the organizational table. Particularly in smaller and flatter corporate structures, a single executive may be responsible for the management of all of these functions. When this is the case, the executive in charge can use Compstat to orchestrate and coordinate the functions of each, since each of these departments is concerned with responding rapidly to geographically diverse problems and incidents, and each is concerned with quality-of-life issues.

As will be described below, because the security force typically has an existing communications system and is usually widely distributed across the geographic area of responsibility, its members are in a unique position to take the lead in reporting and acting upon problem incidents. Rather than merely dealing with crime or other incidents that traditionally fall within security's purview, they should be used to report other quality of life problems to the appropriate persons or office. The Broken Windows concept that immediately attending to minor crime and quality of life problems creates an environment of civility and prevents the development of more serious crime and quality of life problems applies equally well in the private sector. It also makes for a good business practice.

The patrolling security guard who sees fresh graffiti can use his or her radio to immediately summon custodial staff to remove it; he or she can similarly notify the maintenance staff of a broken water fountain or overflowing trash barrel. By filing a brief report that records the locations these problems occur, Compstat technology and the Compstat management style can be used to monitor the speed of the response and the permanence of the corrective action taken. Where the use of a radio communications system is inappropriate for making these notifications, or when a member of the public complains about a problem, the brief report can serve as the trigger for a work order directed to the maintenance department.

In either event, a Compstat approach allows the problem and the response to be memorialized, and may point to an appropriate tactic or strategy to reduce or eliminate the problem. If the graffiti is promptly removed but keeps appearing day after day, the appropriate course of action may be to at least temporarily alter the security officer's patrol patterns. The executive may also wish to notify custodial and maintenance staff to look out for the problem at that or other locations as they go about their regular business. If the same water fountain repeatedly breaks down, the manager may decide that it is more cost-effective to replace it with a new unit than to continually dispatch a plumber for repairs. A rapid Compstat-style response to these quality of life problems and public complaints clearly communicates management's concern and commitment to staff as well as to clients. It builds good will, fosters the perception that management is responsive to public needs, and enhances cost-effectiveness.

One reason Compstat-type management principles work especially well in smaller, flatter structures is the lack of formal organizational boundaries – all or most of the necessary resources are under the control of one executive. Because the organization is smaller and less bureaucratic, it is inherently easier to mobilize in order to solve individual problems, and is inherently easier to transform.

The Practical Application of Compstat in Private Security

As their names imply, an important difference between private security and public policing is that private security personnel work to achieve the interests of the private individuals or group paying their salary while the police work to serve the interests of society as a whole. The primary goal of private security is the protection of assets rather than the overall public good. This is not to say that the security industry is *not* concerned with issues of public good, but that their principal focus is on the welfare of the corporation or the group that employs them. Similarly, the fact that police are primarily concerned with the public good does not mean that they are completely unconcerned with the protection of private assets.

Hess and Wrobleski (1996, p. 29) describe private security as "a profit-oriented industry that provides personnel, equipment and/or procedures to *prevent* losses caused by human error, emergencies, disasters, or criminal actions" (italics in original) The fact that the security industry operates largely according to private sector principles of profit and loss (i.e., it is primarily geared toward increasing the "bottom line" of corporate profits by protecting against the theft, loss or erosion of the employer's assets) bodes well for its adoption and adaptation of Compstat paradigm management practices, because Compstat promotes efficiency in the deployment of personnel and other resources. Generally speaking, private sector entities as a whole are already more oriented than police agencies to the kind of contemporary business practices involved in Compstat management, and private sector corporations may be either less resistant to or more acquainted with the kind of innovative changes necessary to make the paradigm flourish.

As applied in the policing environment, Compstat certainly affects the police agency's "bottom line" – it reduces crime, fear of crime, and public disorder conditions, and it improves the quality of life within the municipality where it is practiced. In the private security environment, Compstat management also has great potential for increasing the corporation's "bottom line" – profitability – by reducing the loss of corporate assets through "inventory shrinkage," simple theft, sabotage, or other risks. As discussed below, Compstat also has the potential to reduce the loss of corporate assets through negligence lawsuits. Because Compstat improves the quality of life in areas where it is applied, it can actually improve profitability. In the retail business, for example, the importance of location has long been recognized as a factor in sales and profitability, and the attractiveness and perceived safety of a business's location is an important part of the business's profitability. Quite simply, customers may go elsewhere if they do not feel safe.

This dynamic was succinctly described in a recent *Security Management* article:

Sometimes, the mere perception of potential danger can keep shoppers away. For example, if groups of teens are loitering in public areas, customers may feel intimidated even if the teens are causing no trouble.

Customers who have a negative experience at a shopping center – whether based on real or imagined threats – are unlikely to return. Moreover, they are likely to tell others of their views, creating a ripple effect that leads even more shoppers to go elsewhere. And once customer confidence is lost, the loss of revenue is not far behind. Security programs must, therefore, be preventive and custo-mer-service oriented.

While every mall's needs are unique, certain issues pertain across-the-board. They include the need to gather information, tailor programs to those findings, provide customer service, create a code of conduct, and develop partnerships with law enforcement (Thompson, 1998).

In this section, we will use a shopping mall as our example for establishing a hypothetical Compstat-type security management system. This example was chosen because most readers will be generally familiar with the types of security problems malls face, and because shopping malls are often geographically dispersed environments with several specific types of territory that require different security strategies and tactics. The point must again be clearly made, though, that Compstat-type security management would apply equally well to a Business Improvement District, a single high-rise office or apartment building, a hotel or resort, a college campus, a corporate complex or industrial park, a factory, a military base, or virtually any other installation or complex with people or assets that require protection.

In addition, although the remainder of this chapter will focus on the mechanics of establishing a Compstat-type management system in the private security area, it will not reiterate or even discuss many of the important management issues and variables covered elsewhere in this book. This chapter could, for example, provide an overview of the history of private security and its impact on contemporary security management practices, or discuss personnel screening, selection, hiring, training and promotion practices in private security and how they also affect corporate operations. It will not discuss these admittedly important issues in detail, since the book is primarily about police management and is primarily geared toward police managers and students of police management. This chapter assumes that the security executive who desires to incorporate this management paradigm in his or her organization knows enough about these important variables to account for them properly, and it assumes that most other readers are more concerned with glimpsing the paradigm's broader applicability outside policing than with learning about the security industry *per se*.

Security executives may wish to attempt the in-house design and imple-mentation of a Compstat-type incident tracking system, but it will probably be less expensive and more efficient to retain a specialized consultant who combines knowledge of the security industry with familiarity in the practical aspects of implementing and using Compstat-type management and technology systems.

Data Collection

One of the first concrete steps to introducing a Compstat-type management system in private security is to establish or refine an existing data collection system. All too often, private security companies or contract guard agencies do not require their patrol personnel to prepare many written reports documenting their activities, and this presents a problem for Compstat-style management. Except in exceptional or unusual circumstances (the security officer effects an arrest, for example, or he or she responds to an incident in which an employee or visitor is injured), security managers often know very little about the specific activities a guard performs or the interactions he or she has with others. Even in security operations where guards or patrol staff are dispatched to respond to reported problems or disturbances, the records often consist solely of a dispatch record log noting the time the call was received, the time the call was dispatched, the identity of the guard, and the disposition – usually something like "problem corrected" or "gone on arrival." When a guard takes some action on his or her own initiative, many companies do not require him or her to record or memorialize the nature of the problem or the action taken. Such policies deprive executives of important management information, they complicate efforts to ensure accountability, and they invite lawsuits.

This kind of data collection (or lack thereof) is wholly insufficient for adequate strategic management in the Compstat mode, and security operations that maintain such rudimentary records systems also expose themselves to potential liability: the records can be subpoenaed and introduced in a criminal or civil proceeding. If the security records betray a lack of adequate sophistication or a tendency to assign the same disposition to every incident, you can be assured that if the plaintiff has retained a good attorney, he or she will seize upon it as evidence of lax security and lax security management. In order to avoid or limit liability in a potential negligence lawsuit, the company will have to show that it made at least a good faith effort to anticipate the likelihood of problems and took reasonable steps to head them off. More will be said about liability abatement, but the point should be clearly made that the availability and accuracy of records affects the likelihood of a successful defense in a negligence lawsuit.

At the same time, care must be taken that the report preparation process does not bog down the security officer with paperwork to the extent that it prevents him or her from fulfilling the primary mission of ensuring a safe and secure environment. The security manager who places too much emphasis on report preparation may inadvertently lead the organization toward the kind of excesses and problems that characterized the Professional Model in policing.

Adequate data collection does not require extensive written statements or narratives, but it does require that certain important items of information are obtained. Despite significant advances over the past several years, one of the issues that continues to face the private security industry is the quality of its personnel. In some states, security guards must now be screened through a criminal records check and receive pre-employment training. As part of their ongoing efforts to raise industry standards, security industry leaders in New York State, for example, successfully lobbied the State Legislature to impose minimum training and registration standards for security personnel, which became effective in January 1994. Security officers must take an eight-hour introductory course and pass a licensing examination (Hoffman, 1996). Although this and other similar legislation is an important step in the right direction, a great deal remains to be done to raise standards. For the most part, contract guard service employees and even proprietary security guards are still not particularly well-paid, education requirements are few, and the average guard's writing skills may be lacking.

Fortunately, extensive narrative reports are not always necessary. Security patrol personnel can be furnished with relatively inexpensive specially-designed snap-out forms or two-sided pre-printed index cards that collect the necessary items of information in a check-off or fill-in format with a brief section for a narrative description of the incident. The information in each box corresponds to a data field in the computerized incident database, and the information items can be entered into the database by a data-entry clerk. The essential thing is that the forms are designed to capture the kind of data managers need to identify chronic and emerging problems and to make their deployment and operational decisions.

What Kinds of Data Do We Need to Capture?

Optimally, we should know *when* incidents are occurring, *where* they are occurring, *who* is involved, *what* kind of incident occurred, *how* it occurred, and if possible, *why* it occurred. Because we are primarily interested in determining spatial and temporal relationships between particular types of incidents, however, we are primarily interested in *when*, *where* and *what kind* of incident occurred. Although all of the above-listed items are important and should be included in the incident report, these three will be most useful to us in terms of mapping incidents and developing incident trend analyses.

The "when" of an incident is easy enough – filling in the date, day of the week and time the incident occurred will usually suffice. The issues of "where" and "what kind" of incident require a bit more thought and planning.

Let us imagine that we are developing an incident report form for a large suburban shopping mall comprised of about one hundred shops and stores. There are several types or categories of places where an incident might require the attention of security personnel. An incident might occur in a parking field, in a particular store, in a storage area or loading dock, in the mall area itself, at one of the kiosks in the mall area, and perhaps at other locations as well. In a practical sense, the problem of "where" is essentially a problem of geocoding the location so that the mapping software can display the incident at its actual place of occurrence. This is not usually a problem in policing, since police officers usually respond to known addresses. Simply coding the location as "inside the mall area" is insufficient, since the mapping software has no way of knowing whether to display the incident at the north end, the south, or the middle of the mall, much less a more specific location. At the same time, the security executive should avoid making the geocoded locations too specific. These issues should be discussed with the software consultants retained to design the system.

A simple way of circumventing this limitation is to create a security map of the mall with some sort of coordinates superimposed or with certain places marked with a location marker code number. Everyone has been to a mall and has seen those large "you are here" display maps showing the locations of various stores. Often the stores are indexed with a number that corresponds to a place on the map, and some use a color-coding scheme as well. The incident report form and geocoding system might use a similar system, but it is probably more advisable to discretely display special location codes throughout the open mall area – each supporting pillar, for example, might bear a small numbered location code plate similar to the mile markers found alongside highways or the numbers seen on lampposts and utility poles in some urban areas. The security officer would simply list the location code from the nearest pole in the appropriate box on the form. As long as the location codes are appropriately spaced - so that they will give the necessary amount of precision to the mapping software – and easily observed by the security officer, it matters little whether they are placed on poles, flowerpots, floors, or storefronts.

Because incidents can occur inside stores, each store in the mall should also have a location code, and especially in long, narrow stores it may be advisable to include a code distinguishing whether the incident occurred in the front or rear of the store. In larger stores it may be advisable to assign location codes to each quadrant or sales department. The ability to distinguish whether the incident occurred in the front or the back of the store is essentially one of determining whether it could have easily been observed by an officer patrolling the public mall area, which in turn effects the deployment and assignment of security officers as well as the patrol instructions they are given. If incidents are taking place in the back of a particular store, the security guard needs to know that fact if he or she is to patrol effectively.

Location codes are less of a problem in parking lots, since most parking lots are already coded for the ease of shoppers. Most parking lot light poles already display a letter-and-number coordinate to help shoppers find their cars. Depending on a variety of factors, the existing parking lot location codes may need adjustment to make them identify locations more precisely. Security directors should be aware that over the past several years a tremendous number of negligence lawsuits against malls and other installations have come from parking lot incidents, and this fact points to the need for special care and attention.

In particular, lighting conditions in parking lots are an area of specific risk. If the overall site security plan calls for (as it should) the scheduled replacement of all security lighting bulbs at regular intervals - generally at three quarters of the bulb's rated life – the Compstat system can be used to automatically track required changes as well as to record locations where lighting devices and bulbs are particularly prone to breakage or vandalism.

Loading docks and storage areas are frequently the sites of incidents, particularly thefts and intrusions, and they also need to be location coded. In short, every area of the mall – whether it is a public or private space – needs to be adequately identified by a location code that is readily available to the security guard for entry onto the incident form. The same location coding principles apply to other types of complexes and locations (hospitals, college campuses, etc.).

The concept of the "adequacy" of location coding depends upon a variety of factors. A great deal depends upon the physical layout of the facility, the types of incidents one considers important, and the limits of the security force's jurisdiction. If the mall only provides security guards for public spaces and the security department is not concerned with what goes on in individual stores, for example, it is obviously not important to code each store's stock room. In another facility operated under different conditions, it might indeed be necessary to code each and every room, stairwell and public area. Geocoding is not a particularly difficult matter, and most off-the-shelf mapping software will easily accommodate a large number of coded locations.

The issue of *what kind* of incident occurred is perhaps the most difficult to deal with on the incident data form, since there would seem to be literally thousands of types of incidents that could conceivably occur at a shopping mall, hospital complex or other installation and require a security response. Determining how exhaustive the list of potential incidents should be is, again, largely determined by the conditions at a particular site. In a practical sense, the number of incident types is limited only by the available space on the form and the coding scheme used. If the security manager is only interested in a few types of incidents, a single-digit coding scheme may suffice. Up to ten types of incident, coded 0 through 9, can be enumerated on the form if a single-digit coding scheme is used. If the number of incident types is ten or more, a double-digit coding scheme (00 through 99) allows up to one hundred different incident types. These incident types and their corresponding code should be listed on the form, or perhaps on the rear of the form if the list is extensive.

The form should collect information about the incident as well as the person or business involved, and these should be collected as separate variables. This limits the need to have extensive lists of specific incident types. For example, many types of theft often occur at malls - the thefts can be of store property, customer property, employee property, or mall property. One could list four or more incident categories for theft, but it is probably simpler to have separate boxes for "incident type" and "victim." When necessary, database and mapping software can combine these variables and determine relationships quickly and easily.

Another consideration is the mutual exclusivity of incident types and the need to balance specificity with simplicity. This means that the list of incident types should be easily understood and written in such a way that the officer does not feel compelled to choose between two categories in deciding how to list the incident, at the same time the incident category should adequately describe the event. The incident types should be fairly simple and straightforward, and at the same time the list should include the kinds of incidents that occur most frequency. Although it is probably easier to simply list a single "theft" category rather than specifying "pickpocket," "shoplift," etc., the goal of simplicity must be weighed against the degree of precision you hope to achieve. In this specific case, it is important that the security manager differentiate between these types of theft because the offenders usually have different *modus operandi*, and because the intervention strategies used to address them are also different. Pickpockets usually operate in fairly crowded outdoor areas, while shoplifters almost invariably work indoors and depend upon the hope that no one will be close enough to directly observe them. Pickpockets are often skilled professionals, while most shoplifters are amateurs; pickpockets usually take wallets, while shoplifters are less discriminate in what they will steal.

For effective analysis in other security settings, it is probably important to break out and distinguish between different types of theft: office thieves who prowl office buildings taking unattended laptop computers and wallets, restaurant thieves who lift wallets and handbags, and construction thieves who take tools, building supplies and other valuable items. Each of these offenses demands a different kind of security response, and different strategies may need to be developed for each.

Security managers should also use the Compstat-type system to identify linkages and causal connections between different events. To continue with the example of the pickpockets and shoplifters, the managers should consider the thief's *modus operandi* and its possible connection to other crimes. If a pickpocket steals a wallet, how does he or she dispose of the credit cards? Attempting to analytically link the times and locations of wallet thefts with the specific times and locations that the credit cards are used can identify a potential pattern and dramatically increase the likelihood that the pickpocket or a member of the team can be apprehended.

Again, the development of a useful data collection form will depend on a number of factors, including the number and type of incidents occurring most frequently, the physical environment, the amount of available space on the form, and the kind of incidents the security executive is most concerned with.

It is recommended, though, that the incident report collect intelligence information about a variety of incident types that concern security and management, and not simply those incidents to which a guard responds. It might, for example, be used to report the placement of graffiti as well as to memorialize the response of cleaning staff, and the report itself could also serve as the automatic trigger for a custodian's work order. As discussed elsewhere in this book, the appearance of the physical environment has a great deal to do with our perception of safety, and graffiti can easily create the false impression that an other-wise safe area is dangerous. This impacts profits if people avoid the place and frequent other merchants. The most cogent tactic in this area is probably to instruct security staff to immediately report graffiti or other quality-of-life problems and, if possible, ensure that they are addressed immediately. Preparing an incident report is necessary because it memorializes the event and allows managers to determine where and when such incidents occur, as well as to determine how quickly the problems are being addressed by other corporate divisions. The incident report can be used to report any type of information or intelligence that managers should be made aware of.

Once completed by the security officer, the incident forms should be reviewed for accuracy and completeness by a supervisor and submitted to the security office as soon as possible. The supervisor's review ensures awareness of the incident, permits him or her to take additional action if necessary, and allows him or her to give the guard additional instructions, guidance, feedback or informal on-the-spot training. After the report is reviewed, a consecutively-numbered incident tracking number should be assigned. At some point the form will be entered into the software database by clerical personnel. Every effort should be made to ensure that the data entry is prompt and accurate. Daily entry is recommended, since batching large amounts of data entry tends to increase error rates.

Analysis of Data

Various options exist for the security manager to analyze the data. Depending upon conditions, the manager may forego holding a formal Compstat-type meeting and simply use the database and mapping software to develop electronic pin maps. These computer-generated pin maps can be posted in or near the security office as a sort of crime information center, and it is probably useful to post these maps in an area where other employees of the operating company can see them. Is probably not advisable to post them in public areas where every customer or every store employee can review them, but the crime information center should be available to cleaners, maintenance workers and other employees of the operating corporation so that they can be aware of conditions and act as the "eyes and ears" of the security division. Given the propensity of some mischievous employees to monkey with them or to post unauthorized comments, the bulletin boards holding the pin maps (especially if they use old-fashioned push-pins) should be protected or encased behind glass.

The security manager has the option of holding a regularly scheduled crime and quality of life strategy meeting attended by shift supervisors, store security personnel, mall management, local police, and just about any other stakeholder or interested party in the public safety and loss prevention spheres, including maintenance, custodial and guard personnel. Fancy techniques – video projection screens, for example – are less important than getting the message across. While a large- screen video monitor (say a 22- or 24-inch color television) is the preferable method of displaying the maps and data analysis charts (since they allow a contemporaneous interactive exploration of the crime and quality of life landscape), flip charts or even handout packets of prepared photostated charts will do. The key element is not how elegantly the data is presented, but what the manager does with it to discern trends, to plan strategies, and to ensure accountability.

Compstat and Civil Liability in Security

The security executive's responsibility to protect the employer's assets extends to protecting or insulating the employer from losses associated with negligence lawsuits. Nemeth (1995) points out that businesses are besieged with premises liability lawsuits alleging negligence through the failure to provide a safe and secure environment for employees, customers and others legally entitled to be on the premises. Current legal standards make it easier for plaintiffs to win negligence lawsuits, and he cites a 1993 study which showed that the average jury verdict for an on-premises rape was $1.8 million and the average jury verdict for a death was $2.2 million (p. 131). Jury awards today are undoubtedly even higher, and will undoubtedly continue to increase. Even an out-of-court settlement can be costly, though. The *New York Times* reported that a famous New York department store settled a lawsuit brought by a female employee who was raped in a storage area by an intruder. The settlement, estimated at about $500,000, came after the store failed in its claim that the case should be covered by worker's compensation (*New York Times*, April 12, 1998).

Negligence is a complex legal concept, and a comprehensive discussion of it is beyond the scope of this book. In order to win a negligence lawsuit, though, it suffices to say that the plaintiff will have to demonstrate that a business had a duty to protect the plaintiff, that the duty was breached, and that the harm had a proximate cause which could have been prevented through due diligence. A jury is likely to consider whether the crime or incident was foreseeable, whether the business had reasonable and prudent security measures in place, and whether a lack of adequate security was the proximate cause of the victim's injury.

In determining culpability as well as in assessing damages, a jury will almost certainly consider the forseeability of an incident and whether the business took reasonable steps to prevent it. The concept of reasonability is also complex, but the point is that the business does not usually have to go to extraordinary lengths to foresee or prevent an incident. Although the key question in preventing liability may be whether the business complied with or met the threshold of prevailing security industry standards, it is clear that practices which exceed industry standards demonstrate that the business exercised an even higher level of due diligence than was required of it or that most others practice. Going beyond industry standards to identify foreseeable events and take prudent steps to prevent them may be the key to a solid defense.

Nemeth (1997, p. 133) says that the areas of duty and foreseeability come into sharper focus in the area of parking lot security. The law requires landowners to take affirmative actions to control the wrongful acts of third parties which threaten persons legally entitled to be on the premises when the owner has reasonable cause to anticipate the acts and the probability that injury will result from them.

> Such affirmative action would seem to mean that the owner or possessor of a parking facility should take reasonable security measures, such as adequate lighting and the presence of security guards, and, if practical, additional measures such as strategically placed television cameras or alarm systems, warnings, and the availability of escort services.
>
> Discerning past and present criminal incidence rates is crucial to the owner's knowledge of what might occur.
>
> An important matter that should be investigated is the availability of statistics concerning crime in the neighborhood where the crime occurred and, more specifically, in the parking lot facility itself (Nemeth, 1997, p. 133).

There is perhaps no better or more effective way of avoiding premises liability, in parking lots or elsewhere, than for security executives to be able to demonstrate that they went beyond prevailing industry standards to identify and address foreseeable problems and incidents. There is no management tool that can realistically assess threats and analyze vulnerabilities as effectively or as inexpensively as Compstat. Compstat analysis provides hard data about actual incidents, spatially identifies security threats and vulnerabilities, and points up the kind of security countermeasures that should be implemented. In any cost-benefit analysis, Compstat is a winner. A relatively small investment in a Compstat-type technology system, coupled with cogent management and effective deployment, may well save a business millions of dollars by averting or by providing for the successful defense of a potential negligence suit payout.

Summary and Conclusions

Compstat technology and the Compstat paradigm seem particularly well-suited to security management. Police and private security share many similarities in their structures, mandates, and operations, and in many venues police and private security organizations have forged close alliances to solve mutual problems. Because Compstat management increases efficiency and cost-effectiveness, it can have a dramatic impact on profitability and can give a security business the edge it needs to thrive in a competitive industry. Because it accurately captures and memorializes incident data, and because it points the manager toward specific policies, practices and deployment strategies that address these incidents, Compstat can be used to identify potential threats and to respond effectively to them. Used intelligently, the security manager may preclude or abate the organization's potential liability in a negligence lawsuit, saving considerable assets.

In this chapter, we described how Compstat can be used to manage security in a shopping mall or in a Business Improvement District, and how such security organizations can use Compstat to enhance their effectiveness as well as their relationships with the public and their partnerships with local police. Compstat systems can be used to manage a host of crime, public order and quality of life problems that security organizations face, and can be adapted to include other problems that do not traditionally fall within the scope of the security function.

Recommended Readings

San Luis, Edward; Louis A. Tyska and Lawrence Fennelly **Office and Office Building Security, (2nd Edition)**, Alexandria, VA: American Society for Industrial Security, 1994.

Nemeth, Charles P. **Private Security and the Law (2nd Edition)**, Cincinnati, OH: Anderson, 1997.

Cunningham, William C., John J. Strauchs, and Clifford W. Van Meter "Private Security: Patterns and Trends," National Institute of Justice: National Institute of Justice *Research In Brief* series, August 1991.

Cunningham, William C. and Todd H. Taylor **Crime and Protection in America: A Study of Private Security and Law Enforcement Resources and Relationships: Executive Summary**, Washington, DC: US Department of Justice, National Institute of Justice, May 1985.

Questions for Discussion and Debate:

1. Specifically, what kinds of data do police and private security need to share? Other than criminal records information, what kind of police data would you want access to if you were a security manager? What kind of security data would you want access to if you were a local police chief?

2. Considering the data collection needs described in this chapter, develop a prototype data collection form for a hospital. What types of data would you want to collect, and why? How would you geocode the hospital?

3. You are the security director for a large urban university. The university does not have a campus, *per se*, but rather it uses about twenty-five separate buildings spread out over a fairly large area of the city. Is it possible to use a Compstat-style security management system for this university?

4. This chapter focused primarily on how to develop and implement a Compstat-type process for solving the crime and disorder problems security managers confront. Based on what you have learned in other chapters, how can this process be used to amplify and extend the accountability of security managers and supervisors for their efforts and results?

Chapter 9
The Future of Compstat

A s our exploration of the Compstat paradigm draws to a close, it is useful to attempt a glimpse into the future. We've seen the organizational environment that preceded Compstat in the NYPD (and, more generally, in American policing as a whole), and we've seen the paradigm's impact on the agency as well as the fundamental changes it effected and the powerful results it achieved. As evidenced by the number of police and other public service agencies that continue to adapt and / or adopt the paradigm and implement its methods and principles, we can see that Compstat has made its mark and that it is fairly well entrenched across the broad landscape of public sector management. But because the Compstat paradigm continues to evolve, to adapt, and to find new areas of application, it would be premature to end our exploration without some speculation about its future.

At the same time, speculating about the future – especially about a phenomenon as dynamic and still-evolving as the Compstat paradigm – can be a perilous venture. In the first place, one risks the embarrassment of having predictions turn out to be wrong: the political, legal and social forces that shape the policing environment can shift rapidly, and the premises and assumptions upon which the predictions are based may no longer have as powerful an influence. New problems and new mandates for the police can arise with little or no warning – the events of September 11, 2001 are a case in point – and they can also change the future. Attempting to predict the future can certainly be a risky business, but taking reasonable and well-informed risks is what the Compstat paradigm is all about.

Further, and notwithstanding these caveats, there is a great deal to be optimistic about concerning Compstat and the Compstat paradigm, since the paradigm's greatest strength lies in its capacity for flexible response to new and emerging trends. Just as Compstat has proven its effectiveness in rapidly responding to new crime trends and rapidly changing crime conditions, it is likely to be effective in overcoming any other complicated exigencies the future may hold. The devastating and entirely unanticipated September 11, 2001 attack on the World Trade Center, for example, has immutably changed American policing, and the threat of terrorism is likely to be among the primary challenges American policing and American government faces in the coming decades. As discussed below, at least one well-regarded observer of police has already suggested that Compstat management practices may be the solution for policing's compelling need for timely and accurate intelligence, rapid deployment, effective tactics and relentless follow-up to prevent and/or react to future terrorist events (MacDonald, 2001). In this concluding chapter, we will briefly explore some of the directions Compstat has taken and some of the directions it may take as it continues to evolve.

Variations on the Compstat Theme

It was noted in an earlier chapter that over the past several years hundreds of police agencies across the nation and throughout the world have visited the NYPD to learn about Compstat (Gootman, 2000). It was also noted (in the context of 'cargo cult management') that many of these visitors returned to their agencies and implemented some variant of what they learned and observed, and it was suggested that the rapid wholesale importation of unfamiliar management methods and strategies might ultimately damage their organizations and organizational cultures. Indeed, significant motivation for writing this book, and for outlining the history and clarifying the under-lying philosophy of Compstat, derived from the recognition of the damage this powerful management tool could do in the hands of inept or unethical executives. Compstat management empowers executives, managers, super-visors and line officers, and that power could easily be subverted – especially by unethical or self-serving executives – to corruptly suppress the ideals of democratic policing, to intimidate or harass personnel, or to diminish human rights and American freedoms. In less democratic nations or police systems, the virtues of Compstat (especially its efficiency and effectiveness in collecting information and responding to issues that concern police executives) could be corrupted and used to increase the power of an authoritarian regime.

Despite a wealth of superficially descriptive material about Compstat in the academic sphere and in the general news media (material that is usually quite laudatory but often factually or philosophically inaccurate in its details), there have been few real research studies about Compstat and its impact on the police agency and its culture. We simply do not know how many American or overseas police departments are currently practicing a variant of Compstat. We do not know how thoroughly the paradigm has infiltrated the management mindset or how significant its impact has been on police operations and strategies, and we do not know how its implementation has affected the agencies' organizational cultures. There have been many success stories, however, and these examples provide an optimistic picture

of Compstat's future. What many of these positive examples have in common is that the Compstat management processes and techniques were introduced to the agencies by individuals who were part of its development in New York – by individuals who thoroughly understood the subtleties of its philosophy and practice. Where Compstat has worked well, there was no cargo cult management taking place.

Many of the success stories come out of police agencies where Bratton, Maple and others involved in the development of Compstat and the turnaround of the NYPD had a direct influence. When Bratton left office in April 1996, he, Maple and several other 'founding fathers' of the Compstat paradigm became successful consultants – other municipalities wanted to achieve the same kind of crime reductions and quality of life improvements New York City had.

Jack Maple and John Linder, for example, took on a major consulting project for the New Orleans Police Department – an agency with a reputation for being notoriously corrupt and perennially mismanaged. Working closely with newly-appointed reform Superintendent Richard Pennington, they helped reorganize the agency by following many of the transformational and re-engineering principles practiced in New York and described in elsewhere in this book. They also introduced a Compstat-type crime management system. Reform in the New Orleans Police Department is ongoing (all effective reform initiatives should be a matter of a continuing process rather than a programmatic effort), but tremendous strides have been achieved in changing the agency and reducing crime: since 1997, the New Orleans Police Department has reduced major crime by forty percent (www. nopdonline.com). Maple and Linder also introduced Compstat crime management systems and Compstat paradigm management practices in Newark and Baltimore, among other cities.

For his part, Bratton's consulting group reorganized police departments including Birmingham, Trenton, and Stamford, as well as various cities in Europe and South America. John Timoney, who served as Chief of Department and First Deputy Commissioner during Bratton's tenure, became Philadelphia's Police Commissioner and introduced the Compstat management style. In each municipality, management systems based on the Compstat paradigm were instituted, and they have achieved remarkable results. The successes these departments have had derive from the expertise of the consultants (or, in Timoney's case, from the chief executive) who adapted Compstat principles to the agencies' needs and to the organizational cultures, as well as from the quality and extent of executive commitment to

Compstat paradigm management principles. In each case, Compstat was tailored to the unique history, culture, mandate and organizational structure – it was not imposed in 'cookie cutter' fashion. In each case, an agency-appropriate Compstat variant was developed in conjunction with a thorough top-to-bottom analysis that gave the consultants and the chief executive a comprehensive detailed understanding of the department. In each case, the Compstat paradigm and the Compstat process expanded and grew, adapting and incorporating the lessons learned earlier.

One of the most notable and most ambitious variations on the Compstat theme is Baltimore's Citistat. In Baltimore, every city agency was re-tooled to operate according to Compstat paradigm principles, and every agency developed statistical measurement and reporting systems for key performance data. Every city agency gathers performance data and conducts a weekly in-house management meeting modeled after the NYPD's Compstat Crime Control Strategy meetings, and every agency head attends a citywide meeting chaired by Mayor Martin O'Malley every two weeks. Jack Maple and John Linder were key consultants in this process, and Edward Norris (a Maple protégé who became the NYPD's Deputy Commissioner for Operations when Maple left) was appointed Baltimore's Police Commissioner in May 2000.

While Compstat in police agencies usually focuses on the seven major crimes as well as other indicators of violence, disorder and quality of life, agencies operating under Citistat focus on issues of concern to their particular mandate. Baltimore's Department of Health, for example, includes statistical measures of the number of food establishments inspected and the number of violations found, the number of HIV tests conducted and the number of positive results, the number of active clients in methadone treatment programs, and even the number of animal carcasses removed from city streets. Among the data items Baltimore's Housing Authority collects are the number and percentage of vacant public housing units, the number of work orders issued for apartment repairs, and the number of apartments inspected, as well as overtime earned by staff at each housing project. The Bureau of Recreation and Parks captures data on attendance and revenues generated at public swimming pools as well as skating rinks and golf courses, the number of youths participating in various city-sponsored sports leagues, and the number of senior citizens participating in sponsored bus trips, as well as numerous other performance indicators.

In line with the Compstat paradigm's emphasis on public accountability through transparency, Baltimore's municipal agencies make these and other key performance data available on the city's web site – www.baltimorecity.

gov/news/citistat/index.html. The web site also contains an excellent description of the Citistat process and a number of links to related news articles and press releases. In addition, the Baltimore Police Department's website (www.baltimorepdonline.org) has a searchable database of reported crime – users can enter an address or neighborhood and call up a detailed pin map showing the spatial distribution of various crimes. The Philadelphia and New Orleans Police Departments also have extensive crime and quality of life data available on their websites (www.ppdonline.org/ppd_compstat.htm and www.nopdonline.com). Although the NYPD makes some data (including modified Compstat reports for each precinct and for the city as a whole) available on its website (www.nypd.org), the site currently has no mapping capability.

Since implementing Citistat, Baltimore has realized substantial declines in crime. Between 1999 (the year before Edward Norris assumed the position of Police Commissioner) and 2001, overall violent crime declined 24 percent; homicides declined 15 percent; shootings fell 34 percent and robberies fell 28 percent; rapes declined by 20 percent and assaults fell 21 percent. Similar results have been obtained in other city agencies, and by monitoring overtime, sick leave and other expenses Baltimore saved more than $13 million in its first year of operation. Citistat's technology piece is inexpensive and highly cost-effective, according to the city of Baltimore: the computers and construction of a special conference room for Citistat meetings cost about $20,000 (www.baltimorecity.gov/news/citistat/index.html).

A host of other municipalities have followed the Compstat model. Houston, for example, has implemented ServiceStat. In an August 2001 press release, Mayor Lee Brown – the NYPD's former Police Commissioner – noted that the initiative was based on the NYPD Compstat model and described it in this familiar way:

> "The ServiceStat module is built on a four-block foundation," Mayor Brown added, "First, accurate and timely intelligence to ensure the most complete analysis possible; second, rapid deployment of resources to quickly address City problems; third, effective tactics and strategies to ensure proactive solutions; and fourth, relentless follow-up and assessment to ensure that problems do not reoccur.

Although it is based on Compstat and is quite similar to Citistat's inclusion of multiple agencies, ServiceStat is linked to Houston's 3-1-1 Service Hotline, a kind of central 911 system for non-emergency matters. By tying the 3-1-1 Service Hotline to a Compstat accountability system, every citizen complaint about service can be tracked and monitored to ensure that the complaint is resolved to the caller's satisfaction. Aggregated and categorized statistics can also help identify the issues of greatest public concern – have the overall number of inquiries about trash pickups increased, or have complaints about potholes tapered off? – and permit executives to identify emerging trends. Once these trends are identified, agency heads can be held accountable for resolving the issues.

The Compstat model was successfully adapted to manage New York City's jail system. Bernard Kerik, who was at that time New York's Corrections Commissioner, developed the Total Efficiency Accountability Management System (TEAMS) initiative to measure, track and control incidents of inmate violence as well as other critical management problems. Once again, the results were remarkable: in the initiative's first four years, inmate violence was reduced by an astounding ninety percent, overtime expenses were reduced by half, sick time among corrections officers declined by 25 percent, and morale improved tremendously (O'Connell & Straub, 1999).

In 2001 Compstat was brought to bear in managing New York City's mammoth and highly bureaucratized Board of Education. Given the nature and scope of the Board of Education's management problems and its long history of institutionalized resistance to accountability, this initiative will present a significant challenge to Compstat. Since practically every other effort in recent history to rein in the Board of Education bureaucrats and to hold educators accountable for the performance of students has largely failed, Compstat's success or failure will depend greatly upon the commitment and perseverance of the Schools Chancellor and middle management superintendents.

Clearly, the Compstat paradigm is beginning to take hold in municipal government, and new applications for the paradigm are being developed. From the accelerating pace of its acceptance and implementation as well as from the positive results it is bringing about, it is a fairly safe prediction that the paradigm will continue to develop and grow. It is also a safe prediction that it will continue to achieve outstanding results in agencies headed by committed executives who properly implement it and wisely use the transformational power it affords them.

Compstat and the Terrorist Threat

One of the most significant impediments to effective law enforcement response to terrorism is the problem of competing interests between and among law enforcement agencies – in other words, 'turf wars' based on the control of crime intelligence information. The American system of law enforcement is incredibly complicated and incredibly decentralized: there are more than 17,000 separate local, state and federal law enforcement agencies in the United States (Bureau of Justice Statistics, 1995; Reeves, 1995), and for the most part there is little real interaction or sharing of crime intelligence between and among them. Notwithstanding the availability of information networks like the National Crime Information Center (NCIC) and their databases for stolen property, outstanding arrest warrants and other criminal records, there is no centralized authority that establishes and enforces standardized policies and practices for these agencies. No central authority holds these agencies accountable for cooperation or for sharing information.

This decentralization and the autonomy of the 17,000 agencies has always been an important and ultimately desirable feature of American law enforcement – decentralization and independence tends to ensure that police power will not be consolidated under the control of a few people who might abuse that power. Totalitarian regimes tend to have highly centralized and very powerful national police forces (as well as a tendency to use these police forces to coerce and control the public and to suppress human rights), but with a few notable exceptions democracies tend to have decentralized and fairly weak systems of law enforcement.

Along with this decentralization, though, is the tendency toward competition and the withholding of information. Turf wars over information occur between and among (as well as within) law enforcement agencies for a variety of reasons, but primarily because the control of organizational information translates into the control of organizational power. If one agency (or one unit or even an individual within an agency) withholds critical information from others, it impedes others' ability to perform their functions and, ultimately, diminishes others' opportunities to receive accolades for performing their function well. In the long run, withholding intelligence information diminishes the likelihood that crimes will ever be solved.

There has always been a kind of tension or rivalry between federal and local law enforcement agencies, as well as a reluctance to share information. This historic reluctance has caused many conflicts and has been the subject of much debate over the years, but the issue reached an unprecedented level of public awareness in the immediate aftermath of the 2001 World Trade Center attack. The American public demanded to know how and why the nation's vaunted intelligence community – including the CIA, the FBI and the NSA – had failed to uncover and prevent the terrorist plot. Significant media attention was devoted to the fact that not only did the various federal law enforcement agencies fail to share information among themselves, but they failed to share it with state and local law enforcement. When Congress met in October 2001 to hold hearings and to draft comprehensive anti-terrorism legislation, it heard testimony from local law enforcement officials (including Baltimore Police Commissioner Edward Norris) calling for greater communication and more information sharing between federal agencies and their state and local counterparts. The final legislation, however, mandated that the various federal agencies share intelligence information but did not require that the information be passed along to the state and local agencies that might be affected by it.

As Heather MacDonald (2001) notes, Joint Terrorist Task Forces (JTTFs), comprised of federal, state and local officers and overseen by the FBI, exist in New York City and several other large municipalities. The idea behind the JTTFs is simple: use the resources of local law enforcement, which typically has significantly more investigative personnel and often more or better sources of local information than the federal agencies, to coopera-tively gather terrorist intelligence. By agreement, the JTTFs have exclusive jurisdiction over terrorism investigations, a situation that gives the FBI *de facto* control over the collection and dissemination of intelligence. As MacDonald describes, however, the FBI has not shared that intelligence – at least not to the satisfaction of local police officials. Interagency turf wars – not unlike the internal turf wars that once prevented the NYPD from effectively fighting crime – are inhibiting the investigation and prevention of terrorism.

The solution MacDonald (2001) proposes is Fedstat – regularly sche-duled meetings of agency heads to monitor ongoing terrorist investigations and other intelligence-gathering operations, to share intelligence information, and to better utilize the resources each agency brings to the table.

The FBI's anti-terrorism efforts should be Compstated in every city where the bureau operates. Where a Joint Terrorist Task Force exists, the commanders of the agencies represented should meet on a biweekly basis to interrogate taskforce members about the progress of their investigations. Where JTTFs don't exist, the FBI should assemble cooperative meetings with all relevant agency heads. The new Fedstat meetings would have two purposes: to ensure that each ongoing investigation is competently pursued, and to share intelligence. The only fail-safe defense against terrorism is information, but it must be made available to those who can best use it. In many cases, that will be local law enforcement (MacDonald, 2001, p. 42).

Can Compstat principles be applied in the fight against terrorism? MacDonald (2001) makes a persuasive case that it can, but once again Compstat's effectiveness in managing terrorism will be a test of the skill, commitment and philosophy of those who apply it. Based upon Compstat's previous track record as well as its inherent capability to disseminate information and to serve as an early warning system, it is a fairly safe prediction that a series of Fedstat processes taking place in cities across the nation would be effective in preventing or responding to terrorist acts. If properly implemented, Fedstats would not only help share critical intelligence data, but they would empower the various agencies involved just as Compstat has empowered middle managers in the NYPD. Agencies could better utilize and better coordinate their resources, and they could focus their investigative and enforcement activities in the most productive areas. The same strengths that make Compstat work to reduce crime or to manage an entire city can easily be brought to bear on the threat of terrorism, with the same potential for success.

A Final Note

As this book goes to press, the Center for Civic Innovation at the Manhattan Institute has released a comprehensive study by George Kelling and William Sousa that addresses one of the primary tenets of the Compstat paradigm. The study, entitled "Do Police Matter? An Analysis of the Impact of New York's Police Reforms," addresses the question of whether the sharp crime declines that occurred in New York City during the 1990s were the result of economic factors, demographic factors, a reduction in drug abuse, police activities, or some combination of these factors. After reviewing and statistically analyzing a host of empirical data the authors concluded that police activities – in particular, the NYPD's operationalization of 'Broken Windows' policing strategies – played a major role in reducing crime.

More specifically, Kelling and Sousa (2001) conclude that 'Broken Windows' policing is significantly and consistently linked to declines in violent crime and that 'Broken Windows' policing prevented over 60,000 violent crimes between 1989 and 1998. In terms of demographic arguments about crime causation, they determined there was no statistical association between crime and changes in the number of young men of high-school age (i.e., the demographic group most often identified by criminologists as responsible for a disproportionate number of crimes). Neither was the decrease in the use of crack cocaine associated with a decline in violence. Case studies conducted in six NYPD precincts showed that the new tactics and strategies the department employed had an impact in reducing crime: Compstat, which the authors describe as "perhaps the single most important organizational / administrative innovation in policing during the latter half of the 20th century (p. 2), permitted commanders to identify and address specific crime patterns, and the statistical frequency of these crimes declined when commanders employed carefully devised strategies and tactics.

Is Compstat, along with the timely and accurate intelligence, effective tactics, rapid deployment and relentless follow-up it entails solely responsible for the decline in crime? No, say Kelling and Sousa (2001), but Compstat and the cops who use it make a critical difference. In an Op-Ed piece in the New York *Post*, Kelling and Sousa (2001a) wrote:

> Make no mistake, we did not find that police did it all. New York City's drop in crime was also the result of the actions of community groups, business improvement districts (BIDs), the faith community, the evolution of community courts and prosecution – and, yes, in some neighborhoods, changing demography, economics or drug-use patterns. But police remain a critical factor. The strength and direction of crime rates is always dependent upon their local context, and police activities help shape that context.

Kelling and Sousa's (2001) study is a thorough and comprehensive analysis of crime's decline in New York – far too thorough and comprehensive to completely analyze here. The study's findings are important, though, because they dispel many criminological suppositions about crime and disorder and advance the ideas – central to the Compstat paradigm – that police *do* matter and police *do* make a difference. Further, the study suggests that the difference police make is substantial.

In their conclusion, Kelling and Sousa (2001) make the following observations:

> First, despite the root-cause theories that have dominated criminological, criminal justice and much popular thinking about crime control, police can have a significant impact on crime levels

in neighborhoods and communities. One singularly important way of doing this is by restoring and maintaining order, through 'broken windows' policing. While this may come as a shock to many criminologists and media elites, it is nothing new to citizens and residents of neighborhoods... (p. 18)

Second, basic shifts in policing strategies – especially the decentralization of problem analysis and problem solving – have had a significant impact. Because crime has been increasingly deemed a local phenomenon that requires localized analysis, considerable organizational pressure now exists to move away from stock and "cookie cutter" responses... (p. 18)

All of which argues, of course, for establishing a baseline expectation of public order through "broken windows" policing, and for the kind of planning and accountability that is entailed in Compstat when it is rigorously conducted (p. 19).

As additional studies of the Compstat Paradigm's effectiveness and its impact on crime and quality of life are conducted, and as crime continues to decrease in agencies that have successfully adapted the paradigm, the new paradigm's value and importance will become even more apparent. The Compstat Paradigm has already had a dramatic, lasting and tremendously beneficial impact on American policing, as well as a tremendous impact on crime and quality of life in the municipalities that have successfully adapted and implemented it. While the Paradigm's future is not entirely certain – this emerging management model could still be derailed through improper implementation or misunderstanding of its precepts and practices – most indications are that it will continue to thrive and flourish. As is the case with any other management paradigm, Compstat's success depends greatly on the commitment, experience, wisdom and integrity of those who put it to practice.

Recommended Readings

Kelling, George L. and William H. Sousa, Jr. "Do Police Matter? An Analysis of the Impact of New York City's Police Reforms," New York: Manhattan Institute for Policy Research Civic Report series, #22 (December 19, 2001). [Available Online: http//: www. Manhattan-institute.org/cr_22.pdf)

MacDonald, Heather "Keeping New York Safe from Terrorists," *City Journal*, 11 (4), (Autumn 2001). pp. 58-68.

Esserman, Dean "How to Decentralize Control and Get Police Officers to Love Their Jobs," Washington, DC: Heritage Foundation *Executive Memorandum #707*, July 1, 2001.

O'Connell, Paul E. and Frank Straub "Why the Jails Didn't Explode," *City Journal*, 9, 2 (Spring 1999), pp. 28-37. [Available Online: http://www. city-journal.org/html/9_2_why_the_jails.html].

Questions for Debate or Discussion

1. In terms of Gladwell's observations about tipping points, what will be necessary for Compstat to become the dominant Paradigm in American Police management? What social forces and what evidence will be necessary to credit the kind of 'critical mass' the Compstat Paradigm will need to overcome and replace current Police Management mindset?

2. How can cookie cutter management and cargo-cult management inhibit Compstat's growth and acceptance?

3. Considering MacDonald's (2001) views on Fedstat as a way to control and respond to terrorism, what agencies should attend the Fedstat meetings? What agency should take the load in chairing the meeting and coordinating the activities that result from it and why? How can that agency ensure the cooperation and compliance of other agencies?

4. Discuss the ways Compstat could be misused by police in a foreign dictatorship to suppress human rights. How could a dictator use Compstat to increase his or her political power? Could an unethical or corrupt police chief or mayor in the United States misuse Compstat to deprive people of their civil rights? Should these inherent dangers preclude the further development and refinement of the Compstat Paradigm?

5. If you had the choice of working as a police officer on patrol in an agency that fully practiced the Compstat Paradigm or in agency managed in a more traditional style, which would you choose? Explain your reasons.

NOTES

Chapter 10
The Compstat Paradigm: Summary of Basic Principles and Precepts

1. Police *can* and *do* make a difference.

1.1 The police manager who does not wholeheartedly believe in the capacity of the police organization and the individual officer to make a difference is in the wrong line of work. A lack of faith in this basic premise will undermine the respect and legitimacy he or she needs from rank-and-file officers.

1.2 Operational officers are the backbone of the police enterprise, and they are more important to the attainment of its goals than most executives would like to admit.

1.3 Most cops sincerely want to make a difference, and would make more of a difference if their agencies permitted them to. Police work is unlike other occupations because, for the most part, officers have aspired to become police officers: they believe implicitly in their own capacity to make a difference and to benefit society.

1.4 The idealism, and enthusiasm and positive outlook that most rookie officers bring to police work is quickly eroded and replaced with cynicism. The cynical outlook is engendered by a host of factors, many of which are within the capacity of police executives and managers to control. Executives and managers can preserve and maintain the enthusiasm and idealism of rank-and-file officers, if they choose to do so. They can also capitalize on a powerful source of motivation if they permit cynical and demoralized cops to rediscover the excitement and joy of doing the kind of police work they initially aspired to do.

1.5 The most important and most inherently motivating rewards of police work are obtained when officers know that they do make a difference, and when they are acknowledged publicly and among their peers for doing so.

1.6 Under the right circumstances, police work can be a great deal of fun. There is nothing intrinsically inconsistent with having a highly focused and highly accountable police agency and permitting officers to have fun.

2.   Four principles underlie effective crime reduction and quality of life problem abatement:

- timely and accurate intelligence;
- effective tactics;
- rapid deployment of personnel and resources; and
- relentless follow-up and assessment to ensure that the problem has been solved.

2.1 The ability to make effective use of timely and accurate intelligence is greatly enhanced through the potential of technology systems to quickly gather, collate, analyze and present raw crime intelligence data. Crime and quality of life intelligence data identifies the problem, its source, the times and places it occurs most frequently, and potential solutions. Police personnel must look beyond the raw intelligence to see causal connections between different kinds of crime or quality of life events.

2.2 Effective tactics are those that have proven over time to achieve the desired result. The tactics used must be flexible and adaptable to local conditions and local environments. Most of these effective tactics are already known to members of the agency – experienced operational officers are the primary source of effective tactical solutions, but managers and executives must excavate these practices and make them the organizational norm.

2.3 The capacity to deploy resources rapidly and effectively is greatly enhanced when the kind of organizational and administrative barriers that characterize most traditional police bureaucracies are removed, and when accountability systems demand that enforcement, support and ancillary units work together in a coordinated fashion.

2.4 Relentless follow-up and assessment means that executives, managers and operational officers do not prematurely conclude that a problem is solved simply because its symptoms abate. Follow-up includes the continual adaptation of tactics and adjustment of resources dedicated to solve a problem. The ability to continue to gather accurate and timely crime intelligence through technology systems enhances the accuracy of the assessment process.

3. Middle managers in field commands are in a far better position to make everyday operational decisions than headquarters executives.

3.1 Middle managers in field commands are better acquainted with the crime and quality of life problems within their jurisdiction, and they are better acquainted with the strengths and abilities of the officers working for them. In order to make cogent operational decisions, middle managers need crime intelligence, practical police experience and problem-solving skills. Middle managers also make more accurate and effective decisions when they incorporate the wealth of information, tactical knowledge and experience possessed by other members of their commands.

3.2 Middle managers must be given the authority to make important decisions without prior review by administrative higher-ups. Careful managerial selection and assignment processes and a viable accountability system will tend to ensure that middle managers make appropriate decisions.

3.3 Middle managers must be empowered in each of the five bases of power that exist in police organizations. Coercive and reward power demand that middle managers exercise substantial control over the disciplinary and reward system. Expert power demands that commanders have expertise and operational experience, or access to the expertise that resides among the officers they command. The commander's legitimate rank and position in the organizational hierarchy must correspond to the amount of legitimate power he or she needs to command the unit or function. Managers who demonstrate fairness in administering the discipline and reward systems, who acknowledge the source of the expertise that informs their decisions, and who generally uphold the valued and positive attributes of the organizational culture will typically be afforded respect and the referent power that accompanies it.

4. The police occupation's culture is not a singular, unchanging and monolithic entity.

4.1 The occupational culture is the heart and soul of the police organization, the glue that often holds the agency together, and one of its greatest strengths. The executive who understands how to manage culture can achieve tremendous results. If the executive does not manage the organizational culture, it will manage him or her.

4.2 In many dysfunctional police organizations, two distinct cultures can be discerned: a 'street-cop' culture and a 'management-cop' culture. When the ideas, attitudes, belief systems, values and goals that characterize these cultures are disparate or contradictory, the agency's executives and managers face formidable challenges and the agency is unlikely to approach or achieve its full potential.

4.3 In many or most cases, the values, belief systems and goals espoused by the 'street cop culture' are more in line with effective policing than those of 'management cop' culture. Especially in larger agencies, executives are often accurately characterized as out of touch with the culture of rank-and-file officers and the world they inhabit. Effective management demands that the differences between cultures be diminished, usually in favor of the 'street cop' culture's best attributes.

4.4 Police executives must manage the organization's culture as they would manage any other valuable resource. Elements of the organizational culture that facilitate the achievement of organizational goals must be acknowledged and rewarded, and elements of the culture that interfere with the attainment of goals must be identified and re-shaped. Few police executives pay sufficient attention to nurturing and developing the organization's culture.

4.5 Rites and rituals that celebrate the positive attributes and values of the police culture (e.g., heroism, fidelity to the ideals of good police work, personal and professional integrity, etc.) tend to draw disparate elements of the culture together and reinforce the importance of the attributes and values.

4.6 Cultures thrive on symbols and images, and a great deal of police activity is as well understood through its symbolic content as through its manifest appearance. Executives and managers must be aware of the latent symbolic content of their own behavior and the messages it conveys to the rank-and-file. The executive or manager who communicates his or her message through symbols and images as well as through words increases his or her power.

5. Accountability is the key to performance.

5.1 Agency-wide accountability systems must be used to identify each member's level of performance, regardless of rank or position. These systems must also function to reward high performers and discipline low performers.

5.2 Transparent accountability systems – systems in which performance objectives are clear and objectively measurable, and in which accountability processes take place in public – are the most effective. Accountability systems that are not open to the scrutiny of those affected by it breed suspicion and distrust of executives' motivation and legitimacy.

6. **In a high-performance police organization, the lines and boxes on the organizational table are largely irrelevant. They are most useful for budget and administrative purposes – a tiny portion of the agency's overall activities – and have less bearing on the important operational aspects of police work.**

6.1 The greater the sense of collegiality, teamwork and commitment the executive is able to generate throughout the organization, the more irrelevant the lines and boxes become.

6.2 A far more effective organizational model would eliminate horizontal and vertical lines, with units and functions structured in a seamless web design: each unit and function should have a direct line of connection to every other unit and function.

7. **Executives must engage in measured risk-taking and reward it within the middle- and upper-management ranks. Operational officers are, by temperament and by the nature of their work, generally risk-takers. Middle managers who take reasonable and measured risks will gain the respect of the rank-and-file.**

7.1 Encouraging risk-taking means that executives must be highly tolerant of well-intentioned and sensible experiments that nevertheless fail. These well-intentioned failures must be seen as opportunities to develop a tactical and operational knowledge base, and they should be carefully analyzed to identify the reasons why they failed to achieve the expected results. Repeated failures, however, indicate poor judgment or poor management skills and point up the need for accountability systems.

7.2 The entire organization can learn as much from experiments that fail as from experiments that succeed.

7.3 Middle managers must ensure that sufficient controls are placed on operational officers' risk-taking, without stifling cops' initiative and ingenuity.

8. **If police executives could divorce or distance themselves from internal and external politics, many elements of the Civil Service system in policing would become anachronistic.**

8.1 Although the Civil Service system often serves to limit the police executive's ability to promote officers on the basis of merit and performance, the potential for nepotism, political favoritism and other abuses make Civil Service a necessity.

9. **Timid or indecisive executives should not conduct a cultural diagnosis or otherwise assess the work-related attitudes prevailing in the organization. They probably will not like to hear what the rank-and-file have to say.**

9.1 The executive who consults with subordinates and with the rank-and-file – honestly seeking input and opinions as to how the agency could be better managed – does not in any way compromise his or her power or authority.

9.2 The executive who consults with the rank-and-file in developing policies, strategies and organizational goals will engender cynicism and suffer a loss of legitimacy and respect if he or she does not follow-through on a significant number of the rank-and-file's recommendations.

10. **Fear has no place in Compstat paradigm or the Compstat meeting. The manager who uses fear either misunderstands or misuses the Compstat paradigm.**

10.1 The Compstat paradigm provides executives and middle managers with an array of exceptionally powerful management tools and capabilities. Like any other powerful management tools, they can be used to build the organization and its culture or to destroy it.

10.2 Compstat is, or should be, all about improving police performance in order to enhance public safety and achieve the goals of good policing. It can, however, be used by unethical, unprincipled or ignorant executives and middle managers to undermine the democratic values upon which good policing is based.

10.3 Compstat vastly increases the power of executives and middle managers. Unethical, unprincipled or ignorant executives can use their power to achieve personal goals that are unrelated to public safety. These personal goals can include settling personal scores and humiliating subordinates. Executives and middle managers who use Compstat in this way illuminate their own weaknesses and lack of commitment to democratic ideals of good police work.

10.4 Executives and middle managers who rely upon fear and coercion at Compstat meetings to manage the organization lose the ability to effectively utilize other bases of power. Ultimately, they undermine their own overall power, losing legitimacy and respect throughout the agency.

NOTES

Bibliography and References Cited

NOTE: Links to many of the documents cited in this bibliography can be found at John Yohe's Compstat website – www.compstat.com.

Anderson, David C. "The Mystery of the Falling Crime Rate," *The American Prospect,* 32 (May-June 1997), pp. 49-55. [Available Online: http://epn.org/prospect/ 32/32andefs.html].

Anderson, David C. "Why Crime is Down," *New York Times Magazine*, February 9, 1997; pp. 47-52.

Babbie, Earl **The Practice of Social Research (6th Edition)**, Belmont, CA: Wadsworth, 1992.

Babbie, Earl. **Survey Research Methods (Second Edition)**, Belmont, CA: Wadsworth, 1990.

Bahn, Charles "Police Socialization in the Eighties: Strains in the Forging of an Occupational Identity," *Journal of Police Science and Administration*, 12, 4, 1984; pp. 390-394.

Banas, Dennis W. and Robert C. Trojanowicz *Uniform Crime Reporting and Community Policing: An Historical Perspective*, East Lansing, MI: Michigan State University, National Center for Community Policing, 1985.

Barker Joel A. **Paradigms: The Business of Discovering the Future,** New York: HarperBusiness, 1993.

Bayley, David *A Model of Community Policing: The Singapore Story*, Washington, DC: US Department of Justice, National Institute of Justice *Research Report*, March 1989.

Bayley, David and Egon Bittner "Learning the Skills of Policing," *Law and Contemporary Problems*, 47 (1984), pp. 35-59.

Bendix, Reinhard **Max Weber: An Intellectual Portrait**, Garden City, NY: Doubleday Anchor, 1962.

Bennis, Warren and Patricia Ward Biederman **Organizing Genius: The Secrets of Creative Collaboration**, Reading, MA: Addison-Wesley, 1996.

Bittner, Egon "The Police on Skid Row," *American Sociological Review*, 32 (October 1967), pp. 699-715.

Bittner, Egon **The Functions of the Police in Modern Society**, Cambridge, MA: Olegschlager, Gunn and Hain, 1980.

Blakely, Edward J. and Mary Gail Snyder **Fortress America: Gated Communities in the United States**, Washington, DC: Brookings Institution Press, 1997.

Blumenthal, Ralph "Brown Says Community Policing Will Endure," *New York Times*, August 6, 1992; p. B4.

Bouza, Anthony **The Police Mystique**, New York: Plenum, 1990.

Bouza, Tony **Bronx Beat: Reflections of a Police Commander**, Chicago, IL: University of Illinois (Office of International Criminal Justice), 1990.

Brady, Thomas V. **Measuring What Matters Part One: Measures of Crime, Fear, and Disorder**, Washington, D.C.: National Institute of Justice *Research in Action* series (NCJ 162205), December 1996. [Available Online: www.ncjrs.org/pdffiles/measure.pdf].

Bratton, William J. "Blood, Sweat, And Databases," *Forbes*, 160, 12 (December 1, 1997), p. S56.

Bratton, William J. "Cutting Crime and Restoring Order: What America Can Learn From New York's Finest," Heritage Foundation Lectures and Educational Programs, Lecture #573, delivered October 15, 1996. [Available Online: http://www.heritage.com/ lectures.htm].

Bratton, William J. "Great Expectations: How Higher Expectations for Police Departments Can Lead to a Decrease in Crime." Paper presented at the National Institute of Justice Policing Research Institute "Measuring What Matters" Conference, November 28, 1995.

Bratton, William J. "Great Expectations: How Higher Expectations for Police Departments Can Lead to a Decrease in Crime." In Robert Langworthy (Ed.). **Measuring What Matters: Proceedings From the Policing Research Institute Meetings**, Washington, D.C. National Institute of Justice Research Report series (NCJ 170610), July 1999. pp. 11-26. [Available Online: http://www.ncjrs.org/pdffiles/170610-1.pdf].

Bratton, William J. "How to Win the War Against Crime," *New York Times*, April 5, 1998; p. A27.

Bratton, William J. "The Legacy Of Detective Sipowicz," *Time*, 155, 9 (March 6, 2000), p. 34.

Bratton, William J. "Why Lowering Crime Didn't Raise Trust," *New York Times,* February 25, 2000; p. A21.

Bratton, William J. and William Andrews "What We've Learned About Policing," *City Journal*, 9, 2 (Spring 1999), pp. 14-27. [Available Online: www.city-journal.org/html/9_2_what_weve_learned.html].

Bratton, William J. with Peter Knobler **Turnaround: How America's Top Cop Reversed the Crime Epidemic**, New York: Random House, 1998.

Brooke, James "Police/Security Partnerships: Privatization Models that Impact Crime," *Criminal Justice - The Americas*, 9, 2 (April-May 1996). [Available Online: www.acsp.uic.edu/index.htm].

Brown, Jeffrey S. "The Ad-Hoc Task Force: Change Made Simple," *FBI Law Enforcement Bulletin*, 62, 8 (August 1993), pp. 17-20.

Brown, Lee P. "Excellence in Policing: Models for High-Performing Police Organizations," *The Police Chief*, April 1988; pp. 68, 70-72, 76, 78.

Brown, Lee P. Testimony before the NYC Council Public Safety Committee's Hearing: 'How to Evaluate the Effectiveness of the Police Department's Community Policing Program.' November 14, 1991.

Buntin, John "Assertive Policing, Plummeting Crime: Epilogue: Crime Falls, Doubts Arise," Harvard University, John F. Kennedy School of Government *Case Study Program* series, #C16-99-1530.1 (1999).

Buntin, John "Assertive Policing, Plummeting Crime: The NYPD Takes on Crime in New York City," Harvard University, John F. Kennedy School of Government *Case Study Program* series, #C16-99-1530.0 (1999).

Buntin, John "The East New York Urban Youth Corps and Community Policing: The Community Security Initiative Gets Underway," Harvard University, John F. Kennedy School of Government *Case Study Program* series, #C14-99-1529.0 (1999).

Bureau of Justice Statistics **Compendium of Federal Justice Statistics, 1993**, Washington, DC: US Department of Justice, Bureau of Justice Statistics, October 1996.

Carlson, Tucker "Safety, Inc.: Private Cops Are There When You Need Them," *Policy Review*, 73 (Summer, 1995).

Champy, James **Reengineering Management: The Mandate for New Leadership**, New York: HarperBusiness, 1996.

Chetkovich Carol A. "The NYPD Takes on Crime in New York City (A)," Cambridge, MA: Harvard University, Kennedy School of Government *Case Study Program* series, #CR16-00-1557.3, 2000.

Chetkovich Carol A. "The NYPD Takes on Crime in New York City (B) Compstat," Cambridge, MA: Harvard University, Kennedy School of Government *Case Study Program* series, #CR16-00-1558.3, 2000.

Chetkovich Carol A. "The NYPD Takes on Crime in New York City (C) Short-Term Outcomes," Cambridge, MA: Harvard University, Kennedy School of Government *Case Study Program* series, #CR16-00-1559.3, 2000.

Chetkovich Carol A. "The NYPD Takes on Crime in New York City (Epilogue)," Cambridge, MA: Harvard University, Kennedy School of Government *Case Study Program* series #CR16-00-1557.1, 2000.

City of New York, **The Mayor's Management Report; Fiscal 1997**, New York: Mayor's Office of Operations, September 1997.

City of New York, **The Mayor's Management Report; Fiscal 2000**, New York: Mayor's Office of Operations, September 2000.

City of New York, **The Mayor's Management Report; Preliminary Fiscal 1998**, New York: Mayor's Office of Operations, February 1998.

City of New York, **The Mayor's Management Report; Preliminary Fiscal 2001**, New York: Mayor's Office of Operations, February 2001.

Clines, Francis X. "Baltimore Uses a Databank to Wake Up City Workers," *New York Times,* June 10, 2001; pp. A11.

Commission to Investigate Allegations of Police Corruption and the Anti-Corruption Procedures of the Police Department (Mollen Commission) **Commission to Investigate Allegations of Police Corruption and the Anti-Corruption Procedures of the Police Department: Commission Report**, New York: City of New York, July 1994.

Couper, David C. "Quality Leadership: The First Step Towards Quality Policing," *The Police Chief* (April 1988), pp. 79-81, 83-84.

Cunningham, William C. and Todd H. Taylor **Crime and Protection in America: A Study of Private Security and Law Enforcement Resources and Relationships: Executive Summary**, Washington, DC: US Department of Justice, National Institute of Justice, May 1985.

Cunningham, William C., John J. Strauchs, and Clifford W. Van Meter "Private Security: Patterns and Trends," National Institute of Justice: National Institute of Justice *Research In Brief* series, August 1991.

Dalrymple, Theodore "What Causes Crime?," *The City Journal*, 8, 2 (Spring 1998), pp. 112-17.

Davis, Edward F. "Turning a Dangerous City Into a Safe One," Heritage Foundation Lectures and Educational Programs, Lecture #681, delivered July 12, 2000. [Available Online: http://www.heritage.com/lectures.htm.]

Davis, Richard J., Joseph E. Gubbay and Rhea N. Mallet *New York City Police Department: The Role and Utilization of the Integrity Control Officer*, New York: Commission to Combat Police Corruption, December 12, 1996.

Deal, Terrence E. and Allen A. Kennedy **Corporate Culture: The Rites and Rituals of Corporate Life**, New York: Addison Wesley, 1982.

Department of Investigation, City of New York (Howard Wilson, Commissioner) *Report to the Mayor: Reports Prepared by the Community Policing Assessment Unit*, 1994.

Dodenhoff, Peter C. "LEN Salutes its 1996 People of the Year, the NYPD and its Compstat Process," *Law Enforcement News,* December 31, 1996; p. 1.

Domanick, Joe **To Protect and to Serve: The LAPD's Century of War in the City of Dreams**, New York: Pocket, 1994.

Duke, Jan R. "Achieving Excellence in Law Enforcement," California Commission on Peace Officer Standards and Training, Command College Project, December 1985.

Dussault, Raymond "Jack Maple: Betting on Intelligence: Former NYPD map master Jack Maple puts his money where his crime stats are," *Government Technology*, April 1999.

Dussault, Raymond "The Taking of New York: Former NYC Police Commissioner William Bratton talks about how technology helped make the streets safe again," *Government Technology*, August 1999.

Eck, John E. and William Spelman "Who Ya Gonna Call? The Police as Problem-Busters," *Crime and Delinquency*, 33, 1 (January 1987), pp. 31-53.

Eck, John E. and William Spelman with Diane Hill, Darrel W. Stephens, John Steadman and Gerard R. Murphy **Problem Solving: Problem Solving Policing in Newport News**, Washington, DC: Police Executive Research Forum, 1987.

Eig, Jonathan "Eyes on the Street: Community Policing in Chicago," *The American Prospect,* 29 (November-December 1996), pp. 60-68.

Fairchild, Henry Pratt (Ed.) **Dictionary of Sociology and Related Sciences**, Totowa, NJ: Littlefield, Adams, 1970.

Finder, Alan "Community Police Officers Cited on Hours and Training: Report Notes Lack of Sunday and Late Shifts," *New York Times,* January 26, 1994; p. B3.

Fogelson, Robert M. **Big City Police**, Cambridge, Mass.: Massachusetts Institute of Technology Press, 1977.

Forbes, Steve "Big Apple's Big Assault," *Forbes*, 157, 1 (January 1, 1996), p. 26.

Fosdick, Raymond B. **American Police Systems**, Montclair, NJ: Patterson Smith, 1920. [1969 reprint].

Fosdick, Raymond B. **European Police Systems**, Montclair, NJ: Patterson Smith, 1915. [1969 reprint].

French, J. P. R. and B. Raven "The Bases of Social Power." In D. Cartwright (Ed.), **Studies in Social Power**, Ann Arbor, MI: University of Michigan, Institute for Social Research, 1959.

Freund, Julien **The Sociology of Max Weber**, New York: Vintage (Random House), 1969.

Gerth, Hans H. and C. Wright Mills "Bureaucracy." In Hans H. Gerth and C. Wright Mills (Eds.), **Max Weber: Essays in Sociology**, New York: Oxford University Press, 1946; pp. 196-240.

Girgenti, Richard *New York City Random Integrity Testing Program: Report to the New York City Commission to Combat Police Corruption*, New York: KPMG Peat Marwick, 1996.

Gladwell, Malcolm "The Tipping Point: What If Crime Really is an Epidemic?" *The New Yorker*, June 3, 1995.

Gladwell, Malcolm **The Tipping Point: How Little Things Can Make a Big Difference**, Boston, MA: Little, Brown, 2000.

Glueck, Sheldon **Continental Police Practice in the Formative Years**, (reprint of 1926 Report to NYC Police Commissioner Arthur Woods), Springfield, IL: Charles C. Thomas, 1974.

Goldberg, Jeffrey "Sore Winner: Police Commissioner Howard Safir Crows About New York City's Plummeting Crime Rate, and Has About As Much Regard for His Critics as He Does For Criminals," *New York Times Magazine*, August 16, 1998; pp. 30-33.

Goldsmith, Stephen "The Coming Digital Polis," *City Journal*, 10, 3 (Summer 2000), pp. 52-61. [Available Online: http://www.city-journal. org/html/10_3_the_coming_digital.html].

Goldstein, Herman "Improving Policing: A Problem-oriented Approach," **Crime and Delinquency**, 25 (1979), pp. 236-58.

Goldstein, Herman "The New Policing: Confronting Complexity," Washington, DC: National Institute of Justice *Research in Brief* series, December 1993.

Gootman, Elissa "Police Department's Allure is Growing," *New York Times,* October 24, 2000; p. B1.

Greenbaum, Thomas L. **The Handbook for Focus Group Research (Revised and Expanded Edition)**, New York: Lexington, 1993.

Guyot, Dorothy "Bending Granite: Attempts to Change the Rank Structure of American Police Departments," *Journal of Police Science and Administration*, 7, 3 (1979), pp. 253-84.

Halbfinger, David M. "In Washington Heights, Drug War Survivors Reclaim Their Stoops," *New York Times,* May 18, 1998.

Hall, Gene, Jim Rosenthal and Judy Wade "How to Make Reengineering Really Work," *Harvard Business Review*, (November-December 1993), pp. 119-121.

Hammer, Michael "Reengineering Work: Don't Automate, Obliterate," *Harvard Business Review*, (July-August 1990), pp. 104-112.

Hammer, Michael and James Champy **Reengineering the Corporation: A Manifesto for Business Revolution**, New York: HarperBusiness, 1996.

Hart, James M. "The Management of Change in Police Organizations." In Milan Pagon (Ed.) **Policing in Central and Eastern Europe: Comparing Firsthand Knowledge with Experience from the West,** Ljubljana, Slovenia: College of Police and Security Studies, 1996. [Available Online: http://www.ncjrs.org/ unojust/index.html].

Hartnett, Patrick J. and William Andrews "How New York is Winning the Drug War," *City Journal*, 9, 3 (Summer, 1999), pp. 29-37. [Available Online: http://www.city-journal.org/html/9_3_a2.html] .

Hatry, Harry T. **Improving the Use of Focus Groups in Police Departments**, Washington, D.C.: Urban Institute, 1986.

Heisenberg, Werner (C. Eckart and F.C. Hoyt, trans.) **The Physical Principles of the Quantum Theory**, University of Chicago Press, 1930.

Henry, Vincent E. "Police Corruption: Tradition and Evolution." In Keith Bryett and Colleen Lewis (Eds.), **Contemporary Policing: Un-Peeling Tradition**, Sydney, Australia: MacMillan, 1994; pp. 160-79.

Henry, Vincent E. "Police Corruption: Tradition and Evolution," *Queensland Police Journal*, September 1993, pp. 37-55.

Henry, Vincent E. "Interview with William J. Bratton," *Police Practice and Research: An International Journal*, 1, 3 (December, 2000), pp. 397-434.

Henry, Vincent E. and Sean Grennan "Professionalism Through Police Supervisory Training." In James Fyfe, (Ed.) **Police Practice in the '90s: Key Management Issues**, Washington, DC: International City Management Association, 1990; pp. 137-150.

Hess, Karen and Henry M. Wrobleski **Private Security: An Introduction,** New York: West Publishing, 1996.

Hoffmann, Terrance W. **Duties and Responsibilities for New York State Security Officers**, Flushing, NY: Looseleaf Law Publications, 1996.

Houstoun, Lawrence O. "Are BIDs Working?," *Urban Land*, 56 (January 1997), pp. 32-36, 57-58.

Iannone, N. F. **Supervision of Police Personnel (3rd Edition)**, Englewood Cliffs, NJ: Prentice-Hall, 1980.

Independent Commission to Investigate the Los Angeles Police Department (Warren Christopher, Chair) **Report of the Independent Commission to Investigate the Los Angeles Police Department**, Los Angeles:

Independent Commission to Investigate the Los Angeles Police Department, 1990.

Jasanoff, Sheila and Ralph Stone "The Knapp Commission and Patrick Murphy (Part A), Harvard University, Kennedy School of Government *Case Study Program* series, (#C94-77-182.0), 1977.

Jasanoff, Sheila and Ralph Stone "The Knapp Commission and Patrick Murphy (Part B), Harvard University, Kennedy School of Government *Case Study Program* series, (#C94-77-182.1), 1977.

Jasanoff, Sheila and Ralph Stone "The Knapp Commission and Patrick Murphy (Sequel), Harvard University, Kennedy School of Government *Case Study Program* series, (#C94-77-182.2), 1977.

Jener, Eric "Computer-Based Crime-Fighting, From the Ground Up," *New York Times,* December 12, 1997.

Jick, Todd D. "Mixing Qualitative and Quantitative Methods: Triangulation in Action." In John van Maanen (Ed.), **Qualitative Methodology**, Newbury Park, CA: Sage, 1983. pp. 135-48.

Johns Hopkins University Institute of Policy Studies *Demystifying Fluctuations in Crime Rates: A Comparative Analysis of Baltimore, Houston and New York*, Baltimore, MD: Institute for Policy Studies *Occasional Papers* series, #20, April 1997.

Johnson, Kirk and Marjorie Connelly "Americans Have More Positive Image of New York City, Poll Finds," *New York Times,* March 13, 1998.

Keith Harries, Keith **Mapping Crime: Principle and Practice**, Washington, DC: National Institute of Justice, *Research Report* series (NCJ 178919), December 1999. [Available Online: http://www.ncjrs.org/html/nij/mapping/pdf.html].

Kelling, George L. and William J. Bratton "Declining Crime Rates: Insiders' Views Of The New York City Story," *Journal Of Criminal Law And Criminology*, 88, 4 (Summer 1998), p. 1217.

Kelling, George "Measuring What Matters: A New Way of Thinking About Crime and Public Order," *The City Journal*, 2, 3 (Spring 1992), pp. 21-33.

Kelling, George "Measuring What Matters: A New Way of Thinking About Crime and Public Order." In Robert Langworthy (Ed.). **Measuring What Matters: Proceedings From the Policing Research Institute Meetings**, Washington, D.C. National Institute of Justice Research Report series (NCJ 170610), July 1999. pp. 27-36. [Available Online: http://www.ncjrs.org/pdffiles/170610-1.pdf].

Kelling, George and Catherine Coles (interviewed by Ryan Nally) "The Promise of Public Order," *The Atlantic Monthly*, January 1997. [Available Online: http://www.theatlantic.com/unbound/bookauth/broken/broke.htm].

Kelling, George L. "Acquiring a Taste for Order: The Community and the Police," *Crime and Delinquency*, 33, 1 (January, 1987), pp. 90-102.

Kelling, George L. "'Broken Windows' and Police Discretion," Washington, D.C.: National Institute of Justice, *Research Report* series (NCJ 178259), October 1999.

Kelling, George L. "How to Run a Police Department," *The City Journal*, 5, 4 (Autumn, 1995), pp. 34-45. [Available Online: http://www.city-journal.org/html/5_4_how-to_run.html] .

Kelling, George L. "Reclaiming the Subway," *The City Journal*, 1, 2 (Winter, 1991), pp. 17-28.

Kelling, George L. and Catherine M. Coles **Fixing Broken Windows: Restoring Order and Reducing Crime in Our Communities**, New York: Touchstone (Simon & Schuster), 1996.

Kelling, George L., Robert Wasserman and Hubert Williams "Police Accountability and Community Policing," *Perspectives on Policing* series, # 7, US Department of Justice, National Institute of Justice, November 1988.

Kelling, George; Antony Pate, Duane Diekman and Charles R. Brown **The Kansas City Preventive Patrol Experiment**, Washington, DC: Police Foundation, 1974.

Kerner, Otto **Report of the National Advisory Commission on Civil Disorders**, New York: Bantam, 1968.

Kirk, Jerome and Marc L. Miller **Reliability and Validity in Qualitative Research**, Newbury Park, CA: Sage (Qualitative Research Methods Series #1), 1986.

Kocieniewski, David "Crime Continues to Drop in New York City," *New York Times,* January 3, 1998.

Kolasky, Bob "Issue of the Week: Cops and Crime," *Intellectual Capital,* June 12, 1997. [Available Online: http://www.intellectualcapital.com].

Krauss, Clifford "Bratton Builds His Image As He Rebuilds the Police," *New York Times,* November 11, 1994; pp. 1, 26.

Krauss, Clifford "Giuliani and Bratton Start Effort To Shake Up Top Police Ranks: Reorganization Will Move More Officers to Street," *New York Times,* January 26, 1994; p. A1.

Krauss, Clifford "Memos Fault Community Policing," *New York Times,* January 24, 1994; p. B2.

Kreuger, Richard A. **Focus Groups: A Practical Guide for Applied Research**, Newbury Park, CA: Sage (*Qualitative Research Methods Series*), 1993.

Kuhn, Thomas **The Structure of Scientific Revolutions**, Chicago: University of Chicago Press, 1970.

Kushner, Harvey W. "Analysis of Factors Generating Nassau County's Low Crime Rate," Unpublished manuscript, Nassau County District Attorney's Office, Mineola, NY. 1995.

Kushner, Harvey W. "Identifying High Crime Areas in Nassau County," Unpublished manuscript, Nassau County District Attorney's Office, Mineola, NY. November 1996.

Langworthy, Robert H. (Ed.). **Measuring What Matters: Proceedings From the Policing Research Institute Meetings**, Washington, D.C. National Institute of Justice *Research Report* series (NCJ 170610), July 1999. [Available Online: http://www.ncjrs.org pdffiles/170610-1.pdf].

Lardner, James "A Mythical Blue Wall of Silence," *US News and World Report*, September 1, 1997. [Available Online: http://www.usnews.com/ usnews/issue/970901/ 1cops.htm].

Lardner, James "Can You Believe the New York Miracle?," *New York Review of Books*, August 14, 1997.

Lardner, James "The New Blue Line: Better Cops, Fewer Robbers," *New York Times Magazine*, February 9, 1997; pp. 44-54, 62.

Lardner, James and Thomas Reppetto **NYPD: A City and its Police**, New York: Henry Holt, 2000.

Lardner, James "The C.E.O. Cop," *The New Yorker*, 70, 48 (February 6, 1995); p. 45.

Lardner, James "The New Blue Line: Better Cops, Fewer Robbers," *New York Times Magazine*, February 9, 1997; pp. 44-54, 62.

Lesley, Elizabeth "A Safer New York City: Commissioner Bratton's Businesslike Crime-Fighting is Paying Huge Dividends," *Business Week*, December 11, 1995; pp. 81-88.

Mac Donald, Heather "America's Best Urban Police Force," *City Journal*, 10, 3 (Summer 2000), pp. 14-32. [Available Online: http://www.city-journal.org/html/ 10_3_americas_best.html] .

MacNamara, Donal "August Vollmer: The Vision of Police Professionalism." In Philip John Stead **Pioneers in Policing**, Montclair, NJ: Patterson Smith, 1977; pp. 178-190.

Mandelbaum, Seymour J. **Boss Tweed's New York**, Chicago, IL: Ivan Dee, 1965.

Manning, Peter K. **Police Work (2nd Edition),** Prospect Heights, IL: Waveland, 1997.

Maple, Jack and Chris Mitchell **The Crime Fighter: Putting the Bad Guys Out of Business**, New York: Doubleday, 1999.

Marks, John "New York, New York: The Big Apple Comes Roaring Back - and Other Cities Wonder How it Was Done," *U.S. News and World Report*, September 29, 1997.

Martin, Douglas "Guys, Dolls and Winning the War on Crime," *New York Times,* August 12, 2001; p. 4W.

Marzulli, John "Community Cops Program a Bust: Memos Show Few Arrests, Fudged Reports," New York *Daily News*, January 24, 1994; pp. 4 - 5, 18.

Marzulli, John "Not Quite What They'd Hoped For from 'Cops on the Beat,'" New York *Daily News*, January 24, 1994; p. 4 - 5.

Maslow, Abraham H. **Toward a Psychology of Being (2nd Edition),** New York: Van Nostrand, 1968.

Maxfield, Michael G. and Earl Babbie **Research Methods for Criminal Justice and Criminology**, Belmont, CA: Wadsworth, 1994.

McDonald, Thomas D., Robert A. Wood and Melissa A Pflug **Rural Criminal Justice: Conditions, Constraints and Challenges**, Salem, WI: Sheffield, 1996.

McGregor, Douglas **The Human Side of Enterprise**, New York: McGraw-Hill, 1960.

McKinley, James C. Jr. "Dispute Flares Over Number of Officers on Patrol," *New York Times,* January 26, 1994; p. B3.

McQuillan, Alice "Bratton Plan Targets Lazy Cops: Says He'll 'Kick Butt,'" New York *Daily News*, January 24, 1994; p. 18.

Melancon, Deborah D. "Quality Circles: The Shape of Things to Come," *Police Chief*, 51 (November 1984), pp. 54-55.

Miller, William Watts "Party Politics, Class Interest and Reforms of the Police, 1929-56," *Police Studies*, 11, 1 (Spring 1988), pp. 42-60.

Mitchell, Alison "Giuliani Urges Street Policing Refocused on Crime," *New York Times,* January 26, 1994; p. A1, B2.

Montgomery, Paul "15 Policemen Keep Money 'Lost' in Test," *New York Times,* November 17, 1973, pp. 1, 8.

Morgan, David **Focus Groups as Qualitative Research**, Newbury Park, CA: Sage (*Qualitative Research Methods Series #16*), 1988.

Murphy, Patrick V. and Thomas Plate, **Commissioner: A View From the Top of American Law Enforcement**, New York: Simon and Schuster, 1977.

Nemeth, Charles P. **Private Security and the Law (2nd Edition)**, Cincinnati, OH: Anderson, 1997.

New York City Commission to Investigate Allegations of Police Corruption and the City's Anti-Corruption Procedures, **The Knapp Commission Report on Police Corruption,** New York: George Braziller, 1973.

New York Police Department **Annual Report, 1918**, New York: New York Police Department, 1918.

New York Police Department *New York Police Department – Plan of Action: Report to the Police Commissioner,* New York: New York Police Department, October 6, 1994.

New York Police Department *Managing for Results: Building a Police Organization that can Dramatically Reduce Crime, Disorder and Fear*, New York: New York Police Department, March 1996.

New York Police Department *Policing New York City in the 1990s: The Strategy for Community Policing,* New York: New York Police Department, June 1991.

New York Police Department *The Year of Change: Taking Hold: The NYPD Agenda for 1995 and Beyond*, New York: New York Police Department, January 1996.

New York Police Department, *Police Strategy No. 7: Rooting Out Corruption; Building Organizational Integrity in the New York Police Department*, June 1995.

New York Police Department, *Staffing Needs of the New York City Police Department*, October 1990.

New York Times, "Macy's Settles Lawsuit By Worker Raped on Job," *New York Times*, April 12, 1998; p. 32.

Newcombe, Tod "Police Winning New York Crime Fight," *Criminal Justice -The Americas*, 13 (6), July, 1997.. [Available Online: http://www.acsp.uic.edu/index.htm].

NewsHour with Jim Lehrer "Crime Watch: Margaret Warner interviews Howard Safir, Paul Butler and David Michaud," January 3, 1997. [Available Online: http://www.pbs.org / NewsHour/ transcripts.htm].

NewsHour with Jim Lehrer "Winning the Battle, But Not the War: Elizabeth Farnsworth interviews Howard Safir, Sam Nuchia and Darrell Stephens," May 6, 1996. [Available Online: http://www.pbs.org/NewsHour/transcripts.htm].

Niederhoffer, Arthur **Behind the Shield: The Police in Urban Society**, Garden City, NY: Doubleday, 1967.

O'Connell, Paul E. "Using Performance Data for Accountability: The New York City Police Department's Compstat Model of Police Management," Arlington, VA: Price Waterhouse Coopers Endowment for the Business of Government *Managing for Results* series, August 2001.

O'Connell, Paul E. and Frank Straub "Why the Jails Didn't Explode," *The City Journal*, 9, 2 (Spring 1999), pp. 28-37. [Available Online: http://www.city-journal.org/html/9_2_why_the_jails.html].

Pagon, Milan **Policing In Central and Eastern Europe: Comparing Firsthand Knowledge with Experience from the West,** Ljubljana, Slovenia: College of Police and Security Studies, 1996. [Available Online: http://www.ncjrs.org/unojust/index.html].

Parker, William H. (O.W. Wilson, Ed.) **Parker on Police**, Springfield, IL: Charles C. Thomas, 1957.

Pedersen, Daniel "'Go Get The Scumbags:' A Very Odd Couple Tries To Clean Up New Orleans," *Newsweek*, 130, 16 (October 20, 1997), p. 32.

Peters, Thomas J and Robert H. Waterman, Jr. **In Search of Excellence: Lessons From America's Best-Run Companies**, New York: Warner Books, 1982.

Peters, Tom **The Circle of Innovation**, New York: Alfred A. Knopf, 1997.

Peters, Tom **Thriving on Chaos: Handbook for a Management Revolution**, New York: Alfred A. Knopf, 1987.

Pettigrew, Andrew M. "On Studying Organizational Cultures." In John van Maanen (Ed.), **Qualitative Methodology**, Newbury Park, CA: Sage, 1983; pp. 87-104.

President's Commission on Law Enforcement and Administration of Justice **The Challenge of Crime in a Free Society**, Washington, DC: GPO, 1967.

President's Commission on Law Enforcement and Administration of Justice **Task Force Report: The Police**, Washington DC: GPO, 1967.

Prince, Frank A. "The Paradigm Shift Process," *Creativity and Innovation Management*, 3, 1 (March 1994), pp. 29-32.

Quinnipiac College Polling Institute "New York City Poll Trends," 2001. [Available Online: http://www.quinnipiac.edu/ polling/nycpolls.htm].

Reaves, Brian A. *Local Police Departments, 1993*, Washington, DC: US Department of Justice, Bureau of Justice Statistics *Bulletin* series, April 1995.

Remnick, David "The Crime Buster," *The New Yorker*, February 24/March 3, 1997; pp. 94-109.

Repetto, Thomas A. **The Blue Parade**, New York: Free Press, 1978.

Reuss-Ianni, Elizabeth **Two Cultures of Policing: Street Cops and Management Cops**, New Brunswick, NJ: Transaction, 1983.

Rich, Thomas F. "The Chicago Police Department's Information Collection for Automated Mapping (ICAM) Program," National Institute of Justice *Program Focus* series, July 1996.

Rich, Thomas F. *The Use of Computerized Mapping in Crime Control and Prevention Programs*, Washington, DC: National Institute of Justice, *Research in Action* series (NCJ 155182), July 1995.

Roberg, Roy and Jack Kuykendall **Police Organization and Management: Behavior, Theory, and Process**, Pacific Grove, CA: Brooks/Cole, 1990.

Rohde, David "Trauma Centers Short of Patients As New York's Crime Rate Drops," *New York Times*, April 20, 1998; p. A1; B6.

Rosenthal, Aaron "NYC's Trouble with Community Policing," *Law Enforcement News*, 20, 412, November 30, 1994; pp. 8, 10.

Rosenthal, Aaron "Problem Solving Policing: Now and Then," *Law Enforcement News*, 19, 377, March 31, 1993; pp. 8, 10.

Safir, Howard "Goal-Oriented Community Policing: The NYPD Approach," *Police Chief*, 64, 12 (December 1997), pp. 31-39, 56-58.

San Luis, Edward, Louis A Tyska and Lawrence Fennelly **Office and Building Security (2nd Ed.)**, Alexandria, VA: American Society for Industrial Security, 1994.

Sherman, Lawrence W. "The Sociology and the Social Reform of the American Police: 1950-1973," *Journal of Police Science and Administration*, II (1974), 3, pp. 255-262.

Sherman, Lawrence W. and R. A. Berk "The Specific Deterrent Effects of Arrest for Domestic Assault," *American Sociological Review*, 49, (1984), pp. 261-272.

Sherman, Lawrence W. and Richard A. Berk **The Minneapolis Domestic Violence Experiment**, Police Foundation Reports, Washington, DC: Police Foundation, 1984.

Sherrill, Martha "Rudy Giuliani is a Colossal Asshole," *Esquire*, 128, 4 (October 1997), pp. 74-86.

Silverman, Eli B. "Crime in New York: A Success Story," *The Public Perspective*, 8, 4 (June/ July 1998), pp. 3-5.

Silverman, Eli B. "Mapping Change: How the New York City Police Department Reengineered Itself to Drive Down Crime," *Law Enforcement News*, December 15, 1996. [Available Online: http://www.lib.jjay.cuny.edu/len/96/15dec/12.html].

Silverman, Eli B. **NYPD Battles Crime: Innovative Strategies in Policing**, Boston, MA: Northeastern University Press, 1999.

Skolnick, Jerome and David Bayley **The New Blue Line**, New York: Free Press, 1986.

Smith, Bruce **Police Systems in the United States (Revised Ed.),** New York: Harper & Row, 1960.

Smith, Bruce **Police Systems in the United States,** New York: Harper & Row, 1940.

Sparrow, Malcolm K. "Implementing Community Policing," U.S. Department of Justice, National Institute of Justice *Perspectives on Policing* series, #9, November 1988.

Spelman, William and John E. Eck "Problem-Oriented Policing," US Department of Justice, National Institute of Justice *Research in Brief* series, January 1987.

Spelman, William and John E. Eck "The Police and Delivery of Local Government Services: A Problem-Oriented Approach." In James J. Fyfe (Ed.) **Police Practice in the 90's: Key Management Issues**, Washington, DC: International City Management Association, 1990.

Stead, Philip John **Pioneers in Policing**, Montclair, NJ: Patterson Smith, 1977.

Stephens, Darrel W. "Measuring What Matters." In Robert Langworthy (Ed.). **Measuring What Matters: Proceedings From the Policing Research Institute Meetings**, Washington, D.C. National Institute of Justice Research Report series (NCJ 170610), July 1999. pp. 55-64. [Available Online: http://www.ncjrs.org pdffiles/170610-1.pdf].

Stouffer, Samuel *et. al.* **The American Soldier**, Princeton, NJ: Princeton University Press, 1949.

Strong, Otto and Joseph W. Queen "Where Are All Those Extra Cops?," *Newsday*, January 25, 1994; p. 5.

Swope, Christopher "Restless for Results: Baltimore Mayor Martin O'Malley is tracking performance on a scale never seen before in local government," *Governing*, April 2001; pp. 24-30.

Tager, Michael "Corruption and Party Machines in New York City," *Corruption and Reform*, 3, (1988), pp. 25-39.

Tapellini, Donna "William Bratton, Digital Crime Fighter," *CIO Insight*, 1, 2 (June, 2001). [Available Online: http://www.cioinsight.com/sections/features/index.htm].

Task Force on Crime Mapping and Data-Driven Management *Mapping Out Crime: Providing 21st Century Tools for Safe Communities*, Washington, DC: U.S. Department of Justice, National Partnership for Reinventing Government, July 12, 1999. [Available Online: http://npr.gov/library/papers/bkgrnd/crimemap/content.html].

Taylor, Frederick Winslow **The Principles of Scientific Management**, New York: W.W. Norton, 1911. [1967 reprint].

Thompson, Gene "Putting Security on the Shopping List," *Security Management Online* [Available Online: http://www.securitymanagement.com), April 1998.

Thurman, Quint C. and Edmund F. McGarrell **Community Policing in a Rural Setting**, Cincinnati. OH: Anderson, 1997.

Treaster, Joseph B. "Bratton Policing Experiment Gets Results," *New York Times*, July 25, 1994; pp. B1, B4.

Trojanowicz, Robert and David Carter **The Philosophy and Role of Community Policing**, East Lansing, MI: National Foot Patrol Center Community Policing Monograph Series #13 (Michigan State University), 1988.

Vaughn, Michael S. "Problem-Oriented Policing: A Philosophy of Policing for the 21st Century," *Criminal Justice and Behavior*, 19, 3 (September 1993), pp. 343-54.

Walker, Samuel "'Broken Windows' and Fractured History: The Use and Misuse of History in Recent Police Patrol Analysis," *Justice Quarterly*, 1, 1 (1984), pp. 57-90.

Walker, Samuel **Sense and Nonsense About Crime: A Policy Guide**, Monterey, CA: Brooks/Cole, 1985.

Walton, Mary **The Deming Management Method**, New York: Perigee (Putnam), 1986.

Webster, William H. and Hubert Williams **The City in Crisis: A Report by the Special Advisor to the Board of Police Commissioners on the Civil Disorder in Los Angeles**, Los Angeles, CA: Office of the Special Advisor, October 21, 1992.

Westley, William A. **Violence and the Police: A Sociological Study of Law, Customs, and Morality**, Cambridge, Mass.: MIT Press, 1970.

Wheatley, Richard "The New York City Police Department," *Harper's New Monthly Magazine*, 74, 442 (March 1887), pp. 7-30.

Whisenand, Paul M. and Ferguson, Fred **The Managing of Police Organizations (Third Edition)**, Englewood Cliffs, NJ: Prentice-Hall, 1989.

Wickersham Commission **National Commission on Law Observance and Enforcement Reports, Report No. 13: The Police,** Montclair, NJ: Patterson Smith, 1931. [1968 reprint].

Wickersham Commission **National Commission on Law Observance and Enforcement Reports, Report No. 11: Lawlessness in Law Enforcement**, Montclair, NJ: Patterson Smith, 1931. [1968 reprint].

Wilson, James Q. "Thinking About Crime," *The Atlantic Monthly*, 252, 3 (September 1983), pp. 72-88.

Wilson, James Q. "Why 'Fixing Broken Windows' Works: An Interview with James Q. Wilson," *Intellectual Capital,* June 12, 1997.

Wilson, James Q. **Thinking About Crime (Revised Edition)**, New York: Vintage (Random House), 1985.

Wilson, James Q. **Varieties of Police Behavior: The Management of Law and Order in Eight Communities**, New York: Atheneum, 1970.

Wilson, James Q. and George Kelling "Broken Windows," *The Atlantic Monthly*, March 1982, pp. 29-38.

Wilson, James Q. and George Kelling "Making Neighborhoods Safe," *The Atlantic Monthly*, February 1989, pp. 46-52.

Wilson, O. W. *A Study of Detroit Police-Precinct Requirements*, Detroit, MI: Citizens Research Council of Michigan, (Citizens Research Council of Michigan Report no. 176), October 1952.

Wilson, O. W. *Distribution of Police Patrol Force*, Chicago, IL: Public Administration Service (Public Administration Service Report #74), 1941.

Wilson, O.W. **Police Administration (1st Edition),** New York: McGraw-Hill (McGraw-Hill Series in Political Science), 1963.

Wilson, O.W. **Police Administration (2nd Edition),** New York: McGraw-Hill, 1963.

Wilson, O.W. and Roy C. McLaren **Police Administration (3rd Edition),** New York: McGraw-Hill, 1972.

Wilson, O.W. and Roy C. McLaren **Police Administration (4th Edition),** New York: McGraw-Hill, 1977.

Witkin, Gordon "The Crime Bust," *U.S. News & World Report*, April 25, 1998.

INDEX

350   Index

Index entries

NOTES